FEED FROM THE TREE OF LIFE

Dedication

To the monks of St Benedict's Priory
Ewu-Ishan, Nigeria
to whom many of these homilies were first addressed

Columba Breen OSB

Feed from the Tree of Life

TWO-MINUTE HOMILIES FOR WEEKDAY MASSES
AND PRAYERS OF THE FAITHFUL

the columba press

First published in 2000 by
the columba press
55A Spruce Avenue, Stillorgan Industrial Park,
Blackrock, Co Dublin

Cover by Bill Bolger
Origination by The Columba Press
Printed in Ireland by Colour Books Ltd, Dublin

ISBN 1 85607 302 5

Acknowledgements

For one who has spent most of thirty years working in West Africa, the preparation of a book for the press by modern methods would have been impossible without the generous 'word processing' expertise of Dame Petra Boex OSB and Martina O'Brien and I am deeply grateful for their help.

Contents

Columba Breen OSB

A biographical sketch by Vincent Ryan OSB

Born in Dublin on 18 October 1917, he was given the baptismal name of Frederick. He received his secondary education at St Flannan's College, Ennis. Shortly afterwards he was enrolled at Clonliffe, the Dublin diocesan seminary. While receiving his priestly training he also studied philosophy with Latin and Greek classics at University College Dublin. A brilliant student, he excelled in his studies. This was followed by a year at the Irish College in Rome. Responding to a persistent call to the monastic life, he sought entry to Glenstal Abbey, Co Limerick. He was received into the novitiate and given the religious name of Columba (Colm Cille) after the great abbot of Iona. He was professed as a monk in February 1941 and ordained priest in December 1943.

Fr Columba served first as junior housemaster and then as headmaster of the Priory School from 1948 to 1953. This was followed by a more academic period when he taught scripture to the young monks and took charge of the library. He spent two years at the École Biblique in Jerusalem where he became proficient in biblical and modern Hebrew. On his return to Glenstal in 1960, he resumed his teaching both in the monastery and secondary school. He was novice master for some years. In the wake of the Second Vatican Council he threw himself wholeheartedly into the biblical renewal, conducting courses and seminars for sisters in Limerick and elsehere. At a more personal and pastoral level, he was a valued spiritual director to both lay people and religious.

The next phase of his life was the missionary one. He was already sixty-two when he heard the call of the Lord of the harvest: 'Go you also into my vineyard.' The move to Africa was prompted by an appeal of Pope Paul VI for European monasteries to implant monasticism in Africa. He was one of the founders of St Benedict's Priory of Ewu-Ishan, Edo State, Nigeria. Initially the idea was to provide a formation team rather than a foundation in the strict sense, but gradually the community evolved on traditional lines and is now a Simple Priory. Fr Columba was its Superior from 1976 to 1982. St Benedict's is now a flourishing native Nigerian monastery with its own Prior, Fr Vincent Mordi.

Fr Columba returned to Glenstal in 1995, having given twenty-six years of his life to the Church in Africa. In spite of advanced age and a serious heart condition, this last phase was to be as fruitful as the previous ones. He had no thought of retiring, at least not fully. He volunteered to join the Columbanus community in Belfast, the well-known ecumenical foundation devoted to the work of Christian reconciliation in Northern Ireland. He spent a prolonged period there, entering fully into the life and activity of the community and encouraging others to join. He was very committed to the peace movement and did all that was in his power to promote it. Each summer he would spend some time in Iona where he established close contacts with the ecumenical community there. In these last years he also revived his knowledge of the Irish language, and enjoyed working holidays in the Donegal Gaeltacht, both learning and teaching the language.

There remained one final task to accomplish and that was the compilation of this book of homilies. He gave it all the time that was available to him during the last two or three years of his life. It was an immense task, but he persevered in it with courage and determination, each day adding a homily or two. Following major heart surgery on his return from Africa, he knew that time was at a premium and that he would need to maintain, and even increase, the pace in order to see the work through. He spent some months with the Benedictine nuns of Stanbrook Abbey where he acted as temporary chaplain while devoting all his free time to the completion of the *magnum opus*. He returned to Glenstal, and now, seeing the goal in sight, renewed his efforts. He managed to put the final touches to the manuscript in the final week of his life. The end came suddenly and peacefully on Sunday 6 February 2000. Vested in alb and stole, waiting to join the procession for the community concelebrated Mass, a faintness came over him, and within a few minutes he had died. It was a fitting conclusion to a life fully spent in the service of the Lord, and surely bore the mark of divine approval.

Foreword

'I will feed from the tree of life' is the promise of the risen Christ to 'those who have ears to hear what the Spirit is saying to the churches.' (Rev 2:7) It sums up what the Second Vatican Council says in several places about the value of the scripture readings in the Mass: 'the bread of life from the *one table* of the Word of God and the Body of Christ'. (*Dei Verbum* 21) But the homily which accompanies the readings 'is to be highly esteemed as part of the (Mass) liturgy itself'. (*Lit. Constitution* 32)

This unpretentious attempt to provide a skeleton formula for the briefest of comments on the *weekday* readings in the Mass is born of the conviction that they can be a real help, if not indeed a necessity, for the many good people who like to attend daily Mass. Even the gospel passages can come more alive for us by the celebrants's two-minute comment on it. Perhaps no more than a thought on the gospel alone is usually needed. But I have also offered a few words on the first reading, at least for variety's sake.

My experience in concelebrating in parish churches is that most clergy find it a help to have an 'already cooked' comment available as a starting point – to be used or discarded, or more often than not, improved. But for the faithful in the pew it should provide at least one brand of butter for the sometimes dry bread of scripture assigned to weekday Masses. The brief 'Prayer-lines' are often but one form of inspiration that the readings can suggest for appropriate enlargement.

Columba Breen OSB

First Week of Advent: Monday
First Reading: Is 2:1-5; Alt. First Reading: Is 4:2-6); Gospel: Mt 8:5-11

Introduction to the Season:
'Our Saviour is coming. Have no more fear.' So runs the entrance antiphon today. And the theme the 'glad tidings' of God's coming, his 'advent', to our aid is echoed daily in these opening antiphons. The readings and the psalms which follow are a rich symphony of the theme of God's saving coming. The key-note, as today, is one of joyful and grateful expectation:

I rejoiced when I heard them say:

'Let us go to God's house.'

First Reading: 'There will be no more training for war ... let us walk in the light of the Lord.' Light and peace are central ideas in our Advent celebrations. But that very central Old Testament idea of peace *(Shalom)* did not at first mean the absence of war. It could also mean success in battle. But gradually peace was seen as God's gift, and given only to those who walk in God's light – the light of his Law. As a memory of a vanished golden age, peace envisaged concord in the animal realm, between individuals and between nations. For Isaiah, whose life was centred on Jerusalem and Yahweh's presence in the Temple, the natural 'school' of this concord in creation, and between creatures and God, could only be 'the mountain of the Temple of the Lord', and the keeping of his Law.

Alternative First Reading: The first reading in these Advent Masses is invariably from Isaiah, the very incarnation of Old Testament prophecy. His message is in a sense a compendium of the prophets' teaching: God's transcendent majesty as 'the Holy One of Israel'; the unworthiness of a chosen people unfaithful to God's covenant with them; his warnings unheeded; the healing punishments that will follow. But, finally God's steadfast fidelity

9

and Israel's restoration by his mysterious coming in power to save them. 'When the Lord has cleansed Jerusalem, he will come and rest on Mount Zion'.

Gospel: The gospel is the culmination of the prophecies. We can easily relate to its message through our long familiarity with Jesus, its centrepiece. Hence we can echo the psalmist's 'I rejoiced when I heard them say, "Let us go to God's house",' but the words of Isaiah too are for us. The Old Testament story is our story too. As Christians we also have been chosen ; covenanted with God by baptism. Not always faithful, but ready to make a new start each year. Confident in God's unfailing mercy and power.

Prayer-lines: Lord, I am not worthy to have you under my roof, to receive you. Just give the Word, and I, your servant, will be healed.

May our Advent season be a firm resolve to spend it walking in the light of the Lord, with the centurion's faith in Jesus' power to heal our weakness.

First Week of Advent: Tuesday

First Reading: Is 11:1-10; Gospel: Lk 10:21-24

First Reading: 'A shoot springs from the stock of Jesse.' Our first reading brings home to us why Isaiah has been called the fifth gospel. In spite of the wretched specimens of kingship that Isaiah has seen reigning in Jerusalem, he is still able to discern a Davidic ruler to come with all the kingly virtues: wise, strong, religious. And with him will come the harmony of the animal kingdom in nature, described in terms of the mythology of Paradise: 'the panther lies down with the kid', and so on. And behind all this lies the mystery of 'the knowledge of the Lord' … filling the country as waters fill the sea'.

Gospel: Today's gospel reveals that this 'knowledge of the Lord' was first given to Jesus. 'No one knows who the Father is except the Son, and those to whom the Son chooses to reveal him.' Jesus came indeed to share our human nature. But only in order to share with us this knowledge of the Father and his plans. For that is the goal of his mission, the other name of salvation. Isaiah can sum up that swelling of the sea of his Father's knowledge in two lines. For Jesus it was the work of a lifetime: from Nazareth to Gethsemane and beyond. So will the knowledge be for us: according to our desire and his will, through our daily Nazareth, perhaps our Gethsemane, to our resurrection.

Prayer-lines: Thank you, Lord, for the blessing of our knowing you through your Son, Jesus. Help us to open up during Advent to the waters of your knowledge, given us through him, and share it with others.

First Week of Advent: Wednesday
First Reading: Is 25:6-10; Gospel: Mt 15:29-37

First Reading: 'See, this is our God in whom we hoped for salvation.' The classic Old Testament image of the day of salvation 'for all the peoples' is the great banquet which God will prepare for them on his holy mountain. For the God who is coming to save is a caring God who will feed a perpetually hungry people in the desert. And his is a life-giving God who will 'destroy death forever'.

Gospel: This saving God of the Old Testament symbolised in the first reading will be made visible and palpable in the Jesus of the gospel. His healing of the lame, the crippled, the blind, the dumb, is part of God's final victory over evil and death. And as the scene is the 'shores of the Sea of Galilee', the crowds that flock to him include the non-Jews of Syria and Lebanon. They represent the 'all peoples' of Isaiah's vision of universal salvation. Perhaps even the seven baskets are a deliberate contrast to the twelve baskets (i.e. of Israel) mentioned in the feeding of the 5,000. In any case, both allusions invite us to 'raise our eyes to the mountains, from where shall come our help', that is God's unflagging purpose of salvation for all humankind.

Prayer-lines: Come quickly, Lord, to save your world, which lives in the shadow of death. You have made a meal our favourite image of salvation and eternal union with you. May our daily Mass build in us a growing longing for that.

First Week of Advent: Thursday
First Reading: Is 26:1-6; Gospel: Mt 7:21, 24-27

First Reading: 'The Lord is the everlasting Rock.' Our first reading shows us Isaiah, the Jerusalemite, at his most characteristic. His strong, dignified imagery of wall and rampart; the rock and steep citadel; the feet of the lowly who trample on the dust. And especially his message of trust in God as 'the everlasting Rock'. And, no doubt, in the gospel too we can catch Jesus' vivid style as a teacher of the crowd. And his basic message: 'Do the will of my Father in heaven'.

Gospel: For house-building is not a bad illustration and visual aid for Jesus' purposes. Men, at least, like to build, if women prefer to adorn. If they grow up near the seashore small children build sandcastles. Sand is easy to handle, and shape when wet. That is all right for a children's pastime. But stupid indeed for the needs of real life. For the worthwhile house we're all called to make and adorn is our lives. There are so many materials for us to choose from : wealth, power, pleasure, fame. And there are so many contractors – especially on the media! – to offer us their services. Today Christ assures us that his words, the gospel, his Good News, are the only material which will stand the test – of the rains, the floods, the gales of life. We are wise if we take Christ as our contractor.

Prayer-lines: God, our Father, thank you for the wisdom of eternal life offered us by Christ. Through the power of the Mass offered daily by your church, make it truly a strong city where all nations may become one with you.

First Week of Advent: Friday
First Reading: Is 29:17-24; Gospel: Mt 9:27-31

Gospel: 'Their sight returned.' One can hardly blame the blind men for forgetting Jesus' stern instruction to tell no one about the miracle which their faith had earned for them. But, as elsewhere in the gospel, Jesus did not seek a reputation as a faith-healer. His mind was on the mystery that lay behind the healing prodigy, the coming of the kingdom in his person and power.

First Reading: And this mysterious coming is the theme of Isaiah's prophecy in our first reading: 'after shadow and darkness, the eyes of the blind will see'. Jesus' life was a continuous struggle against the powers of darkness: not merely the physical signs in bodily sickness, but sin in all its forms. 'Tyrants and scoffers will vanish, and all who are disposed to do evil.' It is important for us today to believe that the kingdom of God in power is not reduced by us to securing merely temporal favours. Isaiah will go on to speak of the greatest favours we ask for in the Our Father: 'They will hallow the Holy One of Jacob, stand in awe of the God of Israel.' We go on to ask God's power to be faithful in the hour of temptation, and deliverance from evil.

Prayer-lines: God our Father, we ask you for an increase of faith whereby Jesus by his coming this Advent may strengthen us in holiness.

First Week of Advent: Saturday
First Reading: Is 30:19-21, 23-26; Gospel: Mt 9:35-10:1, 6-8

Gospel: 'They … were like sheep without a shepherd.' This very traditional image in the Bible for God's people gives us a helpful clue to our attitude to Jesus in our Advent piety. We are familiar with the words of Psalm 22:

> The Lord is my shepherd,
>
> There is nothing I shall want.

It is rare to see sheep without a shepherd in Palestine. Pasture is not plentiful there. Sheep need a guide. Water is equally scarce. The shepherd will know where the wells and the cisterns are. Without the shepherd sheep will stray, or starve, or fall prey to wild animals.

It is a valid picture for our relationship to Christ. History can show how Christians can stray when they look to other guides, other models than Christ. Without his teaching and the sacraments, the life of baptism in us can grow feeble and even die out. And without Jesus' protection we can fall easy prey to the gospel of the world: live for now, for this world, for pleasure, for self. In Advent we shall perhaps hear Isaiah again, in the words of Handel's Messiah, 'All we like sheep have gone astray.'

First Reading: If such a confession rings true for us, our first reading, again from Isaiah, reminds us how God is always ready to receive us back; is always, in Christ the shepherd, seeking for us. 'He will be gracious to you when he hears your cry; when he hears you he will answer … your teacher will hide no longer … you will hear these words behind you: "This is the way, follow it".' Amen.

Prayer-lines: Lord, teach us during Advent to keep our gaze fixed on Christ as our shepherd, our guide.

For all who have wandered from his ways, that the grace of this season may bring them back to his way.

Second Week of Advent: Monday
First Reading: Is 35:1-10; Gospel: Lk 5:17-26

Gospel: 'Who can forgive sins but God alone?' We need to remind ourselves that the gospels are not just records of the past. They are proclamations of the Good News for the present, the present of every generation: the Good News of Jesus' presence in our midst, and of his power as our saviour. In today's gospel it is not merely his power to heal the body, but his power to win forgiveness of sin for humanity. This goal of 'taking away the sin of the world' that we remind Jesus of at every Mass is the key purpose of his becoming man, of the incarnation. This is the great healing that humanity in general, and each of us individually, needs.

First Reading: And this supreme gift of God to us in Jesus' sacrifice on the cross is the reason for the exuberant rejoicing of Isaiah in our first reading. The forgiving of the individual paralytic's sins in the gospel is part of God's plan of universal redemption. 'Those the Lord has ransomed will return.' The blind will see, the deaf hear, 'the lame will leap like a deer', the dumb sing for joy. And the forces of nature will echo this joy of God and of humanity in their own way: the wasteland blooming, the dry land yielding springs of water, and wild beasts will be unknown along the Sacred Way ...' but the redeemed will walk there ... everlasting joy on their faces'.

Prayer-lines: Lord, may the miracles recorded of you in the gospel strengthen our faith in your power to cleanse us from every sin.

Second Week of Advent: Tuesday
First Reading: Is 40:1-11; Gospel: Mt 18:12-14

First Reading: '"Console my people, console them", says your God.' Yes, the tide has turned. Isaiah up to now has swept none of his people's sins under the carpet. From his first chapter he has addressed them as 'a sinful nation, a people weighed down with guilt'. But now in the second part of Isaiah, written two hundred years later (by a spiritual disciple), that people has been condignly punished by seventy years' exile in Babylon. 'Her sin is atoned for,' the prophet proclaims, 'she has had double punishment for all her crimes.' God's message through Isaiah now runs, 'Shout without fear, "Here is you God." The price of your victory is with him.' The victory of God's mercy and forgiveness over humanity's sins.

There will be a new start, 'For the word of the Lord remains for ever'. What word? The word that Israel is his chosen people. As once he led them out of captivity in Egypt to Sinai and the Promised Land, now he will lead them back from Babylon, across the Syrian desert to Jerusalem. 'A straight highway shall be made across the desert' for that homecoming.

Gospel: Such is the prophetic background of today's gospel. Here indeed is your God in the flesh and blood of Christ. He is fulfilling the will of his and your Father in heaven that not one of these little ones should be lost. He will take the risk of leaving 'the ninety-nine on the hillside', the risk of dying as a criminal on the cross in order to save the penitent thief – and the rest of us.

Prayer-lines: Thank you, Father, for the consolation of Advent: the guarantee that your Word stands for ever, that your mercy is greater than our sin.

Second Week of Advent: Wednesday
First Reading: Is 40:25-31; Gospel: Mt:11:28-30

Gospel: 'Learn from me, for I am gentle and humble of heart.' As often in the gospels, we could misunderstand these familiar words of Jesus if we take them out of context. Which context? The context of his life-setting, and his death – 'Learn from me' might conjure up memories of sentimental statues of the Sacred Heart. In the reality of Jesus' life-setting, his words could be dynamite. They could be heard by the Pharisees as blasphemy – for which eventually he would be crucified – 'Shoulder my yoke and learn from me' was part of his repeated criticism of *their* religious practice – which made it so burdensome for ordinary people.

What was Jesus objecting to in it? The Pharisees and Scribes had made their observance of the Law a religion of effort and achievement – with God's reward to follow. Jesus, instead, offered *his* way. A religion of God's free gift of forgiveness, with humanity's tribute of gratitude, of love and spiritual rest. Hence he could truly say, '*My* yoke (or law) is easy, my burden light.' It is a condition of our spiritual growth to accept this Way to God. The other way may seem more righteous, but it only flatters our pride.

First Reading: Our first reading continues yesterday's message of God's consolation for his people in their exile. Their guilt is atoned for, he assures them, but they are still dazed at God's promise of a new start to their covenant-relation to him. Isaiah goes on today to reinforce his astounding Good News by proclaiming God's transcendent power as creator: 'Who made the stars? He creates the boundaries of the earth'. His creative power is no prodigy of the past. He is always at work. He *can*, therefore, make all things new.

Prayer-lines: God, our Father, grant us the grace to follow the law of Christ, the faith to believe, with St Paul, that your strength is best in our weakness.

Second Week of Advent: Thursday

First Reading: Is 41:13-20; Gospel:Mt 11:11-15

Gospel: 'John the Baptist is the Elijah who was to return.' Even secular historians like Josephus pay tribute to John the Baptist's great prestige. Jesus sets his seal on this witness by identifying him with Elijah, the most dramatic prophetic figure of the Old Testament. 'Behold,' cries Malachi, the last of the writing prophets, 'I shall send you the prophet Elijah before the great and awesome day of Yahweh comes.' So the Baptist's witness to Jesus is the climax of Old Testament prophecy and desire. What other prophets could foretell, he could actually see, and point out to others: 'There is the Lamb of God'.

First Reading: And our first reading from Isaiah epitomises this inspiring prophetic forewitness to the coming of God in Christ. 'Do not be afraid, Jacob, poor worm, Israel, puny mite, I am holding you by the right hand.' Well might Israel regard itself a 'puny mite' at that time: tiny remnant as it was of a tiny people in exile under the mighty political power of Babylon. 'I, the God of Israel, will not abandon them,' the prophecy continues.

It is a message in every generation to all who feel overwhelmed by forces which threaten us: in politics, responsibility, in health or temptation. We never need to pretend we are anything but small and puny. All that matters is to retain our faith in God's promises of his presence with us, of his power and his love for us.

Prayer-line: Lord, give us through your Holy Spirit, that constant awareness of your presence with us and in us which is the bedrock of our Christian life.

Give courage and hope to all those who are tempted to despair at the forces of evil in the world, its violence and corruption.

Second Week of Advent: Friday
First Reading: Is 48:17-19; Gospel: Mt:11:16-19

First Reading: 'I, the Lord your God, *teach* you what is good for you.' Yes, God is our teacher as well as our redeemer. 'You come to us,' we tell him as we start our Mass, 'in word and sacrament to strengthen us in holiness.' We are pupils in the school of his service. But what a difficult class we are to teach! 'If only you had been alert to my commandments,' Isaiah continues, 'your happiness would have been like a river'.

Gospel: And in the gospel Jesus tells his generation that they are like peevish children – refusing to join in the games that they are invited to join. John the Baptist they refused to listen to because he was so ascetic. Jesus they reject because he doesn't fast like the Pharisees, and keeps what they regard as disreputable company. How could they both be right? 'Wisdom,' Jesus answers. 'God's wisdom has been proved right by her actions.' Holiness can take different forms for those who are docile to God's Spirit as their teacher.

Prayer-lines: God, our Father and Teacher, grant us always to be led by your Holy Spirit according to the light and grace of each day.

Second Week of Advent: Saturday

First Reading: Ecc 48: 1-4, 9-11; Gospel: Mt 17:10-13

Reading and Gospel: 'Elijah has come already … and they treated him as they pleased.' Elijah is one of the most dramatic figures in the history of the Chosen People. At Mount Carmel he stands out alone and undaunted against the king and people of Israel to insist that Israel can have no other God than the true God, Yahweh. It is easy to see why John the Baptist was identified with Elijah, and not only by Jesus. Both men lived on the edge of society, on the poorest of food, and took no account of the danger which their fearless preaching put them in with the powers that be. But their deepest trait in common is their readiness to be merely God's instrument. Elijah makes it clear that all his miracles are worked by God, not by his own powers. And John the Baptist is equally determined to attract no notice to his own person. He sees himself as merely the voice in the desert foretold by Isaiah, preparing the way for the greater one to come. When his disciples showed jealousy at Jesus' growing prestige, John shows himself at his most attractive: as the friend of Jesus the bridegroom, 'This is the joy I feel, and it is complete. He must grow greater, and I must grow less.' He is the perfect model for a faithful disciple of Christ.

Prayer-lines: God, our Father, help us to learn from Elijah and John the Baptist, to become your willing instruments in promoting your kingdom. May your interests come to predominate in our lives, our own interests diminish.

Third Week in Advent: Monday
First Reading: Num 24:2-7, 15-17; Gospel: Mt 21:23-27

Gospel: 'Their reply to Jesus was, "We do not know".' For Matthew the Good News of the gospel is good news mainly for the Gentiles. For the Jews as a people, especially the religious leaders of today's passage, it is a tragedy – for they will reject it by rejecting Christ, their Messiah. They have had all the chances through the prophets, and finally in the witness of John the Baptist. But their hearts, and therefore their eyes, are closed to the light of salvation. 'They do not know' because they do not want to.

St Matthew will portray this tragedy – of the contrasting reactions of men to Christ, even in Christ's infancy – in the contrast between the Wise Men and the people of Jerusalem. Consulted by Herod about the place where the Messiah is to be born, the chief priests and the scribes have no problem. The answer is, of course, 'Bethlehem'. They know Micah's prophecy by heart – Bethlehem is only six miles from Jerusalem, an easy two hours' walk across the fields. But will they go there? Not they. It is the Wise Men, the truly wise men indeed, who 'come to Jerusalem from the East' and from afar, with only the star to guide them.

First Reading: This is the 'star from Jacob' in the first reading, which St Matthew has in mind, the star seen by the far-seeing eyes of Balaam the pagan seer some twelve hundred years before. The star was a symbol of royalty. But it is also perhaps a symbol of judgement for us Christians if pagans shame us by living better lives than we do.

Prayer-lines: Lord Jesus, grant that we who have not a star, but your Spirit to guide us, may come to you this Christmas with open hearts, ready to give you all that we have, all that we are.

Third Week of Advent: Tuesday
First Reading: Zeph 3:1-2, 9-13; Gospel: Mt 21:28-32

Gospel: 'Tax-collectors and prostitutes are making their way into the kingdom of God before you.' Jesus has come down from Galilee to Jerusalem to present the leaders of his people with a final challenge on his Father's behalf. Yesterday we saw how he reduced them to silence when they asked him about his authority. Today he now takes the offensive with a parable: 'A man had two sons'. The man represents God, his Father in heaven. His sons are Israel, the Chosen People on the one hand, on the other the Gentiles. Israel is the second son in the story. He professed to obey his father, but in fact failed to do his will, especially by rejecting Jesus. The first son, the Gentiles, seemed to have been disobedient from the start by following their false gods; but in the persons of the tax-collectors and prostitutes they have come back to obey God by accepting the teaching of Jesus. But even the return of these 'prodigal' Gentiles did not move Israel to amend its disobedience. Israel thus stands clearly condemned before God.

First Reading: Our first reading, from Zephaniah, reveals the Father's plan in response to men's rejection of the Messiah. Ruin is in store for the rebellious city, for 'the proud boasters'. But he will preserve a faithful remnant, a humble and lowly people 'who will have God as their shepherd'. 'They will be able to graze and rest with no one to disturb them.' This faithful remnant we shall meet shortly in the persons of Mary and Joseph, Elizabeth and Zachariah, and others.

Prayer-line: Create for us a clean heart, Lord, that at your Son's coming among us this Christmas we may be found among the humble and lowly people who are worthy to become his sisters and brothers.

Third Week of Advent: Wednesday
First Reading: Is 45:6-8, 18, 21-26; Gospel: Lk 7:19-23

Gospel: 'Are you the One who is to come, or must we wait for someone else?' St Luke's gospel (which we read today) does not have John the Baptist recognise Jesus at his baptism in the Jordan. His question, therefore, today, 'Are you the one who is to come?' would seem a genuine request for identification from Jesus. John's disciples would have told him of Jesus' growing reputation – as both teacher and miracle-worker. But what a difference in 'style' there was between their messages. 'I baptise you with water for repentance,' cried John, 'but the one who comes after me will baptise you with the Holy Spirit and with fire ... He will gather his wheat into his barn, but the chaff he will burn with a flame that will never go out.' Jesus' message, however, seems otherwise. 'Come to me all you who labour and are overburdened ... I am gentle and humble of heart. Yes, my yoke is easy and my burden is light.' Jesus knew, therefore, that the surest way of reassuring John that he was indeed 'the One who is to come' was to quote for him from the promises made in Isaiah about the Messiah; 'The blind see, the lame walk...' In a word, sickness of every kind is being healed, and the Good News of the kingdom is thereby being truly proclaimed.

First Reading: And our first reading from Isaiah hangs behind the figures of Jesus and John like a great backdrop of God's mystery and benevolent wisdom: that unsearchable wisdom of the transcendent God which both have proclaimed, each in his own way. 'I am the Lord unrivalled. I form the light and create the dark.' God's wisdom, as Jesus has said earlier to the people, has been proved 'right' by all her actions – however at variance with one another these actions may seem. 'From him alone is the power to save ... Turn to me and be saved.'

Prayer-lines: Teach us, Lord, in this season of Advent, to recognise your coming in the varied goodness of the lives of many, and to thank you for their witness to your presence and power in our midst.

Third Week of Advent: Thursday
First Reading: Is 54:1-10; Gospel: Lk 7:24-30

Gospel: 'A prophet and more than a prophet.' If John the Baptist, according to St Luke, is unsure if Jesus is really 'the One who is to come', Jesus himself has no doubts about John's identity and dignity. He pays public tribute to his prophetic greatness, even at the risk of incurring the wrath of Herod Antipas who is keeping John in prison. Yes, John is indeed more than a prophet, for he effectively prepared the way for Christ as no other had done. But he is the climax of only one line of prophecy: that of God's judgement on a sinful people.

First Reading: But our first reading gives us, through Isaiah, the climax of another line of prophecy that Christ will fulfil: God's faithful love even amidst his just punishments. Hosea and Jeremiah before him had already declared this love, but never was it so passionately proclaimed as in today's passage. The mystery of the Sacred Heart, we might say, revealed two thousand years before St Margaret Mary Alacoque.

And the elaboration of the marriage imagery here, (already begun by Hosea), prepares us for the entry of Mary on to the centre of the stage in next week's liturgy. It is important to remember that the gospels saw Mary not so much as the individual girl of Nazareth, but as the fulfilment of these prophecies of Isaiah and other prophets. In her humble readiness to 'hear the word of God and keep it', the mountains and the hills of Israel's infidelity had disappeared, and a new creation had taken place.

Prayer-lines: God, our Father, we thank you for this revelation of your love and forgiveness. Let nothing in our lives or the sins of the world ever shake our faith in that love.

Third Week of Advent: Friday
First Reading: Is 56:1-3, 6-8; Gospel: Jn 5:33-36

Gospel: 'John was a lamp alight and shining.' Next week's readings will bring us to the story of John the Baptist's infancy. It is
appropriate today to hear another testimony to him on the lips
of Jesus, at a time apparently when John had already been be-
headed by Herod. 'John was a lamp alight and shining.' So
much so that earlier in John's gospel we are told that the priests
and Levites had come down specially from Jerusalem to ask if he
was the Messiah. John's reply was that he was not worthy even
to undo the sandal-strap of the one coming after him. (St
Augustine's comment is that John feared that the wind of pride
would blow out the light in his lamp!) How well, then, the early
church could celebrate the Baptist as a model of humble witness
to Christ, in his life and in his death.

First Reading: Our first reading is from the latest part of the Book
of Isaiah, written for the Jews who have by now returned from
their captivity in Babylon. It is remarkable, in foreseeing freedom
for the Gentiles, to share in worship with the Jews. 'My house
will be called a house of prayer for all the peoples.' Jesus will
quote these words when he drives the buyers and sellers out of
the Temple. The Temple of his Body would indeed be a centre of
prayer for all peoples.

Prayer-lines: Give us the grace, Lord, to imitate John the Baptist
in bearing witness to Christ by the shining integrity of our lives.

Advent: 17 December
First Reading: Gen 49:2, 8-10; Gospel: Mt 1:1-17

Gospel and First Reading: Today we acclaim the gospel in the words of the great pre-Christmas antiphon: 'O Wisdom of the Most High, ordering all things with strength and gentleness, come and teach us the way of truth.' And surely the strength and gentleness of God lie hidden behind the long genealogy of Matthew. From Abraham to Christ; from Judah, the lion cub of Jacob's oracle in the first reading, to Mary the Virgin; from the warlike hunger for land that drove the sons of Jacob in to capture Canaan, town by town, from its former inhabitants; from that warlike greed to the vision of justice and peace flowing in today's Responsorial Psalm: the Old Testament forecast of the reign of the Son of Man, the Prince of Peace.

What a revelation of the wisdom of God! '*My* ways are above your ways as the heavens are above the earth.' Yet God makes use of human ways, even human violence and sin, to bring about his will. We may think of murky tales in Genesis, like that of Judah and Tamar. But there are much blacker chapters behind that long *dramatis personae* that Matthew gives us. And the Word of God is our Good News, the basis of our Christian patience and hope and endurance. We may never give way to our human fears. 'The Lord is near. There is no need to worry.' 'Wisdom of the Most High, come and teach us the way of truth.'

Prayer-lines: Lord Jesus, may your coming to live among us this Christmas strengthen our faith in your constant presence, and your unfailing power to help us always.

Advent: 18 December

First Reading: Jer 23:5-8; Gospel: Mt 1:18-24

Gospel: 'She has conceived what is in her by the Holy Spirit.' Matthew here is explaining two points. First, how Joseph figures in the infancy narrative if God alone is Jesus' Father. The answer is: Joseph is Mary's fiancé. Secondly, Joseph's adoption of Jesus is, like the rest of Jesus' infancy, by God's arrangement. There is no allusion to Joseph suspecting Mary of adultery. But the law of Deuteronomy would oblige a just man, as Joseph is, to expose her condition. The idea of putting her away informally is certainly evidence of his compassion, in not exposing her to the rigour of the law. St Jerome takes St Joseph's silence about Mary's pregnancy as a mark of humility and reverence: 'He covered by silence a mystery he could not comprehend.'

Joseph is indeed a person to be studied in the context of Christ's coming into all of our lives. Certainly he had not expected to be foster-father of a son conceived by divine power. Nor indeed the demands this foster-child would make on his life, even from his infancy. But this is the law of Jesus' coming into all of our lives. 'Like a thief in the night' as he will put it himself: unexpectedly and in disguise. It is for us to be always ready in faith to recognise that it is he, and not mere chance, that is making demands upon us: on our health, our patience, our courage, our perseverance.

First Reading: 'I will raise a virtuous Branch for David'. The significant emphasis in the first reading is laid on the activity of God in the work of salvation. Jeremiah is supremely the prophet of Israel's traumatic exile to Babylon. But, like Isaiah before him, he envisages God's power showing in a new Exodus, not from Egypt, but from Babylon. Further, he sees this as a spiritual exodus too: From Israel's past infidelity to a new 'integrity' conferred on it by God's power.

Prayer-lines: Thank you, Lord, for giving us St Joseph as our model. May he help us this Christmas to recognise Christ in whatever guise he takes for his advent.

Advent: 19 December
First Reading: Jgds 13:2-7, 24-25; Gospel: Lk 1:5-25

Gospel: 'He will begin to rescue Israel from the power of the Philistines'. It seems clear that Luke had the account of Samson's birth in mind as he wrote his 'annunciation' of the birth of John the Baptist. The mothers of both men are barren; nazirite abstinence is imposed in both cases, on the mother in one, on John the Baptist in the other. For both children are to be consecrated to God and his saving plans. There is no comparison, of course, between greatness of the two men as characters, or in their function: Jesus himself tells us that there was no greater among the men before him than the Baptist. And we know the miserable downfall of Samson through his infatuation with Delilah.

First Reading: And yet Samson has his own relevance to the Christmas mystery and message. This mystery and message is, of course, one of Israel's salvation. Jesus is the one by name, as the angel told Joseph in yesterday's gospel passage, who will save his people. But Samson, too, in his own small way, was a saviour of his people. His story in the Book of Judges (better translated as 'saviours'), gives an account of the charismatic leaders supplied by God at the critical stage when Israel was trying to consolidate its original invasion of the Promised Land. Scholars tell us that in fact Samson was only a village hero, who made little impact on the Philistine threat to Israel. But what matters is that though he was to prove such a moral weakling, God was prepared to use him as one of his instruments in the many rehearsals for the final deliverance of Israel, and all mankind, from the powers of darkness. Whenever we are tempted to discouragement at our own weakness, failures and mistakes, the story of Samson is there to encourage us. God can use the weakest of us in his work of salvation.

Prayer-lines: Lord, we thank you for the 'hope and consolation of the scriptures'. May they spur us on to use your gifts in us for your glory, yet never to doubt your mercy towards our failures.

Advent: 20 December
First Reading: Is 7:10-14; Gospel: Lk 1:26-38

Gospel: 'The child will be called Son of Man.' Christians down through history have shown keen judgement in treating this scene as the key-point in history. Catholic piety has rightly made the 'Hail Mary' its 'mantra', its bond of prayer with Mary and God. The greatest paintings of the Annunciation have captured something of the awe and mystery of the occasion ... And perhaps the best way to treat the passage is as a great picture that one sits (or kneels) in front of in a gallery, content to admire, and be nourished by it. Certainly there is no need to look elsewhere for Luke's reputation as a painter.

There is no need to be distracted by the frame into which Luke has put his canvas. He has accepted the old traditional frame we met in the annunciations to Samson's mother and the Baptist's father: an angel's greeting; human trepidation; angel's reassurance; promise of a child, and so on. But into that old wineskin Luke has poured an incomparable new wine. Mary's famous question, 'How can this come about?' brings the crowning revelation about *her* Son: Jesus will owe his very existence to the Spirit. The child will be called Son of God.

First Reading: 'God is with us', Emmanuel. This is the sign that God gives to us his people. The sign that Ahaz refused to ask for. The sign of hope for Ahaz and his people and no less the sign of hope for us today. God is with us, he has come among us as one like us. Lord, grant us the grace to accept the sign you have given us.

Prayer-lines: God, our Father, may the coming feast of Christmas strengthen our faith in your Son's presence and protection in our lives.

'The Spirit' — recalls the first moment of Creation;
'The Cloud' — the sign of God's presence in O.T.

Advent: 21 December
First Reading: Songs 2:8-14; Gospel: Lk 1:39-45

Gospel and First Reading: 'Winter is past: the rains are over and gone.' Our first reading today, from the Song of Songs, is well chosen to highlight the significance of the story of the visitation which follows. For the central figure of the visitation – though not visible – is Jesus, the 'blessed fruit of Mary's womb'. Not Mary herself. For the whole purpose of these infancy stories in Luke is to show Jesus as Messiah, not merely from the moment of his baptism, when the Father bore witness to him as such. He is Messiah and Saviour and Son of God from the first moment of his existence. And like the sun, as portrayed in Psalm 18, 'he rejoices like a champion to run his course'. His mission to save and sanctify others begins at once – and with John, his first and greatest human witness.

And our first reading gives us a glimpse of the deeper mystery behind this visitation. Not the solemnity and awesomeness of Jesus' person as announced to Mary by Gabriel. But the delicacy and fragrance of God's love for mankind, already expressed in the story of his walking with Adam and Eve in Paradise. There the springtime of God's love affair with humankind was blighted by sin. Now the winter of his discontent has passed. The second and everlasting spring of his love and saving power is now released, to restore humanity to its original beauty – the image of God in Christ.

Prayer-line: God our Father, we thank you for the marvel of your love. Help us to respond always to it with Mary's faith and the fidelity of John the Baptist.

Advent: 22 December
First Reading: 1 Sam 1:24-28; Gospel: Lk 1:46-56

First Reading and Gospel: Perhaps nothing in Luke's infancy gospel shows more clearly than the Magnificat that Mary is for him primarily the personification of Israel, the old Israel, 'the virgin daughter of Zion'. For the Magnificat is a tissue of Old Testament echoes and reminiscences, especially the story and canticle of Hannah. Hannah is the personification of the oppressed, being barren and childless. The scorn of her rival, Peninnah, clearly echoes the plight of Sarah, Abraham's wife, at the hands of her slave-girl.

The story of Samuel, then, is a paradigm of God's gift of freedom to the oppressed. Samuel's life is God's gift; in return his life is given over to God. As Hannah's song prefigures what God will do for Israel through Samuel, so the Magnificat foretells the liberating mission of her Son.

But Mary is also the embodiment of the new Israel, the church, who continues to sing Mary's canticle daily. We might say that the church uses the Magnificat not only as a prayer, but also as a mirror. Therein she reads all she needs to know. To know first of all, of herself, what she is, God's lowly handmaid in the work of salvation. There too she reads 'the great things the Almighty has done for her' down the centuries. There, above all, she remembers what sort of person God is: 'his mercy reaches from age to age'. But the Magnificat is also a mirror of sin in its basic form: the proud-hearted, the mighty, the rich. There, too, she sees all that is opposed to what Mary stands for; and what the church, and Christians, must never become.

Prayer-lines: God our Father, may we learn from praying the Magnificat with Mary to know the height and depth, the breadth and length of the mercies you have shown us in our lives.

Advent: 23 December

First Reading: Mal 3:1-4, 23-24; Gospel: Luke 1:57-66

First Reading and Gospel: 'What will this child turn out to be?' Jesus would later answer: 'A prophet and more than a prophet.' And to the three apostles after the Transfiguration he would identify John as the 'Elijah' Malachi had spoken of, sent to prepare the coming of God himsel, to purify his people. Malachi indeed, from whose prophecy our first reading is taken, seems to strike a very different note to the comforting rhythms of Israel's promises earlier in Advent. For Malachi spoke at a much later time than these. The people of Judah had indeed returned from exile, but times had been hard and their first religious fervour had waned. They were in danger of slipping back into their old infidelities. John the Baptist at the Jordan was familiar with that prophecy of Malachi, and felt bound to echo it for his own day. 'Who will be able to resist,' he asks, 'the terrible day of the Lord's coming as refiner and purifier of his people?'

Jesus indeed came in a gentler way than John had expected. He had come as the Good Shepherd who will lay down his life for his sheep. As the indulgent father of the prodigal son. And this is the aspect we think most about at Christmas. Yet, even at Christmas, God's coming in Jesus as a new-born child is a coming in judgement. It is an invitation and a challenge to us to accept 'the loving kindness of our God' with repentance and amendment of our lives.

Prayer-lines: God, our Father, may the coming of your Son among us, as one of ourselves this Christmas, turn our hearts in sorrow for our sins, and in sincere amendment in the coming year.

Advent: 24 December
First Reading: 2 Sam 7:1-5, 8-12, 14, 16; Gospel: Luke 1:67-79

Gospel: 'Thus he remembers his holy covenant.' This is what the Benedictus canticle is all about. It is God's nature to be faithful: he is 'the rock', 'the stronghold' of the psalmist. But this faithfulness, Zechariah proclaims, is a work of mercy, a 'salvation through the forgiveness of their sins.' For each of these steps of God's fidelity (Abraham, the father of our faith excepted), is matched by the most dismal contrast of man's unfaithfulness: the kings who followed David; the people who ignored the teaching of the prophets; the Israelites in the desert who could not be brought to trust in God. But, as the psalmist puts it, now 'mercy and faithfulness have met'; God's 'saving justice' and man's peace can now embrace because of the imminent birth of the one who is Faithful and True, God's Amen, and ours, to all his promises.

First Reading: Our first reading gives us the historical context of God's promise to David – the core of Israel's hope of a Messiah. David has brought the Ark of the Covenant up to Jerusalem, his capital city. But he feels it is wrong for himself to be living in a comfortable house of cedar, while the ark is kept only in a tent, as it was at Shiloh. He plans, therefore, to build a proper temple to house the ark, with Yahweh invisibly enthroned on the 'mercy seat' of the ark. David, however, reckons without his host. God lets him know through the prophet Nathan that it is he, God, who will take the initiative. He will do any 'house-building' that's to be done. But the 'house' God has in mind is the dynastic house he will assure to David. That house will never die out, and through it God will assure the *Shalom*, the peace and prosperity of his people for ever.

Prayer-lines: God, our Father, give us an unshakeable faith in your fidelity to what you have promised us in your Son Jesus. Give us a share in John the Baptist's mission to prepare the way for Jesus among those with whom we live.

Christmastide: 26 December Feast of St Stephen

First Reading: Acts 6:8-10; 7:54-59; Gospel: Mt10:17-22

First Reading & Gospel: According to the scriptures, Stephen was the first of all the Christian martyrs. He had been selected by the twelve apostles to assist them when the number of disciples grew and he was subsequently recognised by all as having been endowed by God with grace, and to a very high degree. However, the success he had in preaching the good news of Christ provoked a lot of opposition. In the end he was, not just attacked with words, but led outside the city of Jerusalem and stoned. Yet, as he died, he did what Christ himself had done, he prayed for the forgiveness of those people who were killing him.

This feastday of a martyr, coming as it does just one day after Christmas, seems to introduce a different and, perhaps, an unexpected mood. Yet many of the first disciples knew that to espouse the virgin's child could lead to persecution and to death. They, therefore, needed to commemorate heroic people to sustain their own resolve and Stephen was to be the first of what became an ever-growing list. However, as they told his story, they were able to perceive that, if he did stand firm amid antagonism, it was not by his own strength alone, but also by the powerful presence of the Spirit which was so alive in him. It was, no doubt, that insight which encouraged them the most because they knew that that same strengthening and transforming Spirit had been promised to them too.

Prayer-lines: 'Lord Jesus, receive my spirit.'

Christmastide: 27 December Feast of St John
First Reading: 1 Jn 1:1-4; Gospel: Jn 2:2-8

First Reading & Gospel: In his gospel John refers to a 'disciple-Jesus-loved'. He did not mean by that that Jesus did not love the others. He, in fact, considered all of them his 'friends'; in consequence he told them everything he knew. Moreover, he was ready to lay down his life for them and did. But John, who knew that he himself was loved, may have desired to emphasise that fact. In any case, he offered us an unnamed, loved one who could be a symbol of what all are called to be.

A 'beloved disciple' has, according to St John, a knowledge which consoles and leads to life. Thus he or she can always sense a fruitful presence even if the situation on the surface seems a disappointing one. Such was the case when a disciple-Jesus-loved bent down and looked into an empty tomb. He saw what many others would have missed. Because his heart could not accept that Christ who loved him to the end was not alive, 'he looked in and believed'. St John assures us in another place that each of us is called to have that kind of loving faith and, even without seeing, to be blessed.

In later life St John recalled and spoke about the moments in his own life when he saw with his own eyes and touched with his own hand the one whose love meant everything to him. He knew, of course, that most of those who listened to him when he preached, or who would later read the gospel which he was to write, would not have had that kind of physical experience. He also knew, however, that those very people could have fellowship with him in faith and know the love which comes to us from God. So we, who celebrate his feast today, may now rejoice with certainty that we are one, not just with him and with all other Christians everywhere, but also and most centrally with Christ. We, too, are called to be, with Christ, God's own beloved ones.

Prayer-lines: Lord, may we know that we are loved by you.

Christmastide: 28 December Feast of the Holy Innocents
First Reading: 1 Jn 1:5-2:2; Gospel: Mt 2:13-18

First Reading & Gospel: We often speak about the flight of Jesus into Egypt. The emphasis in the gospel story is, however, on his coming out. That was for Matthew the important point. He thought of Jesus as a second and greater Moses who would lead his followers from the slavery of sin and bring them to a better and indeed a perfect Promised Land.

It is within that context that we hear about the massacre of children. Herod, who is said to have decreed their death, was certainly no saint. The story of what happened is, however, told to echo that of Pharaoh slaughtering the children of his own time and to reinforce the image of a saviour as a new and greater Moses who, escaping death, would guide his followers to freedom and to all their hearts' desire.

Today, however, is a time for gratitude: for giving thanks for being on that journey which will lead us to eternal life, for having found in Christ the one-like-Moses who can lead us on infallibly until we reach that ever-satisfying goal. Perhaps we should remember too those people who have helped us and inspired us up till now. But if we do give thanks for them today, let us remember too all those who, like the children in the gospel, died or were unjustly killed while they were very young. Those little ones have reached their journey's end and so, because they are with God, they cannot but look lovingly and longingly at us. We, therefore, may discover for ourselves not just another, but a very healing, reason to give thanks to God today.

Prayer-lines: Lord, may we follow you with confidence until we reach that Promised Land where those who have preceded us now dwell.

Christmastide: 29 December
First Reading: 1 Jn 2:3-11; Gospel: Lk 2:22-35

Gospel: 'The salvation which you have prepared for all the nations to see.' The presentation of Jesus in the Temple is for St Luke the climax of his story of the infancy. The saviour has been announced by Gabriel to Mary; saluted from womb to womb by John the Baptist; serenaded at Bethlehem by the angels, and venerated there by the shepherds. Now he enters his Father's house, where he will be found, after three days' painful absence, twelve years later – and thirty-three years later in full reality by his ascension to heaven. And in this scene Luke brings together three of the major themes of his gospel: the Paschal mystery; salvation for all; the role of the Spirit. The 'falling and rising' of many in Israel is perhaps not for two categories in Israel. Rather we may read it as the graph of the self-emptying which his disciples must share with him: as John puts it in the first reading, 'the same kind of life as Christ lived'. And as Jesus will put it to the two disciples on the road to Emmaus, 'Had not the Christ to suffer and *so* enter his glory?' As for Matthew, the whole of Jesus' career is summed up for Luke in the events of his infancy.

First Reading: The first Letter of John is directed against disciples who played down the importance of the way Jesus had lived, and therefore the need for imitating his conduct. They felt it was enough to believe that he was the Word of God. For John, Jesus' conduct set a moral standard for all his disciples. 'We know God only by keeping his commandments.'

Prayer-lines: God, our Father, may your Spirit enable us to share in Jesus' self-emptying so that we may also share in his resurrection.

Christmastide: 30 December
First Reading:1 Jn 2:12-17; Gospel: Lk 2:36-40

Gospel & First Reading: 'The child grew to maturity, filled with wisdom, and God's favour was with him.' Twice in his chapter 2 Luke will refer to Jesus' growth: physical, mental and spiritual. He has made a parallel reference to John the Baptist's growth after the account of his birth. In regard to Jesus it is a mystery worth pondering. It brings home to us the reality of the incarnation, of the human nature taken on by the Son of God. Jesus had to grow not only in body, but in mind too. Later on, as a grown man, his teaching shows a deep appreciation not only of the Old Testament but of nature and the ordinary life of simple people. But all this had to come by degrees, through home and schooling and the synagogue. As does every child, Jesus had to learn. To discover his family, his village, its people. Above all he had to discover God: What God was to him, and he to God. This was his spiritual growth: his 'favour with God'.

In much the same way in his Acts, Luke will speak also of the growth of the church. And naturally so, since the church is Christ's 'mystical body', continuing Jesus' life on earth. And with this context we can link our first reading from St John's epistle. In poetic style he addresses Christians as 'children' (as Christ does the apostles at the Last Supper), but also as fathers and young men, according as they are new to Christianity or seasoned believers in it. And as in John's gospel he warns them – and us – against the unregenerate aspects of a sensual and materialistic world.

Prayer-lines: Lord, through the graces of Christmastide, may the life and spirit of Jesus increase in us and in the church to the glory of your name.

Christmastide: 31 December

First Reading: 1 Gospel: Jn 2:18-21; 1:1-18

Gospel: 'It is the only Son that has made God known.' The pro-logue in John's gospel corresponds in a sense to what the two infancy narratives are in Matthew and Luke. It is a summary of the mystery of the full-grown Christ in the gospel which fol-lows. John's Prologue sees the entire sweep of God's revelation in his Word culminating in the life, death and resurrection of Jesus. It refers back not merely to David or Abraham, but to the first word of Genesis: 'In the beginning God created the heavens and the earth.' For Jesus is that Word which God spoke at cre-ation; he is the Wisdom which the book of Proverbs saw playing before God in creation; which the book of Sirach saw coming down to dwell with men in the Law of Moses.

Creation, nature and Law were indeed the light on man's path until Jesus came. But a light, as St Paul says, filtered through 'a glass darkly'. The full light came only with Jesus. 'No one has ever seen God. It is the only Son who has made him known'. And he has shared that light with 'all who receive him'. 'The Word was made flesh ... and we saw his glory'.

First Reading: Yet our first reading does not ignore the shadow side of John's gospel: 'the darkness that could not overpower the light'. The antichrists foretold by Christ have already appeared in disciples who have defected from the true faith in the human-ity of Christ. But the Christians faithful to John's teaching are se-cure in the truth imparted by God's anointing.

Prayers-lines: Father, we thank you for the inexpressible gift of your Word made flesh to live among us. Deepen our knowledge of you through his grace and truth.

Christmastide: 2 January
First Reading: 1 Gospel: Jn 2:22 -28; Jn 1:19-28

Gospel: 'There stands among you the one that is coming after me.' The church's annual 'replay' of events of Jesus' life in the liturgy is not just to stir our imagination but to nourish our faith in the mystery of Emmanuel, 'God-with- us' in Christ. And so after the initial 'aperitif' for faith in the infancy narratives of Matthew and Luke, we turn now to the main course of Jesus' life with the appearance of John the Baptist on the banks of the Jordan. His witness is that he is not the Christ, but implies that the Christ is around, and of infinite superiority to John: 'I am not fit to undo his sandal strap'.

And we note the legal atmosphere which surrounds the witness of John: the personal interrogation of him by the priests and levites sent down from Jerusalem. This will be one of the characteristics of the fourth gospel. The trial of Jesus by the religious authorities, which is placed by Matthew, Mark and Luke at the end of Jesus' life has, for this gospel, begun from the beginning of his public life. And paradoxically, all those who meet Jesus are also being put on trial by their reaction to him.

First Reading: Our first reading, from the first Letter of John, continues its treatment of the darker side of the infancy gospel: the negative reception some will give to the coming of God in Christ, the 'darkness which will not overcome the light'. It is for genuine Christians to 'live in Christ', who is the truth in which they have been anointed.

Prayer-lines: Lord, may the faithful witness of John the Baptist teach us to live no longer for ourselves, but by our lives to bear witness to him who died for us and rose again.

Christmastide: 3 January

First Reading: 1 Jn 2:29-3:6; Gospel: Jn 1:29-34

Gospel: 'Yes, I am the witness that he is the Chosen One of God.'
The Baptist's witness expands over several distinct ways. The
titles he bestows on Jesus are heavy with meaning in the Jewish
context in which John preached. If Jesus is the Chosen One, it is
to take away the sins of the world. And not merely by his own
sinlessness, or a simple act of indulgence. He will be 'the lamb of
God', a reminiscence of the Passover lamb whose blood sprinkled over the Hebrew houses in Egypt will save them from the
destructive plague released by God against the Egyptians.
Reminiscent also of the suffering servant in Isaiah who will be
led willingly 'like a lamb to the slaughter ... and will justify
many by taking their guilt upon himself'. And as the Spirit will
remain on him, filling him completely, he is thereby enabled to
share that Spirit with others.

First Reading: The first reading today outlines the work of that
Spirit in us as Christians. He makes us God's beloved sons and
daughters. It is then for us to live up to this adoption by model-
ling our lives on Christ in freedom from sin.

Prayer-lines: God, our Father, fill us with your Holy Spirit, and
may he come upon the whole world to bring about that kingdom for which we daily pray.

Christmastide: 4 January

First Reading: 1 Jn 3:7-10; Gospel: Jn 1:35-42

Gospel: 'We have found the Messiah.' The goal of John's witness to Jesus is now reached when two of his own disciples follow Jesus. It is a dramatic moment indeed, this meeting of Jesus with his first disciples, and the words are full of meaning beneath their apparent banality. To 'follow' Jesus would come to mean join him, and imitate his way of life. For becoming a disciple means literally one who wants to learn; thus Jesus is addressed as 'Teacher' (Rabbi). The simple verbs, 'coming, seeing, staying', all suggest the gradual growth of the first disciples' faith in Jesus. But as the gospels are written not just as a reportage of past events, but as a proclamation of present realities, we may find here the journey we must all make to find and become attached to Christ. The Spirit of the risen Christ continues to invite us to come and see and stay with him. And then, like Andrew and Philip, pass on the Good News of Christ to others.

First Reading: Our first reading characteristically describes this journey as the matter of loving one's brother. And the resources for this most arduous of journeys are daringly defined as being begotten by God, in our baptism.

Prayer-lines: God, our Father, increase our faith in the reality of being your sons and daughters in Christ, and make us eager to share our knowledge of Christ with others.

Christmastide: 5 January
First Reading: 1 Jn 3:11-21; Gospel: Jn 1:43-51

Gospel: 'From Nazareth? Can anything good come from that place?' The gospels these days recapture the joy of the apostles meeting Jesus for the first time, being called by him and getting to know him. An unforgettable experience, naturally, for those concerned. Very suitable for these days after Christmas, when we can refresh our memories of how and when Jesus became for us a real person. And the gospel marks how quickly the apostles' appreciation of Jesus increases. Yesterday hailed as Teacher and Messiah, today he is also called Son of God, King of Israel. The interesting thing about Nathanael's call is that it starts with Nathanael's prejudice against Jesus as a Nazarene. He will need to be given the salutary shock that Jesus knows him well already. For us, perhaps, that might well serve as a hint that we should come to meet Jesus, (especially in prayer, but elsewhere as well), ready for a salutary revelation about ourselves.

First Reading: 'Follow me' is Jesus' invitation to Philip. But the first reading reminds us of the more important following of Jesus which we must share with the apostles: The message that we are to love one another. For Jesus that love was an historical event too. 'Greater love than this no man has', he fittingly described his death. For us, too, our love of one another must be 'not just words or talk'. Perhaps Christian love will always have a touch of death about it: death to self.

Prayer-lines: Lord Jesus, thank you for your invitation to follow you in love of one another. May our love not be 'just words or talk', but in your Spirit and truth.

Christmastide: 6 January
First Reading: 1 Jn 5:5-13; Gospel: Mk 1:6-11

Gospel: 'He will baptise you with the Holy Spirit.' St Mark's gospel has no infancy narrative. Jesus' public life is prefaced only by John the Baptist's proclaiming of repentance at the Jordan. But there is no embarrassment, (as in Matthew's gospel), about Jesus undergoing John's baptism with his fellow Nazarenes. For Mark the importance of the baptism episode is the identification which follows it. The heavens are 'torn apart', allowing direct communication from heaven to earth and earth to heaven; fulfilment of a plea made in the prophecy of Isaiah many years before. The dove-like descent of the Spirit recalls the Spirit hovering over the waters of chaos at creation. 'My Son, the Beloved', echoes God's praise of Abraham at being ready to sacrifice his only son, Isaac, in obedience to what he felt was God's command. Finally, God's favour rests on Jesus as the suffering servant in the well-known prophecy of Isaiah.

First Reading: Our first reading, from the first Letter of John, is a final warning for the secessionists from John's community. 'Jesus Christ, who came, not with water only, but with water and blood' echoes John's gospel account of the piercing of Jesus' side with the lance after his death. The secessionists had wrongly identified Jesus' saving act as his baptism, with the Spirit descending on him. But John's gospel clearly says elsewhere that the life-giving Spirit of Jesus would not be given till he had been glorified by death and resurrection.

Prayer-lines: God, our Father, may we, through our baptism, open our souls to your Spirit, so that we may ever more faithfully serve you.

Christmastide: 7 January

First Reading: 1 Jn 3:22-4:6; Gospel: Mt 4:12-17; 23-25

Gospel: Today the gospel speaks of Jesus as a light in Galilee and, in particular, within the tribal lands of Zebulun and Naphtali. It thereby indicates that Jesus was, for many of the early Christians, the expected messianic person whom Isaiah had foretold. Deep and indeed long-simmering desires were consequently seen by them as being realised in Christ.

As we now listen to this gospel passage of today, we may be struck by how it calls us to repent: we may be given hope by hearing of the healings which took place when Jesus was acknowledged by the people of his time. But, what is also being offered to us is the grace to recognise within ourselves, not only the desire for a Messiah, but a deep capacity to welcome him as well.

Then in his presence, darkness will give way to light.

First Reading: Light is an image which the author of this letter often used. However, in the sections which we have today he speaks, not of the light, but of the spirit which is being offered to us all. Unlike the godless spirits which are able to lead us astray, this is the Spirit which can lead us all to Christ, which will enable us to do what he commands and which unites us with all those who welcome it. It seems that many people at the time were arguing that Jesus could not be the Son of God in human form and by such thoughts effectively denying that their human natures could be divinised. St John insisted, for their benefit and ours, that Jesus Christ, who is of God, has come in human form and, therefore, that all who receive his Spirit have the power, in their humanity, to love as he commanded and to have and to enjoy his own eternal life. So may that be.

Prayer-lines: Lord, in your light may we see light and may your spirit flow through each of us.

Christmastide: 8 January

First Reading: 1 Jn 4:7-10; Gospel: Mk 6:34-44

Gospel: 'They all ate as much as they wanted.' The gospels of this season are based on the theme of 'epiphany', or 'manifestations' of Jesus' royal, messianic dignity and power. No other episode in Jesus' life is so popular with all four evangelists. The reason for this is not far to seek. By the time the gospels came to be written, from thirty to sixty years after the resurrection, the Eucharist was the central celebration of the faith for Christians. The Acts of the Apostles tells of the early Christians meeting every day in their houses for the breaking of bread. This took place, at that time, in the crowded streets of Jerusalem, not on the pleasant lakeside in Galilee. But what mattered was unchanged. Jesus was back with them again, the Good Shepherd feeding his flock – by his word as by the Bread of Life.

First Reading: And, as the first reading today makes clear, this daily feeding of the flock was the daily revelation of the Father's love, 'who sent into the world his only Son, so that we could have life through him'; and after his example, that we should love one another.

Prayer-lines: Lord Jesus, by our eucharistic celebration deepen our faith in your presence among us, and strengthen our mutual love.

Christmastide: 9 January

First Reading: 1 Jn 4:11-18; Gospel: Mk 6:45-52

Gospel and First Reading: 'They had not seen what the miracle of the loaves meant.' Unlike the other evangelists, Mark never spares the disciples' slowness to catch what Jesus is at. Luke will make excuses for them: they sleep during the agony of Jesus in the garden because of their sadness. Matthew always treats them with reverence. His account of the same episode ends up with their profession of faith, 'Truly, you are the Son of God.'

Perhaps we should not be too quick to dissociate ourselves from the slowness of faith which Mark emphasises in Jesus' disciples, for today's gospel scene is also a parable of the Christian life. So often in our lives we feel we are 'at sea', 'worn out with rowing' against the winds of trouble – of mind or body. Jesus is never absent, but we can act as if he had forgotten all about us, as if he were only 'a ghost'. We find it easy to 'believe' in him once the trouble is past, the problem solved. In the meantime we must practise the Christian solution offered us in the first reading: 'No one has ever seen God; but as long as we love one another, God will live in us, and his love will be complete in us.'

Prayer-lines: Lord Jesus, increase our faith in your saving presence at all times, and deepen that faith by our love for others.

Christmastide: 10 January
First Reading: 1 Jn 4:19-5:4; Gospel: Lk 4:14-22

Gospel and First Reading: 'The Spirit of the Lord has been given to me.' Our last two gospel passages were 'manifestations' or 'epiphanies' of Jesus through his power over nature: the multiplication of loaves and fishes; the stilling of the winds at sea. For Luke, the epiphany of God in Jesus is something deeper: the revelation of his possession by the Spirit; firstly at his conception; then at his baptism and his overcoming Satan in the desert. All this, as the text shows, reveals Jesus as the messianic prophet of Isaiah. It is a stirring programme for the simple people of Nazareth to hear: good news for the poor, freedom from oppression, healing for the disabled. But it is at a price: the price of accepting the word of the son of Joseph, the carpenter. We know from the sequel that they were not prepared to pay that price.

We too must be prepared to accept the reality of God in our lives – as he has chosen to come, not as we have planned or imagined it. And that will be the 'good news' that changes life for us; that sets us free; that heals our blindness.

Our first reading assures us that this programme is not beyond us. We are given the power to live up to it; 'His commandments are not difficult … This is our victory, our faith … that we have been begotten by God.'

Prayer-lines: God our Father, grant us the grace to accept the reality of your presence in our lives, so that we may be set free to live according to your Spirit.

Christmastide: 11 January
First Reading: 1 Jn 5:5-13; Gospel: Lk 5:12-16

Gospel and First Reading: 'Your healing ... as evidence for them.'
Our gospel passage gives us an example of God's 'epiphany' in
Jesus that most attracted the crowds and enhanced his reputation: his power to heal the sick. The revised rite of 'Anointing of
the Sick' and the miracles of healing that God still works on sick
people are a guarantee of his continuing saving will.

When Jesus tells the cured leper to show himself to the priest
with an offering 'as evidence for them', he is, of course, following the law of Moses.

But our first reading shows that there is a deeper evidence in
his new-found freedom from leprosy being given. 'This is God's
testimony, given as evidence for his Son'. Ten times in this short
passage from the first Letter of St John the same word is used as
Luke does for 'evidence'. We are, of course, familiar with the
first two syllables of that Greek word 'martyr', because he is the
primary witness for us of God's saving love: shown to us in the
Spirit and water of our baptism, and in the blood of the
Eucharist. It is, indeed, by our faith in that witness, that 'martyrdom' of Jesus in *our* lives as Christians that, John tells us, we
overcome the world.

Prayer-lines: God, our Father, deepen our faith in the reality of
our baptism, and the presence of Jesus' Spirit which it gives us.

Christmastide: 12 January
First Reading: 1 Jn 5:14-21; Gospel: Jn 3:22-30

Gospel: 'He must grow greater, I must grow smaller.' Tomorrow winds up our celebration of the mystery of the Epiphany, that is, God's showing of himself in Christ at Jesus' baptism in the Jordan. The liturgy will portray this many-sided mystery as the wedding of Christ and the church. They are both given the (traditional Jewish) bridal bath in the Jordan. They are laden with the wedding gifts brought by the Magi. And at Cana they are gladdened by the abundant wine provided by Christ. Jesus himself will later on pronounce he is the bridegroom, and thereby excuse his disciples from fasting while he is still with them. And today John the Baptist is only too happy to claim the role of best man at his wedding.

Jesus has left us many striking paradigms of discipleship, but perhaps no more attractive model for us as Christians than this one. We are all called to be Christ's 'best man' at Christ's daily wedding with mankind in the church. It is for us to rejoice at our privilege, and to see that he grows daily in us, and through us in others, while we and our self-centredness daily decrease.

First Reading: Our first reading reminds us that we are assured of being heard if we ask God for anything that is in accordance with his will. Surely he wills that we can play our part in his ongoing wedding with the church.

Prayer-lines: God our Father, as you have granted us through Christ to know you as you are, may we grow daily in that knowledge till we come to see you face to face.

Introduction: 'Be reconciled to God. Now is the favourable time.' Up to now our scripture readings have treated of the mystery of sin in the world at large, and the role of Christ in undoing that sin in its consequences. With Lent we concentrate our gaze on how we ourselves share in that dual mystery of being sinners and being redeemed from sin by Christ, of 'being reconciled to God' through him. It is very important to reach a proper synthesis in our attitudes to Lent. It is a time of our special personal involvement in overcoming sin in our lives. But we do this only through sharing with Christ in his work of 'taking away the sin of the world' – by his Easter mystery of death and resurrection.

Ash Wednesday

First Reading: Joel 2:12-18; Second Reading: 2 Cor 5:20-6:2;
Gospel: Mt 6:1-6. 16-18

2nd Reading: 'Be reconciled to God. Now is the favourable time.'
We started with a quote from the second reading, from the second letter to the Corinthians. Brief though it is, this extract sums up the meaning of Lent: a favourable time of being reconciled with God; a day of salvation; that, in the sinless one, Christ, we may become the goodness of God. So, the aim of Lent is not self-punishment, but the victory of goodness in us.

1st Reading: Yet the Old Testament appeal in the first reading is relevant too. Here Joel stresses the important aspect that our Lent is a corporate undertaking with the whole church. 'The people together: the community', the young and the old, the laity and the priests. And he assures us of the welcome we receive on our return to him from a God who is 'all tenderness and compassion, rich in graciousness, taking pity on his people'.

Gospel: The gospel, finally, warns us not to parade our special efforts in Lent to impress anyone but God. 'Your Father, who sees all that is done in secret, will reward you.'

Prayer-Lines: God, our Father, thank you for granting us this favourable time for being fully reconciled with you. Unite us more fully these days with your Son, Jesus, in his work of reconciling humanity to you. Amen.

Thursday after Ash Wednesday
First Reading: Deut 30:15-20; Gospel: Lk 9:22-25

1st *Reading:* 'Choose life ... in the love of your God ... for in this your life consists.' Today we enter deeper into the mystery of this 'joyful season of Lent' (Preface) which prepares us for rising with Christ at Easter. There is a gap of some six hundred years between our two readings, but they have an essential message in common. They are both begging people to make a right choice before it is too late. Moses, in the first reading, is pictured giving his last warning before the Chosen People cross the Jordan to enter the Promised Land. He has had ample experience of the unreliability of his people in being faithful to the covenant of Sinai and the ten commandments. And yet their whole future depends on a loving fidelity to God, the God who had brought them out of slavery in Egypt. 'Choose life, then', he begs them, 'in the love of your God'.

Gospel: In the gospel too Jesus utters a warning to every generation. To all he said, 'Anyone who wants to save his life will lose it.' A follower of Christ must follow the Son of Man who 'is destined to suffer grievously, be put to death, and be raised up on the third day.' In the gospel this challenge comes shortly after his question to the apostles, 'But who do you say that I am?' Lent, in particular, is a time for asking ourselves, 'What is Christ to me?' If he is really our Saviour, the centre of our lives, then we must, as his Father bid us at the Transfiguration, 'listen to him'. By the power of his Spirit who raised him from the dead, we must be willing to share the glory of his sufferings as well as of his rising.

Prayer-Lines: God, our Father, we thank you for this sobering as well as joyful season of Lent. May our attendance at Mass teach us to follow Christ through the narrow gate of his Passover mystery.

Friday after Ash Wednesday
First Reading: Is 58:1-9; Gospel: Mt 9:14-15

1st Reading: 'The sort of fast that pleases me: to share your bread with the hungry.' Our readings today are a good example of how the gospel completes the Old Testament without weakening its message for us. It is clear enough from the first reading that our fasting or self-denial is of no value before God if it is not a sign of conversion of heart. And Isaiah lists the various signs of this conversion of heart. We can sum them up in practical goodness to one another, especially those who are in greater need.

Gospel: But Jesus' comment on the question of fasting goes further, though he speaks in the language of allusion and metaphor: 'The Bridegroom' was another name for the Messiah. The messianic age, when God would come to save his people, was conceived as a great wedding feast, the wedding of Yahweh with his people, a day of great joy, therefore.

Does that mean, therefore, that fasting and self-denial are not for Christians? Not so. 'When the bridegroom is taken away, then they will fast.' Scholars tell us that this sentence was added by the early Christian church after the resurrection, when the anniversary of Christ's passion was formally marked by a Christian fast. It is a happy corollary of Christ's words. Our Lenten penance, then, should always be seen in the light of Christ's death on our behalf, as our share in the Bridegroom's death. As St Paul puts it, we were baptised in Jesus' death to enable us to live a new life; to share in Christ's risen life in the eternal feast of his resurrection.

Prayer-Lines: Lord Jesus, may our Lenten observance deepen our knowledge and love of you, our Bridegroom, and make us more sensitive to the needs of those around us.

Saturday after Ash Wednesday
First Reading: Is 58:9-14; Gospel: Lk 5:27-32

Gospel: 'Who needs the doctor but the sick?' It was astonishing enough for the Pharisees and Scribes, who thought themselves the religious elite, that Jesus should include among his disciples a tax-collector. It sounds a neutral enough job-description for us, but in Jesus' world, especially for the religious leaders, it covered almost the sense of the 'untouchables'. The tax collectors' profession kept them in constant touch with Gentiles, and therefore ritually unclean. Jesus and his disciples would incur the same defilement. Jesus justified his actions by his motivation. He was there as a healer of the unhealthy. Which attitude can we detect in ourselves? Lent is a good time for considering the matter.

1st Reading: Our first reading continues yesterday's enumeration of what God considers genuine conversion of heart. He identifies himself with the disadvantaged, the hungry and the oppressed. He will reward our practical concern for them by his guidance and comfort in our own distress. Nor is Isaiah's insistence on observing the Sabbath irrelevant in today's climate of liberalism. Honouring the Lord's day is a privileged way of expressing our fidelity to the covenant of our baptismal promises. It proclaims our acknowledgement of all we owe to God, our Creator and our Saviour. The day consecrated to him must come before any human concerns.

Prayer-Lines: Lord Jesus, help us during this Lent to expose our weakness to your healing power, and share in your care for the underprivileged.

First Week of Lent: Monday
First Reading: Lev 19: 1-2, 11-18; Gospel: Mt 25:31-46

Gospel: 'Be holy, for I, the Lord your God, am holy.' The Old Testament injunction in our first reading is also a key to our gospel. 'You whom my Father has blessed', in Jesus' words, are the ones who have imitated Jesus' Father as he has described him in the Sermon on the Mount.

It is the Father's universal goodness and compassion that these blessed ones on Jesus' right hand on the Last Day have imitated. How? In giving food to the hungry, drink to the thirsty, clothes to the naked, visiting the sick and the imprisoned. All these acts of spontaneous charity are the talents the Father has given them to trade with. Those who failed in these duties of charity are the ones who have hidden their Father's talent in the ground; have borne no fruit for him.

1st Reading: With the Book of Leviticus, from which our first reading comes, we are at the roots of Israel's moral life – and ours. Its overall theme is God's holiness, which he wishes to share with his people as he dwells in their midst, through worship with which the whole book is largely concerned. But through a worship where we meet God's presence as a dynamic power. And no empty ritual, but a worship which commits us to mirror his holiness in personal, effective concern for our fellow-creatures. 'You must love your neighbour as yourself.' The weaker members of society, the labourer, the dumb, the blind, must be shown God's preferential option for them. Another relevant case in the same chapter that might have been included in the reading runs: 'If you have resident aliens in your country, you will not molest them. Love them as yourself, for you yourselves were aliens in Egypt.'

Prayer-lines: God our Father, help us by our Lenten observance to mirror your compassionate love for us all, especially towards those most in need of our care.

First Week of Lent: Tuesday
First Reading: Is 55: 10-11; Gospel: Mt 6:7-15

Gospel: 'In your prayers do not babble as the pagans do.' If Lent is meant to be a time for making up for our slackness at other seasons, it must naturally apply especially to our prayer. Prayer in every form. Therefore vocal prayer too. Even the Our Father. We might be embarrassed today at Jesus' admonition 'not to babble'. A problem with the Our Father may be its very familiarity for us, which dulls our sensitivity to its meaning. Perhaps one way of 'reviving' it is to see how much it is the prayer of Jesus: perhaps the summary of all his prayers.

'Father', the first word, is the hallmark of all Jesus' prayer, as 'the kingdom' is the theme of his preaching. The rest can be found in his prayer at the Last Supper, and in Gethsemani. He prays to the Father there to save his disciples from the Evil One. At Gethsemani he tells them they should be awake and praying not to be put to the test ('temptation'). Finally, he asks that his Father's will may be done, not his own.

First Reading: In the first reading we hear, 'the Word that goes from my mouth does not return to me empty.' The Our Father, as Jesus' prayer, is the word of God-made-flesh. When we say the Our Father as speaking for the church, especially at Mass, we are wielding a mighty power. God's triumph over the rule of Satan becomes more real. The 'daily bread' of our material life is transformed into the bread of everlasting life. We are reconciled to God as to one another. We are clothed in his armour against apostasy in the final trial.

Prayer-lines: Lord Jesus, thank you for teaching us to pray with you through the Our Father. Help us to understand more fully and desire the graces it asks for.

First Week of Lent: Wednesday
First Reading: Jon 3: 1-10; Gospel: Lk 11:29-32

First Reading: 'And the people of Nineveh believed in God.' The book of Jonah is a fascinating example of 'protest literature'. Jonah was indeed an historical character, but barely mentioned in Israel's history. The story here told in our first reading belongs to a much later time. Israel has now returned to Palestine from exile, and is clinging in extremist fashion to its exclusive rights before God. Jonah is painted as being very reluctant to obey God's command to go and preach to the great city of Nineveh. At first he tries to run away. In today's passage he actually goes, but does his minimum of preaching (he made only a day's journey into it!). He is hoping they won't repent, and will, therefore, be destroyed. Nineveh, however, led by its king, does repent seriously, and wins the reward of God's forgiveness.

Gospel: 'Something greater than Jonah is here.' Jesus, in the gospel, is referring not to himself directly so much as to the kingdom, the potent presence of God in his own words and deeds. 'Something greater' is, of course, a monumental understatement. But it brings home to us that Jesus' reproachful finger is pointing as much at our generation as at his own. We say at Mass, 'You come to us in word and sacrament to strengthen us in holiness.' But how far do we live by that word, and by the power we receive in his sacraments? No doubt we might also examine our conscience in the light of the Book of Jonah. Are we too, like the Jews returned from exile, complacent in the many graces we have received by our Christian faith and dismissive of the greater virtue often shown by other denominations in their way of living?

Prayer-lines: May the season of Lent bring home to us the many blessings that are ours who live 'in the fulness of time'. May the words of the gospel blot out our sins.

First Week of Lent: Thursday
First Reading: Est 4: 17; Gospel: Mt 7:7-12

First Reading: 'My Lord, come to my help, for I have no helper but you.' This is certainly a prayer 'out of the depths', of one well-nigh in despair. Queen Esther is a young Jewess who has been taken into the harem of the king of Persia. Her uncle, a faithful Jew, has informed her that the first minister has persuaded the king to order the extermination of all her people. He begs her to intercede with the king. But she knows that it is a mortal offence to approach the king unless one is sent for. Hence her heartfelt cry to God. 'Give me courage when I face the lion.' Her prayer, of course, is heard, and the Jews are saved.

Gospel: People say that even a professed atheist is capable of praying in a moment of desperation. But Jesus' injunction in the gospel, 'Ask and it will be given to you', teaches us far more about prayer than that. 'It will be given' is one of the Jewish reverential ways of saying 'God will give it to you.' And God, he says, is 'our heavenly Father', much more eager to give good things to those who ask him. St Paul says 'we don't know how to pray as we ought, but the Spirit personally makes petition for us…' We should have that constant image of God pushing or pulling us, not only to do good deeds, but to ask him for good things. And not just for a prayer of quiet and contemplation, or even for thanks and praise for his endless benefits, but to ask for good things. Not to ask God for good things does not leave him the richer: it simply impedes his action in the world.

Prayer-lines: God our Father, through the Our Fathers prayed by all Christians, may your kingdom come, may your will be done on earth as it is in heaven.

First Week of Lent: Friday
First Reading: Ezek 18: 21-28; Gospel: Mt 5:20-26

1st Reading: 'Am I to take pleasure in the death of a wicked man?' The context in which Ezechiel is preaching is all-important. He is preaching in Babylon to the Jews who have been exiled there from Jerusalem for their failure to listen to the prophets and give up their idolatry. Their spiritual horizon is now indeed a bleak one. Up to now their ideas on sin and punishment have been largely corporate. The individual must suffer for the sins of his ancestors. But Ezechiel here defends God's love for each individual. 'Thus says the Lord: when the sinner renounces sin he shall certainly live; he shall not die.' But what of the upright man who lapses, and becomes a sinner instead? 'For this he shall die.' But is that fair? Yes, because the life in question is not physical life but the life of communion with God. That communion has been broken deliberately by man, not by God. God will not cancel our freedom even if we prefer to abuse it.

Gospel: 'If your virtue goes no deeper than that of the Scribes and Pharisees ...' It is a danger not only of the past, but is always with us. Today's gospel shows us the pillars of that virtue: a fixed law ('thou shalt not kill'), and material sacrifices. Even the Old Testament realised how inadequate such a negative commandment was. The positive command was added: 'you must love your neighbour as yourself'. So Jesus is only half-correcting the commandment here by forbidding anger and abuse. He will add the full correction later on: 'Love your enemy', as God does his! The nature of Christian sacrifice has changed, but the spirit condemned by Jesus may linger on. Can we, for example, think our prayers are of value in God's eyes if we still deny our brothers or sisters the love that proves our love of God?

Prayer-lines: Lord, by the grace of Lent may all Christians learn to forgo all resentment and live at peace with one another.

First Week of Lent: Saturday
First Reading: Deut 26:16:19; Gospel: Mt 5:43-48

First Reading: 'These laws you must keep with all your heart and all your soul.' Deuteronomy is a summit of Old Testament teaching. It purports to be Moses' last address to the Chosen People before they entered the Promised Land. But it was edited again long after Moses was dead and the desert left behind. Now looking back over Israel's laws and troubled history, it did two things. One, it simplified this complex of laws by reducing it to one basic one: Thou shalt love the Lord the God with all thy heart. Secondly it interiorised the Law. It made Israel's religion a religion of the heart: 'with all thy heart' recurs in the text constantly. Its one fatal flaw was to link religious fidelity to God's temporal reward. We shall see the contrast in the gospel.

Gospel: 'You have learnt how it was said.' Jesus has taken six examples from the Law – the touchstone of holiness for the scribes and Pharisees – to show how far it falls short of the holiness required of his disciples. Today's example is the climax: 'Love your enemies and pray for them.' Where will you find that in the Law, the prophets or the psalms? For the enemies of the just are the wicked, and the only prayer for them is for their destruction. Such was the last blow Jesus gave to current Jewish ideas of holiness. And now he reveals the only possible justification for such a superhuman programme. 'You are sons of God, and you must be like your Father.' He shows love to his enemies. You can do no less. As someone has said, 'All Christian holiness is summed up in *Abba*.' If we really treat God as our Father, the rest will follow.

Prayer-lines: God, our Father, grant us an ever-greater share in the Spirit of our adoption, that we may love even our enemies with your love.

Second Week of Lent: Monday

First Reading: Dan 9: 4-10; Gospel: Lk 6:36-38

c.165 3c.

First Reading: 'To us, Lord, the look of shame belongs. To the Lord God, mercy and pardon belong.' Poignant prayer, fed by the prophets' unique intimacy with God, was the great gift of the Jews in the ancient world. Few, if any of them, can surpass this prayer of Daniel, the young Jewish visionary at the court of Babylon. In the book to which he gives his name he voices the pleas of his exiled people who have seen what they feel is the ultimate in a people's humiliation: the destruction of their city, Jerusalem, and their temple, and their deportation to distant Babylon. It might even seem to overstate the case if we fail to see in it a genuine sense of Israel's infidelity down the centuries to its covenant with its God at Sinai. Nor is it too difficult to make that confession of guilt our own, as we reflect on all the violence and corruption of the 20th and earlier centuries in a so-called Christian era.

Gospel: And yet, today's gospel assures us, that is only half the story of 'the sin of the world'. Daniel indeed could recognise that 'God has kindness for those that love him'. But Jesus can even enjoin on us to share and show our Father's compassion, 'for he knows the stuff of which we are made'. We are not condemned to the instinctual reactions of nature, which the Old Testament could accept: 'an eye for an eye and a tooth for a tooth'. By the Spirit of Christ which we have received we are capable of not judging others; of not condemning; of granting pardon for offences; of giving (and forgiving) generously beyond the measure of mere justice. That compassion is a genuine sharing in God's fatherly understanding of the frailty of the human condition. Our imitation of him, in the footsteps of Christ, is indeed the proof that the kingdom of God is here.

Prayer-lines: God, our Father, we thank you for forgiving us in Christ. Fill us with your Holy Spirit that we may be compassionate with others, as you are with us.

Second Week of Lent: Tuesday

First Reading: Is 1: 10, 16-20; Gospel: Mt 23:1-12

Gospel: 'The greatest among you must be your servant.' Scripture's message is for every generation. We too can be heirs of the Pharisees' weaknesses. There is a perennial danger of making religion (a) a matter of rules; (b) a tool of power and prestige. Jesus' teaching is clear in the second half of this passage. Religion is a matter of our personal relationship with Jesus, and with God as our Father. God is the only Master that matters. The only one whose approval of us counts. And Jesus is the only Teacher to enlighten us. We have constantly to check our spiritual bearings to see if our relationships with the Father and the Son – sustained in us by the Spirit given us in baptism – to see if these relationships are our guidelines in life. And the practical test of that orthodoxy is given us in the final word: 'The greatest among you must be your servant.'

First Reading: 'Take your wrongdoing out of my sight.' Advent and Christmas have made us familiar with Isaiah as the prophet of hope. But his starting-point in today's reading is in a sinful Jerusalem, to which he is passionately attached. And his opening vision of God is as 'the Holy One of Israel', sitting invisibly enthroned in the Temple surrounded by the heavenly court perpetually acclaiming his holiness. The appalling contrast between this holy Presence in the heart of a sinful people fills Isaiah with horror. And yet his message is not one of despair. God is still eager to use the power of his holiness to transform this guilty people into a worthy one. Isaiah's immediate concern is for social justice: 'help the oppressed, the widow and the orphan'. In a world of so much social injustice as ours, even on a global scale, Isaiah's message has lost none of its relevance for us.

Prayer-lines: Lord, may this Lent deepen our sense of your presence in our midst, in word and sacrament and people. Send forth your Spirit, Lord, to give us a new heart and a new spirit.

Second Week of Lent: Wednesday

First Reading: Jer 18: 18-20; Gospel: Mt 20:17-28

Gospel: 'The Son of Man came to give his life as a ransom for many.' Today's gospel brings us to the primary theme of Lent: our preparation for the mystery of the death and resurrection of Christ. But we still find ourselves (for we can always identify with the disciples, as well as with the Pharisees) in the toils of self-interest. Bad enough to find that it is the sons of Zebedee, two of his first disciples that are involved, but so are all twelve of them. 'The ten were indignant with the two brothers.' The laws of group dynamics are patent. Their assessment of the egoism of the two is faultless, but they can't see, as Jesus does, that the 'beam' of egoism is in their own eyes too. He has to reprove them all. The rewards of high places that all of them are seeking have been allotted by his Father. They are not for him to give. It is for him, the Son, the Beloved Servant, to give his life for all of them. Well may St Paul write to the Philippians: 'Make your own that mind that was in Christ Jesus.'

First Reading: If Isaiah is pre-eminently the prophet we link with Advent, Jeremiah (our first passage today) is the one to keep company with in Lent. 'Who do men say that I am?' You remember that to some of his contemporaries Jesus had seemed a second Jeremiah. And apart from David there is no individual in the Old Testament that we know as fully as Jeremiah. In today's reading he is fully conscious of being plotted against by his own people: 'They are digging a pit for me'. This is the people he was devoted to and prayed for, to turn God's wrath away from them. Passages like this must have made Jesus' future rejection by his people daily more clear to him. Even Jeremiah's bewilderment at God's apparent readiness to let his enemies have their way: 'Should evil be returned for good?', foreshadows Jesus' last words on the cross: 'Why have you forsaken me?'

Prayer-lines: God our Father, give us this Lent some share of Christ's self-giving for the salvation of all.

Second Week of Lent: Thursday

First Reading: Jer 17: 5-10; Gospel: Lk 16: 19-31

Gospel: Today's gospel story contrasting the destiny of rich and poor is another instance of the 'option for the poor' in Luke's gospel. 'Blessed are you poor' is its version of the Beatitudes. It is also appropriate reading for Lent, as almsgiving is, together with prayer and fasting, a traditional Lenten practice. The story of the rich man and Lazarus is, apparently, a well-known folk-tale from Egypt. But Luke adds on to it an allusion to the lack of faith of Jesus' generation. If the rich are unprepared to follow the basic Old Testament teaching (of Moses and the prophets) what chance have they of accepting the mystery of the kingdom in Jesus' person, and the resurrection? 'They will not be convinced even if one should rise from the dead.' The practice of even Old Testament virtue is a necessary foundation for believing in the Good News of Christ.

First Reading: Perhaps that too is part of the message of the wisdom sayings in our first reading. 'The man who relies on things of flesh' will bear no fruit for God. 'He is like dry scrub in the wastelands. If good comes, he has no eyes for it.' On the contrary, 'the man who puts his trust in the Lord (and therefore obeys his commands) never ceases to bear fruit.' These are not prophetic oracles on Jeremiah's lips: they are proverbial sayings, which we meet elsewhere. But they may well reflect the rueful tenor of Jeremiah's tortured thoughts on the perversity of his hearers. Certainly, both for him and for Jesus, the springs of true religion can only be found in the human heart, not in mere outward observance.

Prayer-lines: Through the hearing of your word, Lord, may we come to know you in our hearts, and live according to your will.

Second Week of Lent: Friday

Friday – 2ⁿᵈ Week,   FEED FROM THE TREE OF LIFE

First Reading: Gen 37; Gospel: Mt 21: 33-43, 45-46

Gospel: 'The kingdom of God will be taken from you, and given to a people who will produce its fruit.' Our gospel from this on will illustrate the growing conflict between the religious leaders and Jesus, a conflict that will lead to his death. The religious leaders of Israel, who are the tenants in our parable, had failed down the generations to make of Israel a people capable of accepting God's designs as embodied in Jesus and his teachings. Their privileges, therefore, would be taken from them and given to the Gentiles. Is there, perhaps, a lesson here for a post-Christian Europe whose failure to bear the due fruit of the Christian ideal to the world will see their long-lived privileged position in the faith transferred to other regions of the world?

First Reading: Joseph, in our first reading, is a rare but welcome arrival on our liturgical screen. He is the ideal man of the Old Testament, outstanding in the moral virtues, patience, chastity, wisdom and mercy. As such he is indeed a prefiguration of Christ. But he is such even more in his story. Heartlessly sold into slavery by his brothers, he is providentially enabled by God to become a potentate in Egypt, and thus the saviour of the family of Jacob, the nucleus of the Chosen People. After the death of Jacob in Egypt the guilt-stricken brothers come to ask his forgiveness. He greets them in compassionate tones worthy of Christ. 'Do not be afraid. Is it for me to put myself in God's place? The evil you planned to do me has by God's design been turned to good, to bring about the survival of a numerous people.

Prayer-lines: God, our Father, may our Lenten scripture readings deepen our sense of sin, and of confidence in your mercy.

Second Week of Lent: Saturday

First Reading: Mic 7:14-15, 18-20; Gospel: Lk 15:1-3, 11-32
                    ᵉ 7ₐᵢ — 7ₒ).

Gospel: 'This man welcomes sinners and eats with them.' It is important for us to remember that Jesus is the father of the two sons in the parable. The prodigal's words make Jesus' identity clear. 'I have sinned against heaven and against you.' 'Heaven' is the Jewish reverential way of speaking of God. And yet, of course, Jesus is not distinguishing his conduct from that of his 'Father in heaven'. He knows (in Paul's words) that 'God (namely the Father) is in him (Jesus) reconciling the world to himself.'

The elder brother represents the Pharisees and the scribes with their disdain for 'the tax-collectors and sinners' that Jesus is welcoming. The contrast with the 'father' is glaring. And yet the father does not condemn them. Jesus assures them that they too are the object of his love. But he reminds them of their family bond with the prodigal: 'Your brother here was dead, and has come to life.' With which attitude towards sinners do we identify?

First Reading: Our first reading, from the prophet Micah, confirms the compassionate nature of God. 'What God can compare with you: delighting in showing mercy?' Our passage has been described as a liturgy of repentance. For, on the whole, Micah's prophecy is one of denunciation and doom. He prophesied one hundred years before Jeremiah. 'Israel', that is, the northern kingdom, has already been deported into exile. Judah is now repeating Israel's sins of social injustice, oppression of the poor. So Micah (prophetically) sees Israel's punishment in store for Judah too. Only in the thought of God's mercy (and in the prophecy of a saviour to be born in Bethlehem) can Micah find any consolation.

Prayer-lines: Lord Jesus, may our Lenten readings of scripture send us speedily back to you to find forgiveness.

Third Week of Lent: Monday
First Reading: 2 Kgs 5:1-15; Gospel: Lk 4:24-30

Gospel: 'No prophet is ever accepted in his own country.' Today's gospel has truncated the full account (according to Luke) of Jesus' first preaching in his own town, Nazareth. Invited to read the statutory Sabbath reading from the prophets, Jesus chooses Isaiah. There he selects and reads out the Good News of the coming of God's Spirit to free the poor, the sick and the social outcasts. Sitting down then as the preacher, he assures the congregation that these prophetic promises are being fulfilled in his own person and his powers. At first his listeners marvel at his eloquence and his assurance. Then their familiarity with their townsman breeds suspicion. And parochialism. Why has he worked all these wonders and built up such a reputation at Capernaum instead of his home town? Jesus steadfastly insists that God's goodness is not restricted to the people of Israel. It extends to all who are afflicted. The climactic reaction of the Nazarenes is a striking foreshadowing of Jesus' later rejection in Jerusalem.

First Reading: Our first reading exemplifies the idea of the prophet as a dominant figure in Israel's 'salvation history'. The story of Naaman significantly shows a prophet using his miraculous powers in favour of a Gentile, and for an enemy people at that. Typical too are the contrasts emphasised. The apparently insignificant means God uses to bring healing to the humanly mighty: the little Israelite captive girl sets the wheel of General Naaman's healing in motion. The bathing in the modest river Jordan gives Naaman back 'the flesh of a little child'. The punchline, of course, for its contemporaries is the last: 'Now I know there is no God in all the earth but in Israel.'

Prayer-lines: God, our Father, deepen our faith in your presence in others, and give us a share in your love for the afflicted.

Third Week of Lent: Tuesday

First Reading: Dan 3:25, 34-43; Gospel: Mt 18: 21-35

Gospel: 'Forgive him not seven, but seventy-seven times.' There are no ambiguities in this parable. No need for the disciples to ask Jesus for an explanation afterwards. There is no problem about identifying the characters in the drama, or the debts involved, be they towards God or to ourselves. The only question that seems worth asking is: How could the first servant have been so merciless after receiving such overwhelming mercy from his master? The answer, insofar as the parable indicates it is, I think, in the words 'He went out...' He went out from the master's presence and thereby became a different man. I am reminded of St.John's account of Judas at the Last Supper. 'As soon as he had taken the piece of bread, he went out. It was night'. Conversely, the key to being merciful, seventy-seven times, is never, in thought or spirit to go out from the master's presence.

First Reading: Our first reading from the Book of Daniel is a worthy pendant to Jesus' incomparable parable on mercy, God's ineffable mercy which should be the model for ours towards our 'fellow-servants'. 'Treat us gently,' Azariah prays, 'as you yourself are gentle.' The prayer is made in a dramatic setting. The three young Judaeans have refused to worship the statue of the king of Babylon, and are thereby thrown into the blazing furnace. There they are untouched. An angel, representing God, joins them there to assure their safety. A salutary reminder again of the need to keep God's nearness in mind in 'overheated' situations in life.

Prayer-lines: Lord Jesus, may this season of Lent, which recalls us to all you have suffered to atone for us, be a season of heartfelt forgiveness and reconciliation among all Christians, and throughout the world.

Third Week of Lent: Wednesday
First Reading: Deut 4:1, 5-9; Gospel: Mt 5:17-19

First Reading: 'No other people is as wise and prudent'. Deuteronomy, which gives us our first reading, means literally 'a second
law'. In fact it is a kind of second edition of Israel's laws, already
given us in earlier books: Exodus, Leviticus, Numbers. In the
meantime the 'editors' (shall we say) have been enriched by the
teachings of the prophets and Israel's wisdom books. Hosea, for
instance, will have emphasised that what God wants is not just
external conformity to laws so much as heartfelt love of God. For
God is essentially a loving God, a giving God, who gives land
and life, and 'laws and customs that lead to life'. The Ten
Commandments were not regarded as a burden, restrictions on
conduct, but as a gift, a revelation. In fact, they represented
God's guiding presence with his people.

Gospel: With all this in mind we can better understand Jesus'
words in the gospel about the Law and the prophets: 'I have not
come to abolish, but to complete them.' Jesus is indeed the full
presence of God with humankind, giving us not new laws, but a
deeper motive for keeping them, a deeper gratitude than
Israel's. This is the sense in which his commandments are to be
treasured: as the expression of our love for him as God's continuing presence and power in our lives. At first sight the insistence
of St Matthew on the permanence of the Law as binding might
seem a direct contradiction to Paul's teaching on Christian living
in the Spirit. But Paul's critique of 'the Law' refers more to detailed pharisaic prescriptions than to the commandments. And
Matthew's approach is a positive counter balance for his time to
a view that might be open to libertinism. At all events, in all our
conduct Christ remains the model: for Paul more than anyone
else.

Prayer-lines: God, our Father, thank you for your presence with
us in your commandments. Make us wise by our fidelity to
them.

Third Week of Lent: Thursday
First Reading: Jer 7:23-28; Gospel: Lk 11:14-23

First Reading: 'Here is the nation that will not listen to the voice of its God.' In yesterday's reading from Deuteronomy we heard Moses' assurance to his people that the world would envy their wisdom in having such 'laws and customs' as they had been given at Sinai. All the more searing, therefore, is God's denunciation of that people through Jeremiah. 'They did not listen ... They turned their backs on me.' Judah's sins were sins of social injustice, oppression of the poor. But our present passage follows a blistering indictment of something else: Judah's insincere Temple worship. 'When I bought your ancestors out of Egypt.' God tells them, 'I gave no orders about sacrifices and burnt offerings.' And, he goes on to say: These were my orders: 'Listen to my voice; then I will be your God, and your shall be my people.' These are, of course, the basic terms of the Covenant at Sinai. But now, he continues, 'Sincerity is no more; it has vanished from their mouths.'

Gospel: In the light of this total condemnation, it might seem as if all were lost for the Chosen People. But the gospel still remains God's Good News for us. Jesus can assure us that if he casts out devils, the reign and the kingdom of God has overtaken us. Yes, while Beelzebub, the prince of devils, was 'the strong man guarding his own palace (even amid God's people), his goods were undisturbed'. But now Jesus, the stronger one, has attacked and defeated him, and shares out his spoils. Let us never cease to glory in this dearly-bought victory of Christ over evil and man's infidelity.

Prayer-lines: Lord Jesus, strengthen our faith in you as our 'stronger one' in our lives: able and eager to overcome all power of evil in us and in society.

Third Week of Lent: Friday
First Reading: Hos 14:2-10; Gospel: Mk 12:28-34

First Reading: 'I will heal their disloyalty, I will love them with all my heart.' After Jeremiah's denunciation yesterday of God's people for its insincere worship, Hosea's message of comfort is a welcome change. Once Israel responds to God's appeal to 'Come back', he will forget and heal their sin. For he is the one in whom 'orphans find compassion'. Yahweh, in his forgiveness will show them that he is the source of all nature's blessings. 'I will fall like dew, bloom like the lily, spread abroad like the poplar, the corn, the vines, the wine of Helbon'. Hosea's distinctive contribution to our image of God is his presentation of him as Israel's husband (Baal in Hebrew!). So, to convey the strength and tenderness of God's marital love Hosea uses the language of Israel's love-songs: 'fragrance of Lebanon; dwell in the shade; wine and lily'. The whole line of Christian mysticism is in debt to Hosea.

Gospel: 'Seeing how wisely he had spoken, Jesus said, 'You are not far from the kingdom.' We share Jesus' satisfaction today at meeting for once a scribe who is both friendly and wise in his acceptance of Jesus' teaching: making love God's primary commandment. That primacy of love is indeed the highest wisdom of the kingdom. This was indeed Old Testament wisdom too, as Hosea, and after him Deuteronomy proclaimed. But there was a constant danger for Israel of making God's will predominantly a man's observance of the law of the covenant. (It can be a danger for us too.) But love has been made easier for us by God showing us his face in Jesus of Nazareth. And Jesus tells us we see that face too in all the underprivileged and marginalised. How wise are we in practice?

Prayer-lines: God our Father, teach us to recognise you as always as the God of love, in the face of Christ and of others, and even in our own chequered lives.

Third Week of Lent: Saturday

First Reading: Hos 5:15-6:6; Gospel: Lk 18: 9-14

First Reading: Yesterday we were cheered by Yahweh's promises to restore his loving favour to Israel. That was from the end of Hosea's book: 'the end of the affair'. But we need also to hear today of the stormy passages of their love-affair that preceded this promised reconciliation. Yahweh has declared his anger at their disloyalty – their idolatry in which priests and king and people have all indulged. He will treat them, therefore, like an angry lion till they return to him. But even this return, he knows, is only a show, a lip-service. It is not their temple sacrifices (lawful though they be) that he wants of them, but their love from a sincere heart.

Gospel: 'Knowledge of God, not sacrifice' might well do as the title of Jesus' parable in today's gospel. 'Let us set ourselves to know the Lord', was the insincere slogan of Israel in Hosea's time. And surely the knowledge of God is the one thing necessary for us all. But there is a catch. Knowledge of him means really love of him. Accepting him as he is; and ourselves as we are. And that is the price that the Pharisee in us can find too high to pay. It means giving up all self-esteem, as did the tax-collector. 'When we have done all that we ought,' Jesus tells us elsewhere, 'we are only poor slaves.' This means trusting in nothing but God's mercy. We have our choice. The self-respecting religion of merely outward observance of the Pharisee, or the 'God, be merciful to me a sinner' disposition of the tax-collector. And only he 'went home again at rights with God'.

Prayer-lines: Lord, create for us a pure heart that we may know your will and follow it in sincerity and truth.

Fourth Week of Lent: Monday
First Reading: Is 65:17-21; Gospel: Jn 4:43-54

Gospel: 'Your son will live.' And he and all his household believed. As we enter the fourth week in Lent, our gospel readings
change from Matthew, Mark and Luke (the synoptic gospels) to
that of John (the fourth gospel). Written down later than the others,
at the end of the first century AD, it reflects the deeper understanding of Jesus and his mysteries which the early church
acquired by its pondering on them. In a later chapter than
today's passage Jesus will say, 'I came that they might have life,
and have it to the full'. And the very last line of the whole gospel
explains why it was written: 'that you may believe that Jesus is
the Christ, the Son of God, and that believing, you may have life
in his name.' Today's account of a second miracle in Cana in
Galilee is one example among other 'signs' which John has chosen of the life-giving faith which Jesus' deeds evoke. His first
sign in Cana, we remember, which gave that faith to his disciples, was the changing of water into wine.

First Reading: And in our first readings too we turn from our
three weeks pondering with the prophets on the mystery of sin
in God's Chosen People to the final stage of God's restoration,
when punishment is ended. 'I create a new heavens and a new
earth.' God is now taking over in a work which he alone can do:
transformation of the universe. Not merely will this new creation be 'Joy for Jerusalem and gladness for her people'. God too
will be happy with them. 'I shall rejoice over Jerusalem and
exult in my people.' It will be the last word in that long and
chequered history of that marriage bond contracted at Sinai between God and Israel.

Prayer-lines: Lord, deepen our faith in your presence, in the second half of Lent, that we may be filled with your life at your
Son's resurrection.

Fourth Week of Lent: Tuesday

First Reading: Ezek 47:1-9, 12; Gospel: Jn 5:1-3, 5-16

First Reading: 'Life teemed wherever the river flows.' In our first reading Ezechiel, portrayed as writing among the exiles in Babylon, is describing the new Jerusalem to be restored by God when the exile is over. The heart of this new Jerusalem will be the new Temple. Ezechiel describes in loving detail its dimensions, its surrounds and its cult, which had been so defiled before the exile. Once it has been restored by God to its proper cultic holiness, it will be a life-giving source for the restored people. Its imagery is drawn from the account of creation in the book of Genesis. In the Near and Middle East water and life are nearly synonymous. The river in Eden is described as branching into four great streams. The river issuing from the new Temple will bring with it life and healing and fertility in abundance. It is a worthy climax of Ezechiel's vision of the restoration of God's presence to his formerly unfaithful people.

Gospel: Ezechiel's river-of-life vision is also an appropriate pendant for the gospel. In St John's gospel Jesus has already presented himself as the new Temple. And from now on he will show himself increasingly as a source of healing and of life. But in using his healing power on the Sabbath he will incur the hostility of the religious authorities. Their ongoing 'persecution' of Jesus for such infringements of the Law prepare us for the climax of his arrest, passion and death. As individuals in John's gospel are intended to have symbolic value in their relationship to Jesus, our paralytic would seem to be allied more with Jesus' opponents that with his followers. Where do we stand? We too are invited by the fourth gospel to declare our allegiance, for or against Jesus.

Prayer-lines: Lord Jesus, strengthen our faith in you as healer of our sins and source of our eternal life.

Fourth Week of Lent: Wednesday
First Reading: Is 49:8-15; Gospel: Jn 5:17-30

Gospel: 'The Son can do only what he sees the Father doing.' From now on our weekday gospel readings in St John will show us Jesus on trial by his enemies. Yesterday we saw him accused of healing a man on the Sabbath. Today he is guilty of a far greater sin. 'He spoke of God as his own Father, and thus made himself God's equal.' Scholars agree that in these self-defence discourses of Jesus we have (as elsewhere in the four gospels) a 'double-exposure', so to speak, of the film. We are given not only Jesus' words, but also echoes of the debates of the early church with the Jews at the end of the first century. The case for defence smacks very much of a synagogue debate. The Pharisees in this matter of the Sabbath would agree that God himself worked on the Sabbath by enabling people to be born, and others to rise from the dead for judgement. It is a precious glimpse for us both of Jesus' day, and of the problems of the early church in later decades.

First Reading: However, if the gospel shows us clouds of hostility gathering over Jesus' head, Isaiah in our first reading has prophetic good news to counterbalance the gathering storm. The greater reality lying behind Jesus' ultimate rejection by the people of his day is God's continuing love for his people. 'Even if a woman forgets her baby at her breast, I will never forget you.' And God's agent in this great saving victory is the mysterious figure of the 'Servant of Yahweh'. 'I have formed you and appointed you as covenant of the people.' This faithful Servant of God's strategy of salvation will come fully into view in our Holy Week readings. For the moment we are just assured that the victory will be his. A victory with land restored and people consoled, cattle feeding in rich pastures. A worthy reason indeed for heaven and earth to rejoice together.

Prayer-lines: God, our Father, thank you for revealing yourself to us in the person and words of Jesus. Help us to listen to him with faith in his power over all our ills, of body and soul.

Fourth Week of Lent: Thursday
First Reading: Exod 32:7-14; Gospel: Jn 5:31-47

Gospel: 'There is another witness who can speak on my behalf.' Jesus is still on trial today before the Jews, both for his healing the paralytic on a Sabbath, and especially for calling God his Father. But Jesus does not need to mount his own defence. He can now bring in four formidable witnesses. John the Baptist, of whom they had once been proud. God himself has witnessed to him. So do the scriptures, which are for them the very source of eternal life. And, fourthly, Moses, their great Lawgiver. 'If you refuse to believe what he wrote how can you believe what I say?'

First Reading: But who are the Jews whom Jesus is addressing? Not merely those of his own day. Like so much else in John's gospel 'the Jews' are symbolic: a symbol of all who refuse to believe in Jesus. And insofar as we too lack faith, Jesus' words are addressed to us. The Jews of Jesus' time thought they were far removed from their ancestors of our first reading who had made a golden calf in the desert. They knew God was invisible and transcendent. The 'calf' (or probably a young bull) was a symbol of Yahweh's power. But they wanted to 'harness' that power, to domesticate God by a visible image. They did not want an unpredictable God who would shape their lives by his unpredictable word. Neither did the Jews of Jesus' time want a God that spoke through a carpenter of Nazareth. How far are we prepared to let our lives be ruled by this unpredictable Word of God?

Prayer-lines: God our Father, thank you for sending us the words of eternal life in Jesus Christ. Give us the faith to live by his words.

Fourth Week of Lent: Friday
First Reading: Wis 2:1, 12-22; Gospel: Jn 7:1-2, 10, 25-30

Gospel: 'The Jews were out to kill him'. John's gospel, as we saw, presents Jesus' public life as an extended trial by the Jews. But also as a rehearsal of his death and resurrection. So today he speaks of the Jews intent to kill Jesus even though we are only at the feast of Tabernacles, some six months before his actual death. John does this because he is less interested in the actual motives of his enemies (the jealousy of the Pharisees; materialism of the Sadducees) than the deeper mystery of 'the sin of the world' (that we recall daily before our Communion). 'The light that shines in the dark' is how John speaks of Jesus in his Prologue. Today we read of one symptom of that darkness in which men live, with an illusion of knowing the truth: that of Jesus' origin. 'We all know where he comes from' they say, (meaning Nazareth). But really, unknown to them, Jesus comes from God: 'one who sent me, and I really come from him'.

First Reading: The darkness of which John's gospel speaks is from the devil. As Jesus will say of him: 'a murderer from the beginning'. Our first reading accurately portrays the thoughts of the devil's disciples. 'Let us lie in wait for the virtuous man. He boasts of having God for his Father... If he is God's son, God will take his part ... Let us condemn him to a shameful death.' This picture of the virtuous man as the victim of the wicked is based on Isaiah's description of the suffering servant. The liturgy invites us these days to enter compassionately into the deeper aspects of Jesus' death and final victory over the powers of evil, the power of darkness in the world.

Prayer-lines: God, our Father, we thank you for calling us in Jesus into the Light of the world. Help us to grow in his light, and to shun all feelings of resentment coming from the powers of darkness.

Fourth Week of Lent: Saturday
First Reading: Jer 11:18-20; Gospel: Jn 7:40-52

Gospel: 'So the people could not agree about him.' Something unusual about today's gospel. Is something missing? Yes. Jesus himself. As if we were watching a play on the stage and all the lights go off. Confusion follows. Jesus, as we saw, is for John 'the Light of the world', and when he 'moves off stage', as here, John indicates the confusion and uncertainty that follows. Some said, 'He is the Christ'. But others said, 'Would he be from Galilee?' 'Some would have liked to arrest him.' But even the police are overawed by his presence. The chief priests and the Pharisees, however, remain rigid in their antagonism, even when the timid Nicodemus urged that Jesus be given a fair trial. How right Jesus was, as John reports earlier about the success of his first miracles in Jerusalem: 'He did not trust himself to them … He could tell what a man had in him.'

First Reading: Yet in the liturgy today Jesus is not completely off the stage. We see him in the first reading, standing as it were in a corner, listening to what men say of him. 'Let us cut him off from the land of the living so that his name be quickly forgotten.' Jesus is there in the person of Jeremiah. It is not an invention of the liturgy, or even of the gospels, that Jesus was seen as a reflection of Jeremiah. Jesus himself saw that he would have to fulfil the role that Jeremiah played six hundred years earlier. His part, too, was 'like a trustful lamb being led to the slaughterhouse'. The great difference between them would be that Jesus, being God and not mere man like Jeremiah, would not call for vengeance, but for mercy.

Prayer-lines: God, our Father, thank you for the willing death of Jesus on our behalf. Help us to live no longer for ourselves, but for him who died for us and rose again.

Fifth Week of Lent: Monday: Year A
First Reading: 2 Kgs 4: 18-21, 32-37; Gospel: Jn 11: 1-45

Gospel: 'Through this sickness the Son of God will be glorified.'
John's Gospel presents Jesus' public life as a series of 'signs', culminating in the seventh sign, his death and resurrection.
Today's sign, the raising of Lazarus is the sixth. It is told in great
detail because it is also a rehearsal of Jesus' resurrection.

'The Son of God will be glorified through it.' The resurrection
of Lazarus plays two roles. First, it fulfils all that Jesus has hitherto said of himself and his mission. He is the light and the life of
the world. 'He who follows me will have the light of life.' Jesus
gives the water of life and the bread of life: and now life itself.
'The hour is coming when the dead will leave their graves at the
sound of his voice.' But Lazarus is also a symbol of the Christian:
'he whom you love is ill'. His resurrection is a pledge of all our
resurrections.

And, above all, Lazarus' rising from the dead is a pledge of
Jesus' own rising. Jesus is walking into certain danger of death
by coming as far as Bethany. Only a mile and a half from
Jerusalem. And, in fact, according to John, Lazarus's resurrection is the decisive factor in the Jews' decision to kill Jesus. But, if
Jesus can raise others from the dead, it is only because he is himself the resurrection.

Do you – like Martha – believe this?

First Reading: Our short first reading is a truncated version of an
Old Testament story of a resurrection, by the prophet Elisha. But
it has interesting points of contact and contrast with St John's.
The Shunammitess is an impressive figure of womanly initiative
and resource on a par with Martha. But the physiotherapeutic
ritual Elisha has to invoke to perform the miracle highlights the
unique power of Jesus' simple word of command: 'Lazarus!
Come out.'

Prayer-lines: God our Father, penetrate us with the message of
Jesus' love for us in this marvelous story, and of his power to
save.

Fifth Week of Lent: Monday: Years B and C

First Reading: Dan 13; Gospel: Jn 8:1-11

First Reading: Our first reading today is one of the moral folk-tales added to the original book of Daniel, which circulated among the Jews of the last pre-Christian centuries. Its primary purpose is to show the triumph of virtue over vice by God's help. In its liturgical context today, however, as a pendant to the reading of chapter 8 of John, we may well treat Susanna as a symbol of the old Israel; a symbol of Old Testament fidelity – to the Law of Moses. Hence she is here vindicated and saved by God's miraculous intervention through the boy, Daniel.

Gospel: But the Law, St Paul tells us, was to be our guardian until the Christ came. And today's gospel presents us with a typical trap set by Jesus' enemies. 'They asked him this as a test, looking for something to use against him.' A parallel to their question about the lawfulness of paying tribute to Caesar. The death penalty was forbidden to Jews by the Romans, whereas, if Jesus let the adulteress go free, he would be breaking the Law of Moses. We might see Jesus' solution of the dilemma as a parallel to his parable on the Pharisee and the tax-collector praying at the same time in the Temple. There, you remember, it was the tax-collector's prayer, 'O God be merciful to me, a sinner' that was approved. The scribes and Pharisees in today's gospel would claim to be at rights with God. But they slipped away, one by one, each with his guilt-complex, instead of confessing it and being freed by Christ's Word. She who remains, however, in full admission of her guilt, leaves at one with God.

Prayer-lines: God our Father, thank you for your mercy, come to us in your Son, Jesus. May we always, especially in Lent, come to you in search of your mercy rather than your just judgements on us.

Fifth Week of Lent: Tuesday
First Reading: Num 21: 4-9; Gospel: Jn 8:21-30

Gospel: 'When you have lifted up the Son of Man then you will know that I am he.' Today's gospel is a fragment of a long dialogue between Jesus and the Jews. It will be continued through the week, for it really represents the material of Jesus' trial later on before the Sanhedrin. But for John it is really the Jews who are on trial. The Light is shining in the darkness, and the darkness cannot comprehend it. So this dialogue is an echo and an illustration of the gospel's Prologue: 'He came unto his own, and his own received him not.'

Jesus was received only by those who believed. Believed what? Believed that he was Son of God, in the beginning with God, and was God. And the 'sign', both to challenge that faith and confirm it, was his 'raising up'. How? Raising up indeed on the cross. But also raising up to glory through the cross. Only the cross and its sequel, the resurrection, can reveal what Christ is, 'God so loved the world that he gave his only son.'

First Reading: 'Moses fashioned a bronze serpent which he put on a standard. If anyone was bitten by a serpent, he looked at the bronze serpent and lived.' In a religious reform in Judah about 700 BC Hezekiah is said to have smashed a bronze serpent in the Temple area to which the people had offered incense. This story of Moses having erected it in the desert may well be the legend explanatory of this cultic object. In the Near East, images of snakes as protective deities were sometimes attached to temples. Another example of biblical symbols 'leading us back to silence and unknowing'.

Prayer-lines: Lord Jesus, increase our faith, that we may experience the healing power of your death and resurrection over the wounds of our sins.

Fifth Week of Lent: Wednesday
First Reading: Dan 3; Gospel: Jn 8:31-42

Gospel: 'If God were your Father, you would love me.' Our last gospel passage ended with the statement that many of the Jews that Jesus spoke to 'believed in him'. But the progress of the dialogue betrays how shallow is that faith. Discipleship, Jesus assures them, will lead them to the truth, and that truth will make them free. At this they bridle. Are they not free already? Their slavery, Jesus explains, is to sin: 'You want to kill me.' Truth will set them free if they confess their sin.

And truth would also make them sons of God, as Jesus is the Son of God. To accept that is full truth and full freedom. Freedom to love. 'If God were your Father, you would love me.' Tomorrow we shall hear the sad sequel of this. His listeners take up stones to kill him. 'Though the Light has come into the world, men have preferred darkness to the light.'

First Reading: The open threat of death in today's gospel accounts for another Old Testament story of faithful Israelites resolutely facing up to painful death rather than betray their allegiance to the one true God. The full story, not given in our reading, tells how God sends an angel to join the three Israelites who have been cast into the furnace in their bonds. As a result their bonds are consumed, and all four of them joyfully proclaim God's praises as they walk about their harmless sanctuary. This echoes the theme of the book of Jeremiah, that God redemptively shares in the sufferings, both of body and spirit of his faithful witnesses.

Prayer-lines: Lord, we thank you for sending us your truth and love in your Son, Jesus. Help us through his Spirit to make his words our home.

Fifth Week of Lent: Thursday
First Reading: Gen 17:3-9; Gospel: Jn 8:51-59

Gospel: 'Before Abraham ever was, I AM.' With today's gospel we come to the climax of Jesus' self-revelation to his people. Up to now he has avoided 'exposing' them to the full mystery of who he was. People in the dark are blinded by very strong light. So he shows himself to the Jews indirectly – through what he brings them, what he can do for them, give them freedom, light, life. For those ready to listen to his word and keep it, Jesus' person and deeds are revelation enough. But, bent on rejecting all Jesus' claims, the Jews press him for a straight answer. And, in obedience to the truth (which he is) Jesus gives it. He applies to himself the name for himself which God had given to Moses at Horeb (Sinai). 'Tell them, I AM has sent me to you.' Abraham's joy at seeing Jesus' day reflects the rabbinical belief that the patriarchs would rejoice at seeing the day of salvation. The listeners' attempt to stone Jesus is the final proof that they are not children of Abraham's faith.

First Reading: Our first reading gives us God's formal ratification of his covenant with Abraham. The latter has shown his trust in Yahweh who had called him at 75 years of age to 'leave his country, his kindred and his father's house' for a land that Yahweh would give him. Stage by stage Abraham had traveled down from Syria towards Egypt, offering sacrifice at each stage to this God who had entered his life. At the time of today's reading he is ninety-nine years old, but still trusts in Yahweh's promise not merely of land, but of a son and myriad descendants through his aged wife Sara. As Paul would say, 'Be sure then that it is people of faith that are Abraham's children'.

Prayer-lines: God our Father, thank you for the gift of faith. May we foster it, and share it with others by living according to its light.

Fifth Week of Lent: Friday
First Reading: Jer 20:10-13; Gospel: Jn 10:31-42

Gospel: 'The Father is in me, and I am in the Father.' Jesus, we see, is still on trial by his opponents. But in today's passage he is speaking at a later feast, Hannukah. It celebrates the reconstruction of the Temple, and the dedication of its altar after its desecration under Syrian rulers. Jesus now claims to be 'the one the Father has consecrated and sent into the world'. 'The Jews fetched stones to stone him' for this blasphemy. We are in the heart of the sinister struggles of 'the Light shining in the darkness, and the darkness could not overpower it'.

We recall that, like so may of St John's symbols, the phrase 'the Jews', while historically referring to the Jewish leaders of Jesus' time, is a symbol of humanity's resistance to the Good News of Christ. For the gospel to be fully effective with us today, we must not dismiss the truth of our own infection by this 'darkness'. Passiontide is a privileged time in the Christian year for letting the sacramental power of Jesus' death and resurrection overcome the dark places of our soul: anger, resentment, untruth and the rest.

First Reading: In our first reading Jeremiah is portrayed like a man drowning amid tempestuous waves, and clinging desperately to a rescuer. He is a fair prophetic prototype of Jesus' feelings in his passion. Condemned by his prophetic calling to foretell Jerusalem's imminent ruin, Jeremiah feels he stands alone against the whole people. But then he recalls Yahweh's initial promise to be with him in spite of this universal hostility. And confiding in this promise he can rise above the waves of fear to cry exultantly, 'Sing to the Lord, praise the Lord.'

Prayer-lines: God our Father, open our hearts these days of Lent to let the light of Christ shine on them and dispel all that is in them that is opposed to your will.

Fifth Week of Lent: Saturday
First Reading: Ezek 37:21-28; Gospel: Jn 11:45-56

Gospel: 'It is better for one man to die for the people.' We have come to the end of the preliminary skirmishes between Jesus and his enemies, between the light of the world and darkness, Jesus has become more and more outspoken in his claims of a unique relationship with God; but his enemies were unable either to stone or arrest him. In today's meeting of the Sanhedrin it is the Sadducees who clinch matters. The Pharisees were mostly merchants and craftsmen. (Paul was a tent-maker.) Sadducees were priests or wealthy landowners. If the Pharisees felt threatened by Jesus in their prestige, the Sadducess feared for their social security. It was important for them to keep well in with the Romans to avoid taxation or confiscation. The priests depended for their livelihood on the safety of the Temple. And, with their worldly wisdom, as St Augustine says, 'they took counsel. But they never thought of saying, "Let us believe." They feared to lose temporal goods; they did not consider eternal life, and so they lost both'. 40 years later in fact the Romans did destroy the Temple. But by then Jesus' death and resurrection had 'gathered into the unity of the church the scattered children of God'.

First Reading: Our first reading gives us Ezechiel's prophecy of restoration that Jesus' death and resurrection would fulfil. The exiles would return and form again one people of north and south under one king as in the days of David and Solomon. The land would now be cleansed of its idolatry, and all will observe God's laws, for he now will be living in the midst of his people in a permanent and peaceful relationship. 'I will be their God; they shall be my people.'

Prayer-lines: Lord Jesus, we celebrate in the Mass the unity of your scattered people which you bought with your blood. Help us to strengthen that unity by living at peace with one another.

Holy Week: Monday
First Reading: Is 42:1-7; Gospel: Jn 12:1-11

First Reading: 'I have appointed you as light of the nations.' Holy Week, of all weeks, is a time for concentrating on the person of Jesus. 'Here is my saviour whom I uphold.' We have met this 'Servant' two weeks ago as the mysterious agent of Yahweh's strategy of salvation – not merely for Israel, but for the nations too. Naturally the New Testament writers will identify him with Jesus. But this identification is not just a discovery of the early church. For Jesus himself in the gospels has applied words of these Servant Songs of Isaiah to himself. And it is clear that he must have meditated on the words of Jeremiah and other prophets. Here, if anywhere, have we a guide to Jesus' inmost thoughts and feelings during his last week in Jerusalem, after the evanescence of his triumphal entry to the waving of palms and the messianic acclamations of the crowds.

Gospel: Today's gospel, dated only six days before Jesus' death, makes it carefully clear that his mind is now filled with his approaching death. Once arrived at Bethany (only a half-hour's walk from the eastern wall of Jerusalem), he is fully inside the danger zone. He had consciously entered it on the last week of his life. While Mark and Mathew will dilate on the merit of Mary's anointing of Jesus, John prefers to end the episode with Jesus' poignant prophecy of an impending death: 'You will not always have me with you.' May Mary of Bethany be our model this week in our awareness that we will not always have Jesus with us as we have him these days, and lavish on him accordingly the fulness of our attachment.

Prayer-lines: Lord, may the power of the saving mysteries we celebrate this week purify, unite and strengthen the whole Christian church for the salvation of humankind.

Holy Week: Tuesday

First Reading: Is 49:1-6; Gospel: Jn 13:21-33, 36-38

Gospel: 'I shall not be with you much longer.' Yesterday we saw how Jesus' thoughts were already at Bethany, preoccupied with his death. Now his passion is only a few hours away, and the fear that overwhelms him at Gethsemani is already beginning. We may note here one of the major psychological elements in his passion, namely, solitariness. Not only is one of the twelve about to betray him, but their chief spokesman will deny him later on that night, and the others desert him. Yet, amid all this gathering Dark Night of his soul Jesus remains captain of his soul. It is he who sends Judas out to set his 'hour' in motion. It is he who offers Judas the morsel of special concern; and will give Peter the promise of his future restoration. 'Truly', as the centurion on Calvary would say as Jesus died, 'this man was a Son of God.'

First Reading: 'You are my servant (Israel) in whom I shall be glorified.' This time the Servant of Yahweh is speaking for himself. Another Jeremiah, he tells us that he was called by Yahweh before his birth. His prophetic preaching will be effective, 'a sharp sword' in Yahweh's hand. But the Israel he will bring back will be a mere remnant. He had been losing heart in the face of the difficulties of his mission. But Yahweh proclaims that through him salvation will 'reach to the ends of the earth'.

Prayer-lines: Lord Jesus, may our celebration of your passion give us a share of your unshakeable confidence in the Father in all the trials of life.

Holy Week: Wednesday

First Reading: Is 50:4-9; Gospel: Mt 26:14-25

First Reading: 'Each morning he wakes me to hear, to listen like a disciple.' The Servant Songs of Isaiah are read not just as interesting parallels to the passion narrative of Jesus and its theological purpose. On the evening of his resurrection, as he walks with the two disciples to Emmaus, Jesus will explain how all these prophecies referred to him. He must have brooded over them from his youth, and they must have recurred to him especially during his passion: 'I did not cover my face against insult and spittle.' We know he was sustained in the ordeal of his passion by the Spirit, the power of God. But his passion also reveals the sustaining power of the Word of God, which Jesus was himself, though made flesh for our salvation. In Isaiah's words: 'The word that goes from my mouth will not return to me empty without carrying out my will.'

Gospel: 'In truth I tell you, one of you is about to betray me.' In stark contrast to yesterday's anointing of Jesus by Mary of Bethany, Judas goes secretly to the chief priests to seek a reward for the betrayal he has already planned. Thirty silver pieces is the legal indemnity for an injured slave. For Matthew, it fulfils a prophecy of Zechariah.

The Passover meal would be for Jesus the culmination of all his former meals of intimacy with his disciples. As the Passover meal it would be their sacramental sharing in their people's salvation from Egypt, the high-point of national joy. By his words over the unleavened bread and the wine Jesus would transform this ancient celebration into his own saving death and passing-over to the Father.

Prayer-Lines: Lord Jesus, forgive us our past betrayals of you, and carry us over, by the sacred mysteries we celebrate, from this world together with you to the Father forever.

THE SEASON OF EASTER

Easter Week: Monday
First Reading: Acts 2:14, 22-23; Gospel: Mt 28:8-15

Gospel: 'To this day, that is the story among the Jews.' It is only Matthew's gospel that tells of this attempted cover-up of Jesus' resurrection by the Jewish authorities. The resurrection is a matter of faith, not of proof. We recall the parallel contrast in Matthew's infancy narrative between belief and disbelief in the persons of the Magi and Herod. Here the contrast is between the women at the tomb and the chief priests and elders. The women in today's gospel are the models for our celebration of Easter. We too are to be filled with awe and great joy, and run to spread (by our lives) the Good News that Christ is risen. And coming to meet us – in our Christian living – is Jesus himself. Now exalted in glory, but friendly and approachable as ever. 'Do not be afraid,' he tell us, 'but go and tell my brothers' (no longer deserters), they are invited to a family reunion with me in Galilee.

First Reading: 'God raised this man Jesus to life, and all of us are witnesses to that.' With the Acts of Apostles, which we read throughout Eastertide, we cross the bridge between the gospel story and the rest of the New Testament. It starts with Jesus ascending into heaven, and leaving his programme to the apostles. But first we hear Peter's witness in Jerusalem. For Peter (as later for Paul) this witness must begin with the person and story of Jesus. God had already borne witness to Jesus by his public life; he had surrendered him to his unlawful death; but then, as David had foretold in the psalm, God had raised him up again. In tomorrow's Mass we will hear the dramatic effect of this apostolic witness in the conversion of 3000. The infant church (of Jerusalem) is born.

Prayer-lines: God our Father, we thank you for the Good News of the Paschal mystery. Grant us always to live no longer for ourselves, but for him who died for us and rose again.

Easter Week: Tuesday
First Reading: Acts 2:36-41; Gospel: Jn 20:11-18

Gospel: 'I am ascending to my Father and your Father.' When we read John's gospel we have to remember that he is writing theology as well as history. So today he is putting the theology of the resurrection in dramatic form. Firstly, why is Jesus only slowly recognised by Mary? Because he has been transformed by the resurrection. He has entered into a new state, with a new body. As St Paul puts it, 'what is sown (he means, in death) is a natural body, and what is raised is a spiritual body'. Secondly, this calls for a new attitude on the part of his disciples, a new relationship with him: no longer merely the earthly one: 'do not cling to me'. Most importantly, though, are Jesus' last words to Mary about his resurrection: 'I am ascending to my Father and your Father.' He is ascending to heaven not only for his own sake. It is to make his disciples share his sonship; share his Father (as on Calvary he shared his mother). This is to be the new and eternal covenant, which he promised them at the Last Supper. His God will be their God, and they his people. His final prayer at the Last Supper is now granted him: 'that they all may be in us, as you, Father, are in me, and I am in you.'

First Reading: Our first reading ends with the climax of Peter's first witness to Christ's resurrection. The Jesus whom the Jews had rejected has now been made by God not merely the Messiah (the 'Christ') but Lord and King of all the world. The effect of this burning witness is dramatic. Awareness of their crime in putting the Messiah to a shameful death brings deep compunction to the listeners, and thereby openness to God's forgiveness. With baptism, Peter assures them, they will be forgiven, and receive the Spirit of the risen Christ. And henceforth the power of the Spirit, so manifest in Jesus' preaching will recommence in the apostles.

Prayer-lines: God our Father, we thank you for our adoption through Jesus' resurrection into your family. May your Spirit enable us to bear your family likeness in all we do.

Easter Week: Wednesday
First Reading: Acts 3:1-10; Gospel: Lk 24:13-35

First Reading: Our first reading meets us today, with a typical Christlike miracle. Seeing this crippled beggar being left at the Temple threshold – Jewish law forbade their entering it – Peter is inspired to do the Christlike thing. 'In the name of Jesus Christ the Nazarene, get up and walk.' ('Name' in the Bible is a synonym for power). The words are the words of Peter; the power is the power of the risen Jesus. 'Peter then took him by the hand, and raised him up.' Another gesture of the gospel Jesus, you remember. And with that the cripple is no longer debarred from the Temple. He enters it 'walking and jumping and praising God' – exactly as Isaiah foretold for the days of messianic salvation.

Gospel: Like John in yesterday's gospel, today we find Luke equally capable of explaining Jesus' paschal mystery, his death and resurrection, in dramatic form. This time we are not standing but walking. Luke, you remember, structured his gospel on a journey from Galilee to Jerusalem. This time it will be a different kind of journey: a journey of faith, or rather from incomprehension and a lack of faith, to vision – vision of the truth. From 'You foolish pair! So slow to believe the full message of the prophets' to, 'they recognised him, at the breaking of the bread'. The key to the gate of faith, and vision, lies in the words, 'Was it not ordained?'. That passive voice is the Bible's way of speaking of God's action. 'Hadn't God planned it all?' And finally, we recall that, like the rest of his gospel, this story was written by Luke to be read at the early Christian Eucharist. So here we have an early Christian portrait of ourselves at Mass. Jesus in our midst; unrecognised by face; but explaining the contents of our faith to us through the Bible; and then giving himself to us 'in the breaking of bread'.

Prayer-lines: Lord Jesus, may we daily grow in faith in your presence and the power of your Spirit within our lives.

Easter Week: Thursday
First Reading: Acts 3:11-26; Gospel: Lk 24:35-48

Gospel: 'A ghost has no flesh and bones as you can see I have.' It is Luke's gospel that gives the most orderly presentation of the gospel accounts of the resurrection. So, in this chapter 24 Luke proceeds from the discovery of the empty tomb by the women and the news of the resurrection by the angels, to the first appearance of Jesus at Emmaus to two of his followers. In today's passage he reaches his climax by returning to the twelve (now only eleven), in the fulcrum of his whole gospel, Jerusalem. It is now the eleven, above all, who have to be led through the scriptures to accept their astonishing fulfillment in Jesus' triumph over death. And for the eleven a new point is made in addition to the discourse on the way to Emmaus. If Jesus' resurrection is in one sense a finale, in another it is only a beginning. A beginning of the preaching of its fruits for all humanity: repentance, that is, a turning from the blindness of past ages; and, on God's side, the fruit of his forgiveness of sins. As for ourselves, while we share in the 'dumbfounded' joy of the apostles, our joy is tempered too by compunction as Jesus shows us his hands and feet – that our sins have pierced.

First Reading: In our first reading, from Acts, by the same St Luke, we recall, we find Peter fulfilling this commission of preaching the paschal mystery. It is worthwhile recalling the special importance for us of these apostolic discourses in Acts. Scholars agree that they are faithful substantially to the first preaching of our faith in Jerusalem. One proof of this lies in the primitive titles given to Jesus, which soon dropped out of current use. But they are titles that we should hold on to for our prayer life in Christ, if we want to touch him with the mind of his first disciples. Jesus must be for us too, especially in this paschaltide, our 'Holy One', our 'Just One', our 'Prophet', our 'Prince of Life'.

Prayer-lines: Lord Jesus, thank you for coming so close to us in these Easter readings. May you be for us no 'ghost', but 'you who are truly bone of our bones, and flesh of our flesh.' Amen.

Easter Week: Friday
First Reading: Acts 4:1-12; Gospel: Jn 21:1-14

Gospel: Jesus said to them, 'Come and have breakfast.' Some scholars feel that our gospel today describes that first appearance of Jesus to Peter after the resurrection, so strangely undescribed elsewhere in the New Testament. Jesus is mysteriously transformed, and therefore unrecognised till he gives a sign of who he is. And yet he is indubitably the same friendly, attentive Master as before.

But perhaps the aspect of today's story most spiritually helpful to us is to treat it as an allegory: of the church's life, and of our own. How often can we too, like the seven disciples, seem to be 'at sea'; no thought of Jesus in our minds; frustrated by our efforts to 'make a go' of things. And suddenly Jesus, standing all the time within earshot, gives us a sign of his presence; perhaps a shock of some kind. And the 'beloved disciple' in us realises that 'it is the Lord' – waiting to welcome us ashore; to feed us not merely with bread and fish, but with his Body and Blood.

First Reading: 'Peter, filled with the holy Spirit, addressed them.' What a transformation the power of the Spirit has wrought in Peter too. This fisherman from the sea of Galilee, who had lacked the courage to face the query of a servant girl in the courtyard of Annas a few weeks ago, is now fearlessly addressing the rulers and the high priests of Jerusalem. Jesus' promise at the Last Supper of the help of the Holy Spirit in facing any opposition is now fulfilled. The Sadducees did not believe in any resurrection of the dead. They accepted only what was found in the first five books of the scriptures (the Pentateuch). In the gospels we see how Jesus had been able to point out that even in the Pentateuch God had revealed himself as God of the living; of Abraham , Isaac and Jacob able to overcome death and give life in every form. And that is the Good News brought by Jesus' resurrection too.

Prayer-lines: God, our Father, deepen our faith in the presence and power of the loving, risen Christ with us, that our lives too may bear witness to the resurrection.

Easter Week: Saturday
First Reading: Acts 4:13-21; Gospel: Mk 16:9-15

First Reading: 'What are we going to do with these men?' Yes, our first reading shows that the rulers in Jerusalem too share our astonishment at the transformation of Peter and John since the death of Jesus a short time before. As we saw in the gospel passage the day before Holy Week, they take counsel. But, as St Augustine observed, they failed to say, 'Let us believe.' And now they firmly seal their unbelief, in stark contrast to the mass of the people who 'were giving glory to God for what had happened.'

Gospel: 'Proclaim the Good News to all creation.' As is well known, today's gospel passage is not from Mark's hand. Our passage is clearly not a continuation of that and is mainly a compilation of material from the other gospels.

But it has some details that are not in the other gospels. That Mary of Magdala found the apostles 'mourning and in tears'. That they still disbelieved even after the two disciples return from Emmaus. There is also a typical Markan touch in Jesus reproaching the eleven 'for their incredulity and obstinacy'. This reproach has in fact the ring of truth , for Matthew softens their disbelief by making it: 'Some of them doubted.' And Luke, indulgent as ever, says 'they doubted because of their joy', as he had them sleeping at Gethsemani from grief! But this ring of truth in Mark's unflattering portrait of the apostles is also comforting for us, as we face out from the rather heady rejoicing of Easter week into another year of trying to live up to our faith in the resurrection. For, in spite of their disbelief, Jesus does not revoke their commission – or ours! – to 'proclaim the Good News', nor take back the assurance of his presence and power with them and with us.

Prayer-lines: Lord Jesus, may the Good News of your resurrection remain always in our minds to fill us with joy and courage in our lives as Christians.

Second Week of Easter: Monday

First Reading: Acts 4:23-31; Gospel: Jn 3:1-8

Gospel: 'You must be born from above'. The Eastertide gospels might seem to turn the clock back by revisiting Jesus' pre-resurrection days. But we remind ourselves that we read our scriptures at Mass not primarily for their historical interest or novelty, but for their ever-present sacramental value for each generation. Jesus' words today are addressed to the Nicodemus of every generation, to me and you. To share in the new life of Jesus' resurrection we must be 'born again'. For Nicodemus the life of salvation meant belonging physically to descent from Abraham. Jesus corrects him. No, it is by descent from God: a supernatural gift. Only by expressing God's love to others in our lives are we truly 'born again', and 'children of the resurrection'.

First Reading: In our first reading Peter and John hurry to share with the community their experience of the Spirit working in power in them before the Sanhedrin. Spontaneously they all burst into a common prayer – to God as creator ('who made heaven and earth'), and speaker ('who spoke through David in the psalms') – for the fulfilment of his promise ('this is what has come true'). The murderous alliance between Jew and Gentile which caused Jesus' death was according to God's plan. And now they ask him to continue through their proclamation of the resurrection the marvels he had already worked through Jesus. God's answer to their prayer comes at once in another palpable experience of the Holy Spirit (without, however, the ecstatic speech of Pentecost day). This dramatic experience would be followed by others recounted in the rest of the Apostles' Acts.

Prayer-lines: God our Father, thank you for your gift of your Spirit to us in the sacraments. By the power of that Spirit may we show forth in our lives the mystery of your Son's resurrection.

Second Week of Easter: Tuesday
First Reading: Acts 4:32-37; Gospel: Jn 3:7-15

Gospel: 'Jesus said to Nicodemus.' We recall that in the liturgy we all stand in the shoes of Nicodemus. Yesterday we were told that he was one of the Pharisees. In the gospels we often find them castigated by Jesus. For what? Their root fault was they sought to be holy through their own activity. We remember the parable of the two men at prayer in the Temple. Only the tax-collector, Jesus declared, went home again 'justified', that is 'made holy'. Why he? Because he relied on God's 'activity', namely his mercy. Easter is, of course, the celebration of God's greatest 'activity', his mightiest deed, namely Jesus' resurrection. And the resurrection was also God's activity in us, by giving us his Spirit, by whom all of us are born again. We must take time off these days to meditate on this deed of God in and for us. And not only in us individually, but as a community, especially in our relations to one another.

First Reading: 'The whole group of believers was united heart and soul.' This idyllic portrait in the first reading of the early Christian community might seem a far cry from the gravely mysterious words spoken by night to Nicodemus by Jesus. But they are two aspects of the same reality; of the same Good News. This 'unity of heart and soul'; and the 'great power' by which the formerly ineffectual apostles now give witness to the fact and meaning of the resurrection. All this sudden newness in Jerusalem and eventually in the whole world is the sign of that re-birth in the Spirit which is such a mystery for Nicodemus. *Prayer-lines:* God, our Father, increase our faith in the presence and power of the risen Christ in our community and in our lives.

Second Week of Easter: Wednesday
First Reading: Acts 5:17-26; Gospel: Jn 3: 16-21

Gospel: 'God loved the world so much that he gave his only Son.' What an astonishing utterance! And so it is meant to be. Paschaltide above all tides is one for our increasing astonishment at God's love for us. 'The world' has a special meaning in John's gospel. It is not the material creation, or merely men. It means humanity as opposed to God through self-sufficiency and refusal to admit dependence. It is a world that prefers the darkness of this attitude to the light of God's fatherhood. And yet God loves this world. It is noteworthy too that these words are addressed to Nicodemus, a Pharisee. They too belong to 'the world' in two ways. By claiming self-sufficiency for 'righteousness' and by despising others. And yet Nicodemus was one of the better Pharisees. So we should not be surprised to find traces of Phariseeism in ourselves. Lacking concern, for example, for the morally unattractive and undeserving. In such a discovery we turn with trust to Jesus. 'Have courage,' he says, 'I have overcome the world; the world in you.'

First Reading: 'Tell the people all about the new Life.' Our first reading shows us the preaching of the Good News by the apostles becoming ever more confident by the power of the Spirit. And the growth of their adherents among the people is large enough now to deter the Temple police from using force against them in public. As in John's gospel narrative Jesus in person was being constantly being put on trial, his trial now continues in the person of his followers. As Paschaltide is a special time for marveling in gratitude for God so loving us as to give his Son to save us, so is it equally a privileged time for proclaiming by our standards and conduct the new life for everyone ushered in by Jesus' resurrection.

Prayer-lines: God our Father, give us a share of your unfathomable love for 'the world', and an ever-increasing trust in the help of your spirit.

Second Week of Easter: Thursday
First Reading: Acts 5:27-33; Gospel: Jn 3:31-36

First Reading: 'We are witnesses to all this, we and the Holy Spirit.' The witness of the apostles to the life and death and resurrection of Jesus of Nazareth is twofold. It is firstly the witness of their senses, what they have seen and heard and touched. But besides this physical experience which they are bound to share, they have also had a spiritual experience: the power and confidence of the Spirit of Jesus in them. That spiritual experience we too share with them through the sacramental power of the liturgy, especially of the Mass. And we have already noted the plus value of the earliest names these first Christians gave to Christ. For the high priest Jesus is simply 'this man'. For us, as for the apostles, Jesus is our leader and our saviour. May we so treat him in all the problems of life.

Gospel: 'The Father loves the Son and has entrusted everything to him.' To his disciples, who take exception to the Baptist's former followers now flocking to Jesus instead, John takes the opportunity to bear his last witness to him. Jesus, he has already said, is Israel's true bridegroom, as Messiah; he himself, only the bridegroom's friend. Still more, Jesus, as God's Son, has been given the fulness of the Spirit. 'The Father loves the Son.' A new angle on the mystery of Jesus for us to ponder. Not merely what Jesus is to us, but what he is for us to the Father. Not merely eternally, in his divinity. But concretely and visibly in time, through his incarnation, as Jesus of Nazareth. All through John's gospel Jesus will speak of his being sent by the Father: sent in the form of a man, as St Paul reminds us; in the form of a slave; to accept death on a cross.

Prayer-lines: God, we thank you for sending your Son, the Beloved to die for us. Help us to believe that in him we too are your beloved children. May this Eucharist express our thanks to you through your beloved Son, Jesus.

Second Week of Easter: Friday
First Reading: Acts 5:34-42; Gospel: Jn 6:1-15

Gospel: 'Where can we buy some bread for these people to eat?' (With 5 barley loaves for 5,000!) In such a context, only from him who creates the seeds. But Jesus provides the bread not only by a miracle, as creator. It calls in this context for a special deed. 'It was shortly before the Passover.' 'He himself knew exactly what he was going to do' to feed the 5,000. The Passover of his death, a year later. 'Where can we buy?' Jesus himself knew the price. ('Not by gold or silver,' St Peter writes, 'but by the precious blood of a lamb without spot or stain.') This feeding of the 5000 is a great sign of how Jesus still feeds us today, in his word as with his Body and Blood. Let us hold on to this reality of Jesus' presence and power with us – for every need, in suffering and in joy. Because, unlike the occasion in the gospel, Jesus is now the risen Christ, sharing with us the power of the Spirit that raised him from the tomb.

First Reading: 'You might find yourselves fighting against God.' This unexpected intervention of Gamaliel is appropriate for a Pharisee. Paul, in fact, Gamaliel's pupil, was a good witness, in his persecution of Christians, of the truth of Gamaliel's words. And there is a practical lesson there for us all. Often in the church's history even well-meaning Christians have persecuted causes that proved in the event to be God's causes. In our own century we may think of great Catholic scholars who were vindicated only by Vatican II. The lesson, therefore, is not only one of judging others with charity when their views conflict with ours. Perhaps it is primarily humility: not being too quick to believe that God is dependent on our efforts to vindicate his cause. On the other hand, our reading also indicates the programme for the persecuted: joy and honour in suffering for Christ.

Prayer-lines: May our paschaltide eucharistic celebration fill us with charity for others and joyful patience under trial.

Second Week of Easter: Saturday
First Reading: Acts 6:1-7; Gospel: Jn 6:16-21

Gospel: 'Dark by now, and Jesus had still not rejoined them.' No doubt he had promised to do so as they were embarking. But John, like the other evangelists, did not tell these stories about Jesus as mere reminiscences of the past. They are told for all later generations to reveal what Jesus is still doing. Today's gospel is a parable of the church in every generation. The wind against the bark of Peter is always strong, the sea is often rough. It is better so. As Jesus had told the apostles when news was brought of Lazarus's illness: 'It is not unto death, but it is for God's glory, that through it the Son of God may be glorified.' Yes, the disciples may indeed be frightened in any era by the violence of the waves; and by the mysterious way that Jesus chooses to come eventually across the waters. But once he has come, the arrival at their destination is assured.

First Reading: Our first reading is an illustration of the 'rough sea' that the church has had to face from its earliest days. The Hellenists were Greek-speaking Jews in Jerusalem, immigrants returned from the Jewish Diaspora in Egypt and elsewhere. Their widows, in particular, could be vulnerable as the distribution of food was done by the local Aramaic-speaking Christians. A practical solution is found by the appointment of seven Hellenists to look after this side of everyday life. More conversions, even of priests, follow. But a new storm breaks when Stephen (and later Philip) engage in 'the service of the word'. His zeal, learning and courage lead to new and worse persecution. The boat for a time looks like sinking. Yet out of that apparent disaster, with the scattering from Jerusalem of the Greek-speakers, salvation really begins for the Gentile world.

Prayer-lines: Lord Jesus, increase our faith in your presence at all times, and grant peace and courage to all Christians facing real persecution in the world today.

Third Week of Easter: Monday
First Reading: Acts 6:8-15; Gospel: Jn 6:22-29

Gospel: 'You must believe in the one he has sent.' On Saturday
we saw the apostles set off in their boat for Capernaum. Today
we are among the crowd who follow them, eager to see more of
this marvellous teacher and wonderworker. We are surely doing
the right thing, in search of our Messiah, our saviour. But how
did he get here before us? Jesus ignores our shallow curiosity,
and goes straight to the one thing that matters. 'You are not
looking for me for the right reasons. You had all the bread you
wanted to eat.' You did not see the sign it was – the better food
the Son of man wants to give you. 'But, what must we do then,
to please God?' we ask him urgently. 'God asks only one thing
of you: faith. You must believe in me, the one he has sent.'
Believe in me as one living in you:,with you at all times, sharing
my Spirit with you to show you the way to think, to speak, to
act, to suffer. Hear me murmuring constantly in your heart:
'Come with me to the Father.'

First Reading: In the first reading Luke has portrayed Stephen as
a complete contrast to the shallow crowd of the gospel. He is,
outstandingly in the early church, one who has 'believed in the
one whom God has sent'. His life is therefore modelled on that
of Jesus. And so, will be his death. Filled with the Spirit of his
baptism, it is the Spirit who prompts what he says; is the source
of his power, his miracles and signs. Looking at him, his face
shining with angelic light, we are ready to hear how he passes on
the prophetic message of his Master to an unbelieving people.

Prayer-lines: Lord Jesus, grant us during this Easter season to
come to you as the Bread of Life that we may bear witness like St
Stephen to the power of your resurrection.

Third Week of Easter: Tuesday

First Reading: Acts 7:51-8:1; Gospel: Jn 6:30-35

First Reading: 'Saul entirely approved of the killing.' St Luke likes to drop a trail-blazer for coming events. Saul is a man we shall meet again. But meanwhile our first reading gives us the electric conclusion of Stephen's great discourse before the Sanhedrin. Starting with the patriarchs he traces the long history of God's caring guidance of the Chosen People down to their own time. At every stage God's saving work was met by infidelity and resistance, notably by the killing of his prophets. The climax had come in their own day by their murder of 'the Just One', the Messiah. As the infuriated mob rush forward to lynch him, Stephen is rewarded by a vision of Christ, standing in heaven to welcome his faithful witness to his Father's throne. Christlike to the end, Stephen repeats Jesus' own last words, commending his spirit to Christ in glory, and asking forgiveness for his killers.

Gospel: 'What sign will you give? What work will you do?' We marvel at the obtuseness of a crowd that only yesterday has seen 5,000 fed by one pair of hands from five barley loaves and two fishes. This demand for more signs exposes the shallowness of their faith. 'Can he procure bread from heaven as Moses did, if this man claims to be the Messiah?' A current Jewish belief at that time was that manna would reappear in messianic days. Jesus then reveals the 'sign' that underlay his feeding of the 5,000. The bread they had eaten was God's gift, as the manna was not Moses' gift. And again, God's gift is a gift of the present, not of the past. God's is a life-giving bread, the Bread of God. It is Jesus himself, and his words. As he will tell them a little later, his words are spirit, and they are life, eternal life.

Prayer-lines: God our Father, thank you for the words of eternal life you have given us in your Son, Jesus. May we treasure them, and let them guide us at all times.

Third Week of Easter: Wednesday
First Reading: Acts 8:1-8; Gospel: Jn 6:35-40

Gospel: 'All that the Father gives me will come to me.' Jesus is certainly leading his listeners into deep waters of revelation. Yesterday he shifted their attention from Moses to God, as the real giver of manna in the desert. And it is God too who has given them the real bread from heaven, the Bread of Life in Jesus himself. But today he speaks of the Fathers' gift to Jesus himself: the gift of disciples. There are those who will believe in Jesus and unite with him for what he is: the One sent by the Father to bring them to eternal life. On his part Jesus is committed to this saving role given him by his Father. 'Whoever comes to me I shall not turn away, but raise him up on the last day.' Our destiny, then, is always our relationship with Christ. Who do we say he is? What does he mean in my life?

First Reading: 'Everyone who had escaped fled to the country districts.' But what desperately bad news our first reading starts with: 'a bitter persecution broke out against the church in Jerusalem'. And all, it seemed because of Stephen and his provocative speech before the Sanhedrin. The apostles, it is true, were allowed to stay on in Jerusalem, and that was vital for its continuity with the past. But how they must have taken alarm at the apparent recurrence of the Calvary tragedy so soon. And now even the Pharisees, with Paul at their head, were on the warpath against them. Yes, it was indeed a dark day for these Nazarenes in Jerusalem. But, wait: ('westward, look, the land is bright.') Philip, another of those controversial Hellenist converts makes off for Samaria. And there the seed falls at once on good ground, and conversions follow. 'There was great rejoicing in that town as a result.' God can indeed write straight with crooked lines.

Prayer-lines: Lord Jesus, increase our faith to recognise you coming to us not merely in word and sacrament, but in all the ups and downs of life.

Third Week of Easter: Thursday

First Reading: Acts 8:26-40; Gospel: Jn 6:44-51

Gospel: 'No one can come to me unless he is drawn by the Father.' We came away from yesterday's gospel with the question, 'what does Jesus mean to me? Who do I say he is?' Ever since the feeding of the 5,000, Jesus has been trying to raise the minds and fixation of the 5,000 from the material food, which preoccupies them. From that to God, the person who has fed them. When they raise the question of the manna which, they say, Moses gave his people in the desert, Jesus points out that it was God, not Moses, who gave it. And it is the same God his Father who has sent him not merely to feed them bodily in the desert, but to lead them to eternal life – the ultimate goal of all food. In uniting with Jesus by faith they will achieve the higher reality behind the meal they had enjoyed in the desert, that is, they will, by sharing Jesus' life, become immortal. 'The bread that I shall give is my flesh.' Jesus is now about to speak of the Eucharist, that sacramental food that will achieve this life – giving union with him.

First Reading: Our first reading gives us a graphic illustration of the abstract gospel wording about the Father leading people to Jesus. There is nothing haphazard about this encounter of the deacon Philip with this Ethiopian official on his way home after his pilgrimage to Jerusalem. He has just reached the part of the scripture, which refers directly to Jesus' saving death. 'Starting, therefore, with this text of scripture Philip proceeded to explain the Good News of Jesus to him.' And now we note the fulness of the new life brought by Jesus. The whole Trinity of the Godhead is involved. It is the Spirit that has directed Philip to meet the chariot. In Philip's role we can see the programme of our own life as Christians. Our union with Jesus and his Spirit by our baptism must enable us to play our part in drawing all those we meet into the company of Father, Son and Holy Spirit.

Prayer-lines: Father, may the zeal of the first Christians stimulate us to share the Good News of Christ with others.

Third Week of Easter: Friday
First Reading: Acts 9:1-20; Gospel: Jn 6: 52-59

Gospel: 'He taught this at Capernaum, in the synagogue.' It might seem at first sight that all this Galilean teaching of Jesus is drawing us away from the paschal mystery we have been celebrating: Jesus' passion, death and resurrection. It would be wrong to think we have left that central mystery of our faith in these gospel readings. Led by the Spirit we plunged down into the heart of that mystery. For it is no longer a mystery of the past but of the present – for every generation of believers. A present too that leads us on to the future. 'Whoever eats my flesh and drinks my blood, has eternal life.' That life which Jesus eternally draws from the Father, and shares with us in the Eucharist. 'Anyone who eats this bread will live forever.'

First Reading: Our first reading today is no doubt the most dramatic story in the Book of Acts: the conversion of Saul, arch-persecutor of the infant church. His conversion, but also his vocation, his calling for his mission. And like the Old Testament prophets (Isaiah, for instance), his whole mission and teaching will be coloured by that initial revelation: 'I am Jesus whom you are persecuting.' In mathematical terms, the equation: Christians are one with Jesus. This will be the basis of Paul's teaching on the Body of Christ, and the relations between Christians. When Ananias placed his hands on Saul 'it was as though scales fell away from his eyes'. It was the physical counterpart of his spiritual experience. This faith-experience we must share with Paul. If we have been blind, or even shortsighted in our faith we must now open ourselves to several new truths. a) I and Jesus are one. b) All Christians, especially those around us daily, are also Christ.

Prayer-lines: Lord Jesus, increase our faith in our oneness with you, and, in you, with one another. May our lives bear witness to that common bond between us all.

Third Week of Easter: Saturday

First Reading: Acts 9:31-42; Gospel: Jn 6:60-69

Gospel: 'Lord, to whom shall we go? You have the message of eternal life.' And yet 'many of his followers' found this discourse of Jesus, with its claim to be God's wisdom from heaven, above all the talk of eating his Body and drinking his Blood – they found this 'intolerable language'. Jesus does not demur. But he says that even greater challenges to their faith lie ahead. His 'ascent' is John's code-phrase for Jesus' death and resurrection. We are here at the start of Jewish rejection of Jesus. But it is also the start of the apostles' (and therefore the church's) faith in Jesus. The future was no clearer for them than for others, but they would cling to Jesus as their only hope. 'Lord to whom shall we go...?' It is not yet perfect faith; for a future denial is in store, even for Peter. But the 'grain of mustard seed' had been sown. So it can be for us at times, when our faith is seriously challenged: a vital decision to make; an illness to accept, and so on. Like the apostles, we are always free to 'go away'. But with even a grain of faith (which he will supply if we ask for it) we can cling to Jesus, and go through any trial to share his resurrection.

First Reading: 'The churches were filled with the consolation of the Holy Sprit.' After the dramatic story of Saul's conversion, the Acts give us a breather before the next great phase in the church's expansion: the mission to the Gentiles. But this mission had first to be launched by Peter, who had already reinforced the evangelisation of Samaria by Philip. Here too his miracles follow the pattern of those wrought by Jesus, for they are worked in Jesus' name: 'Aeneas, Jesus Christ heals you... Tabitha, stand up.' Faith in the power of Jesus' name is both the prerequisite of the miracle, and the fruit of the healing for those who hear of it.

Prayer-lines: Lord Jesus, increase our faith in you, that we may experience in our lives the power of your resurrection.

Fourth Week of Easter: Monday

First Reading: Acts 11:1-18; Gospel: Jn 10:1-10

First Reading: 'What God has made clean, you have no right to call profane.' This story of the conversion of the pious centurion (Gentile, therefore) is a hinge in St Luke's history of the spread of the gospel. Luke emphasises its importance by telling twice how it happened: to us, first; and today to the critical Jewish Christians in Jerusalem. And he tells in detail about the vision in Jaffa that followed Peter's prayer. The declaration of the 'cleanness' of God's animal creation (which contradicts diet regulations of the Old Testament) refers by extension to the acceptability of non-Jews in God's saving plans. We can see how hard a pill this was for even Christian Jews to swallow. Eating with Gentiles was the ultimate taboo for Jewish feelings. But Peter's story, especially the precipitate way the Holy Spirit had descended on Cornelius and family before Peter's address to them, had finally clinched the case. Gentile admission to Christianity would be ratified soon after at the council of Jerusalem. As Peter put it, 'Who was I to stand in God's way?'

Gospel: 'I came that they may have life, and have it to the full.' Two parables here: Jesus as the gate (that is, the only sure way to the truth and the life); and he is also the model shepherd. In the gospel these parables follow directly on the long story of the blind man, healed by Jesus, but expelled from the synagogue. The identity of the true and false shepherds is very clear there. But Jesus as 'the gate' strikes us as parallel rather to our first reading. 'I have other sheep that are not of this fold.' By the initiative of his Spirit in 'baptising' the Gentiles at Caesarea, Jesus is showing up the defectiveness of the Jewish exclusion of them from God's plan of salvation. Jesus, the only authentic shepherd is prepared to lay down his life for his sheep 'that they may have life to the full'.

Prayer-lines: God our Father, grant that we may follow Christ in all we say or do, so as not to stand in your saving way.

Fourth Week of Easter: Tuesday
First Reading: Acts11:19-26; Gospel: John 10: 22-30

Gospel: 'The sheep that belong to me listen to my voice.' We are back in Jerusalem in the Temple. The last time Jesus had been challenged there about his identity he had narrowly escaped stoning for what was taken as blasphemy. Today's crowd is less hostile, but they still do not believe in him. And it is only to believers, like the Samaritan woman and the blind man, that Jesus will directly admit his messiahship: 'I am he who is speaking with you.' As he said at Capernaum, when many of his disciples drifted away, it is only by the Father's gift that believers come to him. He concludes with the words, 'I and the Father are one.' At the Last Supper he will declare that he shares that oneness with his believers.

First Reading: Our first reading describes how the Father drew Gentile believers (which means you and me) to Jesus. It brings out how the Spirit worked to bring the Gentiles into Christ's sheepfold. Jewish Christians from the island of Cyprus, and Cyrene in north Africa, were more cosmopolitan than those of Jerusalem. They had no qualms about preaching the Good News of Jesus to the Greek-speaking pagans of Antioch, then the third largest city in the Roman Empire. And 'a great number believed'. At the subsequent 'council of Jerusalem' it will take the strong Spirit-filled words of Peter to have this first unofficial evangelisation approved in Judaea. In the millennia to follow the church has always known this tension between what we may call 'charismatic' interventions and the slow agreement by church leaders. Let us share Christ's desire that the prophecy of our psalm today will be fulfilled: 'Zion (i.e. the Church) shall be called Mother, for all shall be her children.'

Prayer-lines: Lord Jesus, increase the unity of your believers, that through them the world may believe that you are the saviour whom the Father has sent.

Fourth Week of Easter: Wednesday

First Reading: Acts 12:34-13:5; Gospel: Jn 12:44-50

Gospel: 'What the Father has told me is what I speak.' John has very appropriately placed the discourse of Jesus at the end of his public life before he enters on his passion. It sums up the major themes of the earlier chapters, which were outlined in the Prologue. Jesus is the light come into the world; the Word of God made flesh to save the world. Each one of us is classified by our reaction to that light, that Word. The deliberate compression of these fundamental themes can be almost unbearably disturbing. It reminds me of a film where the camera swings from its middle distance shots (say, Jesus changing water into wine, feeding the 5,000, healing the blind man) and suddenly gives us a close-up of Jesus' face filling the whole screen. There is no escaping that look, those eyes, that question. 'Are you for me or against?'

First Reading: 'The word of God continued to be spread.' Luke is now ready to give Paul and his missionary work the centre of the stage for the rest of the story of Acts. Barnabas and Saul were sent down from Antioch with funds for the famine-stricken poor in Judea, and have returned. We now catch a glimpse of the Spirit-filled leadership of the young church in Antioch: prophets and teachers. Assembled there one day at worship, the Spirit gives them the message that they should spread the Good News further afield through Saul and Barnabas. As Antioch had itself received the faith from Cypriot believers, Cyprus is the first place to be rewarded by evangelisation. And, in accordance with Paul's constant programme, the Good News is first preached in the synagogue there – to the Jews.

Prayer-lines: Lord Jesus, thank you for the two-edged sword of your word. May it open our hearts to say 'yes' to your Spirit in every area of our lives.

Fourth Week of Easter: Thursday

First Reading: Acts 13:13-25; Gospel: Jn 13: 16-20

Gospel: 'Whoever welcomes me welcomes the one who sent me.' We have now left Jesus' public life, and are seated at table with him at the Last Supper. In these Last Supper discourses we are being invited into an awareness that in Jesus we meet the Father, and share his Spirit. 'No servant is greater than his master' is the sequel to his washing of the disciple's feet. This breath-taking gesture of his, we remember, abashed them all, especially Peter. Yet, it was Jesus' prophetic way of foretelling the far greater humiliation of the crucifixion he would endure for them (and us) next day. It is for us to pass on that message of God's love by unselfish dedication to others.

First Reading: 'Give some words of encouragement to the people.' This is the invitation given to Paul as he arrives in the synagogue of Antioch in Pisidia. Having finished their first mission in the island of Cyprus they now make for the cities of Asia Minor (our modern Turkey). The network of Roman military roads would remain a useful asset in spreading the gospel in the first centuries. Paul is now addressing a congregation of Jews ('men of Israel') but also a fringe of Gentiles who admired the Jewish ethic and attended their weekly worship without actually becoming Jews (they are the so-called 'fearers of God'). It is an important occasion, and Paul makes the most of it. Like Peter on the day of Pentecost and Stephen later on, he will lead up to Jesus by an outline of Israelite history. In a word, God promised king David a messianic descendant. He is Jesus, and witnessed to by the renowned John the Baptist. The rest of this discourse will come tomorrow.

Pray-lines: Lord Jesus, we thank you for the perennial Good News of our faith passed on to us by your scriptures. May the power of your Spirit make us doers of your word, not merely hearers.

Fourth Week of Easter: Friday

First Reading: Acts 13: 26-33; Gospel: Jn 14:1-6

First Reading: 'We have come here to tell you the Good News.' Paul is continuing the 'words of encouragement' which he was invited to give yesterday in the synagogue at Antioch in Pisidia. His Good News today, he says, is 'a message of salvation'. He had already given an outline of Israel's history, culminating in the witness of John the Baptist that Jesus of Nazareth was the Messiah promised as descendant to David. The sequel, alas, was not welcome by his people. With absolutely no justification they condemned him to death under the Romans, that is, by crucifixion. But here God stepped in miraculously to vindicate his Just One. He raised him from the tomb. The risen Jesus then appeared over a number of days to his Galilean disciples. These disciples are now bearing witness to him before all the Jews. The Good News then is that in the life, death and resurrection of Jesus, God has fulfilled his promises to us.

Gospel: 'I am going to prepare a place for you.' We recall that John's gospel was written some sixty years after Jesus' resurrection and gift of the Spirit. So these Last Supper discourses of Jesus reflect the early Christian meditation on the mystery of Jesus' death and resurrection and ascension, and their fruit in the life of his disciples. So the place that Jesus says he is going to prepare for them is not only in heaven after their death. It is also the place which he will make in them, while still alive, for his Spirit. So the Christian 'Way' is not only the example of Jesus' life in the Spirit. It is also in our imitation of Christ's death and resurrection.

Prayer-lines: Lord Jesus, fill our hears during these days of Eastertide with your Spirit that he may carry us with you through your paschal mystery to your Father and ours.

Fourth Week of Easter: Saturday

First Reading: Acts 13:44-52; Gospel: Jn 14: 7-14

Gospel: 'It is the Father, living in me, who is doing this work.' For Jesus 'this work' is the work of the next twenty-four hours: the work of his passion and death. Yes, in St Paul's words, during these terrible hours of torture and humiliation, the Father, in Christ, is 'reconciling the world to himself'. Nowhere does Jesus speak more profoundly of the relations between himself and the Father. And it is a supreme revelation of our relationship with the Father, seeing him made visible to us in the sufferings of Christ. We come to the Father always through the humanity of Christ, and nowhere more fully than in manifesting in our lives the paschal mystery of Christ, passing from this world to the Father, 'who is glorified in the Son'.

First Reading: 'I have made you a light for the nations.' Paul's address in the synagogue at Antioch in Pisidia had obviously made a deep impression on those who heard it. An even larger crowd came to hear him on the following Sabbath. This apparently aroused the jealousy of the Jews, and they contested all that Paul had said about Jesus being the Messiah. This did not deter the missionaries. They knew that the Good News was destined for the Gentiles too. To the Gentiles, accordingly, they now turned, and the seed fell on good ground. This was going to be a recurring pattern for Paul's preaching wherever he went, even on the last occasion we meet him in the Acts, as a prisoner in Rome. As the Jews fail to believe him as he preached to them in chains, he had to address the parting words: 'The salvation of God has been sent to the pagans. They will listen to it.'

Prayer-lines: Lord Jesus, in these joyful days of Eastertide deepen our gratitude for the gift of your Good News and by its power enable us to live no longer for ourselves but for you who died for us and rose again.

Fifth Week of Easter: Monday
First Reading: Acts 14:5-18; Gospel: Jn 14: 21-26

First Reading: 'Do you intend to show yourself to us and not to the world?' If Eastertide is a reason for exploring the riches of our Christian Good News, today we are helped in this by means of contrast. Our first reading gives us a vivid picture of what un-Christian religion can mean; the gospel brings us into the heart of the Christian faith. The story of how the people of Lystra took Paul and Barnabas to be gods because of the cure of a cripple illustrates the pathos as well as the shallowness of paganism. Religion for paganism was primarily a matter of securing temporal favours from the gods by material sacrifice. And yet today's episode shows a pathetic longing that the gods would show themselves by coming even for a while to live among humans. And Paul and Barnabas are prepared to use these imperfect concepts to point the way to the goodness of God to all his creatures.

Gospel: But what a contrast in the revelation of the true God in the gospel. Surely, as Jude divines, this revelation is too wonderful not to be passed on to the world, even during Jesus' short ministry. There is indeed an exterior and visible side to this religion of Jesus: the keeping of his commandments. But this is only the outward sign of an intense inward relationship to the three persons of the Trinity, each with his own role to play in the mystery of our salvation. The Spirit will continue Jesus' work as Teacher and Guide; Jesus will share with his disciples the love and indwelling of the Father.

Perhaps we cannot take for granted that our spirituality lacks all trace of the merely human attitude of the Lystrans. But we can train ourselves to cultivate the true interior religion Jesus reveals in these Last Supper discourses.

Prayer-lines: God our Father, thank you for the knowledge, the faith and immortality you have made known to us in your Son, Jesus. Help us to grow daily in a true knowledge and love of you, Father, Son and Holy Spirit. Amen

Fifth Week of Easter: Tuesday
First Reading: Acts 14:19-28; Gospel: Jn 14: 27-31

Gospel: 'The world must be brought to know that I love the Father.' If we accept the view of scholars that today's gospel is the end of the Last Supper discourses, we have here Jesus' last words to his disciples. 'Shalom' (peace) is still a farewell word in Israel today. But in the fourth gospel it includes all that Jesus has come to give us: life and light, joy and truth. 'Life' is no woolly term here. It means Jesus' own life, not just in heaven, but also on earth. Think of the setting. Jesus is facing certain death. Judas has gone out to guide his captors. Time is short. It is one of John's equivalents of the agony in the garden described by the other gospels. At Gethsemani Jesus will say, 'my betrayer is at hand. Let's go to meet him.' Here he speaks of 'the prince of this world' who is behind Judas' betrayal. No aspect of the horror of the passion escapes Jesus. Yet he is at peace; his 'own peace'. The source of that peace is his love for the Father.

First Reading: Our first reading gives us a concrete picture of the peace, which Jesus had bequeathed to his disciples, 'a peace, which the world cannot give'. In writing to the Corinthians Paul will refer to this stoning, but not as the only time he was given up for dead. Yet, we are told in today's passage, when his disciples arrive prepared, presumably, to bury him, he simply gets off the ground and returns to the town with them. And, on his return from Derbe later on, he tells the disciples it is all part of the Christian lot. 'We all have to experience many hardships before we enter the kingdom of God.' Back at base in Antioch in Syria, the news given by Paul and Barnabas is not of what they had to suffer, but 'of all that God had done with them, opening the door of faith to the pagans.'

Prayer-lines: Lord Jesus, may your church in our day know your gift of peace and, with justice, make it a primary part of its message to the world.

Fifth Week of Easter: Wednesday
First Reading: Acts 15:1-6; Gospel: Jn 15:1-8

Gospel: 'Make your home in me as I make mine in you.' Perhaps 'making our home' sounds incongruous with the image of Jesus as the vine. But it has the advantage of reminding us that we must cooperate with the life that Jesus gives us. Jesus has indeed 'made his home' in us by sharing his paschal mystery with us through the sacraments, especially baptism and eucharist. How do we cooperate with that gift? By faith in the first place. The initial seed planted in us by baptism, and cultivated by prayer, and reflection on his word. Also by living, doing and accepting according to that word, which includes his example. But Jesus' parable of himself as the vine, the true and faithful one, is in contrast to the prophet's image of Israel as a choice vine planted by God, yet yielding only bitter grapes. And with his Father as 'the vinedresser', we see that our growth in holiness, in union with and likeness to Christ is not so much our work as the Father's, through his Spirit. If Christ is the way, the Father is its goal, and the Spirit leads us to him: a way of the cross that leads to glory.

First Reading: 'Certain members insisting that the pagans should keep the Law of Moses.' Already in the gospels we see how vital it was for Pharisees to keep the Law of Moses strictly. Paul himself before his conversion would be completely with them in that. And even Pharisees converted to Christ still felt that the law should still hold good for all. But Jesus had shown by his life and teaching that religion was a matter of loving God, and one's neighbour as oneself. Jesus could not have revealed himself and the mystery of his cross to Paul without sharing this insight with him. And, of course, since Pentecost the Spirit had shown that the pagans had free access to the Good News of Christ's salvation without even knowledge of the Law. We shall see tomorrow how he will make this clear at the highest level in the church.

Prayer-lines: God our Father, make us true branches of your Son, the true Vine, in being open at all times to the guidance of his Spirit.

Fifth Week of Easter: Thursday

First Reading: Acts 15:7-21; Gospel: Jn 15:9-11

Gospel: 'That your joy be complete.' Jesus is always the model of our lives as Christians. In his deeds, of course, as washing his disciples' feet, but also in his words, even where he reveals his inner life at its deepest, as he does today. We may distinguish four elements in it. First, he knows he is the object of his Father's love. Then, as he puts it, he 'remains' in that love. How? By, thirdly, obeying his Father's commands. For 'remain' has a deep meaning. So that obeying does not mean earning his Father's love, but living with the Father, unlike the Prodigal Son who leaves him. And the final element is the joy of such a life lived in conscious adherence to the Father's will. Blessed indeed are we who hear this word, if we can also keep it.

First Reading: 'The discussion had gone on for a long time.' Our first reading, about a church council meeting, may seem a far cry from the mystical intimacy of today's gospel. And yet they are different aspects of the same reality, remaining in Jesus' love.

Things had been much simpler when Jesus was with the twelve in Galilee. Now, however, they were not twelve, but thousands. And for the ex-Pharisees, observing the Law was a vital way of pleasing God. How could there be any hope of unity between such 'arch-conservatives' and a 'progressive' like Paul? Today's reading shows clearly how the Spirit worked among them – and can still work. First by experience: that of Peter at Caesarea confirmed by Paul and Barnabas further afield. Then St James brings the light of scripture to bear on the problem. And, thirdly, James comes up with a practical compromise. This will leave the Gentiles free of an intolerable yoke, and yet not offend the deeper susceptibilities of the Jewish Christians. Christ has truly shown his risen presence in the church through the guidance of his Spirit.

Prayer-lines: Lord Jesus, thank you for your continued presence with your church. Make us always open to your voice and to your Spirit.

Fifth Week of Easter: Friday
First Reading: Acts 15: 22-31; Gospel: Jn 15:12-17

Gospel: 'Love one another as I have loved you.' Is Jesus really asking too much of eleven men (with Judas gone off to betray him), men who were constantly bickering about who would be first in the kingdom? Jesus admits that he is asking for a love that has no greater kind: loving to the point of willing death on behalf of another. Yes, before the Spirit comes, he is obviously asking too much. But with the gift of his Spirit, Jesus' love unto death and beyond will remain the foundation and the source of their love of one another. And now with the new status of 'friends', their major responsibility will be not so much the faith he asked of them before, as 'bearing fruit' – for the Father.

First Reading: 'Some of your members have disturbed you.' Let's see if there is any trace of Jesus' intimate love surviving amid the tensions of the early church. Has anything gone wrong? After all the same people are there too as at the Last Supper, the apostles. Recall first the background of this 'council'. The great confront-ation between the conservative (Jewish) and liberal (Greek-speaking) wings of the infant church. Many of the former, Paul included, brought up as Pharisees. Who are they sending their decisions to? People even shortly before regarded as untouch-ables. How will they address them? 'The apostles and elders, your brothers ... send greetings to the brothers of pagan birth. Some of our members have disturbed you.' (We are sorry, we apologise.) No attempt to sweep the wrong under the carpet. Firm steps are taken to rectify the wrong. The gist of the practical measures decided upon is 'not to saddle you with any burden beyond the essentials'. Truly, this random account of practical administration in the early church shows how really it is living up to Jesus' command to love one another.

Prayer-lines: Lord Jesus, by your holy Spirit, teach your church at every level to make your commandment of love the keynote of its life.

Fifth Week of Easter: Saturday
First Reading: Acts 16:1-10; Gospel: Jn 15:18-21

Gospel: 'If the world hates you, it hated me before you.' A sharp contrast this gospel with yesterday's Good News of being Jesus' friends, no longer mere servants; with easy access therefore to the Father. From this lagoon of mutual love and friendship we are thrust uncertainly into a rough sea of hatred and persecution from the world. No mere prophecy this in John's time with Nero's savage persecution in the 60s AD, and final rupture with the Jews after Jerusalem's fall in 70. Yet our gospel passage also illustrates yesterday's passage. The world's hatred proves the Christian's closeness to Jesus – as his friend. And this means too that the Christian must share Jesus' positive and active attitude to the world, 'which God so loved'. It means, therefore, being in the world as Jesus was, as it saviour – though not *of* the world.

First Reading: 'The Spirit of Jesus would not allow them.' The Book of Acts has been described as 'the gospel of the Spirit'. And in many places we are struck by the similarity of the role which the Holy Spirit plays in the early church to the guidance of Jesus when on earth with the twelve. So, in today's reading we see Paul and his companions being obliged, they feel it is by the Spirit, constantly to change their travel plans. Possibly it was a disappointment for Paul not to be able to evangelise in Bithynia on the Black Sea coast. But a momentous message was waiting for him instead at Troas: 'Come across to Macedonia and help us.' For Christianity it was historic as the scene of St Paul's first venture into Europe, to whose cities his most important letters would later be addressed.

Prayer-lines: God our Father, strengthen our faith in the presence of your Spirit in our lives, and make us always docile to his guidance in our problems.

Sixth Week of Easter: Monday
First Reading: Acts 16:11-15; Gospel: Jn 15:26-16:4

Gospel: 'When the time for it comes, you may remember that I told you.' How many young people, at this time of year – and at others – are desperately trying to remember what they have been told, been taught, in view of an impending examination? And examination in the sense of a testing or trial is not a bad symbol of our Christian life. The first trials of Jesus' disciples, we remember, were punishment by the Sanhedrin, expulsion from the synagogue, even killing, like Stephen. Their support under trial, as St Peter's first letter shows us, was to remember what was done to Christ, and how he endured it. 'He was insulted and did not retaliate with insults.' Christians are other Christs; Christ still present in the world. And a specific task of the Spirit is to remind us of our Christhood, and of the passion as the pattern of Christian life. 'Was it not ordained,' runs the Alleluia verse today, 'that Christ (and therefore we) should suffer?' We forget so much we should remember. The Mass is our dramatic, effectual 'memory' of Christ and his death.

First Reading: The Good News of the Spirit has geography as well as a history for St Luke, dictated by the itinerary given by Jesus before his ascension. 'You will be my witness in Jerusalem, Judea, Samaria and to the ends of the earth.' And today's part of the journey of evangelisation, as we saw, was the momentous one of bearing the Good News into Europe. And a particular element to note in today's passage is the important contribution of women in St Paul's work. Luke's account of Lydia is brief, but none the less distinctive. A practical businesswoman, somewhat reminiscent of Martha in the gospel. Used to getting her own way. 'Would take no refusal' of her offer to put up Paul and his companions. No small concession this on Paul's part.

Prayer-lines: Lord Jesus, may your church always allow women full scope for their enormous potential in spreading your Good News.

Sixth Week of Easter: Tuesday

First Reading: Acts 16:22-34; Gospel: Jn 16:5-11

Gospel: 'Unless I go, the Advocate will not come to you.' Yes, it is natural for the disciples to be sad at Jesus' going. But they should keep in mind that he is going to the Father: 'the one who sent me'. Moreover, Jesus knows that there is another person for the Father to send, in order to complete his great plan of salvation. This is the Holy Spirit. Jesus calls him 'the Advocate'. For the Spirit will be his counsel for the defence. Jesus has been judged by the world and condemned. Now it is time for God to judge the world. To confront it first of all by its sin of disbelief in Jesus. To downface the world by showing the victory of Christ in his exaltation by the Father. To challenge the world by the downfall of its prince, the devil. All this the Spirit will do through Christians, to whom he is given in baptism. The institutional church, of course, is bound to bear witness to the values of Christ's Spirit by its pronouncements. But how many of the challenges to the world's selfishness, materialism and corruption have been given down the ages by individual charismatic Christians!

First Reading: Our first reading is not a bad example of how the Spirit bears witness to Christ through the disciples. This time it is the Roman citizens of Philippi who have Paul and Silas scourged and thrown into prison. Their spirits, however, are in no way cowed by this unjust ill-treatment. They bear witness to their faith by 'praying aloud and singing God's praises', to the astonishment, no doubt, of the other prisoners. And their submission to their unjust imprisonment proves the occasion of conversion for the gaoler and his family – as rapid a reception into the faith as was that of Cornelius on his meeting with St Peter.

Prayer-lines: Lord Jesus, fill us with your holy Spirit that we may be emboldened to uphold Christian values at all times.

Sixth Week of Easter: Wednesday
First Reading: Acts 17:15, 22-18:1; Gospel: Jn 16:12-15

Gospel: 'The Spirit will lead you to complete truth.' Yesterday we heard that the Spirit was to come as our Advocate. Today as our Teacher. The Father has already given us Jesus as the Way, the Truth and the Life. The Spirit has first to lead us into the truth about Jesus. We can see from the New Testament how quickly he got to work. At Pentecost we hear Peter preaching about Jesus of Nazareth as 'a man...'. Less than 30 years later Paul will quote a Christian hymn (in Philippians) saying, 'though his state was divine'. These were giant steps in truth. No less striking was the guidance of the Spirit in matters like the observance of the Law of Moses. Not only had all the first disciples practised it; so had Jesus too, and never disowned it. And yet a few decades after the resurrection the 'council of Jerusalem' can dispense Gentiles from observing it in the words, 'It has been decided by the Spirit and ourselves...' Nor should we forget the 'second Pentecost' that was Vatican II. Nor that the Spirit is also given to us for our private tuition – so far as we let him.

First Reading: At first sight our two readings might seem poles apart: Jesus speaking intimately with his disciples in the gospel; in our first reading Paul selling the rudiments of Christianity in Athens, the heart, we might say, of Greek paganism. As Jews, of course, the disciples would boast that there was no 'unknown God' for them. And yet, at the same Last Supper we hear Philip asking Jesus, 'Show us the Father.' The disciples will not laugh at the mention of the resurrection; but they are equally at a loss before its mystery. And how far can we, 2000 years later, claim we know God, and understand the resurrection? However, more important than our common ignorance is the truth expressed by the Greek poet, and approved by St Paul: 'We are all his children.'

Prayer-lines: God our Father, grant that your church may always be open to the guidance of your Sprit into the fulness of your truth.

Sixth Week of Easter: Thursday
First Reading: Acts 18:1-8; Gospel: Jn 16:16-20

Gospel: 'In a short time you will see me again.' Jesus' last words to his disciples, and therefore to us, are words of consolation. But they are also realistic: a description of the Christian life after his ascension to heaven. In John's time, when his gospel was being written, persecution by both Jews and Romans had already become a reality. Jesus meant his disciples to see this time of stress as another way of seeing him again. For the Spirit was sent to reproduce in Christians Jesus' life on earth. Unfailing fidelity to 'the one who sent him' – and that would mean suffering at the hands of a 'world' that rejected him. It is the pattern of a Christian life in every generation. We may not be suffering persecution, though in parts of the world other Christians are. But there can always be some unwelcome side of life for us. This is not so rare. We must see it, as Jesus did, as part of God's plan of salvation. We must seek to find his presence in it; and the power of his Spirit, leading us to the final joy of the resurrection, but already, leading us to peace in our faith in his presence.

First Reading: We have Paul's very enlightened attempt to graft the Good News of the risen Christ on to the soil of Greek culture and philosophy of Athens. Not many, it would seem, were converted. Paul would therefore naturally push on to the nearby city of Corinth, capital city of the Roman province. Here today we find him immersed in one of his most important missions in a very cosmopolitan context. We marvel to note that it is truly twenty years since Jesus' resurrection. Paul still feels bound to preach in the synagogue but, as the Jews still contest his Good News about Jesus, he can now, as he says, 'with a clear conscience give all his attention to the Gentiles'.

Prayer-lines: Lord Jesus, help us by your Spirit, to reproduce in our lives your loving acceptance of your Father's will amid the trials of life.

Sixth Week of Easter: Friday
First Reading: Acts 18:9-18; Gospel: Jn 16:20-23

Gospel: 'When that day comes you will not ask me any questions.' Above all the great question, 'Why the Cross?' (alias, 'The Problem of Pain.') Cyril of Alexandria speaks of the 'typical joy and courage that Jesus showed in his passion'. A deep mystery indeed, but clarified by Jesus' parable of 'a woman in child-birth', willingly bearing the suffering at the thought of the child she will deliver. Jesus' passion was therefore a 'child-birth', a begetting, of a new humanity. More an activity than a passivity: a 'labour' indeed. And Jesus' deep joy in the passion was that too of a man at hard work: a work He alone could do. The image of childbirth is already found in the messianic prophecies – of the birth of the new People of God. But why the pain? Because it was also a bitter conflict with the prince of this world, the powers of darkness. We too must accept our share in this vital, saving work of sharing in Christ's 'labours', of bringing humanity out of the dark womb of sin into the light and joy of redemption.

First Reading: Our first reading gives us a graphic glimpse of how the birth of the important church of Corinth was safeguarded by the unexpected intervention of the Roman authorities. Jewish antagonism to Paul had apparently reached its peak and they hoped to use the new Roman proconsul as their tool. They framed their accusation against Paul ambiguously in the hope that Paul would be punished as a civil law breaker. But Gallio, brother of the famous Roman philosopher, Seneca, saw through the ruse and washed his hands of a religious dispute. The tables, therefore, were turned against Paul's opponents and the Good News vindicated. We may never be hailed before a court for our faith, but we all share Christ's assurance to Paul, 'Fear not. I am with you.'

Prayer-lines: Lord Jesus, help us by your holy Spirit to glory, like Paul in sharing the mystery of your cross for the world's salvation.

Sixth Week of Easter: Saturday

First Reading: Acts 18:23-28; Gospel: Jn 16:23-28

Gospel: 'Now I leave the world to go to the Father.' Words spoken at the Last Supper, but how appropriate too for the mystery of the ascension, when the church is still clinging to Jesus in thought before he disappears from sight. And only as he goes does she begin to realise who he is and what is his message. He has indeed fulfilled the prophecy of Isaiah: 'Just as the rain and snow come down and water the earth, so the Word does not return to me fruitless without accomplishing my purpose, and succeeding in the task I gave it.' Jesus' parting request of us, 'Ask and you shall receive', he has already made in the other gospels. But it has a new depth now as he enters on the last stage of his career: re-union with his Father. He wants to share all he is with his disciples. So we are to ask not merely for temporal needs, but for that union with the Father which is the heart of Christian life. In other words, it is to ask for the Spirit, the life-stream uniting Jesus with the Father.

First Reading: 'An Alexandrian Jew named Apollos.' St Paul still remains for Luke the key figure of Acts while he revisits his original bases, Antioch and Galatia. But Luke must also mention a new and distinguished preacher of the Good News whom God sends from Alexandria. This was the major centre of Jewish learning and culture outside Jerusalem, so we are not surprised to read that 'he was able by God's grace to help the believers considerably'. Like the first Hellenist converts in Jerusalem earlier on, his conversion was a considerable help to the more educated Jews. At Ephesus Prisca and Aquila would take care to acquaint him with the major lines of St Paul's teaching. We find no trace here of the rivalry between the followers of Paul and those of Apollos mentioned in the first Letter to the Corinthians.

Prayer-lines: God our Father, increase our faith in Jesus' guarantee that as we are your children we have only to ask your gifts in order to receive them.

Seventh Week of Easter: Monday
First Reading: Acts 19:1-8; Gospel: Jn 16:29-33

Gospel: 'Be brave. I have conquered the world.' The mystery of
the ascension we've already celebrated can be viewed under
two aspects. One is the triumph of Jesus. The 'world' he has conquered is not, of course, the world of nature, God's creation. It is
for John the 'world' of which Satan is the prince; the world of
men who prefer darkness to light; who echo Satan's, 'I will not
serve'. It is the world which will hate Christians as it hated
Christ. Yes it cannot destroy the peace, which Jesus gives them
through the Spirit. The other aspect is the presence of Christ
with his Father in heaven in the fullness of his humanity. At the
Last Supper, and all through his life on earth, he could sincerely
say, 'I am not alone, because the Father is with me.' Both aspects
are food for our prayer, food of our peace who are in Christ.

First Reading: Our first reading gives us another example of Jesus
conquering the world through the visible manifestation of his
Spirit. Apollos, as we have already seen, had been a disciple
only of John the Baptist at Alexandria, but at Ephesus he had
quickly assented to Jesus as the true messiah to whom John had
borne witness. Apollos had left for Corinth when Paul arrived at
this prestigious city of Ephesus, one of the greatest in the Roman
Empire. Here he met other disciples of John the Baptist. They
had, therefore, received only John's 'baptism of repentance', but
not that of Jesus, with the conferring of his Spirit. Once Paul had
given them this baptism in Jesus' name, the same manifestation
of the Spirit had occurred as at Pentecost in Jerusalem. No doubt
we have still to learn from this early Christian generation some
of their fervent faith in the Holy Spirit as a real person continuing in us the life and work of Jesus.

Prayer-lines: Lord Jesus, increase our faith in ourselves, the temple
of the Holy Spirit in which you are continuing your work as
saviour of the world.

Seventh Week of Easter: Tuesday
First Reading: Acts 20:17-27; Gospel: Jn 17:1-11

Gospel: 'Let him give eternal life to all those you have entrusted to him.' John places this sublime prayer of Jesus at the Last Supper, as prelude to his passion, his 'hour'. We may read in it Jesus' thoughts and feelings as he ascends to the Father. While a prayer, it is also a revelation of both the Father and Son. We might, perhaps, imagine Jesus turning with relief to the Father to escape from the wretchedness of humanity he has had to live with for thirty odd years. But these are only human thoughts. God's thoughts are selfless. So are Jesus'. He does indeed rejoice to be coming to the Father to receive as man the glory and intimacy he always had as God's Son. But the whole purpose of his manhood (his incarnation) has been to share his divinity with all humankind. If he leaves the world to go to the Father, it is only to enable us to do the same.

First Reading: 'You see me already a prisoner in the (Holy) Spirit.' Our first reading is a fitting pendant to Jesus' farewell prayer at the Last Supper. Paul has finished his 'third missionary journey' and is on his way back to Jerusalem. He summons to meet him at Miletus the leaders of the church at Ephesus, where he had laboured for three years in building up the church. He wants to bid them farewell, as he does not expect to see them again. It is his only speech in Acts to Christians. It forms a hinge between his mission and the passion which he is convinced lies ahead. He looks back with a clear conscience on how he has served (Christ) the Lord, in imitation of Christ's service of his Father. And he looks forward to what lies ahead. As Christ followed the programme 'ordained' for him by the Father, Paul is equally impelled by the Spirit of the risen Christ to imitate his Master.

Prayer-lines: God our Father, strengthen our faith in Jesus as the one who has come from you to share with us, through his Spirit, your mutual love.

Seventh Week of Easter: Wednesday

First Reading: Acts 20:28-38; Gospel: Jn 17:11-19

Gospel: 'For their sake I consecrate myself.' One of the most striking differences between John's and the synoptic gospels is the absence in John of the eucharistic formulas of the Last Supper, 'this is my Body; this is my Blood'. But, (apart from the earlier discourse at Capenaum on eating his flesh and drinking his blood) we have John's equivalent here: 'I consecrate myself.' Consecration means broadly to separate something from its secular state and usage to a state of belonging to God and his service. Jesus has always been consecrated to God ('I do always the things that please him'), but this consecration by his death is the culmination of it. And its fruit is to share that consecration with his disciples. This will make them 'other Christs'. If the Christian vocation can take many forms, lay, religious, clerical, these three prepositions sum up what is common to all of them: 'Other Christs in the world; not of it, but for it'.

First Reading: 'Feed the church of God which he bought with his own blood.' This, of course, is the heart of Paul's farewell address to the elders of Ephesus. They have the example of Christ, the Good Shepherd who laid down his life for his flock. Imbued with the prophetic Spirit who filled him, Paul then looks forward and foresees heresies arising after his death. And history has proved him right. Paul then confides the Ephesians to the care of God and the power of his divine Word. It is worth noting that it is the church which is confided to the Word of God, and not the word confided to the church. Vatican II then will be able to declare that the word of scripture should be the heart of theology. And, finally, these 'overseers' ('bishops' in St Luke's Greek) are to be free from all self-seeking. Paul himself has given them an example here, but so above all has Christ. As Paul will remind the Corinthians, 'he made himself poor to make us rich'.

Prayer-lines: God our Father, enable us like St Paul to fulfill our Christian calling, by living no longer for ourselves but for him who died for us and rose again.

Seventh Week of Easter: Thursday

First Reading: Acts 22:30, 23:6-11; Gospel: Jn 17:20-26

Gospel: 'I pray also for those who will believe in me.' Usually in the gospels we are listening to Jesus' words indirectly, meant for us indeed, but addressed directly to the disciples or others. Not so here. We are directly spoken of here. We are 'those who believe in Jesus through the words of the apostles'. Here it is we for whom Jesus is praying to the Father. And what is he asking for us? He asks for a mysterious 'oneness'. But he goes on to clarify that word by his thrice repeated phrase, 'you loved me'. Jesus is asking for us the 'oneness' he enjoys himself. And if it is Jesus' own 'oneness', then we know it's shape – the shape of the cross. He is one with the Father not only by trust and affection, but by the bond of filial obedience, even unto a death on a cross. And he is one with all other sons and daughters of God by the same blood-kinship. But the explanation, 'you loved me' shows us that this oneness is a dynamic thing, visible enough to challenge the world – by an obedience to the Father like Jesus' own, and a dedication to our brothers and sisters on Jesus' model too.

First Reading: Paul is now in Jerusalem. He is brought on trial before the Sanhedrin. Paul takes advantage of the potential sympathy for the Good News of the resurrection among Pharisees. Paul's ruse works, and the Pharisees take his part. Yet the ensuing fracas puts Paul in mortal danger. Again he has to be taken into custody by the Romans. And in a vision Jesus advises him that he must next be a witness for him in Rome. Rome was the last stage he had mapped out for the apostle's mission before his ascension.

Prayer-lines: God our Father, may Jesus' prayer for our oneness with him and you to be granted: so that by our oneness with you and each other we may bear witness before the world.

Seventh Week of Easter: Friday
First Reading: Acts 25:23-21; Gospel: Jn: 21:15-19

Gospel: 'Lord, you know everything: you know I love you.' The last time Peter had protested his love to Jesus was at the Last Supper, when Jesus had foretold his denial of him that night. Peter had indeed learnt that Jesus knows everything. But Jesus here is not just probing Peter's feelings; he is giving him a chance to disclaim his three denials, while implicitly forgiving them. And he is proving this forgiveness by renewing Peter's special responsibility for Jesus' lambs and sheep. Yet he would do this, not without foretelling the price which Peter would have to pay for his primacy of love: his martyrdom: 'the kind of death by which he would give glory to God.' .

First Reading: 'A dead man called Jesus, whom Paul alleged to be alive.' We have seen many instances of St Luke's literary skill: for example, his compression of the original apostolic preaching on Jesus' lips to the disciples walking to Emmaus. In today's reading he sums up our Christian faith in one line: 'A dead man called Jesus whom Paul alleged to be alive.' And, with brilliant effect, he puts his summary on the lips of the Roman governor, Festus. That is, indeed, our faith as Christians. We believe in a dead man who is alive. And this captures the difference between a Christian and a pagan. For the pagan Jesus is a dead man, of ancient history; for us as Christians, as for Paul, Jesus is alive. 'For me to live is Christ.' Perhaps we can even say, the contrast reflects the barometer of our faith. In proportion as our faith is weak, Jesus is for us a figure of the past. If our faith is strong, Jesus is alive. Like Paul, we live in Christ, Christ lives in us. May the Holy Spirit of our baptism make that true for us all.

Prayer-lines: Lord Jesus, grant us in your mercy to undo our denials of you by our love for you and witness to you before we die.

Seventh Week of Easter: Saturday

First Reading: Acts: 28: 16-20, 30-31; Gospel: Jn 21:20-25

Gospel: 'Jesus had not said ... He will not die ... but stay behind till I come.' Today we reach the finale of John's gospel. If this last chapter began with the joy of breakfasting with Jesus by the Sea of Galilee, today it seems to sound a note of tragedy. Peter's death has already been foretold, and it would seem, already fulfilled. Death too of the Beloved Disciple would also seem to be implied. Were our last links with Jesus, therefore, to be broken? The apostles had seemed to be indispensable as the living witnesses to the Word made flesh. Jesus' answer to this vital question is 'no'. For the Beloved Disciple is more than a historical person of the past. He is also a symbolic (theological?) person. He is the eternal Christian, beloved of Christ (and of his Father), filled and led and comforted by the Holy Spirit. Some would say he is the incarnation of the Holy Spirit in the world.

First Reading: Our first reading too might seem to strike a despondent note at the end of St Luke's great Acts of the Apostles. Paul is now a prisoner in Rome, 'in the lion's mouth'. He too, like Peter, will die there in the same persecution. But he is free to welcome all who come to visit him He is still proclaiming the kingdom of God and teaching the truth about the Lord Jesus Christ with complete freedom and without hindrance from anyone. This is the great triumphant truth which dispenses Luke from satisfying our modern curiosity about what happened to Paul in the end. Don't worry about Paul, Luke tells us. What matters is that Christ's last injunction before his ascension has been carried out. 'You will be my witnesses to the ends of the earth.'

Prayer-lines: Lord Jesus, thank you for the consolation of your scriptures. Help us to live as your beloved disciples, faithful witnesses to you till the end of our lives.

Week 1: Monday

Cycle 1: Heb 1:1-6; Cycle 2: 1 Sam 1:1-8; Gospel: Mk 1:14-20

Gospel: 'Follow me. I will make you fishers of men.' And so we leave the Jordan and follow Jesus in Galilee. Galilee is certainly more beautiful than the arid Jordan valley, but our trip is to be no 'picnic'. 'After John had been arrested ' is a sinister time signal. Jesus knows now that the time is short. 'The kingdom of God is close at hand' (in his person), yet the kingdom of Satan is not going to yield if it can – until it is forced to, until 'someone stronger attacks and defeats' it. Jesus knows he has to be that 'someone'.

'Repent'; reform, because his call is to a new way of life. Jesus' way is not the way of the world. The four disciples today give us a practical example of what this 'Repent' can mean. 'They left their nets and followed him.' There is nothing wrong with fishing for a livelihood. No taint of the dishonesty that is attached to the tax-collectors and the shepherds. But even what is good must now yield to what is better. The 'time of fulfilment' has come, to complete the merely partial, to perfect the imperfect. Catching men for God's saving net is better than catching fish. – Little, of course, did the four disciples know all this new 'fishing' would involve. It is only after the Resurrection that Jesus tells Peter openly of martyrdom ahead. Nor do we know all that is ahead of us in the New Year. And, secure in the One who calls us, we gladly follow him.

Cycle 1: Our first reading is taken from the Mass of Christmas Day. A salutary reminder that as we embark on a new Christian year in Jesus' footsteps, we carry with us all the riches and encouragement of the Christian revelation with us.

Cycle 2: Our first reading brings us back to a major stage in 'the time of fulfilment', with the appearance of the scene of Israel's history of the prophetic figure in the person of Samuel. He and his successors will keep alive the people's awareness of Israel as the chosen people of God.

Prayer-lines: God, our Father, may this New Year be a time of faithful following of Jesus in his work of salvation.

Week 1: Tuesday
Cycle 1: Heb 2:5-12; Cycle: 2: 1 Sam 1:9-20; Gospel: 1:21-28
Cycle 1: 'The leader who would take them to their salvation.' Perhaps it is best to take Hebrews (our first Reading for the next two weeks), more as a homily to us than as a letter to these Jewish Christians in Rome. The practical point the preacher wants to make is that Christ be the centre of our lives: our go-between with God, our great 'high-priest'. Coming after our Christmas celebrations it is easy to accept Jesus' greatness: as the Word in the beginning; as God's last word to the world. Easy for us then, (if not for all first century Christians apparently), to see Jesus as superior to any angel. But it is equally important to see him as human: as one of ourselves. He needed to be fully human to save us; to be our high-priest, which was his task, his mission. And that meant to be able to suffer, like us. We must never forget that Jesus still suffers, with us, as well as for us.

Cycle 2: Our first reading shows us God's saving power at work in that ever-present affliction of maternal sterility. Trusting in the blessing and reassurance of Eli, the high-priest at Shiloh, Hannah is granted a son. She, in turn, will fulfil her promise of dedicating him to God's service, and that Son, Samuel, will inaugurate the prophetic line of Israel's self-awareness of God's Chosen People.

Gospel: Our gospel today shows Jesus in action as our high-priest. He teaches us as one who knows perfectly what God is like, and what he wants of us. But he has also the power to save us from our weakness, even in this life.

Prayer-lines: Lord Jesus, we thank you for putting aside your glory in order to share our sufferings. May your submission to death to save us be the foundation of our love for you and the Father.

Week 1: Wednesday

Cycle 1: Heb 2:14-18; Cycle 2: 1 Sam 3:1-10, 19-20; Gospel: Mk 1:29-39

Cycle 1: 'Long before dawn he went of to a lonely place and prayed there.' Our first reading from Hebrews is still exploring the flesh and blood reality of Jesus' humanity. To be able to atone, as high-priest, for our sins, he had to be completely like us. He had to be able to offer God a complete human nature, human life and human death. So much we are used to hearing , and can accept. But how could he actually go 'through temptation'? What sort of temptation could Jesus have?

Gospel: Our gospel gives us a good example. Briefly, on the evening of the Sabbath Jesus has been a sensational success in Capernaum, especially by healing. Simon and his other disciples would obviously be thrilled by this. But, to their dismay, when they awake, they find he is not there. They rush after him in pursuit (according to the verb Mark uses). It is clear from the implicit reproach in their words, 'Everybody is looking for you' that they are pressuring Jesus to come back and keep it up; to be a spectacular Messiah. But Jesus has been praying for light and strength, and sees that for him God's will is different. And for him that is what matters. 'I do always the things that please him.' 'Because that is why I came.'

Cycle 2: Our first reading continues the story of Samuel's growth in the sanctuary at Shiloh. It will be the literary model for St Luke in referring to Jesus' growth as a boy, just as Hannah's canticle is a model for Mary's Magnificat. In today's gospel Jesus is now a man of thirty, setting out on his mission to preach the Good News of the kingdom. But Jesus needs no Eli to teach him to say, 'Speak, Lord, your servant is listening.' He lives in constant alertness to his Father's will.

Prayer-lines: Lord Jesus, teach us by your example, always to be attentive and docile to your guidance of us by your Holy Spirit.

Week 1: Thursday
Cycle 1: Heb 3:7-14 Cycle 2: 1 Sam 4:1-11; Gospel: Mk 1:40-45

Cycle 1: 'If only you would listen to him *today*.' Hebrews is reminding the Jews in Rome of the story of their forefathers in the desert. On their way to the Promised Land, so Moses told them, but they were fed up with the daily drudgery of collecting the lightweight manna to eat, and water being hard to find: they longed for the 'fleshpots' they had had in Egypt. They longed for the 'place of rest' ahead in the Promised Land. But the weariness of the Today in the desert overcame their trust in God in their midst, in the Ark of the Covenant. They continually 'tested' him. Tested his patience by their grumbling. It can be a salutary lesson for every generation, even our own. 'If only you would listen to him today': to trust in his love and power to help.

Cycle 2: Our first reading continues the story of Israel's painful growth into statehood in the Promised Land. Today it is the story of a crushing defeat by the Philistines, apparently an irretrievable disaster, for the Ark of the Covenant is captured. Has Israel's God deserted her? The sequel, of course, will prove otherwise. Apparent disasters in our lives can turn out later to be blessings. We must turn to God with the faith of the leper in the gospel.

Gospel: The gospel, too, we remind ourselves, was written down as a message for every generation, for today, not merely as a record of the past. We too, like today's leper, can come to Jesus with whatever weakness we need to be rid of, and say to him: 'If you want to, you can cure me.' And Jesus, feeling sorry for each of us, too, will say: 'Of course I want to. Be cured.' The time of our cure he knows best. All he wants from us is our faith.

Prayer-lines: Lord, let not the difficulties of our life on earth weaken our faith in your presence in our midst, and our trust in your will to save us.

Week 1: Friday

Cycle 1: Heb 4:1-5, 11; Cycle 2:1 Sam 8:4-7, 10-22; Gospel: Mk 2:1-12

Gospel: 'The Son of Man has authority on earth to forgive sins.'
We can miss much of the Gospel's saving power if we allow ourselves to be distracted by factual details, (the lowering of the
paralytic through the roof, etc.) and not to hear the story as did
the first Christians. For them the important thing was not 'what
happened', but 'what does it mean'? The key sentence of the
passage is the one we began with ... the point of this episode is
not what Jesus did, or even said on this occasion, but what it reveals in him. God has forgiven man in Christ ... In the power of
Jesus, here made visible, God has thrown a bridge across the
gulf of man's powerlessness to save himself. In Jesus' words the
Last Things have already come to pass: judgement and salvation.
The curing of the sick man's paralysis is not a proof of the inner
forgiveness (which is not open to proof) but a symbol of
mankind's recreation in Christ to a new life, eternal life.

Cycle 1: It is this eternal life, 'the place of rest' which is the theme
of the first Reading. The Promised Land was something more in
God's mind for his people than Palestine. That eternal rest
shared by God is the real goal for which we must strive, and to
which the personal saving power of Jesus is the way, the bridge.

Cycle 2: Our first reading records a major turning point in
Israel's history: the institution of kingship in place of the earlier
prophetic guidance. The pros and cons of being a kingdom,
written down at a later date, reflect the varied fortunes of the
kingship that was to ensue. The final line is the key one: 'Obey
their voice and given them a king.' God will always remain a
control of history, and can 'write straight with (our) crooked
lines.'

Prayer-lines: God, our Father, thank you for so loving the world
as to send your Only Son to be our Saviour. Increase in us daily
our faith in his power to forgive and save us.

Week 1: Saturday

Cycle 1: Heb 4:12-16; Cycle 2: 1 Sam 9:1-4, 17-19; 10:1; Gospel: Mk 2:13-17

Cycle 1: 'The word of God is something alive and active, it cuts like any two-edged sword.' The Word of God had always been alive and active for Israel, people of the Bible, of the Book. Especially as spoken by the prophets. 'It shall not return to God empty, fruitless, without carrying out the work God gives it to do.' Like Wisdom and the Spirit, the Word of God has almost become a person even in the Old Testament. Certainly the concept prepared for the Incarnation, when 'the Word was made flesh and dwelt among us.'

Cycle 2: Our first reading will, optimistically, introduce us to the first in the long line of kings in Israel's history. It obviously comes from circles favourable to the idea of kingship. Even in physical appearance Saul seems to be the ideal man to 'rule the Lord's people and save them from the enemies surrounding them.' But later history, written in prophetic circles, will bear out the psalmist's warning of trusting in human resources rather than God's help.

Gospel: And in today's gospel we can check on how that Word fulfils its mission in human form. The Word utters two 'words' today: 'Follow me', and 'I did not come to call the virtuous but sinners.' A two-edged sword indeed, dividing not the good from the bad, but those whom Jesus came to call, and would answer that call, from those deaf to that call, The Sword of that Word turns the Pharisees' philosophy of life upside down, by making the 'sinners' (of the Pharisees' dictionary) God's privileged ones, the blessed of the Father, called to possess the kingdom. – And the choice is always before us: do we want to see ourselves as virtuous, the healthy, or as sinners, the sickly; always waiting in Jesus' surgery for that two-edged lancet of his that heals our wounds as well as exposing them?

Prayer-lines: God, our Father, may we learn from your Word in Scripture to trust, not in human power or virtue, but only in your saving help.

Week 2: Monday

Cycle 1: Heb 5:1-10; Cycle 2: 1 Sam 15:16-23; Gospel: Mk 2:18-22

Gospel: 'New wine, fresh skins.' As so often in the gospels what is at stake is the true and false attitudes to religion. For Pharisees religion must involve sacrifice, in this case fasting. One's motivation while fasting was not important. Here Jesus corrects them. What God really wants (in other words, religion) is a person to person relation to him, and that will mean a lot more than fasting. It will mean facing up to the new demands for God's sake made on one. One day this can be rejoicing, because 'the Bridegroom is with them'. Another day it will mean fasting in memory of Jesus' death. 'New wine, fresh skins.' The new wine of our love of God will keep the 'skin of our religion always fresh, authentic.

Cycle 1: Our first reading from Hebrews gives us the supreme example in Christ of true religion. He waited for his father in heaven to appoint him our high priest, and by his obedience through his Passion he won us, in his resurrection, eternal redemption.

Cycle 2: 'Obedience is better than sacrifice' is the prophet Samuel's pointer to Christ's future teaching. The first book of Samuel does not conceal Israel's admiration for Saul and his genuine achievements. But by the time it was written down Israel had lived through some 400 years of predominantly disastrous kingly rule, and Israel's disenchantment with kingship in general is reflected back on Saul's portrayal. In the story of Saul's fall from grace we can also hear our Lord's warning about our own need for vigilance, lest our anointing (by baptism) be damaged.

Prayer-lines: God, our Father, may our religion and our practice of it be always filled with your new wine, a source of life to ourselves and others.

Week 2: Tuesday

Cycle 1: Heb 6:10-20; Cycle 2: Sam 16:1-13; Gospel: Mk 2:23-28

Gospel: 'The Sabbath was made for man.' By whom? By God, of course. In the Bible the passive voice is often the reverential Jewish way of mentioning God's action. It is God who decides the priorities in religion. Once again we are listening to Jesus' teaching on the nature of true religion, of what God wants of us. Apart from the case of putting human need first, (a regular feature of Jesus' clashes with the Pharisee perspective), like hunger or illness, the service of God is not merely a matter of the punctilious observance of rules, (often merely man-made). Jesus, Master of the Sabbath, is the model of true religion vis a vis God. In keeping him company, as disciples, and following his example, we cannot err.

Cycle 1: Our first reading from Hebrews, will confirm this serenity in our relations with God. Jesus, we are told, is the 'sure anchor for our soul'. He has entered beyond the veil, and is acting there in God's presence as our high priest.

Cycle 2: 'God does not see as man; man looks at appearances, but the Lord looks at the heart.' This distinction between God's perspective and man's is a constant theme of the Bible, in the New as in the Old Testament. 'My ways are not your ways ...' The Chosen People had indeed the very real light about God from the prophets. But this light was often obscured by unnecessary human regulations. With Jesus' coming, the 'true light that enlightens every man', we are now enabled to share God's perspective on how he wants us to live in the likeness of Christ.

Prayer-lines: Lord Jesus, teach us by your Holy Spirit to follow you faithfully in the liberty of children of God.

Week 2: Wednesday
Cycle 1: Heb 7:1-3, 15-17; Cycle 2: 1 Sam 17:32-33, 37, 40-51; Gospel: Mk 3:1-6

Gospel: 'They were watching him.' At least in this we may imitate the Pharisees. We cannot watch Jesus' actions and reactions in the gospel too closely if we wish to know and imitate him. And this is a highly dramatic scene: Jesus consciously courting death by stoning for healing on the Sabbath. He had already had his warning about picking corn on the Sabbath. Now there would be no more warning. To Jesus' explicit disclosure of his view of religion, of God's will for us: 'Is it against the law on the Sabbath day to do good or to do evil?' they have nothing to say. There is only one way to deal with such a downright challenge to *their* ideology. 'At once they began to plot how to destroy him.'

Cycle 1: We would seem to be in a totally different world of thought when we turn to our first reading, where Jesus is declared in Old Testament terms our unique high priest. Hebrews has already declared him to be superior to the angels; now to Moses and the official tribal priesthood of Levi. It remains only to call him another, superior Melchisedek, who was great enough in Jewish thought to be revered by Abraham. Yet Jesus is our priest, our go-between, not only in virtue of his 'indestructible life'. Also because he has borne into heaven for us the same nature that, in the gospel, will look angrily round at the impassive obstinacy of the Pharisees, but also face fearlessly the murderous hatred of theirs he knows he is incurring.

Cycle 2: The story of David's victory over Goliath is one of the Bible's best known folk tales. It is part of 1st Samuel's preparation for David's eventual accession to kingship. Its religious point lies in David's reliance on God for whose honour he is fighting, and on whose help he is utterly reliant. 'I come against you in the name of the Lord of hosts.' (As a footnote we may note that elsewhere the Bible shows a sling in experienced hands like David's was the equivalent of a good modern rifle.) (Jgs 20:16).

Prayer-lines: Lord Jesus, may the human nature you have deigned to share with us be also filled with your Spirit, so that we may always seek to do good and not evil.

Week 2: Thursday

Cycle 1: Heb 7:25-8:6; Cycle 2: 1 Sam 18:6-9; 19:1-7; Gospel: Mk 3:7-12
Cycle 1: 'The power of Jesus to save is utterly certain.' What the first reading will communicate to us in remote theological terms, the gospel passage will bring to light in a vivid visual tableau. Thus today's passage from Hebrews will sum up Jesus' superiority as our go-between with God, as our high priest, over all the worship in the Old Law. For him there is no daily repetition of the sacrifice as theirs needed. No need for him to offer sacrifice for himself because he, unlike all former priests, is utterly sinless. In a word, Jesus' priesthood is of an infinitely higher order than any previous ministry.

Gospel: All this abstract terminology comes to life in our gospel passage. From Jerusalem, Judaea, Idumea, Transjordania, and the region of Tyre and Sidon – what we would today call the Near East and the Levant – many came to him. He even had to have a boat ready in case he would be crushed to death by this crowd. What an extraordinary pen-picture of afflicted humanity crowding in on Jesus from all sides. Surely it is a sort of parable of the history of salvation – all men, of all times and regions surging however confusedly towards him 'whose power to save', as Hebrews puts it, 'is utterly certain'. 'The true light that enlightens every man coming into the world.' A picture of what humanity is seeking, even unwittingly. And also a picture of what we, who do know who Jesus is, should be doing: pressing continually on Christ, in our thoughts, our prayers, our affections, to draw more life and health from him. For at no stage does Jesus cease to be our Saviour.

Cycle 2: Our first reading introduces us to the first stirrings of Saul's jealousy of David's growing reputation with the people. Saul's growing paranoia in David's regard is highlighted by his son Jonathan's intercession for David. Some of the lamentation psalms are attributed to David suffering from Saul's unjust persecution. But David too will be capable of grave sin, and only on Christ's lips will these psalms be really fulfilled.

Prayer-lines: God, our Father, grant us and all humanity today a true hunger and thirst for the salvation you have sent to us in Jesus Christ your Son.

Week 2: Friday
Cycle 1: Heb 8:6-13; Cycle 2: 1 Sam 24:3-21; Gospel: Mk 3:13-19
Gospel and first reading: 'Jesus summoned those he wanted, and he appointed twelve.' Why twelve? Because Jesus was establishing the new covenant promised to Jeremiah in our first reading. That covenant was made with the twelve tribes of Israel at Sinai. The apostles should be our clearest reflection in the gospels. Here they are only introduced on the scene, yet even this has a significance for us too. 'He summoned those he wanted', we are told. The same can be said of each of us. 'You have not chosen me. I chose you.' 'They were to be his companions.' Again an identikit for us as Christians. Reminiscent perhaps of St Patrick's Breastplate: 'Christ be with me, Christ within me ..., etc. He knows them by name, and soon enough, as we say, 'by heart'. By temperament, by character, by failure.

Cycle 2: 'I will not raise my hand against the anointed of the Lord.' Whatever serious sins David will be guilty of later on, his reverence for Saul's anointing by God's prophet shows him worthy to ascend the throne of Israel himself. Yet Saul's recognition of David's magnanimity also goes some way to redeem his neurotic prejudice against his rival.

Prayer-lines: Lord Jesus, we thank you for calling us to be your disciples. Fill us with your Spirit that we may be faithful to our calling to spread the Good News.

Week 2: Saturday

Cycle 1: Heb 9:2-3, 11-14; Cycle 2: 2 Sam 1:1-4, 11-12, 17-19, 23-27;
Gospel: Mk 3:20-21

Gospel: 'They set out to take charge of him.' 'Quite a change from our last snapshot of Jesus. There he was laying the foundation-stones of the church, the people of the new covenant, by calling twelve companions. He summoned them: they came to him. Here we find a very different human reaction to Jesus. Back in Nazareth the discovery by his relatives that he is a celebrity is completely news to them, 'What on earth has happened to our carpenter cousin, Jesus? Has he gone mad? Let's go and look after him before he does himself damage.' We'll hear the rest of the story later on. As for now we note that while these relatives are not hostile to Jesus, as will be the Scribes and Pharisees, other attitudes besides hostility can hinder faith. 'Familiarity', we say, 'breeds contempt' – even, it would seem, of the sacred. Those of us who have been born into an atmosphere and tradition of cosy familiarity with Jesus must beware of thinking that we have nothing new or startling to learn of him in our lives, as indeed his fellow Nazarenes had in the events which followed.

Cycle 1: Meanwhile, our first reading from Hebrews, starts at the other end of the spectrum of Jesus' mystery. Using the imagery of the most solemn part of the Jewish liturgy, when once a year the high-priest went into the Holy of Holies to sprinkle the blood of sacrifices over the ark of the covenant. Jesus is here portrayed as the one and only real high-priest of humanity entering into the Holy of Holies in heaven. Thither he brings the blood of his own sacrifice, which washes away the sin of the world.

Cycle 2: David's elegy over Saul and Jonathan brings Saul's ill-starred reign to a fitting and dignified conclusion. David's grief, especially for Jonathan, is obviously sincere. And the path now lies clear for his own eventual accession to kingship over all Israel.

Prayer-lines: God, Our Father, no one knows the Son fully but you. In your mercy, enable us by your Holy Spirit to grow daily in that knowledge of Jesus which surpasses all understanding.

Week 3: Monday

Cycle 1: Heb 9:15, 24-28;Cycle 2: 2 Sam 5:1-7, 10; Gospel: Mk 3:22-30
Gospel: 'He has tied up the strong man first.' We may well admire Jesus' serenity in demolishing the two charges levelled against him by the scribes: namely that Jesus himself is possessed by a devil; that the power, (which they can't deny), shown by his miracles is of evil origin. This simple logic is irrefutable. But more interesting is the theological reality he unveils. Yes, he implies: the sickness and cure are indeed the evidence of an evil power. Satan has been 'the strong man' in the world up to now. Can you not see then that I am the stronger one of my parable? By my healings I have made my way into Satan's house, tied him up and made off with his possessions. Did not John the Baptist, whom the people revere as one sent by God, testify that I was stronger than he?

Cycle 1: This aspect of Jesus as the 'stronger one' is perhaps an aspect we may overlook or undervalue in our devotion to him. There is no attempt to conceal Jesus' weakness in the Agony. But the dominant image of Jesus for the early Christians is the risen Jesus, with 'all power given to him', the Lamb in the Apocalypse indeed, but also the Lion of the Tribe of Judah. This majestic power is also the image projected by our first reading from Hebrews. He appears in the actual presence of God on our behalf. At his second coming it will be to reward with salvation those who are waiting for him.

Cycle 2: 'David captured the fortress of Zion.' The concept of God's salvation coming through an Anointed king, a 'Messiah', is earlier than kingship in Israel, but from David's time on this Saviour has always been linked with David's name. May not we, therefore, see in this vital capture of Zion by David a forecast of the capture of Satan's stronghold in men's bodies and souls by Jesus, Son of David in the gospels? The Good News of the New Testament lies hidden in the womb of the Old.

Prayer-lines: God, our Father, thank you for overcoming Satan by the death and resurrection of your Son, Jesus. Help us to open our lives fully to the power of Christ's victory.

Week 3: Tuesday

Cycle 1: Heb 10:1-10; Cycle 2: 2 Sam 6:12-19; Gospel: Mk 3:31-35

Cycle 1: Sacrifice has always been for man the clearest expression of religion; 'bull's blood and goat's blood', and the rest. But what did these sacrifices mean? For St Thomas religion is part of the cardinal virtue of sacrifice: giving God what is his due. Man gives back to God part of God's gifts to him, by which he lives. But if God is a moral God: concern with good and evil in men's lives – as well as maker of heaven and earth, then the gift to him that really makes sense is the total gift of one's own will, by doing God's will. As our reading from Hebrews says, 'This will of Christ was made holy for us by the offering of his body.'

Gospel: And this simplifies for us today's gospel where Jesus seems to be repudiating his natural family. 'Who are my mother and my brothers?' Family relationships were vitally important in Jesus' world and time. Jesus himself could not deny that. But he is establishing a new priority: his family in the kingdom of God, the kingdom he personified in himself, was constituted not by natural ties, but by 'doing the will of God'.

Cycle 2: 'They brought the ark of God with great rejoicing to the Citadel of David.' This transfer of the Ark of the Covenant to Jerusalem was a turning-point in Israel's history and religion. God had now a permanent home amid his people. For many this would seem the last word about their religion. It would be for the prophets to show that what God wanted was something deeper. 'Thou shalt love the Lord thy God with thy whole heart, with all thy soul, with all thy strength.' This is the teaching Jesus echoes in the gospels. Yes, God wants us in his family, and he in ours. But that can only be if we do his will.

Prayer-lines: God, our Father, thank you for showing us in Jesus Christ the true way to you. Help us to adore you in Spirit and truth by doing your will in all things.

Week 3: Wednesday

Cycle 1: Heb 10:11-18; Cycle 2: 2 Sam 7:4-17; Gospel: Mk 4:1-20

Gospel: 'Some seed fell into rich soil and produced a crop.' A parable normally makes one point. Jesus and the apostles were sowing the seed of the gospel. There would be many obstacles to its growth, and apparent failures. But the final success of the sowing was assured. The Word of God would ultimately bear fruit. – But the parable ends with a warning: 'the worries of this world will choke the Word.'

Cycle 1: We should be listeners to every part of the gospel: alert to its special meaning for each of us. And here, our first reading, from Hebrews, is an encouragement. By Christ's self-offering, we are told, he has achieved the eternal perfection of all whom he is sanctifying. This is the new covenant God has promised us through Jeremiah.

Cycle 2: David had been planning to build a house for the Ark of the Covenant, still placed in a mere tent. But God sends him word through Nathan that he is not dependent on David for anything, nor has he ever been so. He, God, will do the 'building'. He will build for David a dynasty that will last for ever. This promise would remain a vital guarantee right into New Testament times.

Prayer-lines: Lord Jesus, thank you for the seed you have planted in us by Baptism. Grant us the light and faith we need to bear the fruit you want for us.

Week 3: Thursday

Cycle 1: Heb 10:19-25; Cycle 2: 2 Sam 7:18-19, 24-29; Gospel: Mk 4:21-25
Gospel: 'You will put a lamp on the lampstand.' The parable of the seed and the sower emphasises the innate power of the word to bear fruit, despite obstacles. Today we have the symbol of a lamp. The stress now is on *our* contribution to the growth of the seed, the spreading of the light. We are bound to pass on the light to others:- by example, and when possible, by instruction. 'Be sensitive', St Paul says, 'to the kind of answer each one requires'.

Cycle 1: Our short passage from Hebrews in the first reading sums up such a programme for Christian living. It was written, as we saw, for former Jews. They saw life, like the history of the chosen People, as a journey to meet God. They are now assured they have 'got there', to journey's end, by the sacrifice, 'the blood of Christ'. As Christians they can now go confidently into God's presence. Not just, as did the high-priest in the past, into the Holy of Holies in the Temple, but into heaven itself. All they need now is faith in what Christ has done to purify them; hope that his promises will come true; love for all men for whom Christ has died, and in whom he is found.

Cycle 2: Yesterday we heard of God's historic promise to David that rather than having David build a temple for him, he, God, would assure a perpetual dynasty for David. Today's passage gives us a wonderful heartfelt thanksgiving prayer. David's opening words, 'Who am I, Lord, and what is the house of my father that you have led me as far as this?' ... This humble thanksgiving is an ancestor to that of Mary in the Magnificat: 'He has looked upon his lowly handmaid ... the almighty has done great things for me.'

Prayer-lines: God, our Father, we thank you for sharing with us your Word, who is the Light of the World. May that Light shine through us in all we say and do.

Week 3: Friday

Cycle 1: Heb 10:32-39; Cycle 2: 2 Sam 11:1-10, 13-17; Gospel: Mk 4:26-34

Gospel: 'The seed is growing ... how he does not know.' Once again in the gospel, Jesus draws on the workings of nature to describe the mystery of God's kingdom. That its growth is assured has already been emphasised in the parable of the sower. But how does this growth come about? The farmer does not know. Only God knows, and this 'how' is God's secret ...

Cycle 1: Our first reading, from Hebrews, throws some light on the mystery with regard to the Christians who are the growing seed of the kingdom. We are given no clear indication of the nature of the persecution which occasioned such sufferings for the Jewish Christians being addressed. But these sufferings are certainly part of the means by which God brings about the growth of the kingdom. The happiness of these Christians in being despoiled of their goods is a sign that they are aware of God's positive purpose in these trials. They knew, Hebrews puts it, that they 'owned something that was better and lasting'. They are encouraged to persevere in their patience, because their deliverance will not be delayed.

Cycle 2: The secret of God's kingdom is deepened by our first reading, from the Book of Samuel. We have heard in the last two days of God's magnificent promise to David of a perpetual dynasty; and David's humble thanksgiving for such a favour. The scene seems set for a stained-glass portrayal of David's subsequent life as the model king, (we think, for example, of St Louis of France), till he can pass on his throne to his sons. The adultery which he tries in vain, (due to Uriah's superior virtue), to cover up; and then the cold-blooded murder in battle. That is perhaps the deepest aspect of the kingdom of God. God will not rule through man's virtue, and its reward, but by forgiving his sin.

Prayer-lines: God, our merciful Father, thank you for the mystery of our redemption. May we come to know you more and more through your forgiveness of our sins.

Week 3: Saturday

Cycle 1: Heb 11:1-19; Cycle 2: 2 Sam 12:1-7, 10-17; Gospel: Mk 4:35-41

Gospel: 'How is it that you have no faith?' We can sympathise with the apostles at hearing this reproach from Jesus. The gospel story conveys quite clearly what they had just been through. The very real danger of drowning: not every fisherman can swim. And then the incredible sight of Jesus lying fast asleep in the midst of it all, his head on a cushion. No one, apparently, had realised how exhausted he was after preaching all day. And then the sudden shock of relief when he stood up and, at a word, calmed the waves. But how unreasonable his rebuke for their panic! And yet, Jesus had given them the example of his perfect confidence in God. By the time Mark's Gospel was being written down this story of Jesus' power to still a storm would be read at a deeper level during the frightful persecution of Christians under Nero. And, of course, it remains as an encouragement for every generation in the church. Jesus is always with his church, even when, at times he may seem to be asleep 'in the boat'.

Cycle 1: Our first reading from Hebrews, will echo this call of the gospel for faith. The example of the patriarchs' faith in God's promises is humbling for us whose eyes have seen in Christ, what their eyes were unable to see. They 'died in faith before receiving any of the things that have been promised.'

Cycle 2: 'Then Nathan said to David: you are the man.' David's two great sins we read of yesterday showed him up as a typical near Eastern despot: sensual and ruthless. Nathan is risking his life by saying, 'You are the man'. But, by God's grace, David is bigger than his type; he breaks the mould with his ready confession: 'I have sinned against the Lord'.

And the stature of his faith increases when we see the sincerity of his fervent prayer for the child of his adultery. In spite of his guilt, God remains for David a person, a friend, a forgiving father; not merely a judge. 'For his mercy is without end.'

Prayer-lines: Lord Jesus, we ask you to increase our faith so that we may feel the power of your saving help and forgiveness.

Week 4: Monday

Cycle 1: Heb 11:32-40; Cycle 2: 2 Sam 15:13-14; 30; 16:5-13; Gospel: Mk 5:1-20

Gospel: 'Swear by God you will not torture me.' St Mark follows his account of Jesus' teaching in parables by four miracle stories. We have seen the deep impression made on the disciples by Jesus' power to still the storm at sea by a mere word of command. Miracles of healing are to follow. The first is the most dramatic, and told with great elaboration of details. We have not to go into the various problems which scholars have found in some of these details. Enough for us to share the simple faith of Mark and see in the miracles of healing a further illustration of the mystery of Jesus' life-long struggle with the powers of evil. Once again Jesus proves to be the 'stronger one' in the contest.

Cycle 1: Our first reading concludes the list of those heroes of faith in the Old Testament. There are some notable phrases about them worth holding on to. 'They were too good for the world.' And once again, their faith pricks *our* conscience. '*They* did not receive what was promised. ... Since God had made provision for us to have something better; and they were not to reach perfection except with us.'

Cycle 2: The first reading from the second book of Samuel portrays David in flight from his son, Absalom, who is seeking to take over the throne. Nathan's prophecy of God's punishment for David's crimes of adultery and murder is now being fulfilled: 'I will stir up evil for you out of your own house.' David sees his evil plight as his well-earned punishment, and will do nothing to avert it. But he still clings to his faith in God's mercy: 'Perhaps the Lord will look on my misery, and repay me with good for his curse today.'

Prayer-lines: Lord, teach us to be grateful for all you have done for us, and to trust in your power to heal all our weaknesses.

Week 4: Tuesday

Cycle 1: Heb 12:1-4; Cycle 2: 2 Sam 18:9-10, 14, 24-25, 30-19:3;
Gospel: Mk 5:21-43

Gospel: 'The child is not dead but asleep.' It is a hallmark of St Mark's Gospel that he inserts one miracle into the narrative of another. And he is also famous for giving us unnecessary details that Matthew and Luke will omit. Like the ineffective medical treatment the women of the first episode had received. Both miracles foreshadow Christ's salvation from death: 'Your faith has restored you to health.' And, 'Little girl, I tell you to get up.' Mark's policy is to keep Jesus' messiahship secret – until his resurrection. Only then will it be fully seen that Jesus is victor over death.

Cycle 1: Miracles in the gospels are the reward of faith. And our passage from Hebrews sequel to the long list of Old Testament heroes of faith gives us all the same message 'With such a vast number of women and men of faith, let us not lose sight of Jesus, who perfects us in our faith.' He not only worked miracles through the faith of others. He is our great example by the way he believed that his death on the cross would issue in the resurrection. Engaged as Christians in this struggle with evil, we cannot yet claim to have bled for our witness of faith.

Cycle 2: 'My son, Absalom! Would I had died in your place.' Once more David's characteristic weakness for his children comes across in his heartfelt lament. But also something much more. In yesterday's reading we noted David's meekness under the curses of a follower of Saul. Perhaps David, then, was not fully sure of God's pardon for his two great sins. Today gives him his full answer to any such misgivings. Not through a prophet this time, but through his own heart. Through his unconditional love for his own worthless, faithless son. 'Would I had died in your place.' From his own love as father David learnt what God's love was like. He had been given the message of the Prodigal Son parable one thousand years before Jesus spoke it.

Prayer-lines: Lord Jesus, increase our faith, especially in your boundless love for us sinners. Amen.

Week 4: Wednesday

Cycle 1: Heb 12: 4-15. Cycle 2: 2 Sam 24: 2, 9-17. Gospel: Mk 6:1-6

Gospel: 'And they would not accept him'. For St. Mark this episode at Nazareth is a summary of his whole Gospel: the mystery of Jesus' rejection by his own people. This latter was a constant puzzle to early Christians, for St. Paul a 'thorn in the flesh'. He sees it, optimistically, as a mysterious part of God's plan to save the nations: the stone rejected by Israel becomes the cornerstone of faith and salvation for the Gentiles. It is true what the Nazarenes say 'Jesus is the carpenter' etc. And they ask the right questions, 'Where did the man get all this?' etc. But they are blocked from giving the right answer by this preconceived idea of the Messiah; of God, therefore, and his way of salvation. Therein lies the message of this story for us. Only the humility born of faith and faith born of humility can reveal to us the hand and person and wisdom of God in the details of our human situation.

Cycle 1: Our first reading, from Hebrews, will extend that message into the area of the trials of life. We should, with faith and humility, be able to see them as God's way of moulding us in the image of Christ. He is the leader of our faith; his sufferings are the chart and means of our salvation. 'Suffering is part of your training'.

Cycle 2: 'David's heart misgave him for having taken a census of the people'. This curious episode of the census ends the second Book of Samuel. The census would, no doubt, in practice be the basis of the various forms of centralisation, taxes, conscription, etc – as Samuel had warned the people would follow from their having a king. For Samuel this kingship would blur the reality of God's primary kingship of the people. The balance of the two sovereignties would be redressed by God's punishment and David's repentance.

Prayer-lines: God, our Father help us to recognise and accept your active presence in the course and events of our life.

Week 4: Thursday

Cycle 1: Heb 12:18–24 Cycle 2: 1 Kgs 2:1-12. Gospel: Mk 6:7-13

Gospel: 'Then he summoned the twelve and began to send them out'. Our last Gospel passage ended with Jesus' amazement at his native Nazarenes' lack of faith in him. This immediate sequel smacks of a sense of urgency on Jesus' part. As if to say, 'Well, in that case there is no time to lose. Someone must spread the Good News, and the sooner the better.

Here, at least, Mark presents the apostles in a positive light. Entrusted with Jesus' own message and mission, they are given his authority over unclean spirits and sicknesses.

Dependent entirely on God to support them, they must travel as light as possible. Like Jesus, they too may not be everywhere welcomed. But by their deeds of power, they too will show 'the Kingdom of God is at hand'. In every generation, no committed Christian may feel him/herself dispensed from sharing in this mission.

Cycle 1: Our first reading is one of the most famous passages in 'Hebrews'. It is obviously a reminder to us of our privilege as Christians: 'where everyone is a first born son and a citizen of heaven'. It is a sort of summary of the Good News we get else-where in the New Testament, St John too speaks of our divine adoption. St Paul too reminds us we are citizens more of heaven than of earth. But we must remember its original context; written to converts finding it hard to live up to their Christian faith. As Jews they are told that Christianity is not a religion of fear, as it seemed at Mount Sinai. But there is still a judgement to be faced. We have, indeed, come to Mount Zion and the city of the living God – but he is also the Supreme Judge of us all.

Cycle 2: Our first reading brings David's colourful career to an end. The later editor of the Books of Kings takes care to stress the new king's obligation to the Law of Moses – something not men-tioned in God's promise of a perpetual dynasty to David – Nor did David in fact 'sleep with his ancestors', for they were buried in Bethlehem.

Prayer-lines: Lord Jesus, grant us a constant sense of our oblig-ation to live up to the missionary commitments of our baptismal adoption.

Week 4: Friday
Cycle 1: Heb 13:1–8 Cycle 2: Eccles 47:2-11. Gospel: Mk 6:14-29
Gospel: 'It is John ... he has risen from the dead'. Mark's main in-terest in giving us the gruesome story of St. John the Baptist's be-heading in prison by Herod is to give us a brief rehearsal of the death and resurrection of Jesus that lie ahead. For Mark, it was indeed fitting that Jesus' precursor should share beforehand his master's violent fate. It is a reminder for us too that as Christians we must be ready to share in some way in Jesus' sufferings, if we wish to share also in his glory. If we are, naturally, appalled at the ferocity displayed in the story by those concerned, we have only to think of parallel cruelties inflicted, and on an even vaster scale, in our own days. And to resolve to do whatever we can in our lives to deepen the respect for human life, which is the nec-essary ingredient of peace.

Cycle 1: 'Remember your leaders ... Imitate their faith'. If, for the most part, Hebrews has the character of a homily or sermon, it ends up like a New Testament letter, with a moral exhortation. As one gets older it is often easier to remember the distant past more vividly than the recent past; one's teachers at school, for instance. Hebrews here advises us to remember those to whom we owe the knowledge of the faith. But in the positive way of imitating their good example. Above all to remember Christ, the 'leader of our faith, who is the same in every generation. His Sermon on the Mount is never out of date. The gate by which we must enter the kingdom is always the narrow gate.

Cycle 2: Our first reading looks back over King David's life through the eyes of Ben Sira, some 800 years later, about 200BC. Things have vastly changed for the Chosen People since the story of David, with all its flesh and blood qualities, was written. David's military achievements are remembered as legends; his political ones have been blown away, his sins are passed over as forgiven by God. For Ben Sira his greatest legacies to the Chosen People are, first the hope of a Davidic Messiah; and second the liturgy of praise, which was the core of life in Jerusalem in Ben Sira's day. For those great legacies, we too must be equally grateful.

Prayer–lines: Thank you, Lord, for all the help you have given us to salvation. Make us zealous in bearing fruit for you in our lives.

Week 4: Saturday

Cycle 1: Heb 13:15–21. Cycle 2: 1 Kgs 3:4-13 Gospel: Mk 6:30-34

Gospel: 'They were like sheep without a shepherd'. Sheep and shepherd are biblical symbols to conjure with. They evoke at once the nomadic life of so many people in the Near and Middle East from earliest times even to the present day. They are evocative too of their desert background where pasture and especially water are such vital and rare commodities. Mark thus sets the scene for Jesus' next great miracle, the feeding of 5,000 in the desert. But even before that remarkable episode we see the image of the Good Shepherd emerging in Jesus. When the apostles return to tell him of their missionary work, his first thought is to give them the rest they need. 'Come away to some lonely place and rest for a while'.

Cycle 1: Our first reading brings our three weeks sampling of the letter to the Hebrews to a close. It too echoes the theme of Jesus as the shepherd. Not merely the shepherd of the embryo church in Galilee, while he is still on earth, but as risen from the dead (after giving his life for his sheep) to be 'the Great Shepherd' of all humanity. This in fact is the image St Matthew will give us of Christ's second coming – a judgement – where he will separate the sheep from the goats. And the hallmark of the sheep that are his is a life of grateful praise; a generous sharing of goods with others; and cheerful obedience to church leaders.

Cycle 2: Our first reading gives us the optimistic dawn of Solomon's reign. His first act is to show his fidelity to Yahweh by offering, lavish sacrifice (one thousand whole-burnt offerings) at Gibeon. Until the temple was built, sacrifice at sacred sites, often on hill-tops like Gibeon, was legitimate. But one of Solomon's glories will be the magnificent temple he plans to build at Jerusalem. The dialogue he has with Yahweh in his dream is a rich theology of the ideal of kingship under Yahweh, and the duties of a faithful King: 'discerning judgement' to rule wisely God's people.

Prayer-lines: God, our Father, in your mercy grant us the wisdom always to follow the guidance of your Son Jesus, our Great Shepherd.

Week 5: Monday

Cycle 1: Gen 1:1-19 Cycle 2: 1 Kings 8:1-13 Gospel: Mk 6:53-56

Gospel: 'All those who touched him were cured'. This brief vivid snapshot of Jesus' public life in Galilee: the crowds flocking round from all sides to touch even the hem of his cloak. We might well take it as a parable of our daily Mass. For through the Mass we are all able to touch Jesus through word and sacrament and be cured, redeemed. May we always come to our Mass with desire for that.

Cycle 1: And this week and next we touch him in a special way by our readings from the first eleven chapters of Genesis. What we call 'primeval history'. It is important for us, however, to listen to it with a 'biblical' curiosity. That is, asking not 'what actually happened?', but 'what does the narrative mean?'. Much confusion was caused in the last century when read as if it had been written a hundred years ago, that is, as a scientific account of the beginning of things. No, Genesis 1-11 is a teaching about God and humanity, and nature as known to faith. 'In the beginning God', sums up its first message: that is, not a matter of time but of priority of importance and reality. And the restrained, tabular account of the creation in 'six days' ends in 'Let us make man in our own image'. There you have the two truths that matter: God over all, and us in his image. We can never get to the bottom of that mystery: of God and his image.

Cycle 2: 'I have built you a dwelling, a place for you to live in forever'. The Bible is all about the presence of God, from Paradise in the book of Genesis to Paradise regained in the book of Revelation. Solomon thought that his temple in Jerusalem was the 'last word' on the presence of God. A later prophet would give a different perspective. 'With heaven my throne and earth my footstool, what house could you build me?' The Gospel would reveal that God is fully present in a person, Jesus. All the former 'presences' are summed up in him. The 'kingdom of God', which was Jesus' Good News was God ruling over evil in every form through Christ.

Prayer-lines: Lord, through the Spirit of your son Jesus, fill us at all times with a grateful awareness of your presence in us, in others, and in all you have made.

Week 5: Tuesday

Cycle 1: Gen 1:20–2:4 Cycle 2: 1 Kings 8: 22-30 Gospel: Mk 7:1-13
Gospel: 'Lip-service, while their hearts are far from me'. We remind ourselves that the Gospels were written for the present of each generation, not just to record the past. If so, we must look for ourselves not merely in the crowds flocking to be healed by touching Jesus: but also in the scribes and Pharisees whom he rebukes today. The Scribes and Pharisees were the religious Èlite of Jesus' time in Palestine. The danger for them was that of thinking they were the only ones who really practised the law, and were, therefore, holy in God's sight. But Jesus proclaimed, like the psalmist before him, that it was to the 'brokenhearted', the contrite, the repentant tax collector and sinner that God was close, by his mercy and love. God grant that we may always practise our faith as an affair of the heart, and not just of ritual observance.

Cycle 1: Our first reading today recounts the fifth and sixth days of 'the origins of heaven and earth when they were created'. For the ancient Near East, familiar to the biblical authors, the origins of a people's history were a privileged moment. But the bible account is free from any allusion to conflict between superhuman

powers at this moment of origins. God alone is in supreme control, and order serenely replaces chaos. God said: 'Let the waters
teem and so it was' by his word. And 'God saw that it was good'.
The climactic point is reached on the sixth day with the creation
of humanity. 'In the image of God he created him, male and female he created them'. 'God saw all he had made and indeed it
was very good'.

Cycle 2: 'From heaven, where your dwelling is, hear – and forgive. The temple has now been built by Solomon and God has
taken possession of it. We have here a shortened form of the full
prayer of dedication. Here Solomon recalls God's promises of a
dynasty to David. The later editors, however, aware of
Solomon's later lapses from fidelity to Yahweh, are careful to in-
sert references to the Covenant and the Law which it entailed.
'As you hear, Lord, forgive', our faithlessness.

Prayer-lines: God our Father, thank you for creating us in your
image. Give us also the grace to live in faithfulness to our dignity,
as your sons and daughters.

Week 5: Wednesday
Cycle 1: Gen 2:4-17 Cycle 2: 1 Kgs 10:1-10 Gospel: Mk 7:14-23
Gospel: 'It is what comes out of man which makes him unclean'.
Jesus continues in today's Gospel his plea for a religion of the
heart as against a mere observance of outward ritual. The 'heart'
is the biblical term for man's mind: his intentions that lead to his
conduct. No use, in God's eyes, in keeping human regulations
about food being clean or unclean if your thoughts are not rooted in love of God and your fellow-humans.

Cycle 1: Our reading from Genesis invites us back to the very
'origins' of religion, of the relationship between God and humanity. Today's passage narrates the preparation of the envi-
ronment for this crown of God's creation, the human community.
For it God plans a garden. There must be water, then, for plants
to grow in it . And what a picture of beauty then emerges. 'Every
kind of tree, enticing to look at, and good to eat'. Man's task is to

cultivate this lavish beauty. But why not 'eat of the tree of the knowledge of good and evil'? 'Good and evil' is a code phrase for 'everything'. And 'knowledge' in the Bible means experience. This knowledge, then, can belong only to God. The reality, the truth of things remains that man is a finite creature, fashioned from dust by God. But, as we shall see tomorrow, God has even more blessings in store for him than this.

Cycle 2: Solomon has now built his temple for God. And last week we heard how God had promised him not merely the wisdom Solomon asked for, but also 'riches and glory as no other king ever had'. Today we catch a glimpse of how God fulfilled that promise. Yes, indeed, Solomon had an answer for all of the Queen of Sheba's questions. She is left breathless, we are told (even for any more questions?) by the magnificence both of his palace and the temple. – But we note that the prosperity has obviously accumulated on Solomon himself, not on his people. The reference to his wives foreshadows the religious corruption they will lead to in Judah. And the only reference to 'dealing out law & justice' is on the lips of Sheba's queen. There are indeed, clouds gathering on the horizon of Solomon's glory.

Prayer-lines: Create for us a clean heart, Lord, and give us a spirit of grateful fidelity to you.

Week 5: Thursday
Cycle 1: Gen 2:18-25 Cycle 2: 1 Kgs 11: 4-13 Gospel: Mk 7:24-30
Gospel: 'For saying this, you may go home happy'. In several ways this is a strange story. It is one of the few cases where Jesus works a miracle at a distance. It is also the cure of a pagan. Again, the apparent coldness of Jesus: the children should be fed first. (The 'house-dogs' image is not so harsh as it sounds, though. They are pets in the family). What really matters is that Jesus does work the miracle, as if in spite of himself. It is almost a contest between Jesus and the mother – and the mother wins (as at Cana, if you like).

Anyway, we may take the story of what our relations with

Jesus should be: faith in his power to help us: humility in know-ing that we don't deserve his favour: and perseverance as a sign of both.

Cycle 1: 'It is not good that the man should be alone'. This second account of creation is not content with summarising human ori-gins in one phrase, 'male & female he created them'. It prefers the story form and with the happy ending, the first love affair. A miniature, we might say, of the love-story of creation. Yes, the Garden of Eden is magnificent; the animals are all at man's bid-ding; it was for him they were made. And yet the man's nature is not yet complete. He is destined to be a sociable being, with an-other, a partner to share the joys of living, and by his God-given power, the joy of continuing his posterity. The man awakes from his 'deep sleep' to the joyful vision of God's final gift. 'This at last is bone from my bone and flesh from my flesh'.

Cycle 2: Our first reading now pulls back the curtain fully on Solomon's fall from grace. His heart had turned from the Lord God of Israel. This part of Israel's history was written by the later prophetic circles that had seen the ruin which such idolatry had caused in Israel. And yet, such total failure on Solomon's part is less significant than God's fidelity to his promises. What the Bible calls his 'justice'. 'For the sake of my servant David, I will leave your son one tribe'. God's last word to us is not judge-ment, but fidelity and mercy.

Prayer-lines: God, our father, constantly increase our faith, that we may never fail to trust in your loving mercy.

Week 5: Friday
Cycle 1: Gen 3: 1-8 Cycle 2: 1 Kgs 11;12 Gospel: Mk 7:31-37
Gospel: 'He makes the deaf hear and the dumb speak'. Yesterday we marvelled at the Syro-Phoenician woman who 'forced' Jesus by her faith, humility & perseverance to grant her request. Today shows our relationship with Jesus at an even deeper level. The clue is in the word Jesus uses, Ephatha, 'be opened'. When we are baptised, Jesus says the same word to us through

the priest. 'Be opened'. For Baptism is the opening up of our whole being to the power and presence; to the love and life of God. We are used to the ideas of Baptism as re-birth. It is a basic image. Before our baptism we are locked in the womb of merely natural life – a life destined to death. By baptism we are born into the new world, where we can hear God calling us, telling us the Good News. 'You are my son/daughter. This day I have begotten you'. And, like a newborn child we give our first cry in reply: 'Abba. My beloved Father'.

Cycle 1: Our first reading dramatises the origins of sin. But not so much as history as in its timeless actuality; in all of us still, therefore. As God has not so much created the world in the past, but is still creating it, holding it in being, in its slow ascent to its fulfillment. So is Eve's sin and Adam's sin in all of us. Our sin, like theirs, begins in using our freedom to walk away from our conscience, instead of being guided by it. A great mystery, indeed, in them and in us. Two other things about sin in our passage. That it can be contagious, infectious. And that it estranges us from our trusting relationship with God. 'They hid from the Lord God among the trees of the garden'.

Cycle 2: The history of salvation, which the bible gives us is the history of sin and estrangement. We have seen it at work even in a specially favoured kingship like David's. It has gathered momentum in the idolatry which Solomon's reign unleashed on the Chosen People. Today it climaxes in our first reading, in the schism of ten northern tribes (henceforth called 'Israel') from the single tribe of David, Judah, with its capital at Jerusalem. It is a schism, which will never be repaired before both kingdoms, north and south, are carried into exile. A schism that mirrors the many divisions that still plague humanity today.

Prayer-lines: God, our Father, grant us the peace and unity of your Son's kingdom into which we are baptised.

Week 5: Saturday

Cycle 1: Gen 3:9-24 Cycle 2: 1 Kgs 12; 13 Gospel: Mk 8:1–10

Cycle 1: 'Some have come a great distance'. If we take this Gospel phrase symbolically, we might measure that 'great distance' to Jesus by looking back to the start of humanity's Great Trek in our first reading, the sequel of humanity's primordial sin. Yes, the first fruit of sin, as this passage suggests, is our sense of nakedness, our destitution in God's presence. And then follows our alienation from others. The man, in this story, puts the blame on his once beloved wife.

She, in turn, blames the tempter. And the Bad News of sin's sequels is to follow. The pains of maternity; for man the age-long struggle with a rebellious soil. Yet God remains faithful to his creative love for his image, 'male and female'. The woman's posterity will avenge her on the deceitful tempter. And the man can still give her a name of promise. Eve, 'Mother of the living'. God will not allow their sin to alter his plan to make them fruitful.

Gospel: Today's gospel can be read, by the biblical mind, as the fulfillment of the Old Testament prophecies of a banquet in messianic times. 'Where could anyone get bread to feed these people in a desert place?' This question of the disciples has already been notably answered by God, for the Israelites in the Sinai desert. There too, 'they ate as much as they wanted' of the manna. Whatever about the similarities between this account and the earlier feeding of five thousand, we cannot deny for St. Mark's generation the potential symbolism of the seven baskets. It could signify the mission to the Gentiles, to the seventy nations of the Old Testament world. At all events, Jesus sharing of food in the gospels is daily being fulfilled by our sharing with him in the Eucharist. The way is opened again for humanity to the tree of life by the sign Jesus gives that he is God-with-us.

Cycle 2: Our first reading shows us the political rupture between Israel and Judah being followed by religious schism. For the Jerusalem temple to remain the centre of worship for the northern tribes would inevitably sap their independence from Judah. New sanctuaries must be set up in the north at Bethel and Dan;

with them new images and a new priesthood. Solomon's infidelities will now reap their full harvest among the people.

Prayer-lines: God our Father, aware of our sinfulness, we take grateful heart from our faith that you sent your only Son, not to condemn the world but to save it.

Week 6: Monday

Cycle 1: Gen 4:1-15, 25 Cycle 2: Jas 1:1-11 Gospel: Mk 8:11-13

Gospel: 'No sign shall be given to this generation'. Jesus has already given ample signs of his power in his miracles of healing and multiplying food for the hungry. It was no part of his mission to proclaim himself as Messiah by spectacular prodigies (in the desert Satan had already tempted him to make that his strategy). The 'sigh that came straight from the heart' is a rare display of Jesus' emotion at the blindness of religious leaders. And the reference to 'this generation' is a loaded one, with echoes of the unbelieving generation of Israel in the desert, still failing to trust God after the wonders he had worked for them – Can we apply these allusions to our own generation, to ourselves? The Good News of Christ has been proclaimed to us even more than to the Pharisees. Have we thanked God enough for all God has done for each of us, from our own creation and Baptism up to now. And do we still fail to trust his loving protective presence with us now?

Cycle 1: Our last reading from Genesis showed us the first fruits of sin in the punishment of Adam and Eve. The later fruits we read of today are even worse. Eve's first son will murder the second son, and this is only the first link in a chain of violence that will follow down the ages. – But even in the darkness of this murder God's mercy shines out as the ultimate reality: God is protector of the innocent: he avenges their blood. Even with the guilty one he is still merciful, protecting him too from man's vengeance – Greatest comfort of all: to Adam and Eve he gives a new line of descendants in Seth – a line reaching down to Noah, through whom the world's first salvation is effected during the flood.

Cycle 2: Our first reading for the next two weeks will be from the New Testament letter of James, no doubt the greatly revered 'brother of the Lord'. He presided over the infant church at Jerusalem till he was martyred there in AD 60. He is writing for a group of Jewish Christians living outside Palestine. It reflects much Old Testament teaching, especially the wisdom books. But it is equally close to Jesus' moral teaching, especially in the Sermon on the Mount. Despite its conservative Jewish stress on observance of the Law, it is especially appreciated today as being the most socially conscious writing in the N.T. His references to the poor and the rich echo the beatitudes of Jesus, especially in the Gospel of Luke.

Prayer-lines: God our Father, make us always alert to the signs of your goodness and mercy in the story of our lives that we may never doubt your loving power to help us.

Week 6: Tuesday
Cycle 1: Gen 6; 7; Cycle 2: Jas 1:12-18; Gospel: Mk 8:14-21
Gospel: 'Are you still without perception?' Yesterday we noted the heartfelt sigh of Jesus at the Pharisees' lack of faith. Today it is his disciples whose blindness dismays him. 'Are your minds closed? Or do you remember?' They are indeed a backward class. Jesus' warning about the 'yeast' (meaning the corrupting influence) of Herod and the Pharisees was indeed called for when they cannot glimpse the presence of God's spirit at work in Jesus in the miracles he has wrought before them. As the sequel will show, they are not to understand Jesus' message till they are shocked into the truth by his passion and death, and finally his rising from the dead. – Are we too slow to remember and accept into our lives that Good News of Christ?

Cycle 1: In our first reading today the themes of humanity's sins and God's mercy come to a climax in the story of the flood. 'I regret having made them, my own creation'. But 'Noah had found favour with God'. We are not told how Noah had done so, but he certainly proved his justice by implicitly obeying without question God's mysterious command. The details of this story of salvation by an ark from a world-enveloping flood are inspired by ancient Near Eastern mythology. In the New Testament it will serve as a symbol of our salvation by the water of Baptism.

Cycle 2: St James's teaching in our first reading is clear and practical. Some would say it bears the mark of early baptismal instruction, rather than allude to 'trials' caused by persecution. The fallacy of attributing temptation to God's intervention has already been unmasked by Old Testament writers. No, it is only good which God provides for us, even when it may seem contrary to our plans or desires. A gospel note is struck by the thought that we are made God's children by the gospel, 'the message of the truth'. The Jewish chord is struck by the reference to being 'first-fruits of creation'. In the Law of Moses these are dedicated to God.

Prayer-lines: God, our Father, increase our faith in the presence of your Spirit at work in our midst, moulding us into the image of your beloved Son.

Week 6: Wednesday
Cycle 1: Gen 8:6-22 Cycle 2: Jas 1:19-27 Gospel: Mk 8:22-26
Gospel: 'I can see people like trees walking about'. We note that, for once, Jesus had to lay hands on someone twice in order to heal him. For Mark this particular healing is a symbol. In our last gospel passage the slowness of the apostles to understand Jesus and his mission was heavily emphasised. 'Are your minds closed?', he asks in frustration. This healing episode serves as a transition from Jesus' ministry in Galilee to his journey south to Jerusalem. It is on that (for Mark) final journey that Jesus will have to try to heal his disciples' blindness to the need for his death and resurrection. We too, may have to take a long while in our lives to learn the necessity for a Christian to share Jesus' death if we are also to share his resurrection.

Cycle 1: Our first reading describes the aftermath of the great flood. The waters eventually recede. Noah leaves the ark, and offers sacrifice to God. The altar will henceforth be the focal point of humanity's relations with God. On his part God revokes his former judgement. Though God recognises the evil intent in man's heart as continuing, he nevertheless decrees a new start, a new creation.

Cycle 2: 'The wrong idea of religion ...'. James in our first reading is dealing with a constant problem that confronted Jesus in his moral teaching. And James is a perceptive guide. When angry, we pass swift judgement on others. But it may not correspond to God's judgement. Our rule of conduct must be the gospel: 'the word, which has been planted in you and can save your souls.' It is not enough to admire that ideal in a mirror, and then ignore it in our actions, especially in our speech. What God wants of us is care for the helpless, and freedom from worldly desires.

Prayer-lines: God our Father, may we carry in our hearts the death of Jesus, so that his life too may be visible in our lives.

Week 6: Thursday
Cycle 1: Gen 9:1-13; Cycle 2: Jas 2:1-9; Gospel: Mk 8:27-33
Gospel: 'But you, who do you say I am?' This was clearly a turning point in Jesus' life. It was of interest to him what 'men' thought of him, and there had been negative as well as positive opinions on that. But 'the big issue', so to speak, for Jesus was what view his own chosen, intimate disciples had of him. Recent episodes we have read in Mark's Gospel didn't suggest they would get very high marks for their answer to that. (You remember his scathing quizzing of them in the boat). Peter indeed does give the right answer. 'You are the Christ, the Messiah'. Jesus does not deny it, but he forbids his disciples to advertise the fact. He can now pass on to revealing that his programme as Messiah will lead through suffering, death and resurrection. When Peter impetuously rejects this harrowing programme, he incurs Jesus blistering rebuke for challenging God's designs. It is a warning for us all, when we shrink from the cost of discipleship.

Cycle 1: The sequel of the Flood story in our first reading is the fulfillment of the Covenant promised already to Noah. The original blessing of stewardship over the earth given to Adam is now repeated for Noah. In addition the flesh of animals is allowed for food. But man, made as he is in God's image, must not be killed. Humanity is once more to be multiplied. The rainbow in the sky will be man's reminder of God's promise never again to destroy the earth by flood.

Cycle 2: James's manner in our first reading is perhaps deceptively gentle. First of all 'my brothers'. Then 'my dear brothers'. But he has a stern lesson for his readers. In a word, he warns bluntly against the hypocrisy of (Christians) being disciples of 'our glorified Lord' (who as St Paul says, 'has no favourites') and yet making class distinctions in practice between their fellow-Christians. 'Come this way to the best seats': or ' You can sit on the floor'. The gospel, of course, preaches the beatitude of the poor. But even the Old Testament binds us to 'love your neighbour as yourself'. Here again is a practical example – in view of Jesus' parable of the judgement day – to ask ourselves in relation to others, the poor especially, how do we answer Jesus' basic question to all of us. 'But who do you say I am?'.

Prayer-lines: Lord Jesus, help us by your Holy Spirit, to be able to say sincerely, you are our Messiah, our Saviour, as we meet you in every level of your creation.

Week 6: Friday
Cycle 1: Gen 11:1-9; Cycle 2: Jas 2:14-24, 26; Gospel: Mk 8:34-9:1
Gospel: 'Must take up his cross and follow me'. As Peter has rejected the idea of a suffering Messiah, Jesus must drive the point home that suffering will be the lot of his followers too. What are we to make of the word 'cross' on Jesus' lips? Execution by crucifixion was far from uncommon in Roman Palestine. The cross then was no mere metaphor as it has since become. 'Taking up the cross' referred to the moment when sentence of death had been pronounced. The condemned man put his shoulder under the patibulum or crossbar and set out for the place of execution

before a usually jeering and unsympathetic, even hostile perhaps, crowd. It is certainly not an aspect of Christianity that appeals to us. And yet it is the programme that Jesus holds out to us. St Paul could escape actual crucifixion by being a Roman citizen: death for him would be by the sword. But it was the image of Christ under and hanging on the Cross that was his continual inspiration. Is it ours?

Cycle 1: Peter was rebuked by Jesus for thinking 'not God's way but man's'. Our first reading gives us another example, on a world scale, of thinking man's way instead of God's. 'Let us build a tower with its top reaching heaven'. The nations, now Noah's descendants, are speaking. Instead of their allotted task (after the flood) of filling the earth to subdue it, they concert to grasp a greatness which is not theirs. It is the primeval sin of pride. Can we recognise it in our (technological) world today?

Cycle 2: 'Faith is dead if it is separated from deeds'. At first sight this trenchant statement could seem an attack on St Paul's insistence (in Galatians and Romans) on reliance on faith in Christ for salvation. 'A person is justified by faith apart from the works of the Law'. – But Paul is speaking on quite a different matter than James. Paul was teaching Gentile converts that it was not the ritual observances of the Mosaic Law (especially circumcision) that would save them. The faith in Christ he wanted also involved a commitment in conduct. James, on the other hand, is aiming at people who claimed to believe in Christ, but belied that belief by failing in practice to show charity. Certainly, in our day too, Christians unconcerned by the need for social justice are also a fair target for his attack.

Prayer-lines: Lord Jesus, may our following of you show itself in our lives, and our concern for the needs of others.

Week 6: Saturday

Cycle 1: Heb 11:1-7; Cycle 2: Jas 3:1-10; Gospel: Mk 9:2-13

Cycle 1: 'It was for faith our ancestors were commended'. All this week our first reading has dealt with the evil fruits of humanity's first sin, culminating in the story of the Tower of Babel. But today's extract from the Letter of the Hebrews casts a look back at the positive glimpses of goodness on that dark horizon. Three figures, Abel, Enoch and Noah are singled out as just: as 'walking with God'. They are commended for their faith in an unbelieving world. They believed in realities as yet unseen: the existence of a God who creates, and rewards the just. A saviour-God.

Gospel: Our gospel today leaps over the gulf between the Old and New Testaments to give us a glimpse of Christian faith. God now not only inspires people inwardly with faith, but speaks audibly from heaven to enjoin it. And the object of faith is no longer God's existence, but his presence in Jesus. 'This is my son, the Beloved. Listen to him'. There is the essential task of the Christian: to believe that Jesus is the Son of God, and to listen to his teaching by obeying it. In the context of the Transfiguration that might have seemed an easy task for the three apostles. Yet trials for their faith lay not far ahead. We know how these trials shattered their faith. Their puzzlement at the phrase 'rising from the dead' foreshadows this. It is no puzzle for us now, but our faith too will be tried in one way or another. May the vision of the Transfiguration stay with us to strengthen us.

Cycle 2: 'The tongue is a whole wicked world in itself'. Sins of speech may seem a far cry from questions of faith. Yet James, in our first reading, is surely right in stressing their destructive power, especially destructive in the vital area of loving one another. And yet even James admits the tongue can have a positive role too: 'we use it to bless the Lord'. The Son of God to whom the gospel today bids us listen comes to us as God's Word. He is a saving word, and if saving others is the motive of our speech, we need not fear to use our tongues.

Prayer-lines: Lord Jesus, help us to listen faithfully to your word, and by our obedience to it may we bring your life and joy more abundantly to others.

Week 7: Monday
Cycle 1: Ecc 1:1-10; Cycle 2: Jas 3:13-18; Gospel: Mk 9:14-29

Cycle 1: The rich variety of Bible readings at Mass brings home to us that the Bible is not just a book, but a library – of great variety. Today we open Ecclesiasticus, one of the last and longest of the wisdom books. Unlike the historical books these wisdom books stem not so much from Israel's historical experience of God as from her contact with older people and cultures. These led them into the secrets and wonders of nature. But for Israel all these came to point to her God as the creator of nature. Also to another form of his presence with humanity. A remote but real preparation, then, for his coming to share our human nature in Jesus.

Cycle 2: 'The wisdom from above shows itself by doing good'. Wisdom in Egypt, to which Israel's wisdom books are much indebted, professed to show men how to get on well in life, in social relations, etc. In Israel the principles of this 'worldly wisdom' inevitably came to reflect its belief in a God concerned with right and wrong, a moral God. New Testament writers are, of course, heirs to this tradition. But they also reflect the teachings of Jesus and Paul. James's concern today for peace and harmony in society overlaps with Paul's efforts to unite rival Christian factions in Corinth. James's disapproval of jealousy and ambition echoes the sharp remonstrances of Jesus to the Twelve. For Jesus, we recall, was himself, in person, 'the Peace that comes from above'.

Gospel: 'Help the little faith I have'. The disciples, Mark has already told us, have already been sent on a mission to the villages and 'cast out many devils and cured sick people'. Yet here they are helpless. The centre of the stage is held by Jesus and the father of the epileptic boy. After the failure of the disciples we can hardly blame the father for his tell-tale, 'If – you can do anything' to Jesus. We can often, certainly be grateful to him for teaching us his second prayer. 'I do have faith. Help the little faith I have'. And Jesus avails of that 'mustard seed' of the father's faith to heal the epilepsy. We note too his characteristic gesture of helping the boy to his feet. Back in the house, when Jesus explains to the Twelve that prayer was the missing element in their fruitless efforts to heal, was he ironically holding up the boy's father as a role-model for them?

Prayer-lines: Lord Jesus, eternal wisdom of the Father, grant us to share in that wisdom by living according to your will.

Week 7: Tuesday
Cycle 1: Ecc 2:1-11 Cycle 2: Jas 4:1-10 Gospel: Mk 9:30-37

Gospel: 'Last of all and servant of all'. Jesus gives us the syllabus for Christian life. But he knows that this basic principle makes little impact on the ambitious dreams of the Twelve. Despite his predictions of his death, they can think of him only as the Messiah, the long-awaited King of Israel. And they themselves could only be his highly placed lieutenants. Jesus decides to give them a visual aid to see what he means: a little child. No ambition there: no pretence of being equal to all the grown men around him. 'That's me', Jesus says 'if you want to welcome me as your Master, this is the image you must have of me – and not only of me, but of the One who sent me, my Father'. Humility, like love, is the definition of God.

Cycle 1: The school of wisdom is a hard one for it means God's service. How serious your search for wisdom is will be tried in many ways. Be ready to be patient, even in humiliation. But trust always in the Lord, and hold on to him. For he is supremely trustworthy, and has never failed to reward those faithful to him. – This principle of earthly reward by God did not go unchallenged in the Old Testament, especially by Job. It would not be vindicated until it was personified in Jesus.

Cycle 2: 'When you do pray, you have not prayed properly.' James is the sort of preacher that won't allow his congregation fall asleep while he is talking. He doesn't put a tooth in what he feels is our defective Christian living. We're prepared to kill, he says, to get our own way. Strong language this, but do the law court reports in the newspapers today give him the lie? I doubt it. Again, if we pray, he says it's for our selfish interests. We are following the world's values. The media makes no secret of these. But James says the remedy is clear too. Come close to God. 'Humble yourselves before Him, and he will lift you up'.

Prayer-lines: God our Father, teach us wisdom by imitating the humility of your incarnate Son.

Week 7: Wednesday

Cycle 1: Ecc 4:11-19; Cycle 2: Jas 4:13-17; Gospel: Mk 9:38-40

Cycle 1: 'Those who serve her, minister to the holy One'. Wisdom in our first reading today is personified as a mother eager to prepare her children for 'the good life'.

'Whoever loves her, loves life'. It is, therefore, an obvious literary personification. Such a literary personification is found elsewhere in the Bible, but nowhere with the same intensity as in these wisdom books. Yesterday Ecclesiasticus identified wisdom with God. He is, therefore, the object of your love and service of wisdom. And at once we recall so much of what Jesus tells us of himself and the Father. And the likeness to Jesus continues today in the account of the trials to which wisdom will subject her sons, only to lead them to security in the end.

Cycle 2: 'You never know what will happen tomorrow'. St James today seems to be preaching at business folk – 'trading and making some money' is their programme. But what he says about 'what will happen tomorrow' can apply to us all. Especially perhaps when we are in good health, and can feel unaffected by the daily news in the media of fatal accidents on the roads or elsewhere. We feel we can plan recklessly for the future. The wise prayer that St James suggests. 'If it is the Lord's will' is apparently one borrowed from pagan and not the Old Testament tradition. But it has been adopted freely in the past in Christian cultures. It is not one, however, to be uttered mechanically. It should be the genuine expression of our humble awareness of our total dependence on God.

Gospel: 'Anyone who is not against us is for us'. The disciples are often taken aback by Jesus' attitudes. Yesterday we saw him rebuke their ambitions by using a child as a role model of humility. Today we feel, it was a bombshell for John to be told. 'You must not stop him', this stranger casting out devils in Jesus' name. And no doubt John was typical of the rest of the Twelve. Their call by Jesus has, they feel, given them rights over him: to protect him (as Peter wanted), to possess him and his powers, exclusively in this case. Jesus reveals himself as devoid of all self-interest. It costs him nothing to share his power over evil with all who want to exorcise evil. It could be a basic text for the ecumenical movement.

Prayer-lines: Lord Jesus, give us the grace to see your Spirit at work in others, especially in those around us.

Week 7: Thursday
Cycle 1: Ecc 5:1-8; Cycle 2: Jas 5:1-6; Gospel: Mk 9:41-50
Gospel: 'Just because you belong to Christ'. Today's miscellaneous teachings illustrate different aspects of Christian living. It is, for example, a comfort to know that the smallest act of kindness we do to anyone, Christian or not, is noted by God in our favour for the day of judgement.

But the major lesson today is about scandal, and in Jesus' strongest tones. No evil, he is saying, is to be avoided so much as coming between another person and Christ. (And we can do this by omission as much as by deed). And no price is too high to pay to avoid losing eternal union with God. In other words, Jesus is urging us to take our Christian life seriously, with its responsibilities towards others and ourselves. 'Have salt in yourselves and be at peace with one another'. We are, after all, called to be the salt of the earth. This should be a fruit of our careful listening to God's word at Mass.

Cycle 1: 'No use to you on the day of disaster'. We miss the pictorial style of Jesus teaching when we turn to the Old Testament wisdom books. But their teaching too comes from God, and is equally for our guidance in Christian living. And who can say that today's recommendations from Ecclesiasticus are not relevant in this secularised consumerist age? Giving our hearts to money!

Uncontrolled pursuits of our appetites of every kind – today so reinforced by the potency of the mass media. Memory flashes of Christian teaching on God's mercy can breed dullness to Jesus' equally forceful teaching to be vigilant, for we know not the day nor the hour of his coming and judgement, 'the day of disaster'.

Cycle 2: 'The answer for the rich', says St James, is 'start crying'. Here he is echoing so many of the Old Testament prophets, not to speak of Jesus'. 'Woe to you who are rich' in St Luke's Gospel. If what James writes is unlikely to catch the eye of the rich themselves, it serves at least as a warning to the Christians who will read him. Both Old and New Testament have inveighed against the injustice of employers towards labourers. But Vatican II has elaborated on the need for maintaining justice on a world scale. 'The cries of the reapers', as James puts it, 'reach the ears of the Lord of hosts'. If peace is as difficult as ever to maintain in our world, how frequently is it not due to the absence of justice on the global scale.

Prayer-lines: Lord Jesus, grant us the grace to show 'we belong to you' by our constant pursuit of justice and peace.

Week 7: Friday
Cycle 1: Ecc 6:5-17; Cycle 2: Jas 5:9-12 ;Gospel: Mk 10:1-12
Gospel: 'What God has united, man must not divide'. Few Gospel topics are more topical than today's. Divorce is still practised among the Jews, despite their high standards of family life. Still more frequent among us Gentiles, but this is not the place to enter into the modern debate. It is worth noting, though, when Jesus challenges Jewish religious traditions – as he does in the Sermon on the Mount. His condemnation today of divorce is part of his regular and remarkable stand for the dignity of woman. This stance was part of his Good News. As one of the Eucharistic Prayers puts it. 'To the poor he preached the good news of salvation, to prisoners freedom, to those in sorrow joy'. Even in Judaism that Good news was needed. Even in Christianity, down the centuries, it is still needed. It is part of the

mission of salvation that clergy especially can be slow to undertake. Like the Twelve, and others in the New Testament, one gets the impression that they are afraid of women. Jesus in the gospels is strikingly the one who is never afraid or embarrassed in his dealings with women. Why so? Because, as his name 'Jesus' implies, he came to save, and to serve – 'and to give his life as a ransom for many'.

Cycle 1: 'Whoever fears the Lord makes true friends'. Nowhere do the wisdom books speak more clearly of human experience than on human relationships. And no other book in the Bible treats of friendship as fully as does Ecclesiasticus. Today it covers succinctly so many of its aspects. The importance of our words. Discretion in seeking advice. Readiness for disappointment. – Our greatest guarantee in this context, we are told, is having a true friendship with Christ – 'from whom all good things come'.

Cycle 2: 'So as not to be brought to judgement'. In the Old Testament wisdom tradition, James stresses the need for patience in everyday social living, where we so easily pass judgement on one another. We are reminded at once of Jesus' words in the Sermon on the Mount: Judge not and you shall not be judged... Unexpectedly James calls on the Old Testament prophets as models of patience under trials. The story of Job was well known even outside the Bible. Again James echoes the Sermon on the Mount in advocating moderation in speech: simplicity and restraint is the ideal.

Prayer-lines: We pray for all married people, that they grow in conviction of their vocation and power to save and sanctify each other.

Week 7: Saturday
Cycle 1: Ecc 17:1-15; Cycle 2: Jas 5:13-20; Gospel: Mk 10:13-16
Gospel: 'Welcome the kingdom of God like a little child'. We are struck by the two conflicting emotions which Jesus shows in today's Gospel: indignation with the disciples; affection for the children. But his words: 'I tell you solemnly', show there is something more important than emotion in question. It is a matter of qualifying for the kingdom, for salvation – the whole purpose of Jesus' saving life. But how could children be a model for this saving quality? We remember that Jesus is continually challenging the opposite quality in the Pharisees – their spiritual arrogance. They would look down (as did the disciples here) on children as unimportant because they would be unable to know and follow the Law: as they looked down on the tax collectors. If Jesus can propose children, as symbolic models, for his religious stance, it is because they were unimportant – in their own eyes. The whole spirit of Christianity is one of littleness before God. The spirit of the Magnificat. The spirit of Jesus' emptying himself of his divinity to be obedient, even unto death.

Cycle 1: From shedding its light on the trials of life wisdom now lifts our gaze to the marvels of God's bounteous dealings with human kind. God has created us in the first place, though only for a limited span of days. But in that limited realm humans are made in God's image, with authority over all animal creation. 'What a piece of work is man', Shakespeare writes. And Ecclesiasticus lists the riches we tend to take for granted: our senses, our minds, our conscience. All these, he says, should be a motive for our grateful praise to God. His crowning gift was the Covenant of Sinai and the Law of Moses, an unfailing guide of conduct.

Cycle 2: From treating of various moral evils in society, and virtues to be practised, James now concludes his letter with a plea for prayer in all life's vicissitudes. Not merely when we are in trouble but also when we are happy. The latter duty, we can so easily forget in a pleasure seeking age. But the Bible gives ample evidence of the power of prayer to obtain major favours. The official prayer and anointing by the elders is regarded as the

Scriptural witness to the sacrament of Extreme Unction. And, finally, a Christian should always keep the spiritual welfare of others at heart, and do whatever is possible to prevent their straying from the path of truth.

Prayer-lines: Lord Jesus, grant us your Spirit of filial gratitude to our Father in heaven for all his goodness to us.

Week 8: Monday

Cycle 1: Ecc 17: 24 -29; Cycle 2: 1 Pet 1:3-9; Gospel: Mk 10: 17-27

Cycle 1: We can see an obvious link between our first reading and the Gospel today. In a way, Ecclesiasticus represents a highpoint of Old Testament wisdom. It is the first wisdom book explicitly to identify Wisdom with the Law, and our rich man in Mark is an embodiment of fidelity to that Law in practice. Repentance, in the sense Ecclesiasticus gives it, of 'return to the Lord and leave sin behind', is a constant refrain of the prophets. It is also the answer St Peter gives on the day of Pentecost when his listeners ask him, 'what must we do?'

'Repent' is his answer. And we maintain this tradition daily by starting Mass by a penitential Act. Compunction must be a basic attitude for a Christian. For Ecclesiasticus this is not a matter of morbid guilt-feelings. Its spirit is a spirit of constant praise of the Lord's mercy 'on all those who turn to him'.

Gospel: All this, we can see our rich man in the gospel has lived up to. True, Jesus lists only the second half of the Decalogue, which refers to relationships with our neighbour; but these presuppose loving God above all as well. And this is why 'Jesus looked steadily at him and loved him'. Yet, to be a follower of Christ demands something more than this Old Testament programme of virtue. To give away all that one has to the poor would be to deprive oneself henceforth even of the merit, and joy, of giving alms. Jesus admits that. Yes, it is asking the humanly impossible. But no more than that. In following Christ, in sharing his Spirit, then God's power comes on the scene -to make it possible.

Cycle 2: 'A new faith and a sure hope'. St Peter's upbeat opening to his exposition of the Christian reality will rise in a few verses to a crescendo. 'You are already filled with a joy so glorious that it cannot be described'. And the cause of this joy is the person of Christ and our love for him. The fact of our not having seen him (our lack of that distinctive qualification of an apostle) is compensated for by our faith, our believing. Believing what? 'The salvation of our souls'. And that salvation is guaranteed first of all by God's raising Jesus from the dead. Secondly, by the new birth which his resurrection gives us as God's children. And, finally, the sure hope of our attaining heaven. Is this a fairy tale theology? No, it is a faith, which will be brought down to earth by trials -by which alone it can be tested and made strong.

Prayer-lines: God our father, strengthen our faith in your power to enable us to follow the teaching and example of your Son, Jesus Christ. Amen.

Week 8: Tuesday
Cycle 1: Ecc 35:1-12; Cycle 2: 1 Pet 1:10-16; Gospel: Mk 10:28-31
Cycle 1: 'The Lord is a good rewarder'. For Ecclesiasticus, as we saw, the height of wisdom was keeping the Law. But the Law also obliges us to God's worship, and worship is also a priority in Jewish life and virtue. But sinless living is a necessary adjunct to Temple worship, to a Temple sacrifice for sin.

Temple worship has as well, its own claims to make. God is pleased with our generosity to the Temple: to cheerful surrender of our first fruits. For God has been generous to you, and will also reward your generosity in his worship. God, however, cannot be bribed as a judge to overlook your sins. For his justice is even-handed and he makes no account of human rank.

Gospel: 'What about us?' Peter asked 'we have left everything and followed you?' We can imagine the relief of the other eleven at Peter's voicing their thoughts. Jesus had just written off riches for those who would enter the kingdom. Clearly the apostles hadn't. Peter's question, would seem to imply, what is the value of the kingdom, then, if it means giving up all, as we have done? Jesus is not embarrassed by the question. His reply is relaxed. Elsewhere he has invited the apostles to share his sufferings, and he mentions them here too. But that's only one side of the story. We needn't be distracted by the list of compensations he gives: houses, brothers, sisters, etc. The basic meaning is certain. Those who throw in their lot with me won't repent it. They will find unsuspected joys and peace of heart – and, after death, everlasting happiness.

Cycle 2: 'Free your mind, then, of encumbrances'. Yesterday, St Peter identified for us the ground of our Christian joy: the sure hope of salvation through Jesus Christ. Today he assures us that his hope is a high privilege that had not been revealed to the Old Testament prophets – greatly though they longed to discern it – or even to the angels. He urges us then to cultivate this hope by eliminating anything in our lives, which would obscure it. Our aim in life should be holiness, for God our Father is holy. He has made us his children by the power of the resurrection, and the power to attain that holiness by the gift of his Spirit, Spirit of adoption.

Prayer-lines: God our Father, increase our faith in our Christian privileges, and our trust in your rewards.

Week 8: Wednesday

Cycle 1: Ecc 36:1, 4-5, 10-17; Cycle 2: 1 Pet 1:18-25; Gospel: Mk 10:32-45

Gospel: 'To give his life as a ransom for many'. Mark's Gospel is well-known for its portrayal of the Twelve as very far from understanding the true nature of Jesus' mission. Today's Gospel is a very clear sample of this. James and John, with Peter, had formed a trio to whom Jesus gave special prominence on several occasions. May one speculate that they could have felt their family ambitions threatened by Peter's apparent priority. St Matthew seems to cloak their indiscretion by bringing in their mother to make their request. What is more important for us is to note the gentleness with which Jesus answers them. He doesn't upbraid them for thinking in terms of presiding in glory when he has already foretold the disaster ahead for himself. When they airily say they are prepared to share his 'cup' (that is, of suffering) he predicts that in fact they will. But, as always, he defers to his Father's will for the question of rewards. And from there, as he sees the rest of the Twelve are just as uncomprehending of his mission, he gives the enduring Christian blueprint of humility and service for all leaders in his 'kingdom'.

Cycle 1: 'Send new portents, do fresh wonders'. Ecclesiasticus is no doubt thinking in terms of a new Exodus for his people as a new revelation to the nations of Yahweh's supreme power and glory. He was, it seems, waiting in a time of religious unease at the threat posed by the prevailing Greek culture of the Near East to Jewish religious values. But we can make this prayer our own in the Spirit in which Pope John 23rd called for a new Pentecost at Vatican II. In the 40 years since then there has been great secular development, opening the gates to gross global injustice and materialism, which threaten our Christian tradition. We may well make this prayer for a new and sanitising intervention by God to show 'there is no God but you, Lord'.

Cycle 2: St Peter continues today to exhort us to keep in mind our dignity as Christians. If we have been rescued from the fruitless existence of our pagan forebears, it was at a great price, the blood of Christ. 'A lamb without blemish', he calls him -Why? Because Jesus is the fulfillment of the lamb whose blood ensured the safety of Israel in Egypt, the night they escaped from their slavery there. No mere human blood this, but the blood of the eternal Son of God. By his paschal mystery, his death and resurrection, the seed of his immortal life has been planted in us. This seed is God's immortal Word, the Good News of our salvation.

Prayer-lines: God our Father, renew your miracles of power and mercy in us, in our church and in the world, that the 'world may believe that Jesus is your Son whom you sent to redeem us'.

Week 8: Thursday

Cycle 1: Ecc 42:15 -25; Cycle 2: 1 Pet 2:2-5, 9-12; Gospel: Mk 10:46-52
Cycle 1: 'Who could ever be sated gazing at his glory?' If Israel could not compete with Greece in philosophy, or with Rome in engineering or military arts, it could yet, through its special revelation from God, soar above both of them in the realm of prayer. As in the books of Job, of Proverbs and Psalms, Ecclesiasticus is here carried away, we might almost say in ecstasy, at his wonderment before God our creator, revealed in the beauty and harmony of the world about him. Not even the angels ('his holy ones') he writes, can take it all in. No secret of the mighty ocean or of human thought ('the deep and the heart') are hidden from him. The variety of God's creation is endless. 'All things go in pairs, by opposites: day and night, darkness and light'. – In this era of massive ecological destruction are we in danger of marring irreparably this divine harmony of our planet?

Gospel: 'He followed him along the road'. The road is, of course, to Jerusalem, the theatre of Jesus' passion: for Jericho is only 15 miles away. The healing of the blind Bartimaeus is a significant one. Mark rarely gives the name of a person healed. But Bartimaeus is a symbol as well as a person. Peter apart, he is the first to address Jesus as Messiah. 'Son of David', At Jesus' summons he responds at once and throws off his cloak. Clothes seem significant for Mark, and this may symbolise his leaving his former life behind. His 'Let me see again' expresses the faith that permits his cure. His prompt following of Jesus 'along the road' (Mark uses the same verb as for the Twelve) is in contrast to their reluctance to share his 'service' unto death. Bartimaeus is certainly a role-model for all of us in our relationship to Christ.

Cycle 2: 'Be living stones making a spiritual house'. The richness of the mystery of Christian life demands mixed metaphors. Peter sees the newly-baptised converts firstly as new-born babies. In their new life they can savour only the purest of food: the milk of the everlasting Word which will nourish them, for their ultimate maturity in salvation. But the psalmists' image of Christ as the living stone chosen by God as the keystone suggests another image. Our union with him by baptism will build up a spiritual temple for God. Therein we can be a new Chosen People, a spiritual priesthood to perform a spiritual liturgy of praise to God for his mercy. And pagans seeing the splendour of this faultless life will be led to praise the true God.

Prayer-lines: God our Father, open our hearts to appreciate the dignity you have given us in baptism, and give you praise by living as the spiritual crown of your creation.

Week 8: Friday
Cycle 1: Ecc 44:1, 9-13; Cycle 2: 1 Pet 4:7-13; Gospel: Mk 11:11-26
Cycle 1: 'Their glory will not fade'. Ecclesiasticus now turns from his praise of God in creation and the marvels of nature to extol the fruits of wisdom in the major figures of Israel's history. Later, in the New Testament the letter to the Hebrews will list a number of these figures as examples of faith and trust in God. In the Christian era Vatican II justifies its celebration of Christian saints as showing in their lives the victory of Christ in his paschal mystery. The aim of Ecclesiasticus, however, some 200 years before Christ, is to encourage the Jews of his day not to compromise with the all -pervasive Greek culture around them; to take pride in their own Jewish heroes, and to remain faithful to Israel's traditions.

Cycle 2: 'Keep a calm and sober mind'. We have no reason to suppose that first Peter was written in time of official persecution. But the author seeks gently to prepare his hearers for its possibility in the future. It is a necessary part of the programme for those who follow Christ. But, as St. Paul would remind the Corinthians, 'everything will soon come to an end'. We must, therefore, be ready for God's judgement in calmness and trust. Charity is of course, the main virtue to be upheld. It makes up for many defects in those who show it. It is practised especially in hospitality, and the service of others according to one's talents. In all we do the goal is to give glory to God through Jesus Christ.

Gospel: 'Get up and throw yourself into the sea'. Can Jesus' words be taken literally here about mountains? The answer of course is 'yes'. We have only got to read parts of Isaiah or Job, or the Psalms about mountains in relation to the power of God: they 'melt like wax before the Lord of all the earth' -to see how tame Jesus' invitation is. Only one mountain? It would hardly make a splash. – Still, the mountain is not the message. As elsewhere in Jesus' teaching the message is that with God nothing is impossible. For us what counts in practice is the metaphorical mountains in my life, real or imaginary, personal or communitarian. As long as they block my view of God or my way to him, we can't pray enough to God to remove them. And if the prayer is 'with no hesitation', even that mountain of my feeble faith God can also remove.

Prayer-lines: Grant, Lord, that we may always keep the truths of faith before our minds so that we still trust you in all the trials of life.

Week 8: Saturday
Cycle 1: Ecc; 51:12 -20; Cycle 2: Jude 17:20-25; Gospel: Mk 11:27-33
Cycle 1: Today we came to the end of our readings from Ecclesiasticus with an autobiographical glimpse of the author. The Greek foreword (which we didn't read) tells us that the original Hebrew was by the translator's grandfather, named 'Jesus'. A few lines on from our present passage it tells us that this Jesus conducted a 'wisdom school' in Jerusalem some 200 years before New Testament times. Here he taught young men how to join ancient near Eastern wisdom traditions with their Jewish religious traditions. He had been a pioneer in this project. Today's extract reveals how he himself had gained wisdom; by praying to acquire it and by scrupulously observing the Law. This Jesus Ben Sira, to give him his full name, if limited by the culture of his time, was a not unworthy foreshadowing of the real teacher of wisdom, Jesus of Nazareth, two hundred years later.

Cycle 2: 'Use your holy faith as your foundation'. Scholars would regard the letter of Jude as from an anonymous Christian towards the end of the first century. It was quite common then to use the name of a revered figure of the past to lend weight to one's teaching. At all events he speaks of the apostles as figures of a past generation. He gives us no clues about the people from whom he is advocating 'apartheid'. But his positive advice is unimpeachable, with so many wild ideas circulating in that period of a religious world in transition. (Is our own any better?). We all need to deepen our faith by prayer 'in the holy Spirit':- Our model here is the prayer of the first Christians united in mutual love and 'waiting for the mercy of our Lord' when he comes again.

Gospel: 'Nor will I tell you my authority'. Mark places this challenge to Jesus in his last week in Jerusalem. We can guess the alarm of the religious authorities there. On the first day of the week (our 'Palm Sunday') Jesus has entered the city to general acclaim as a messianic figure. Then, acting like a prophet, he has driven sellers and buyers out of the Temple area. Both events, they felt, were a direct challenge to their authority on their 'home ground'. But Jesus is not to be trapped into claiming God's authority for his actions. This could easily be used against him as an act of blasphemy. With the wisdom of the Spirit - which he has already promised to his disciples for the days when it is they who would be on trial, he turns the table on his challengers. They dared not assert that John was an impostor. Yet they could not justify their ignoring his message. They fell silent – Jesus' easy mastery here highlights his voluntary submission on Good Friday. As we say at Mass, 'a death he freely accepted'.

Prayer-lines: Lord, may the power of your Word read at Mass deepen our faith in your Spirit within us, and perfect our imitation of your Son, Jesus our Lord.

Week 9: Monday

Cycle 1: Tob 1:1; 2:1 -8; Cycle 2: 2 Pet 1:2-7; Gospel: Mk 12:1-12

Cycle 1: Granting all the merits and virtues of the lengthy book of Ecclesiasticus, it is something of a relief to be given our edification today in the form of a story, the book of Tobit. The Jews were gifted at story telling as well as at praying. And Tobit should be appreciated for its virtues as a story. We should savour the suspense of the plot, the interest of the events narrated, the skill of the character-sketches, and at times a pinch of real -life humour. But, of course, it would not be in the Bible if it wasn't also intended to edify. 'Tobit' means goodness, and Tobias means 'God is good'. The virtues of both father and son are described from the beginning. The highest good work for the Jews was burial of the dead (we remember Jesus' defence of Mary of Bethany at 'anointing' him for his burial in advance). In a word, Tobit describes the Old Testament way to happiness. Not without trials, but with God always near, and ready to answer the prayer of his faithful ones.

Cycle 2: We have already remarked in regard to the letter of Jude on the ancient literary convention of attributing one's writing to a venerable figure of the past. This is equally true of St. Peter. It is however, an inspired book, and 'we do well therefore to take it', like the rest of the Bible, 'as a lamp shining in the darkness'. Unlike other epistles, as it is addressed to no particular church, we can take it as valid for every Christian generation. It begins by our being called by God to a great dignity -to share his divine nature. Primarily, therefore, all is grace, God's gift. Yet, we also have a contribution to make. And here the letter describes a ladder of virtue reminiscent of more than one passage in St Paul: on our faith we build a good life: then understanding of that faith, patience, self-discipline – and finally, love.

Gospel: 'He will give the vineyard to others'. There is no great problem in seeing the drift of this parable in its historical context. The Old Testament had spoken of Israel as God's chosen vineyard. That, Jesus' listeners would easily remember. The logical sequel would be that Israel should bear fruit for God: by being faithful to the Covenant of Sinai, and leading other nations to the knowledge and service of the true God. In fact, however, Israel's history had been one of repeated infidelity: worship of alien gods, and much social injustice. So the parable says that Israel's privileges will be passed on to others – by Mark's time naturally the Gentiles. But we are also entitled to apply the teaching here to ourselves. How far have we, chosen by our Baptism to be God's vineyard been faithful to our privilege and mission -to build up our faith in ourselves and others? We too can forfeit God's gifts by infidelity.

Prayer-lines: God our Father, we ask you daily to give us 'our daily bread'. Grant us to receive in faith and deed the Bread of Heaven, who is your Son, our Lord. Amen.

Week 9: Tuesday

Cycle 1: Tob 2:9-14; Cycle 2: 2 Pet 3:11-15, 17-18; Gospel: Mk 12:13 -17

Cycle 1: 'Everyone knows what return you had for them'. Tobit, we said portrays the Old Testament way to happiness. According to the Psalm: 'many are the trials of the just man'. Tobit would be no exception. Despite the psalmist, affliction in Israel always bore a stigma. Belief in the next life, with compensation for the just who suffered came late to Israel. So reward for goodness had to be received and be seen to be received, in this world. However, Tobit is a story, not a deep study, like Job, of the 'problem of pain'. So picturesque details enliven the tragedy. Inefficient doctors are sniped at, as Mark will do in his gospel. And even Tobit's excessive scrupulosity about the justly earned kid merits his wife's rebuke. Such is the stuff of human life -major sufferings can be greatly aggravated by additional minor ones.

Cycle 2: 'The sky will dissolve in flames and the elements melt in the heat'. What was in St Peter's time conventional apocalyptic imagery has in our nuclear age become a physical possibility . St Peter is endeavoring to rebut current false beliefs that challenge basic Christian teachings like the return of Christ for the final judgement. He will adduce the combined authority of Peter and Paul to uphold the traditional teaching. And its practical relevance for Christians he says is, that 'they live holy and saintly lives'. This is always true, but in our generation a new dimension of moral responsibility is increasingly stressed: the Christians social responsibility. The church is not only the 'People of God'. It is also the 'Church in the modern World' as its saviour. The vocation of Christians today is to release by the purity of their lives the power of God in a world, which is in so many ways 'sick unto death'.

Gospel: 'What belongs to Caesar and what belongs to God'. Unlike the challenge to Jesus' authority in the Temple area, this question of the rightness of paying full-tax to the Romans seemed a copper-fastened trap: a Yes or No answer was unavoidable, thereby losing Jesus the support of either the (mostly Galilean) nationalists or the Pharisees. The poll-tax had to be paid in the Roman silver coinage, stamped with Caesar's head: a constantly galling reminder to nationalists that Romans ruled them. This was a less bitter pill for the Pharisees who could at least claim their freedom to observe their laws. Jesus' reply implied that an official coinage was the sign of valid rule over a country -so it should be paid. But this rule was insignificant beside God's rule, and kingdom, which was imminent, indeed already begun in himself and his teachings. It is an important truth to ponder even today: the validity of some values in the modern world, e.g. liberty of conscience, and the overriding priority of God's values, e.g. of justice and peace.

Prayer-lines: God our Father, may your church always be guided by the wisdom and Spirit of your Son Jesus in upholding your values in the world.

Week 9: Wednesday

Cycle 1: Tob 3:1-17; Cycle 2: 2 Tim 1:1-3, 6-12; Gospel: Mk 12:18-27

Cycle 1: 'Better to die than still to live'. The story of Tobit is now moving to a climax in the simultaneous grief of Tobit and Sarah. Tobit's blindness, as we saw, is aggravated by the sense of guilt, which pervaded his people since the Exile. It is a sign of unbelievable suffering for a just man to ask for death. The psalmists cling to life at all costs, reminding God that they cannot offer him praise in Sheol, the abode of the dead. – But even more extreme is Sarah's grief where she is prepared to contemplate suicide, a thought that occurs to very few people in the Bible, and these few far removed from Sarah's condition. But the storyteller has made his point. Tobit and Sarah, like an infinitely greater character in the Gospels are 'sorrowful unto death'. The solution of the impasse comes in the same way to all three. They turn to God in prayer. And, God takes their sorrow on himself. He sends an angel. 'Raphael' means 'God is a healer'.

Cycle 2: 'Never to be ashamed of witnessing'. Our first reading is from Paul's last letter from his prison in Rome to Timothy, his faithful lieutenant in so many of his missionary journeys. He reminds Timothy that it was from Paul (and no other) that he received his commission to be a witness to the Good News. He now invites Timothy to share the trials of that career of 'witnessing to the Lord'. It is God's power, not their own efforts, that sustains them both. This common Good News is the appearing on earth of Jesus as saviour, and the victory over death achieved by his resurrection. It is Paul's witness to this common faith that has bought him to his present condition in prison. But he is at peace, confident that his missionary work is safe in the care of God.

Gospel: 'He is God of the living'. The Sadducees were the conservative element of the religious leaders in Jesus' time. They accepted only the Pentateuch (i.e. the first five books of the Bible) as inspired, and in them there is no reference to resurrection of the dead. Jesus is easily able to refute them, by showing that even in these books resurrection is implied. The God who speaks to Moses from the burning bush as the God of Abraham,

Isaac and Jacob is a God of the living, not of the dead. That means they must be still alive. But even apart from that esoteric textual proof, the main guarantee is the power of God to give life even to the dead, and to live in heaven like angels, unmarried. It is still important for us as Christians in understanding mysteries of our faith to rely on our basic faith in the power of a creator God who can achieve what is utterly beyond our comprehension.

Prayer-lines: God our Father, grant us the peace of soul which passes all understanding, and is firmly based on your divine power, through Christ your Son. Amen

Week 9: Thursday
Cycle 1: Tob 6, 7, 8 or 6:10-11, 7:1, 9-14, 8:4-9 Cycle 2: 2 Tim 2:8-15;
Gospel: Mk 12:28 -34
Cycle 1: *'It is not good that man should be alone'*. Our first reading gives us a valuable illustration of the Gospel principle: 'love your neighbour as yourself'. One's first neighbour is, of course, one's spouse in marriage. In practice is this principle always so clear to spouses? At all events the theme of our passage is the contrast between the wrong relationship of man and woman in marriage -which brought death to Sarah's seven husbands – and the right relationship, which brought a blessing on Tobias and all his family. It is not good for man to be alone, as the book of Genesis puts it, because one is incomplete as a person without another person to love and be loved by. This mutual love is in total contrast to lust: using another not as a person but as a thing: a means of procuring selfish pleasure. Self-love is indeed the counterfeit coin of true love, which is loving one's Neighbour as oneself.

Cycle 2: Our first reading in 2nd Timothy stresses the distinctive emphasis of Paul's teaching: the crucified but risen Christ. Here he puts Christ's resurrection even before his birth, his descent from David. As in his letter to the Philippians, it is the heart of Paul's spiritual life: 'to know Jesus and the power of his resurrection'. To the Corinthians he writes: 'If Christ is not risen, then our faith is vain, is empty'. But the resurrection, which Christ shares with us, also presupposes that 'we have died with him'. Timothy is urged to insist that the leaders of the churches adhere to this core of the Christian faith, and not to get distracted by niceties of language. The programme for Timothy is to cleave 'a straight course' – as if through a sea – 'with the message of truth'.

Gospel: 'You are not far from the kingdom of God'. A rather remarkable scene this. A scribe genuinely looking for enlightenment from Jesus: welcoming it when it is given, and praising Jesus for such an admirable reply. As elsewhere Jesus can show that God's will is already revealed in the Old Testament -though Jesus adds the injunction to love one's neighbour from a different book of the Bible. The commandment to love God is part of the Jewish Morning Prayer. 'With all your heart and soul, mind and strength'. This means a love both inward and outward: something the prophets often claimed was lacking in the Temple worship. Orthodox Christians have tried to take this commandment literally by means of 'the Jesus prayer'. At all events we find the supreme model of it is Jesus, in his awareness of his Father's presence and will at all times. Face to face with Jesus, our scribe was indeed 'not far from the kingdom of God'.

Prayer-lines: Lord Jesus, share with us your sense of God's presence at all times that we may live constantly in love of Him and our neighbour.

Week 9: Friday

Cycle 1: Tob 11:5-17; Cycle 2: 2 Tim 3:10-17; Gospel: Mk 12:35 -37

Cycle 1: 'Blessed be God. Blessed be all his holy angels'. The liturgy unkindly skips many of the memorable events after Tobias's wedding to Sarah. Today it leaves us on the return journey, and the happy ending is in sight. The credit for all this domestic happiness goes, of course, in Tobit's prayer, to God. (And we may note the current reference to angels at the time as part of God's preparation for the Incarnation). The Incarnation is still undreamt of, still more the indwelling of the Blessed Trinity in the Christian Church. But there is a real faith in the nearness of God through his angles to those who are faithful to his Law, his will; and in his power and concern to help them.

Cycle 2: 'What I have taught, how I have lived'. Paul is once more reminding Timothy of the example he himself had given of the apostolic life, so often in Timothy's company. And he recalls the places, known to us already through the Acts of Apostles where his chief early work had been, Antioch, Iconium, Lystra. It was not only the common Christian virtues of faith, patience and love in all he did. It was also bitter persecution. This is to be the common lot of the faithful Christian. But the great resource of the serious Christian is the wisdom contained in the Bible. – We ourselves are blessed since Vatican II in having easy access to these inspired Scriptures in a way that had for centuries been barred to us.

Gospel: 'David said, 'The Lord said to my Lord'.' Jesus, as we saw, was frequently challenged by his enemies when teaching in the Temple. Here, for a change, he challenges them on the questions of the identity of the Messiah. King David was commonly regarded as the author of all the Psalms. How then can David, in this well-known Ps 110, speak of the Messiah -who was reputed to be his descendant – as also his Lord? Jesus preferred to refer to himself as 'the Son of man'. The blind Bartimaeus at Jericho was the first to call him 'Son of David'. But is Jesus here giving his hearers a clue that, whatever about his Davidic descent, he was also the Son of God? At all events, whenever we hear Jesus speak in the gospels, we can join with the people who today 'heard him with delight'.

Prayer-lines: Lord Jesus, give us increasing faith in your presence and power to help us as we read or hear the Scriptures.

Week 9: Saturday

Cycle 1: Tob 12; Cycle 2: 2 Tim 4:1-8; Gospel: Mk 12:38-44

Cycle 1: 'I am about to return to him who sent me.' We might have thought that God had no more to give Tobit and us than the return of Tobias, happily married to Sarah, and Tobit's sight restored. Yet God has even more good news for us. As Raphael says, it is right to thank God for all his earthly favours. But we are not to limit God's greatness and goodness to these. From Raphael we learn that the God we rightly praise and thank is a God of unimaginable majesty. He commands the services of in-visible beings before whom men are only pygmies. Tobit is one of the late Old Testament books with this special interest in the role of angels. It is a providential preparation of God's people for the supreme 'Angel' (the word in Greek means a messenger) to be sent as God -with-us 'Emmanuel'. – And Raphael today anticipates one of this 'Angel's' last words in St John's Gospel: 'I am about to return to him who sent me'.

Cycle 2: 'Welcome or unwelcome proclaim the message'. Paul is writing to Timothy between his first captivity in Rome de-scribed in the last chapter of Acts, and his second, final trial there. There is therefore a special urgency in these final words of his letter. He begs Timothy to see that in the rising generation Paul's true doctrine will be upheld, however unpopular it may seem. (We think today of how faithful Pope John Paul is to this injunction on so many moral issues of the modern world). For his own lot Paul is at peace. We hear again a number of his favourite images in his earlier letters. His life is being poured out as a sacrificial liquid. He has kept up the contest to the finish, run the race to the end. And now he can securely expect Christ's reward for this, as can all others who have lived with faith in his Second Coming.

Gospel: 'She has put in all she had to live on'. The generosity of the poor widow is in stark contrast to the greed of the scribes 'who swallow up the property of widows'. In Mark's Gospel this little episode is the last before the passion narrative. In that story we shall see Jesus himself giving us all he 'had to live on';

emptying himself to make us rich. This should be a recurring question for ourselves. How far do we imitate Christ in self-giving? Nor can we, at our Saturday Mass, forget another widow who generously surrendered Him who was her all, as she stood beside the Cross.

Prayer-lines: God our Father, deepen our faith in your presence with us through your angels, and keep us always thankful for your daily blessings.

Week 10: Monday

Cycle 1: 2 Cor 1:1-7; Cycle 2: 1 Kings 17:1-6; Gospel: Mt 5:1-12

Cycle 1: 'A gentle Father and the God of all consolation.' We last met St Paul at the end of his life, as a prisoner in Rome. Today, and for another two weeks we listen to him at the height of his powers in one of his greatest epistles. We are in for a unique revelation of what it can mean to be passionately in love with Christ. He will sum it up in a later chapter: 'The love of Christ overwhelms us … that one died for all'. His every line can be memorable. God, whom he knew and served so passionately as a Pharisee is now 'the Father of our Lord Jesus Christ, a gentle Father and the God of all consolation, who comforts us in all our sorrows'. (Later on we'll get a glimpse of these sorrows). But it is not self-pitying piety on Paul's part. No, he cries, God's consolation is given me only to be shared with others, supporting *you* Corinthians, in patiently bearing the same suffering as we bear.

Cycle 2: Our first reading begins a fascinating drama that will be played out for us for the next ten days. With no warning the curtain goes up on the chief character: Elijah of Tishbe in Gilead – across the River Jordan to the east of Samaria, if your geography is hazy. Nothing more to introduce us. No word of his parents or his age. But we quickly find out his era, through his peremptory threat to Ahab, king of Samaria. It is now some sixty years since Solomon died, and the northern half of David's kingdom broke away from Judah in the south. It retained the name of 'Israel', but fell away rapidly into the cult of Baal, the Sidonian god of fertility. Ahab is introduced by the Book of Kings as the latest of a series of faithless rulers of Israel, and as worse than all his pre-decessors. Elijah now confronts him with the news that it is his God, Yahweh, that controls the fertility of Israel. 'Watch for the next episode!

Gospel: 'Blessed are the pure of heart: they shall see God.' Jesus in his Sermon on the Mount has often been compared to Moses as Lawgiver and prophet. But here he uses the language of the wisdom books, ('blessed is he who meditates on wisdom', etc). So the beatitudes are the condensation of Christian wisdom. Where else will you find another advertisement for becoming poor (be it in pocket or in spirit)? For facing life's hardships as something desirable? But Jesus' whole emphasis is not on the unsatisfactory nature of things in this life. It is on the eternal blessedness they can contain: the kingdom; – the comfort, the mercy, the vision of God.

Prayer-lines: Lord Jesus, we thank you for being our Teacher of wisdom in your gospel: thank you for the eternal blessings you promise us in today's reading. Make us worthy to receive them.

Week 10: Tuesday
Cycle 1: 2 Cor 1:18-22; Cycle 2: 1 Kings 17:7-16; Gospel: Mt 5:13-16
Cycle 1: 'With Christ Jesus it was always "Yes".' Paul can some-times bewilder us because of his unique sense of being every moment in the presence of not merely 'God', (which for him al-ways means the Father), but of Christ too and the Spirit. So today he dazzles us by placing a minor incident in this profound theological context. He has been accused of not keeping a promise to visit Corinth, and therefore of being unreliable, a 'Yes' and 'No' man. How could I be that, he explains, when my life is based on God, the all-reliable: the God who wants all to be saved; the God who so loved the world that he gave his only Son, Jesus, who is his 'Yes' to all his promises to humanity? – May we too be so united to Christ that God's sincerity may show itself in all we do or say.

Cycle 2: 'Up and go to Zarephath, a Sidonian town.' Elijah is still living by the 'Word of the Lord', when the wadi Cherith dries up in the drought which God's word had foretold. Elijah must now go to the land of Sidon, of Ahab's wife, Jezebel, and her Baal-worship. There too the same famine rages. Elijah does not challenge the poor widow's tale of woe, but he undoes it by Yahweh's word of hope. 'Jar of meal shall not be spent, jug of oil shall not be emptied before the Lord sends rain on the face of the earth.' The widow and her son will live to have another story told of them.

Gospel: 'You are the salt, the light, the city on a hill-top.' Not a command, an invitation to effort. Rather a statement of fact – what we are as Christ's disciples. 'Christian', cries St Leo at Christmas, 'acknowledge your dignity'. For the moment the Sermon on the Mount doesn't specify how we show this reality: it will later on, and the infinite reality of its ways. Outstanding individuals like Mother Teresa of Calcutta may occur to us. So may followers of other faiths, like Gandhi. But many of those tirelessly working for peace may never make the media at all. And Jesus has just pronounced the Beatitudes to remind us that men react to our light by persecution rather than by giving praise to God; that men will often prefer the darkness to the light.

Prayer-lines: God our Father, thank you for the dignity you have given us as your daughters and sons by Baptism. Help us by your Spirit to live in the likeness of your Son, Jesus.

Week 10: Wednesday

Cycle 1: 2 Cor 3:4-11; Cycle 2: 1 Kings 18:20-39; Gospel: Mt 5:17-19

Cycle 1: 'The written letters bring death: the spirit gives life.' The letter is, of course, the written Law of Moses; the Spirit is the Spirit of the risen Jesus. The tribute in today's gospel to the value of the Law of Moses helps us to understand how Paul had to wage such a relentless battle, a) to persuade the Jews that they should look no longer to observances of the Law to make them pleasing to God, but to acceptance of Jesus as 'the one sent by God'.

And b) as in today's passage, to convince converted Gentiles that despite what some converted Jews had told them, it was not necessary for them to adopt Jewish practices in order to be good Christians.

Our salvation too depends on our attitude to Christ. Do we share his life as much as possible – through the sacraments and our love for one another?

Cycle 2: Our first reading is one of the greatest dramatic scenes in the Old Testament: a public contest between idolatry, (worship of Baal), and Yahweh. Elijah is bidden by 'God's Word' to return to Israel from Zarephath. Here Ahab has been brought to his knees by Elijah's 3-year long drought. He agrees, therefore to a confrontation between Yahweh's prophet and the four hundred and fifty of Baal's. The drama takes place at several levels. Not merely the fire of Yahweh consuming the sodden sacrifice. Not merely Elijah's heroic faith expressed in his confident words. The deepest drama is that of, as Elijah puts it, 'winning back the hearts of his people'. The cues for their gradual return are carefully marked out: from their original silence at Elijah's first challenge to their gradual 'hobbling' agreement to the contest, and co-operation in it; to their final proclamation, 'Yes, Yahweh (and only Yahweh) is God'. We must learn from this tale about the ways God can work with our feeble faith.

Gospel: 'Not to abolish, but to complete them.' By 'the Law and the Prophets' Jesus means the Old Testament. He is saying here, as will St Paul to the Romans, that his teaching does not render the value of the Old Testament for us invalid. But he is going to interpret it better than it has been done, especially by Scribes and Pharisees. He will give some practical examples of that in the passages which follow, e.g. on the question of anger. But especially will Jesus illuminate it to the full by the whole of his gospel teaching, e.g. by his parables like the prodigal son. And especially by his life, his passion, and his obedience to the father unto death.

Prayer-lines: God our Father, help us by the power of your Spirit to imitate Christ in his perfect fidelity to your law of love.

Week 10: Thursday

Cycle 1: 2 Cor 3:15-4:6; Cycle 2: Kings 18:41-46; Gospel: Mt 5:20-26

Cycle 1: 'We are turned into the image that we reflect.' In our first reading St Paul continues the defence of his teaching to the Corinthians in the light of his failure to win over Jewish audiences. He turns back to the Old Testament history of the Covenant. Moses' face, we are told, was so radiant after receiving the law from God that he had to veil his face. But now, Paul says, the veil prevents the Jews from seeing the greater radiance of the gospel. For this is the radiance of God's Spirit ... Christians reflect that radiance through the transforming power of the Spirit in them: the radiance of the glory of Christ. Freed from the Old Testament references to Moses, what a marvellous programme of Christian living that gives us: that our lives be a reflection of the glory in the face of Christ. Not so much a matter of our striving for perfect behaviour, as of letting the Spirit be the guide and inspiration of all we think and say and do.

Cycle 2: 'The hand of the Lord was on Elijah.' Yet another drama of Elijah for us today: the lesson of his private prayer. Yesterday he had shown up the inadequacy of Baal worship. But he had also to produce the rain he had promised Ahab before the contest with Baal's prophets. This was a matter of his private, intense prayer; 'with his head beneath his knees', we are told. His servant is told to look out west over the Mediterranean for the tell-tale rain clouds. 'There is nothing at all', he reports. Elijah's faith does not falter. 'Go back and look seven times', he bids him. At last the report comes: 'There is a tiny cloud.' It is enough for Elijah's faith. 'Run', he says, 'and tell Ahab to get back to his palace in Jezreel before the torrential rain clogs his chariot wheels.' The Spirit in Elijah, however, was stronger than Ahab's horses, and Elijah ran the seventeen miles ahead of them.

Gospel: 'If your virtue goes no deeper.' Yes, if Jesus is a new Moses dispensing the New Law in the Sermon on the Mount, he is not discussing the truth and value of the Old Law, of the Ten Commandments. He is seeking to deepen their observance, to interiorise it. Murder is relatively rare, and ancient Israel did not

consider the Ten Words, (as the Hebrew calls them), an excessive restriction on normal living. But murder is preceded by interior anger. It is these interior forces we must learn to control,
so that they do not lead to deeds of violence. So much of the violence we deplore today, in our own context or elsewhere, can
stem from faulty ideas and ideologies about other groups, ethnic
or other. Let us, therefore, do all we can to settle differences in a
peaceful way before we have to answer before the court of
Judgement day.

Prayer-lines: Lord Jesus, help us to deepen our fidelity to your
commands by listening constantly to the guidance of your
Spirit.

Week 10: Friday
Cycle 1: 2 Cor 4:7-15; Cycle 2: 1 Kings 19:9, 11-16; Gospel: Mt 5:27-32
Cycle 1: 'Such an overwhelming power comes from God.' If
Paul's opponents were claiming that his trials and difficulties
were a countersign of his being an authentic minister of the
gospel, he will explain them differently. They are signs of a
deeper mystery at work: the death of Christ is being shared by
Paul's ministry. And that death of Christ, as they all knew, was a
positive force, the power of salvation. If Paul could be such an
obvious 'earthenware jar', in virtue of his human weakness,
then the success of his ministry among the Galatians must clearly be the power of God at work in him, bringing life to them. For
if, as humans, we share in Christ's mortal faith, we shall also
share in his resurrection, 'and you with us', he assures them.
And the more this gift of life is shared, through Christians suffering, the more glory will be given to God.

Cycle 2: In our first reading Elijah's drama continues. But its
tenor has completely changed. Jezebel, Ahab's wife, has sent
word that in revenge for the slaughter of the Baal-prophets she
will have Elijah's life too. All Elijah's courage seems to desert
him. He flees down south, and out into the desert of Sinai, where
God had first revealed his will to Moses. A forty-day trek. And

here, indeed, God will speak to Elijah too, mysteriously. Not in the traditional setting of storm and earthquake, but in an eerie silence, a 'gentle breeze'. Elijah is challenged for his presence there, ('what are you doing here ,Elijah?'). He defensively explains the impossible state of things in Israel. In return God gives him a fresh commission: a threefold one. He is to anoint the kings of both Syria and Israel; and, as his prophetic successor, Elisha. – God's saving work for his people has not yet ended.

Gospel: 'If your right eye should cause you to sin, tear it out.' A question of priorities. 'If anyone wants to save his life, he shall lose it.' Later, Matthew will tell us of the disciples' dismay at Jesus ruling out divorce. And today there would seem to be a world-wide campaign to exploit man's weakness in the domain of lustful looks, waged by media and advertisement. Exegetes have made attempts to weaken the force of Jesus' demands in the Sermon on the Mount. But the truth would seem to be unavoidable. Jesus is proposing a very high moral ideal for us. But not an impossible one. We have a double guarantee for that. First, the example of his own uprightness in the field of sexuality. And then the teaching of St Paul in our readings from Second Corinthians. That even in the earthenware jars that we are, God's Spirit can reveal in our mortal flesh the glory in the face of Christ.

Prayer-lines: Lord Jesus, in all our human frailties may we not lose hope, but rely on your Spirit to show his power in our weakness.

Week 10: Saturday
Cycle 1: 2 Cor 5:14-21; Cycle 2: 1 Kings 19:19-21; Gospel: Mt 5:33-37
Cycle 1: 'We might become the goodness of God.' Paul in our first reading is revealing to the Corinthians the very foundation of his 'vocation' as an authentic apostle of the Good News. But in doing so he also lays bare the heart of our Christian faith. The loving *death* of Christ for us is the model of how we must *live:* no longer selfishly, ('for ourselves'), but for him – in himself and in

our neighbour. And this of course is a radical change from our conventional human living: it is a 'new creation'. Only God could bring about such a new creation: by making 'the sinless one into sin'. That is, by making Christ stand in the relation to God which is proper to us sinners. But, as in fact, Christ, representing us, the sinners, was in fact sinless – in him we were acquitted, justified, reconciled to God. We are touching on the roots of that holiness, freed from lust and selfishness, which Christ is appealing to us 'to live up to in the Sermon on the mount: 'the goodness of God'.

Cycle 2: 'He then rose and followed Elijah.' Elisha's request to bid farewell to his parents meets a gentler reply from Elijah than Jesus' 'let the dead bury their dead', on a parallel occasion in the gospel. But Elisha is clearly abandoning his guaranteed livelihood by burning his plough and sacrificing his oxen. And there is also an aura of the sacred about Elijah's conduct as he repeats Yahweh's words to himself, 'Go back'. Elijah will indeed remain for future generations a symbol of one, like Moses, caught up in the ambiance of the sacred. But his prophetic mission of presenting God's will to the rulers of his people must now be passed on to another, to Elisha.

Gospel: 'Any more than Yes and No comes from the evil one.' Already the Decalogue had taught his people not 'to take the Lord's name in vain', and 'not to bear false witness'. Jesus here deepens the teaching by forbidding the use of a substitute like 'heaven' for God's name. And he enjoys speaking the truth directly and simply. As his own parables show, this does not forbid the use of figurative language, or oath formulas as long as they are truthful. But already the book of Proverbs has warned that 'in a flood of words you will not avoid sinning'. An oath is a symbol of man's unreliability in word or intention in a world of deception and lies. With the coming of Christ, ('God's "Yes" to all his promises'), that must all change. We are a new creation in Christ and must share in God's fidelity to *his* word.

Prayer-lines: God our Father, may the Spirit of truth enable all Christians to speak truly to one another in heart and mouth.

Week 11: Monday

Cycle 1: 2 Cor 6:1-10; Cycle 2: 1 Kings 21:1-16; Gospel: Mt 5:38-42

Cycle 1: 'Our function as God's servants.' In a way we might be grateful to Paul's opponents at Corinth, for unwittingly they evoked a self-revelation of his life and motivation we might otherwise have lost. He had already claimed that in Christ God had made him 'a new creation'. Today he details how that affects his life as God's (newly-made) servant. The first hall-mark of being one with Christ is suffering, sharing Christ's cross. But behind the outward hardship there is an inner conformity to Christ's inner self, holiness and love. And this is a sign of God's power. The end-result is a life of paradox: indifference to contrasting re-actions from people: reactions of condemnation or of praise. In a word, the paradox of Christ's death and resurrection.

Cycle 2: 'The Lord forbid that I should.' Our first reading gives us a blood-chilling account of a cold-blooded violation of God's law in the Old Testament. It recalls the hot-blooded sin of King David in the past: adultery and murder. The chief agent of today's crime is Ahab's queen, Jezebel, but he is her unscrupulous accomplice. (Shades of Macbeth and Lady Macbeth?) Naboth, whose name recurs fifteen times in the story like a sinister death knell, is portrayed (like Uriah in the David story) as a law-abiding , God-fearing man, obeying the Law, which forbade his selling ancestral land. Ahab, we note carefully, omits this explicit religious motive of Naboth in recounting the story of the refusal to Jezebel. The whole sorry tale is a paradigm of so many sins of injustice being committed in every age, our own not excluded.

Gospel: 'Go two miles with him.' Jesus in the Sermon on the Mount is step by step building up a blue-print of the New Law of the kingdom on the foundations of the Old: reconciliation instead of violence, self-discipline instead of lust, truth instead of insincerity. Even though the 'eye for an eye' law already disciplines the natural urge for excess in vengeance, to a due proportion instead, it still falls short of the ideal: the example God sets us. St Paul will sum up the positive values in non-resistance in his 'master evil with good': the aggressor may be shamed by our non-violent reactions. But even where, as so often happens, evil remains obdurate, there remains for all of us the supreme model of Christ's non-resistance in his Passion. In recalling how this model has shared its power of the Spirit in so many martyrs down the centuries, let our memory be ecumenical and not forget the example of the Anabaptist in Reformation times, of Gandhi and others in our own.

Prayer-lines: Lord Jesus, may Christians everywhere, as they meet injustice in their lives, overcome it by the weapons of love, through the power of your Spirit.

Week 11: Tuesday
Cycle 1: 2 Cor 8:1-9; Cycle 2: 1 Kings 21:17-29; Gospel Mt 5:43-48
Cycle 1: 'To make you rich out of his poverty.'The first Christians in Jerusalem were poor. The Twelve had to make special arrangements, you remember, that the widows were not neglected. And when Paul, after his conversion, visited Jerusalem with Barnabas, the apostles made a point that the two of them should seek help for the Jerusalem poor among the better-off Gentile congregations. Paul had already raised the matter in his first letter to the Corinthians, and he feels it was important for bonding Gentile Christians with their Jewish counterparts. Apparently the converts in Thessalonica and Philippi, in spite of their own problems, had set a high standard of generosity in this regard. Corinth was a much wealthier city than these two Macedonian ones, and Paul is hoping for similar generosity from there. He sees the Macedonian generosity as a symbol of their self-giving. And the primary example of such generosity is Christ, who stripped himself of his glory in order to enrich us by his grace.

Cycle 2: 'Elijah answered: "I have found you out."' Ahab's satisfaction at possessing Naboth's coveted vineyard is short-lived. In an era when Israel had not yet reached belief in an afterlife, where retribution would fall on wrong-doing, God's justice had to be seen to be done in this life. Whenever this failed to happen it presented a major scandal for many – as we see in the Book of

Job and the Psalms. So Ahab's condign punishment is announced in no uncertain terms. His descendants would not
reign after him. – Still more striking is the effect of Elijah's words
on Ahab. He would be spared in view of his repentance.

Gospel: 'I say this to you: love your enemies.' This is the climax of
the series of contrasts between the Old Law and the New in the
Sermon on the Mount. It is not just a matter of keeping the Old
Law more heroically, for even the Rabbis and the Dead Sea
monks could ask for that. For them the motive was God's reward. For Jesus, living up to this high standard was the grateful
imitation of God. The experience of God's mercy, as St Paul says,
overwhelms us. It sweeps one off the terra-firma of human nature:
self-defence and revenge – into the river of God's incredible reaction to his enemies, which, as St Paul reminds us, we were. And
this moral programme is not so much one of *our* doing something
heroic, as of God's power, his Spirit working in us.

Prayer-lines: God our Father, send forth your Spirit to create
Christians whose love will overcome the hatred in the world
today.

Week 11: Wednesday
Cycle 1: 2 Cor 9:6-11; Cycle 2: 2 Kings 2:1-14; Gospel Mt 6:1-6, 16-18
Cycle 1: 'Your almsgiving must be secret', says the Lord'. But
that is not the way Paul is looking at it in Corinth. He wants the
relatively wealthy Christians there to give generously on behalf
of the really poor Christians of Jerusalem. There had been a very
severe famine there a few years before Paul wrote this letter. He
is anxious to make the bond between the once – pagan and the
once – Jewish churches a material as well as a spiritual one. But
the last phrase in today's passage, 'the cause of thanksgiving to
God', shows that even the unity of the Christian churches is not
his primary interest. Paul is the apostle and theologian of
thanksgiving! He never tires of interspersing his letters with
prayers of thanksgiving to God. Thanksgiving was his fundamental attitude towards God. It should be ours, especially at
Mass. Paul's word for thanksgiving is 'eucharistia'. And we can

readily understand why the Mass from the earliest times came to be called the 'Eucharist': the great act of thanksgiving to God through Jesus Christ for all he has given us through him.

Cycle 2: 'Where is the Lord, God of Elijah?' The time has come for the torch of prophecy, charismatic emblem of God's continuing surveillance and guidance of his people, to be passed on to Elisha. Three times Elisha shows his independence, and his devotion to the master, by insisting on going with him to the Jordan. The 'double share' that he asks of Elijah's spirit is the traditional share of the eldest son. – Fire has been associated with Elijah throughout the saga, and in this episode it suggests the realm of the divine proximity which Elijah is entering upon. – When the time comes for Elisha to die, he too will be addressed as 'chariot of Israel and its chargers' – visible signs of God's protective presence with his people. Clothes were regarded as an extension of one's personality, and Elijah's cloak, therefore, still contains his power to divide the waters of the Jordan. It is a reminder of Joshua leading the Chosen People into the Promised Land.

Gospel: 'Reward from your Father in Heaven.' If Jesus' warning here was primarily directed to the Pharisees, it can still be relevant to every generation. There is always the danger of looking for the reward of human approval in what we do, even in the domain of piety. It is not at all that Jesus is dismissive of these three classic exercises of Jewish piety. But he here repeats solemnly three times that what matters in piety is our motivation. What we do must be for his Father, who sees in secret and into our secret heart. Such was his own piety on earth. And that unflagging zeal of Jesus for seeking his Father's approval must be our model at all times. 'O God, you are my God, for you I long; for you my soul is thirsting'. (Psalm 63)

Prayer-lines: Lord Jesus, help us by your Spirit, to imitate you in doing always the things that please our Father in heaven.

Week 11: Thursday

Cycle 1: 2 Cor 11:1-11; Cycle 2: Ecc 48:-1-14; Gospel: Mt 6:7-15
Cycle 1: 'I feel for you God's own jealousy.' The topic of this last part of second Corinthians is so different from the preceding part that it would seem to be a new letter. Paul is defending himself as an apostle against charges that other preachers, latterly come to Corinth, are making against him. If *his* teaching, he writes, is so different from theirs, it was because it was the uncorrupted truth about Christ. What a tragedy for me, he explodes, to see that when any outsider arrives and preaches otherwise about Christ, you embrace his doctrine at once! If they claim that I'm not a good speaker, that may be so. But my *knowledge* of what I preach is incontestable.

Cycle 2: 'Elijah was shrouded in whirlwind, and Elisha was filled with his spirit.' The drama of the two great prophets, Elijah and Elisha, is fittingly concluded for us with their encomium by Ecclesiasticus some two hundred years before Christ. They take their honourable place in Ben Sira's review of the Old Testament 'greats' through whom God's glory has been manifested in Israel's history. These great figures are listed consecutively by him from the early patriarchs like Enoch and Noah, down through Abraham, Moses, kings, prophets and heroes, to reach Sirach's contemporary, Simeon the high priest. The Christian church has rightly followed this tradition by recalling in its annual liturgy not merely the saving events of Christ, but also the lives and virtues of his followers down to the present day.

Gospel: Christians rightly treasure the 'Our Father' as our Lord's own answer to the problem we share with the apostles, 'Lord, teach us to pray'. Repetition can at times distract us from some of its meaning but it is primarily the church with Christ at its head, that is praying in us. Yet it is important to keep in mind the two guiding principles behind its various petitions. First the word 'Father', which hides the boundless familiarity of the 'Abba' on Jesus' lips. For St Paul it is the great sign that it is the Spirit – of our adoption as children – who is praying in us. Secondly, like Jesus' final prayer at the Last Supper, it is the prayer of a people straining upwards towards heaven, with him at our head, leaving this world behind. Yes, we still have world-ly needs. But before, and after them, must come God's plans, the coming of his kingdom. That must be our real concern in life, that God's will be finally done. And that we be ready for his coming by showing ourselves true children of a father whose name is forgiveness and love.

Prayer-lines: Lord Jesus, thank you for teaching us to pray. Penetrate us with your Holy Spirit, that what we ask in your prayer may come to pass, and in the whole world. Amen

Week 11: Friday
Cycle 1: 2 Cor 11:18, 21-30; Cycle 2: 2 Kings 11:1-4, 9-18, 20; Gospel: Mt 6:19-23
Cycle 1: 'Let me boast of my own feebleness.' Once again we are grateful to Paul's opponents for forcing him to give us a glimpse of his heroic apostolate. His ironic opening shows that he is not taking the contest of boasting very seriously. But it also shows us of what his opponents boasted. 'Hebrews' suggests that they were Aramaic-speaking Palestinians (like the Twelve). 'Descendants of Abraham' would suit those who stressed obser-vance of the Law; 'Servants of Christ', Paul goes on to show, must mean suffering, not prestige. And which of them could equal Paul's record which follows. Some of it we already know from Acts. All of it is hair-raising. Jerusalem to Corinth and back, for instance, is about three thousand miles. And, physical sufferings apart, the constant cross he had to carry was his worry about his converts.

Cycle 2: Despite the repentance of King Ahab for Naboth's mur-der, and Elijah's continued prophetic presence, Baal-worship still went on in Israel. Jehu, the army officer, had obeyed God's command through Elijah to wipe it out. But inter-marriage had allowed it to seep into Judah too. Athaliah, the queen mother there, was a daughter of the former king of Israel, and as formidable a promoter of Baal as Jezebel had been. Only the fidelity of

Jehoiada, the Temple priest, had saved the last son of king Ahaziah, from being slain in Jehu's blood-bath. This is not just a record of palace intrigue and violence, a common-place in near Eastern history. In the Bible what is at stake is the all-important fulfilment of Yahweh's promise to David that his dynasty would not die out.

Gospel: Religious hypocrites, Jesus has told us, will seek – and have – their own reward in men's admiration. If Jesus was aiming at the Pharisees of his day it is also relevant for every generation. We Pharisees are an undying race. But the proper place to win admiration, he tells us, is heaven, where 'your Father sees all the good you do in secret'. The good life which Jesus is describing for us in the Sermon on the Mount is a road we must walk to reach that heaven where our treasure is. It is by the light of our inner eye, our basic aim in life, that we see how to tread that way successfully. Our being, our 'whole body' will be filled with light. For light is the property of heaven, and of God. The role model of this singleness of vision is, of course, Jesus himself. The 'light' of *his* life, he tells us, was to do always the will of him who sent him.

Prayer-lines: Lord Jesus, help us always to seek in this life our reward in heaven and not on earth.

Week 11: Saturday
Cycle 1: 2 Cor 12:1-10; Cycle 2: 2 Chron 24:17-25; Gospel: Mt6:24-34
Cycle 1: 'It is when I am weak that I am strong.' Paul's opponents at Corinth apparently also boast of having had visions and revelations. Here, too, Paul can challenge them. But he will do it in the third person, for after all God was the agent involved. But his dating of it, 'fourteen years ago', guarantees the reality of his experience. He could indeed, he says, boast of more than that, but he forbears. For him, all that matters in a genuine apostle is his conduct and his speech. 'A thorn in the flesh' is a biblical image for Israel's enemies in the Old Testament. In our present context it could well be hostility from within Paul's own community. After repeated prayer about it Paul has now come to ac-

cept it. For God's power at work in him is more evident among his apostolic weaknesses. – We too, must sometimes accept the paradox of God's power being effective in us, in spite of our being 'blunt instruments' in his service.

Cycle 2: 'The Lord sees, and he will avenge.' The two books of Chronicles are a priestly interpretation of Israel's history under the kings, from David to the Exile. Events are viewed mainly from the angle of worship, and therefore of the Temple. Kings are assessed according to their fidelity to Temple worship. Our last Old Testament reading stressed the role of the high-priest Jehoiada in saving the boy-king, Joash, David's descendant, from the fury of Athaliah. Once Jehoiada was dead, however, Judah relapsed into idolatry. Zechariah, son of Jehoiada, raised a prophetic protest but is killed, with the connivance of king Joash. God's swift vengeance is seen in Judah's defeat by Syria (Aram), and murder of the king by his courtiers. It is a gloomy presage of Judah's ultimate punishment by Babylonian exile a century and a half later.

Gospel: 'Your heavenly Father knows you need them.' At times we might see the sermon on the Mount as a mountain climb with Jesus at our head. In the opening Beatitudes he sketches out the marvellous vista that will be ours from the top: 'rejoice and be glad' for there is the kingdom! He then leads us first through familiar tracks, the Commandments. But suddenly bids us leap on to a higher ground – especially on to the daunting ledge of loving our enemies. – Surely we must be at the top by now? Perfect as our heavenly Father is! No. There is still the hardest rock-face of all to tackle; perfect trust: 'no to worry'. What! Not to worry about what we are to eat, to drink, to wear? No, he tells us, not to *worry*! That would be to lie down in the meadow with the other master: the other god, Mammon, the 'Celtic Tiger'. It is for you to cling to your Father in heaven. His love you cannot doubt. His power to give you all you need is certain. Set your heart on him – and his will. Love him, that is 100%. And your neighbour as much as yourself.

Prayer-lines: God our Father, thank you for the reproach we deserve in today's gospel. Give us the Holy Spirit to enable us to trust always in your love and concern for us.

Week 12: Monday
Cycle 1: Gen 12:1-9; Cycle 2: 2 Kings 17:5-8, 13-15, 18; Gospel: Mt 7:1-5
Cycle 1: 'All the tribes of the earth shall bless themselves by you.' In our first reading we turn back from St Paul to the Old Testament. For the next nine weeks we dip into the first seven books of the Old Testament, from the call of Abraham to the entry of the Promised Land. We may read it at three levels: a) as the history of God's dealings with Israel, his Chosen People; b) as a miniature of his programme for humankind in general; c) as an outline of the way he is leading each of us to the Promised Land.

There is a link between the three perspectives. Today we start at chapter 12 of the Book of Genesis. Chapter 11 has ended with the building of the tower of Babel. Symbol of man's pride in launching a challenge to God. God had responded by confusing their tongues, and scattering them around the world. Had God, then, abandoned humanity to its fate? Our chapter 12 begins the answer. No! God will restore humanity to his friendship by choosing and testing one man. And through him a people. And through that people all humankind: including you and me.

Cycle 2: 'They despised the covenant he had made with their ancestors.' The covenant of Sinai with Yahweh was the principle that made Israel one people. Entered into under Moses, its basic tenets were: 'You shall be my people; I shall be your God'. By this covenant God had adopted Israel as his special possession 'among all the peoples of the earth'. It was an act of love on his part: they had done nothing to deserve it. But the choice of Israel also imposed on it the responsibility of recognising Yahweh alone as God, and of keeping his commandments. In particular, Yahweh had rescued them from slavery in Egypt, and driven out other peoples from Canaan to make it their Promised Land. Through his prophets, from Moses on, Yahweh had reminded them of their obligations, and the penalty of disobeying the covenant. The instrument of their due punishment was the mighty power of Assyria. The ten northern tribes were deported as far as modern Iran. Would the remaining tribe of Judah heed this awful warning?

Gospel: 'Take the plank out of your own eye first.' Perhaps in the general context of Jesus' moral strictures, this one of not judging others may initially have been aimed at Pharisees, the self-appointed arbiters of moral correctness. But it needs little reflection to see how relevant it is to every generation: how germane it is to human nature to pass judgement on others. Some, indeed, like parents and moral guides, do have an obligation to be judges of right and wrong in the conduct of those in their charge. But first we must be aware of the common human weakness which makes us much more aware of others' faults than of our own. To a degree in fact which justifies Jesus' grotesque (carpenter?) image of the 'plank in your own eye'. And always we must keep in mind the positive example of the sinless Jesus even to the confessedly guilty: 'Neither do I condemn you'.

Prayer-lines: Lord Jesus, our Saviour, help us not to sit in judgement over others, but to imitate you in your desire to save and not condemn.

Week 12: Tuesday
Cycle 1: Gen 13:2, 5-18 ; Cycle 2: 2 Kings 19:9-11, 14-21, 31-36; Gospel: Mt 7:6, 12-14
Cycle 1: Our first reading continues its leisurely portrait of Abraham, harbinger of God's saving plan for humanity. We are struck at once by his peace and humility. For the sake of peace he defers to his nephew, Lot, in the vital matter of choosing pasture for their livestock. A sinister hint is then dropped that Lot's selfish choice will bode ill for him. Abraham's humble deference is rewarded by Yahweh's compensating promise of as much of the land as his gaze can take in. It foreshadowed the consoling vista which God would later accord Moses from the far side of the Jordon at the end of the long exodus from Egypt and from slavery. Abraham , still childless, is also promised an innumer-

able descendance. He now sets up his tent near Hebron where he will bury his wife Sarah. And in token of his faith in Yahweh's promise 'he built an altar to the Lord, and offered sacrifice'.

Cycle 2: 'I will protect this city and save it.' After the fall of Samaria, the northern capital, the camera of Old Testament history is now focussed on Judah and Jerusalem.. How will Judah fare, for it, too, has been defiled by idolatry? King Hezekiah at least, lights the torch of hope. He destroys all the idolatrous hill-top shrines and cult effigies. But when Assyria threatens Judah too, his faith weakens, and he buys them off with Temple and palace treasures. Today's reading tells of a second invasion, and here Hezekiah shows more faith and trust in Yahweh's power to save. In this resolve he is encouraged by the great Judean prophet; Isaiah's oracle assures the king of God's intervention, both for his own divine honour and his promise to David. As a result, the siege of Jerusalem is promtly raised.

Gospel: 'A narrow gate and only a few will find it.' Tobit in the Old Testament had already advised his son, Tobias, 'do to no one what you would not want done to you'. It has been called the Golden Rule, and the world would be a happier place if all tried to observe it. But Jesus raises the standard by making the rule positive: 'Treat others as you would like them to treat you.' It is an invitation to take the initiative in loving, not just in self-defence. We are coming to the end of the Sermon on the Mount, and Jesus is under no illusions about the difficulties of his path for the natural man. The way of Jesus leads through a gate too narrow for the pride of the Pharisees, the avarice of the rich, the sensuality of the many. Jesus urges us not to follow 'the wide and spacious road that leads to perdition'. It is the road of the crowd that so many of the media tempt us to follow. So often the road of the god Mammon. The motive that Jesus gives us else-where for entering the narrow gate is: 'for my sake and the gospel'. He who follows me does not walk in darkness.'

Prayer-lines: Lord Jesus, make us attentive to the breath of your Spirit that we may always choose the way that leads to life.

Week 12: Wednesday

Cycle 1: Gen 15:1-12, 17-18; Cycle 2: 2 Kings 22:8-13; 23:1-3; Gospel: Mt 7:15-20

Cycle 1: 'Abram, I am your shield.' Once more the land and posterity were assured to Abraham. His faith would indeed be rewarded. So well might Abraham raise an objection to God: 'I go childless.' Yahweh's promise of land and posterity was very welcome to the ageing nomad, but Abraham had no son of his own to inherit these promises. Yahweh now reiterates his word by pointing to the stars of heaven – so overwhelming at night against the desert sky. 'Abram put his faith in Yahweh.'

Cycle 2: The covenant whose utter violation had led to the downfall of Samaria is again in question in our first reading. Good king Hezekiah has been succeeded – for fifty-five long years – by the arch-idolater, Manasseh, who flouted all that Moses had preached in the Book of Deuteronomy. In some form this book had been concealed in the Temple during Manasseh's reign, and came to light in the repairs being made in the exemplary reign of king Josiah. When Shaphan had read out before the king the chapters which warned Israel against idolatry, Josiah was appalled at what had happened before this time. A general assembly of all the people was called, the covenant of Sinai was renewed, and fidelity to the law of Deuteronomy was enforced. As we shall see, however, the reform was already too late. Judah would share in the fate of Israel, and be led into exile in Babylon.

Gospel: 'You will be able to tell them by their fruits.' Moses in the Old Testament concluded the terms of the Covenant with exhortations and warnings before his people should enter the Promised Land. So, too, Jesus, having traced the contours of his Way, the new Law, ends with similar injunctions to caution. True prophets in the Old Testament had often to battle with false prophets, usually backed up by those in power. In the new Testament there would also be people claiming to be inspired. Discretion, therefore, is called for. The acid test of prophecy is an upright life. So, after all, there must be someone accredited to judge which conduct is 'good fruit', and what is bad. We need constantly to refer to Jesus' own conduct to assess the soundness of others' lives.

Prayer-lines: Lord Jesus, let us keep your example always before our minds so as to be guided always by your Spirit.

Week 12: Thursday
Cycle 1: Gen 16:1-12, 15-16; Cycle 2: 2 Kings 24:8-17; Gospel Mt 7:21-29

Cycle 1: 'The Lord has heard your cry of distress.' Despite the mysterious covenant of Yahweh with Abram after dark, his faith was to be further tested. Ten years passed in Canaan without a child and Sarah's patience (whatever of her faith) is exhausted. She invokes a current law of those regions which allows her to secure a child through her slave-girl, Hagar. Abram agrees, but once Hagar becomes pregnant she makes no secret of her feeling superior to her mistress. Driven away by Sarah's harsh treatment, an angel finds her resting on her way back to her native Egypt. She too has prayed to God, and her prayer was heard. She, too, will have a numerous descendance. Their name will be 'Ishmaelites', literally 'The God-has-heard' tribe, now known to us as the Arabs.

Cycle 2: 'All the men of distinction were led into exile in Babylon.' The curtain is beginning to fall on Judah, on the house of David. Josiah's gallant attempt to crush idolatry and reform worship in Judah ended suddenly with his death in battle. The new enemy is the rising power of Babylon which has crushed Assyria. Judah's turn for punishment has now come, as the prophets foretold, for Manasseh's long term of corruption. All the portable wealth of Jerusalem is borne away. So, too, is the grandson of king Josiah – to remain captive in Babylon for the rest of his life. So also are all the potential leaders of revolt. The king's uncle, however, is left in charge. His name is changed to Zedekiah to indicate his vassal status. Judah's survival with whatever is left in it will now depend on her loyalty to Babylon.

Gospel: 'A sensible man who built his house on rock.' Jesus is

21621621621621621621621621621621621621216216216216216216216216216216216216216216221621621621621621621621621216216216216216216216216 FEED FROM THE TREE OF LIFE

ending his course on religious wisdom. There will be an exam to pass – not merely on our attendance, our mere listening, but on our putting into practice by our deeds. To put it another way, building won't be an easy job: rain, floods and gales may be expected. Is it worthwhile building? Yes, if we build on a firm foundation, on rock. What style? There are plenty of contractors. The traditional life of our forebears? The advertisements of the mass-media? The example of the world? All no good. The only sure style is Jesus' teaching. Can we outline that ? Yes. Matthew has done so in three chapters: serve God and our neighbour: not only outwardly, but from the heart. Treat God as our Father and our model; and treat others as caringly as ourselves.

Prayer-lines: Lord Jesus, help us to be true disciples, serious learners in your school of wisdom, that you may recognise us as your own on the day of judgement.

Week 12: Friday
Cycle 1: Gen 17:1, 9-10, 15-22; Cycle 2: 2 Kings 25:1-12; Gospel: Mt 8:1-4
Cycle 1: 'This is my covenant.' The covenant which God makes with Abraham foreshadows the one he will make at Sinai with the whole people of Israel. The rite of circumcision, performed subsequently soon after birth is not, as elsewhere, a rite of initiation for boys at puberty, but meant to be a sign of a special relationship with God. It expresses the sacramental character of life in the biblical tradition. God is the author of nature, as of grace, and can choose nature (as, for example, in marriage) as a channel of the supernatural. Not that grace is bestowed as it were automatically through nature, by merely outward rites and gestures. In all our contacts with God, with one another, with the events of life, we must be engaged from our hearts.

Cycle 2: 'He burned down the temple, the palace, and the houses in Jerusalem.' The curtain is finally rung down on the kingdom of Judah. Despite Yahweh's pleading through Jeremiah, the ineffectual king Zedekiah rebels against Babylon, and swift retribution follows. As long as the Temple still stood and a king, however impotent lived in the palace, some hope for the future could remain. Now all has ended in disaster. Unlike the account of Samaria's fall, the historian forbears to comment on the guilt of the people involved. Is it a sign that the story is not yet ended for Judah? At all events, the horrors of the last days of Judah speak for themselves despite the laconic narrative. The famine raging in the city; the futile attempt at escape through a breach in the walls; the king's sons slain before his eyes as he is captured; he himself blinded and led off to Babylon in chains. Tomorrow we shall hear Jerusalem's lament.

Gospel: 'And his leprosy was cured at once.' We have seen Jesus' authority as a teacher. We now see it in his healing power. Matthew keeps a steady balance between Jesus' teaching and now his miracles. Mark, from whom Matthew borrows much, prefers to emphasise the miracles, and puts flesh and blood on them. Matthew is more laconic and will omit reference to feelings. But today he conveys Jesus' readiness to heal, and even to touch what was regarded as unclean. His sending the healed leper to the priest shows his respect for the injunctions of the Law. It is more important for us to remember that the gospels were written not so much to record the past as to reveal the present reality of Jesus' power. We too, can share the faith of the leper in today's story. And we, too, can be certain of Jesus' readiness to hear us and his power to grant our requests.

Prayer-lines: God our Father, increase our faith in your constant presence with us in Jesus, and in your love and power to solve our problems.

Week 12: Saturday
Cycle 1: Gen 18:1-15; Cycle 2 Lam 2:2, 10-14, 18-19; Gospel: Mt 8:5-17
Cycle 2: 'Oh yes, you did laugh.' If our patience (like Abraham's and Sarah's) has surely been tried by God's repeated but unfulfilled promise of posterity to Abraham, it is surely rewarded today by this unique story from Genesis. No need to repeat the skillful narrative. Just to pick out some unforgettable vignettes.

Abraham caught dozing on a hot afternoon at his tent door. He doesn't hear the 'three men' until they are upon him. But his ready hospitality galvanises him – and Sarah inside the tent. Abraham has picked out the central figure of the three. 'My Lord', he addresses him. He stands, alert, while they are eating in the shade of the tree. His guest's divinity shows through in his perceptive references to Sarah, and her desire for a child. And if he did challenge her embarrassed lie about 'not laughing', he surely did so with an understanding smile. Perhaps the best approach of the many – to this delightful tale is to take it as a paradigm, a model of how to meet God in our prayer, and hear his Good News. If we need a visual aid as Christians, we have it in Rublev's immortal icon.

Cycle 2: 'Virgin daughter of Zion, who can possibly cure you?' The second Book of Kings could narrate the fall of Jerusalem in dispassionate prose. The poet who wrote the five Lamentations can wring our hearts with his images of a totally overwhelmed people. As they had fondly imagined, they were God's chosen and beloved people. He had lived in their midst in Solomon's Temple. Now they see him in horror as their implacable enemy overwhelming them in his anger. 'Who, indeed, can comfort you, virgin daughter of Jerusalem?' Today we read only one portion of the Lamentations. They will end, however, on a note of hope. 'Make us come back to you, Yahweh, and we will come back.' So must end all the griefs we are asked to share with God in our lives.

Gospel: 'Many will come from East and West to the kingdom.' Like the leper's cure yesterday, today's is also in response to faith. And like the Canaanite's daughter later on, this one takes place at a distance. Like that miracle too, this one is also remarkable in being wrought for a Gentile, a forecast of the future mission to the Gentiles. If the centurion's faith could be a warning to disbelieving Jews in Jesus' time; in Matthew's time, some fifty years later, and still in our own day, it can equally caution Christians against complacency about inheriting the kingdom. At all events, the liturgy of the Roman Mass has preserved the centurion as a role model for our prayer in the eucharistic words; 'Lord, I am not worthy. Say only the word ...'

Prayer-lines: Lord Jesus, may our daily readings from Scripture increase our faith in their revelation of your Father's love and will to save us.

Week 13: Monday

Cycle 1: Gen 18:16-33; Cycle 2: Amos 2:6-10, 13-16; Gospel: Mt 8:18-22

Cycle 1: 'Shall I conceal from Abraham what I am going to do?' Yesterday we left Abraham showing us how to welcome God into our lives, however unexpectedly he appears. He is still our role model today. God indeed wants us to share our lives with him. Still more, he wants to share with us his plans for humanity. Welcoming God by prayer leads to discussing with him the great problems of human existence. God wants us to debate these with him. Today Abraham has learnt that God is on his way to punish the notorious guilt of Sodom and Gomorrah. But what of the good people there who must therefore suffer with the guilty? Familiarity with God in prayer makes us share in the sufferings of others. Abraham's reverent debate with God, near-eastern style, reveals that even a handful of just folk can save a majority from their punishment. May our prayers, then, be always society-concerned.

Cycle 2: 'For the four crimes of Israel I will not relent.' In our first reading these days we return to Israel, that is the northern tribes which seceded from Judah after Solomon's death. But this time it is not to the fortunes of the kings there as in the colourful days of Elijah and Elisha. We survey the religious decline of Israel through the writings of the so-called 'classical prophets'. The first on the scene is Amos, a rough-spoken herdsman from Tekoa, south of Jerusalem. No professional prophet, then, but simply and suddenly ordered by God to go up north and reproach Israel with its crimes. In God's eyes its greatest crime is social injustice, oppression of the poor in every form. The verdict of guilty is already passed. God's retribution is on its way.

Gospel: 'Master, I will follow you.' In the context of Matthew's gospel this would seem to be a significant occasion. We are still in the wake of Jesus' long Sermon on the Mount. Jesus has shown his unique authority as teacher, and again as healer of physical illness. Lepers, who represent those marginalised in society, and even Gentiles have been healed by him. No wonder Jesus sees a large crowd around him, and decides to cross to the far side of the lake of Gennesareth. A scribe, we are told, in the crowd, that is a student of the Mosaic Law, has been particularly impressed by what he has heard and seen. He has been magnetised by Jesus, and will follow him 'anywhere'. Yet Jesus is in no hurry to encourage such devotees. Are they really prepared to pay the cost of discipleship? To enter by the narrow gate? To be a disciple is to share in the hardships: sickness, bereavement, whatever: are we able to accept them as part of our discipleship, of being followers of Christ?

Prayer-lines: Lord Jesus, grant us a true spirit of discipleship, that we may always give the claims of your kingdom priority in the decisions of life.

Week 13: Tuesday
Cycle 1: Gen 19-15-29; Cycle 2: Amos 3:1-8; 4:11-12; Gospel: Mt 8:23-27
Cycle 1: 'God kept Abraham in mind and rescued Lot.' Abraham's intervention, we saw, will save Sodom if even ten just men are found there. However, the flagrant abuse of the laws of hospitality on the two angels' arrival is taken as proof that there is not even a minimum of justice to be found there. Sodom is, therefore, justly doomed. How to save Lot, though? He is a reluctant evacuee. He makes no attempt to reach the hills as the angels advise. And his wife too will pay the penalty of her curiosity by looking back. Such is the folklore explanation of the rock formation on the shore of the Dead Sea, itself something of a lunar landscape even today. The moral of the tale for ancient Israel was the inevitable punishment by God for people and places where injustice was rampant.

Cycle 2: 'Israel, prepare to meet your God.' 'The Lord speaks: who can refuse to prophesy?' Amos, we saw, is no professional prophet, ready to couch God's message in bland terms congenial to the powers that be. Bluntly he lays bare this basic guilt of Israel. Chosen by Yahweh above all other nations by his rescuing her from Egypt, raised from the gutter, so to speak, she has flouted the marriage bond. Former warnings by military disasters have not been enough to alert her, though they have left her 'like a brand snatched from the blaze'. Therefore, Amos insists, his oracle must come true. Israel must now gird itself to face up to Yahweh as its foe. What Christian society in economic prosperity ('Celtic tigerhood', etc.) can flatter itself, especially in matters of social justice, that it may not incur God's punishments for mass infidelities?

Gospel: 'Even the winds and the sea obey him.' Storms, even today, do break suddenly over the Sea of Galilee. And Mark's gospel, on which Matthew's depends, gives us a more vivid account of the scene. 'Jesus was in the stern, his head on the cushion asleep'. And the disciples are really in a panic, as they shake him with an unceremonious, 'Master, don't you care? We're going down.' High drama indeed. But Matthew's gospel is primarily interested in the church, and he too is right in seeing the episode as a parable. He might even have said, 'The kingdom of heaven is like a boat in a storm, with the skipper fast asleep in it'. And Jesus' reproach to the crew holds good for every Christian generation, 'why are you so frightened, you men of little faith?' For Jesus, even while the boat seems in mortal danger, always has the power to subdue the storm.

Prayer-lines: Lord Jesus, increase our faith in your presence with us and with your church, and in your power to overcome any threat in our lives.

Week 13: Wednesday

Cycle 1: 21:5, 8-20; Cycle 2: Amos 5:14-15, 21-24; Gospel: Mt 8:28-34

Cycle 1: 'The slave-girl is your child too.' At last in today's first reading we see God's promise to Abraham and Sarah fulfilled: Isaac, ('son of God's friendly laughter'), is born. And after three years is weaned – an occasion for a great banquet, for he has now passed the critical stage of infant mortality. Great joy for Sarah naturally, too. But a serious worry for her too, seeing Abraham's and Hagar's boy and *her* son playing together. God's promises, she knows, are for her son. She cannot risk Ishmael sharing them. He and Hagar must leave. Harsh measures indeed, but Sarah is fighting for *her* life too. Abraham's fatherly heart is torn, but God reassures him. He will bless Ishmael too, and make him a great nation as well. We should treasure these signs of God's concern for all peoples. Racism is not according to God's will.

Cycle 2: 'I hate your feasts … let justice flow down like water.' Amos has bidden Israel to meet God as her enemy. 'But what's wrong with us?' they complain. 'Don't we offer sacrifices to him with the best of music in our worship.' Amos parodies the words of their liturgy: 'Seek me that you may live.' 'Seek *good*', he corrects. 'Maintain justice at the gates' – the regular place in Israel for cases to be heard. God, he continues, can take no pleasure in worship that is belied by injustice to the poor. His commandment is: 'Love your neighbour as yourself.'

Gospel: 'They implored him to leave the neighbourhood.' While Matthew's account of this miracle is much shorter than Mark's, it makes the same points: the demonic confession that Jesus is the Son of God; and Jesus' power to expel the devils from the demoniacs. But it may be more to the point to read the episode as a parable of our relations with God. He can show himself in our lives, as Jesus did in this story, in contrasting ways. As he cured the demoniacs, so he may clear up some major problem for us: sickness, an examination or a job. And for this we are truly grateful. But as the loss of a large herd of pigs seemed to their disgruntled owners, God can also inflict some great loss on us at times: the death of some one we love, or the loss of possessions, or our good name. Instinct may prompt us to ask God to leave us alone, as the Gadarenes did to Jesus. *We* can see what a great mistake that was on their part. Let us guard against going it alone. Let us always welcome his presence, for it is always a sign of his love, and for our good.

Prayer lines: God, our Father, increase our faith in your love and providence, and help us to recognise your nearness in all the events of life.

Week 13: Thursday

Cycle 1: Gen 22:1-19; Cycle 2: Amos 7:10-17; Gospel: Mt 9:1-8

Cycle 1: 'God himself will provide.' The story speaks for itself; no reference to feelings is expressed. 'God put abraham to the test', it starts. 'What again?' we exclaim. Yes. This is the last time, the climax of all the others. Rationalists have protested at the callousness of a God thus portrayed. But the readers always know the outcome: 'God himself will provide.' What matters is the theology behind the story. God is the inscrutable master of life and death. But he can be utterly trusted by us. 'Because you have not refused me your only son, I will shower blessings upon you.' Abraham does indeed deserve to be a channel of blessing for all nations. May we pray to imitate his faith in all *our* testings.

Cycle 2: '*You* say: do not prophesy ... Very well, this is what the Lord says.' Our first reading today gives us a narrative interlude in the oracles of Amos against Israel. From it we get a clear idea of the opposition which the prophetic role is pledged to meet in life. Amaziah's 'Go away, seer', expresses his contempt for this sycamore trimmer. 'Get back to the land of Judah', spells out that Amos is a foreigner in this northern sanctuary. 'Earn your bread there.' Amos, as must we, hardens his face against such opposition and proclaims the word of the Lord. Grant us, Lord, the courage always to be true to your word..

Gospel: 'They praised God for giving such power to men.' This was a dramatic miracle on Jesus' part. Matthew does not shirk the challenge which Jesus is giving to the religious sensibilities of the scribes present in saying, 'Your sins are forgiven'. Only God can forgive sins. And at his trial later on, it is for blasphemy that Jesus will be condemned to death. But Matthew's interest is in the church of a later generation too. He is thinking here also of this divine power which Jesus has entrusted to the church after his resurrection. To all of *us*, in the sacrament of Reconciliation, Jesus says, 'Take up your bed and walk' – with me to the Father.

Prayer-lines: Lord, increase our faith in your love for us and the power you can give us to proclaim your truth in our lives.

Week 13: Friday
Cycle 1: Gen 23:1-4, 19; 24:1-8, 62-67; Cycle 2: Amos 8: 4-6, 9-12; Gospel: Mt 9:9-13
Cycle 1: 'Isaac was consoled for the loss of his mother, Sarah.' Our first reading today gives us only the bare bones of a magnificent story to which the bible devotes two long chapters. I recommend them to you as bedtime reading. Abraham, we saw, has proved that he accepts Isaac, the child of the promise, as the gift of God. He now symbolically fulfils the second promise, of possession of the land of Canaan, by buying a plot of land in Canaan for Sarah's burial. It only remains now to see that Isaac responds properly to the promise. He does fulfil it, literally and visibly, by taking a wife Rebekah, from the ancestral homeland in Syria, and settling down with her in Canaan. From what the story tells us of Rebekah's qualities, we can see that she would be a real consolation for him after Sarah's death.
Cycle 2: 'Seeking the word of the Lord, and failing to find it.' Amos' oracles were the great revelation to Israel of Yahweh as the God of social justice. As such they are particularly relevant to us today. When Amos was sent north to preach at Bethel, Israel was revelling in the military and economic benefits of a long and successful reign. The leaders attributed their success to their fidelity in Yahweh's worship (keeping the New Moon feast free from business, etc.). But Amos, insists that this empty worship is valueless. For they can hardly wait to get back to their

business the next day. And their business is a matter of cheating, to make money by false weights and scales. They have failed to see that justice to the poor, especially, is an essential part of the covenant with Yahweh. His punishment, therefore, is decreed and inescapable. Famine on the land thus polluted by injustice, still worse, 'famine of his word'. God will silence his prophets so that they will no longer give the people guidance.

Gospel: 'What I want is mercy, not sacrifice.' A prophetic echo, indeed, on Jesus' lips. The prophets could reveal God only by their oracles. Jesus can reveal him in his person. Today, he starts by calling a tax-collector to join his intimate following. Tax-collecting was one of the trades held to be open to ritual uncleaness, (with camel-drivers, herdsmen, etc.). It was also regarded as collaboration with the Romans. And then Jesus proceeds to join in a friendly meal with these marginalised folk: a gesture unthinkable for a Pharisee. But Jesus here is not trying to flout the law. He is seeking (as 'the one whom God has sent as saviour') to gather in the marginalised, the lost sheep, into God's people. The Pharisees had hardened God's religion into a matter of self-conscious observance of a multitude of petty practices. – Can we find any vestiges of Pharisaeism in our own religious practice today?

Prayer-lines: God, our Father, thank you for revealing your truth to us in the words and conduct of Christ. Help us to live by that truth in our life and judgement.

Week 13: Saturday

Cycle 1: Gen 27:1-5, 15-29; Cycle 2: Amos 9:11-15; Gospel: Mt 9:14-17
Cycle 1: 'May the sons of your mother bow down before you.' The drama of the promises to Abraham continues in today's first reading. It has grown more complex by Rebekah's bearing twins. Progenitors of two rival peoples, she is told, while they are still unborn. Very different personalities, too: Esau, the hunter, preferred by his father; Jacob the stay-at-home, favoured by his mother. Jacob has already tricked the nonchalant Esau out of his first-born birthright, swapped for the famous 'mess of pot-

tage'. Today's reading tells us how Rebekah conspires to win Isaac's farewell blessing for Jacob – again by trickery. God can, we see, write his plans straight with our crooked lines. And the promise will, therefore, pass on to Jacob's family, not Esau's. But Jacob will still have many a trial to endure before he dies. Nor will God's final blessing to us be ours, except according to this pattern.

Cycle 2: 'I mean to restore the fortunes of my people.' Of all the writing prophets of the Old Testament, Amos is the most pessimistic. For him Israel has irredeemably abused its privileges as God's covenanted people by utter political and social corruption, and must therefore pay the penalty. Today's first reading, however, is a direct contradiction of this message. The scholars are therefore agreed that it is an editorial addition to the earlier message of Amos. Its hopeful tone, however, is justified by the overall tenor of the prophets in general. Yahweh's final word is not punishment but forgiveness and restoration. It is a lesson to which we are all entitled when we are oppressed by the sense of our failures.

Gospel: 'The bridegroom is still with them.' The traditional Jewish interpretation of the Song of Songs, the great Old Testament dialogue of two lovers, sees God as the groom. Jesus here interprets his presence among his disciples as a messianic wedding-feast. And this is certainly no time for fasting. Indubitably his teaching has brought a great novelty into the contemporary religion of the Pharisees. This novelty is expressed in the 'Our Father'. The humble but loving fidelity of a son to his father's will, and a confident dependence on him for all his needs. A new 'cloak' indeed for the wearing before God, a new wine to soften the structures of religion. Fasting, however, is a time for expressing grief, and such times will certainly lie ahead for Jesus' disciples. Above all, of course, at his death but always in memory of his Passion.

Prayer-lines: God our Father, thank you for the new garments, the new wine of our Christian faith. May we keep them always new by our constant attachment to the person of Jesus.

Week 14: Monday

Cycle 1: Gen 28:10-22; Cycle 2: Hos 2:16-22; Gospel: Mt 9:18-26

Cycle 1: 'Truly the Lord is in this place and I never knew it.' Jacob, at his mother Rebekah's request, is setting out alone into the unknown. (Haran, his ancestral home in northern Mesopotamia, is no small distance on foot from Beersheba, his home, near Gaza). He needed this night experience of God's universal control (by angels going up and coming down to earth) of human life. And also the assurance of God's special concern for Jacob himself. This is all the more striking in the light of what we have already seen Jacob to be: timid and deceitful, and tied to his mother's apron-strings. And there is more worldly carry-on to follow when Jacob reaches Haran. A consoling contrast this between human frailty and God's kindly power. We can make too much of human weakness – especially in others. As Christ would say to Paul: 'My power is at its best in weakness.'

Cycle 2: 'I will betroth you to myself with faithfulness.' Hosea's message to an idolatrous Israel will resonate down the centuries, into the New Testament and beyond. For he has, it would seem, already lived it out painfully in his own life. Warmly affectionate in disposition, though his own wife has proved faithless to him, he loves her still and is prepared to take her back into their first intimacy. He has no difficulty then in seeing Yahweh's relationship to Israel as parallel. Though Israel has left the true God to whom she was married by covenant, and turned to the fertility cult of Baal, Yahweh still loves her. He will revive in her, her original love for him when he rescued her from Egypt, and cared for her in the desert. Then he will again be her husband ('Baal', in Hebrew). We too can always be restored to God's love and favour through the sacraments.

Gospel: 'If only I can touch his cloak, I shall be well again.' Mark's gospel too has this account of two consecutive miracles in vivid detail. But he takes more than twice as long to retail it. Matthew is, however, more interested in its theological message: Jesus is master not only of health but even of life. And even to touch his cloak with faith brings healing. What a lesson for us today who can eat his Flesh and drink his Blood. And even at the faith-inspired request of another, this time of a child's father, Jesus' touch can restore to life.

Prayer-lines: Lord Jesus, increase daily our faith in your nearness to us, your concern for our well-being, and your power to answer all our needs.

Week 14: Tuesday
Cycle 1: Gen 32:23-33; Cycle 2: Hos 8:4-13; Gospel Mt 9:32-38

Cycle 1: 'Because you have been strong against God, you shall prevail.' Four chapters of Genesis have elapsed since Jacob's dream at Bethel. They detail the very earthy adventures of our hero at Haran, with his uncle Laban and his wives. Twenty years have passed, and Jacob is now returning from Syria to Palestine richer by two wives and two concubines, eleven sons and innumerable cattle. God has indeed lived up to Jacob's prayer at Bethel. And yet Jacob is not to enter the land of promise without a mysterious struggle by night: a struggle imposed on him by God, the God who has tested Abraham so sorely by the sacrifice of Isaac. Jacob, now a new man, is prepared to fight, and even be wounded – but ready to win the blessing by struggle and endurance. It is a lesson for us all.

Cycle 2: 'They have set up kings, but not without my consent.' Hosea continues to reproach Israel (or 'Ephraim', the major tribe of it) for its idolatry. He sees the root of it in the political schism, which began after Solomon's death. Jeroboam, the first king of Israel, had actually been made king and urged by a prophet of Shiloh to revolt against Judah with the ten northern tribes in punishment for Solomon's idolatry. The 'Golden Calves' which Jeroboam set up in the northern kingdom (at Bethel and Dan) were not erected as idols, but as pedestals for Yahweh's invisible presence – to rival his presence in Jerusalem. So reasoned Jeroboam. But with the course of time the people of Israel had drifted into the prevailing worship of nature Gods around them. The proverbs indeed can hold true in our own time – what is begun with harmless intention can often lead to ruin; what is sown as a mere wind, eventually becomes a whirlwind.

Gospel: 'Ask the Lord to send labourers into his harvest.' Jesus' final miracle of healing today causes sufficient stir among the people to arouse the hostility of the Pharisees. This is a dangerous man, they feel, not just a harmless wonder-worker. But for the moment Jesus is free to continue his mission of revealing the kingdom by word and healing power. What he found was disturbing: a general lack of religious leadership, and a consequent lack of people's hope in their relationship with God. It was time, then, for Jesus to send out his own followers to continue his work by power and deed. 'The harvest is rich.' The labourers will always be unequal to the amount of good that needs to be done. They must look to God, 'the Lord of the harvest', both to send more labourers and to give them the grace they need to work untiringly to spread the good news. Only a community of earnest prayer can assure a supply of worthy pastors for the church.

Prayer-lines: God our Father, we thank you for the harvest of salvation which Christ won for us by his dedication to the mission you gave him.

Week 14: Wednesday
Cycle 1: Gen 41: 42; Cycle 2: Hos 10; Gospel: Mt 10:1-7
Cycle 1: 'Go to Joseph and do what he tells you'. Some ten chapters of Genesis have elapsed since we saw Jacob returning to Canaan with his eleven sons. Joseph is the eleventh of them, and these ten chapters tell his dramatic story. Sold by his ten older brothers into captivity, by his virtue and God-given talents he has risen to a position of unique influence in Egypt. When his brothers come down from Canaan for grain they fail to recognise him. But he recognises them, and is moved to tears when he hears of his father Jacob, and his younger brother, Benjamin. He begins to foresee God's plan for fulfilling his promises to Jacob and his descendants. We shall meet him again this week.

Cycle 2: 'It is time to go seeking the Lord. Yes, indeed, as Hosea says in today's first reading. 'Israel was a luxuriant vine' in God's plan, so as to yield plentiful fruit. Hosea was writing at the end of a long and prosperous era in Israel. But her sin was her failure to recognise Yahweh as the author of that prosperity. For Hosea it is Yahweh (and not the local Baals) who is the source of nature's fertility. And their kings have failed them because their true King is Yahweh. How often in history has it not happened that material prosperity has yielded a godless cult of wealth instead of a harvest of integrity and true religion. The Gospel message of Jesus will always remain relevant: seek first the kingdom of God and his justice and all these other things will be given to you as well.

Gospel: 'Proclaim that the kingdom of heaven is close at hand'. Yesterday we saw Jesus sorrowing over a people that were 'like sheep without a shepherd'. Today he begins his campaign to establish the kingdom of heaven for the Lord of the harvest'. The Twelve sent out are not just messengers, but 'other Christs'. For they carry his power and his tasks – to cast out devils and cure diseases – as well as his message, 'the kingdom of heaven is close at hand'. The number twelve is symbolical of the restoration of all Israel, the twelve tribes. The mission to the whole world will not be given until after his resurrection, though it is indirectly implied before that. The 'lost sheep of the house of Israel' will cover especially those marginalised by the religious leaders of the time for 'not knowing the law'. This is a commission entrusted in various ways to Christians of every generation.

Prayer-lines: Lord Jesus, increase our desire to share in every way we can your work for the salvation of all people.

Week 14: Thursday
Cycle 1: Gen 44, 45; Cycle 2: Hos 11:1-3; Gospel Mt 10:7-15
Cycle 1: 'God sent me before you to preserve your lives.' Perhaps nowhere else in the Bible – till we come to some of Jesus' parables – is theology so well served by such narrative skill as the story of Joseph. Where else does so much weeping occur in a single tale? Equally striking is the portrayal of character throughout. What overcomes Joseph's self-restraint so irresistibly is

Judah's narration of Jacob's heart-rending words about Benjamin. For Joseph they revive memories of the special affection his father had for him as a boy. And the final drama of the whole story is now prepared in the reference to the guilty dismay of brothers, who can foresee only that they must now pay the penalty for their heartless crime against their younger brother. But Joseph is more than a model of Old Testament virtue. He is a figure of Christ, and prefigures Christ's role in our redemption.

Cycle 2: 'I am the Holy One in your midst and have no wish to destroy.' This is one of the high-water marks of God's self-revelation in the Old Testament. Through the voice of Hosea he has pitilessly unmasked Israel's sins of idolatry and hypocritical worship, and the retribution for them that must follow. But punishment cannot be God's last word for his people. Hosea is uniquely qualified to portray a father's unconditional love for a sullen child: one he has taught to walk, one he has held against his cheek and spoon-fed. 'My heart recoils from it. My whole being trembles at the thought.' How close it brings us to the mystery of the incarnation. 'God so loved the world that he sent his only Son, not to condemn the world, but that the world may be saved through him.'

Gospel: 'You received without charge. Give without charge.' Our gospel continues Matthew's 'mission discourse' to the Twelve. If it forbids even the footwear or the staff (a defence against robbers or wildbeasts), which are allowed in Mark's gospel, it is in order to emphasise the urgency of their preaching the good news of the gospel. Since Vatican Council II we have been reminded that the whole church is missionary. Can we really say at the end of a century of unprecedented bloodshed and inhumanity that the good news is any less urgent today than in the Roman world of Matthew's time? We must, therefore, bestir ourselves to see if there is, beyond our traditional support for missionary bodies, any new way of spreading the kingdom of heaven. I think, for instance, of the present concern for justice in society and between nations. And also of the need of promoting unity and trust with Christians of other denominations.

Prayer-lines: God our Father, increase in us our love for human-kind, that we may be more active in sharing freely with others the good news of Christ which you have shared so freely with us.

Week 14: Friday
Cycle 1: Gen 1-7; 28-30; Hos 14:2-10; Gospel Mt 10:16-23

Cycle 1: 'Now I can die, now that I have seen you again.' This is Jacob's *Nunc Dimittis* in the first reading. And it does indeed seem the happy ending of the Jacob saga. He has seen Joseph alive and prosperous: the saviour in fact of the whole family. And yet it is only the end of the prologue – at least of the story of God's Chosen People, of Jacob's descendants. This story will begin (next week) in the Book of Exodus. And we know what a chequered history it will be: more black squares than white. But Jacob is not told of this: he has already suffered enough in his own life. ('Few and unhappy have been the years of my life', he will tell Pharaoh when they meet.) He is spared the knowledge of what his descendants will suffer. Not so the Twelve in the gospel, the symbolic descendants of Jacob's sons. But in both readings the keynote is courage, because God is present, and that is enough. Enough too for us, in our legacy of trials.

Cycle 2: 'I will love them with all my heart.' Despite the irrevoc-able sentence which Yahweh has pronounced on his faithless people, Hosea's final message is one of hope. For he foresees that his people will repent. She will renounce her political al-liances (that are bound up with alien gods). She will renounce too her military plans ('we will not ride horses anymore'); and finally put an end to the idols 'which our hands have wrought'. But it is Yahweh who brings about this change of heart: 'I will heal their disloyalty'. He will achieve this by his love. And, to show the strength and tenderness of that love, Hosea draws freely on the vocabulary of Israel's love-songs: 'the fragrance of Lebanon; bloom like the lily; the wine of Lebanon; live in my shade'. All this delightful fertility to follow Israel's repentance will show her that it is Yahweh alone who is the master of life and fertility.

Gospel: 'The Spirit of your Father will be speaking in you.' Yesterday Jesus promised the Twelve they would have in their missionary task the same powers as he had himself over demons and sickness. They would be bringing a message of peace. But today he dispels any illusions about the reception their message would meet. Tomorrow he will urge them, 'Be not afraid.' But today he speaks plainly about the possible motives for fear. 'Beware of men.' Scourging by Jews and worse from Roman governors. Suffering was already experienced by the prophets of old. The Acts of Apostles and St Paul's Letters show how quickly it also became the lot of Christians after the resurrection. The clue to its inevitability – and to coping with it – is the example of Jesus himself. For the same Spirit of the Father by which he bore witness unto death will be in them too.

Prayer-lines: God our Father, increase our faith in the presence and power of your Spirit in us to enable us to bear witness in our lives to the coming of your kingdom.

Week 14: Saturday

Cycle 1: Gen 49:29-33; Cycle 2: Is 50:15-26; Gospel Mt 10:24-33

Cycle 1: 'Is it for me to put myself in God's place?' Our first reading today gives us the happy ending of the Joseph story. And the saga of the patriarchs ends on a note open to the future: God's chosen people in Palestine. Above all, this passage reveals the true greatness of Joseph, the ideal Old Testament figure, not merely in his magnanimity towards his undeserving brothers. (He has to weep again at their fears of his taking vengeance once their father is dead!) Outstanding is his faith in God's active presence in historical events and his consequent humility: 'Is it for me to put myself in God's place?' Is that not a question we might all of us at times put to ourselves? How often do we arrogate the divine prerogative of judgement in our condemnation of others?

Cycle 2: Our first reading for the next few days will introduce us to the greatest of the writing prophets, Isaiah. Greatest in length, indeed, with sixty-six chapters in the Book of Isaiah. But greatest too in other ways: in the span of his message, from the eighth to the fifth centuries BC. We read him *in extenso* in Advent, for in various ways he foreshadows the mystery of the incarnation. He has even been called 'a fifth gospel'. But, like all the prophets, his message is stamped by the historical conditions of his time, and especially by the relationship obtaining in successive periods between Israel and her God. And Isaiah's calling to be God's mouthpiece is unique. He is 'the Holy One of Israel'. Morally holy, indeed, but primarily as transcendentally other to his creation and humankind. This we glimpse in today's account of Isaiah's calling to be God's mouthpiece. No sinecure to be called to bring a sinful people ('of unclean lips') to its senses before the judgement of a transcendent God.

Gospel: 'Do not be afraid.' Fear is indeed a key concept in today's gospel. The disciples' very human dread of having to share their Master's fate: opposition, calumny, even death. Nor should they be afraid, he bids them, even if they should have more to suffer than he. For they will have to preach in public what he has taught them privately: that human fear must be overcome by a deeper impulse than fear of bodily injury. They must above all submit to him who is the supreme power. But this is a totally different kind of fear. Because this all powerful one is a loving Father to whom all his creatures are precious, and none more so than Jesus' disciples.

Prayer-lines: Lord Jesus, grant us a share of your filial love and reverence for your father which will overcome in us all human fears.

Week 15: Monday
Cycle 1: Ex 1:8-14, 22; Cycle 2: Is 1:10-17; Gospel: Mt 10:34-11:1
Cycle 1: 'The more they were crushed, the more they increased.' Today in our first reading we begin the great story of God's deliverance of Israel from slavery in Egypt. Jacob's family, with the passage of time has now become a people enslaved in an alien land.

Yahweh's promises to the patriarchs of Israel about becoming a chosen people destined for a promised land seem now quite forgotten. Pharaoh now seems completely in control of their destiny: hard labour, and even extinction by killing the male children. For the New Testament writers this story was the paradigm, the basic pattern of what God did for us in Christ (which is why we read it at the Easter Vigil service). But it is also the paradigm of our lives as Christians: suffering, prayer for deliverance; God's saving intervention.

Cycle 2: 'Take your wrong-doing out of my sight.' Our first reading today gives us an initial sample of the message that Isaiah has volunteered to give his 'people of unclean lips' on behalf of 'the Holy One of Israel'. While addressed primarily (in the strongest terms: 'you rulers of Sodom') to the leaders, it also concerns the rest of the people. God could not put it more clearly. What time can he have for the people's elaborate ceremonial of worship when it is accompanied by social wrongdoing. Here the prophet is surely echoing the Law of Moses and of the Wisdom books. God makes a special plea for the weaker members of society. 'Help the oppressed, be just to the orphan, plead for the widow'. So God's appeal for justice is allied to his disgust for empty ceremonial. There is still time for the people's repentance. All is not yet lost.

Gospel: 'Not peace I have come to bring, but a sword!' What kind of Good News is this? Not peace'? What of our daily reminder to Christ at Mass, 'My peace I give to you.' Yes, but Christ went on to say (Jn 14:27), 'peace the world cannot give, that is my gift to you'. The Christian message, though Good News, is essentially one of paradoxes, of contradictions and tensions. It is summed up in the great tension between life and death – expressed in many ways. You must lose your life for Christ, to 'find' it. His Good News is for the poor, often materially so, but always for the 'poor in spirit': For those, that is, ready to look to God for their needs. But those who 'find their life' in self-reliance, in creature comforts, even in self-assured goodness, will lose it.

Like the pharisee complacently at prayer in the Temple, they will not 'go home again at rights with God.'

Prayer-lines: God our Father, thank you for teaching us the wisdom of the Cross so often in Scripture. Help us to live no longer for ourselves, but for him who died for us and rose again.

Week 15: Tuesday

Cycle 1: Ex 2:1-15; Cycle 2: Is 7:1-9; Gospel: Mt 11:20-24

Cycle 1: 'The Lord listens to the needy.' Words from the Responsorial Psalm. Our first reading yesterday ended on a note of near despair. Not merely are the Hebrews crushed by hard labour for the Egyptian masters, but the baby boys are sentenced to death by drowning. It is a dramatic context for Moses' birth and deliverance (echoed in Matthew's Infancy Gospel by Herod's attempt to kill the 'new born king of the Jews'). The infant Moses will indeed be thrown into the river, but by God's providence this will give him access to a royal education and 'all the wisdom of the Egyptians' (Acts 7:22). Yet the astutely contrived suckling by his own mother will ensure his ethnic solidarity with the Hebrews. His initial adult attempt to help them, however, will meet with the recalcitrance which will mark every stage of their deliverance at his hands.

Cycle 2: 'If you do not stand by me, you will not stand at all.' Our first reading today gives us a dramatic confrontation between Isaiah and Judah's king, Ahaz. This time it is not a question of hollow worship belying social injustice. It is a question of naked faith in Yahweh, who has promised to guard his people. For Jerusalem is in real crisis. Israel, the northern kingdom, and Syria or Aram have allied together to force Judah into a revolt against Assyria, the super-power in the East. Ahaz and his people panic and prepare for the siege by its neighbours, but will end by calling in Assyria's help. For Isaiah it is an acid test of Judah's faith in the power and protection of Yahweh. Through his prophet, Yahweh dismissed the threat of Syria and Israel (they are shortly to be overrun themselves by Assyria). Only by faith in Yahweh can security be achieved. Otherwise 'You will not stand at all'. For us, too, in life's trials, it is only by faith in God we can be at peace.

Gospel: 'Jesus began to reproach the towns.' St Matthew tells us that after John the Baptist's arrest Jesus left Nazareth and settled in the lakeside town of Capernaum. It was here and in the neighbouring towns of Chorazin and Bethsaida that he had preached and worked many miracles. The fulfilment, as Matthew sees it, of Isaiah's prophecy: 'The people that lived in darkness have seen a great light.' That indeed was the goal of Jesus' life-work: to be the true light; 'to prepare a people fit for God', and thus be a light of salvation for the whole world. The people, however, had failed to accept him, notably after the discourse on the Bread of Life. Jesus here foretells the severity of the judgement they must face for their unbelief. It is a salutary reminder to us that all the many graces we have been given will have to be accounted for on the day of Judgement.

Prayer-lines: Lord Jesus, increase our faith in the part you have been pleased to play in our lives, and make us increasingly ready to do your will.

Week 15: Wednesday

Cycle 1: Ex 3:1-6, 9-12; Cycle 2: Is 10:5-7, 13-16; Gospel: Mt 11:25-27
Cycle 1: 'I shall be with you', was the answer. One of the pivotal events of the Old Testament, indeed, of the whole Bible: the call of Moses, and the proclamation of Israel's deliverance from Egypt. History apart, we can legitimately take it as the pattern of our encounters with God, both in life and in prayer. We note the apparent unexpectedness of God's epiphany. Moses is apparently finished with Egypt, and his thoughts elsewhere. But God's thoughts are with his chosen people in Egypt and their situation under oppression. God can seem to call us 'out of the blue'. But, for Moses, his message is always one of concern, and a promise to save. His call may also be a commission to be an agent of his saving work. And if, like Moses, we shrink from new responsibilities, God's reassuring message will always be the same, 'I shall be with you.'

Cycle 2: 'Woe to Assyria, rod of my anger.' As with Israel's other prophets, Isaiah's oracles are directed primarily to Israel, the Chosen People. But, again, like other prophets, Isaiah never forgets that the 'Holy One in Israel' is God of all the earth, master and judge of all the unchosen peoples. In his wisdom God can use any of these peoples as his agents and instruments for furthering his plans. In punishing Israel, for instance, for its infidelity to his covenant with it. Assyria was a classic example of this in Isaiah's time, as Egypt before and Babylon afterwards. But God will also judge and punish such instrumental peoples for the pride in their power which they may yield to, or their inhumanity. In our own times we may discern similar examples of God's judgements in history. At all events, this truth of God's concern for all humanity must reinforce our ongoing prayer for peace on the whole earth.

Gospel: 'I bless you, Father.' We are gazing into fathomless depths of revelation as we catch Jesus at prayer in today's gospel. Only in John's gospel can we find its equal. 'No one knows the Father except the Son.' Here is the basic expression in the Synoptics of Jesus' divine nature. As Wisdom in the Old Testament rejoiced to be at the Father's side at creation, 'ever at play in his presence, delighting to be with the sons of men', so Jesus rejoices here at being the Light of revelation, the Light of the world to the pure of heart, the poor in spirit. Let us in our prayers share in that mutual joy revealed to us so spontaneously. The joy of the Father at Jesus being his perfect image in mankind; the joy of Jesus in sharing with us the vision of his father's goodness and saving plans.

Prayer-lines: God our Father, we thank you for revealing yourself to us in the Scriptures, and above all in your Son, Jesus. May our whole lives reflect the sincerity of our gratitude.

Week 15: Thursday

Cycle 1: Ex 3:13-20; Cycle 2: Is 26:7-9, 12, 16-19; Gospel: Mt 11:28-30

Cycle 1: 'I am who I am.' God's assurance yesterday to Moses that he would be with him was not enough, Moses thought. He must have the name of the God who is sending him if he is to convince the Hebrews. Scholars debate the exact translation of 'I am who I am', but they agree that it expresses God's intent to display his creative power in Israel's future. He foresees Pharoah's reluctance to let the people of Israel go: but this will provide him with an opportunity to display his irresistible power. *We* also need to allow God to show his concern and power in overcoming the difficulties we anticipate in doing his will. Nor should we be bashful in encouraging others to express their faith in the same way.

Cycle 2: 'Your name, your memory, are all my soul desires.' God's name is not an empty name. When he revealed it to Moses at the burning bush, it was a pledge that he would show his loving concern for his people in their distress, and his power to save them. This he continued to do throughout their chequered history of unbelief, infidelity, repentance and ultimate rescue. 'Lord, you are giving us peace, since you treat us as our deeds deserve.' We should nourish our faith on the memory of what God has been in our lives, even from our childhood. And let this memory grow into an ever-firmer hope for the future. 'Awake, exult ... and the land of ghosts will give birth.'

Gospel: 'And I will give you rest.' In today's gospel Jesus turns to us as Wisdom personified, in fact as God's law, and therefore God's will in person. He quotes an appeal which God had made through Jeremiah before the fall of Jerusalem. An appeal to return to the way marked out by the covenant of Sinai: 'Take it, and you shall find rest', he begs them. Wisdom in the Old Testament is personified as a woman, and there is certainly a maternal tone in Jesus' appeal to us today, as one who is 'gentle and humble', and offering rest. The 'rest', of course, is the kingdom of God. His yoke is his teaching, by word and in person. In comparison to the 613 regulations of the Pharisees his yoke is indeed 'easy and light'. But, of course, it is far more demanding by the total commitment it requires. With God, however, as Jesus assures us, 'all things are possible' and he is with us always.

Prayer-lines: Lord Jesus, give us the faith to come to you in prayer for the rest you promise us, and make us faithful in our commitment to you.

Week 15: Friday

Cycle 1: Ex 11:10-12:14; Cycle 2: Is 38:1-6, 21-22, 7-8; Gospel: Mt 12:1-8

Cycle 1: 'I shall deal out punishment on all the gods of Egypt.' Our Mass readings have skipped the dramatic account of the nine plagues by which Yahweh revealed the meaning of the name he had revealed to Moses at the burning bush: 'I am who I am.' Nothing can replace an intelligent reading of these four carefully crafted chapters on God as Master of creation. We now come to the climactic last plague. Even before the first plague Yahweh's message to Pharaoh had been: 'Israel is my first-born. You refuse to let him go. So be it. I will put your first-born to death.' But the blood of the Israelite's sacrificial lamb, sprinkled on the doorposts would keep them safe. And so we read this passage every year on Holy Thursday to remind us of the Last Supper, where Jesus transformed the shadow into reality. The blood is now the blood of the Lamb of God: the deliverance from Egypt the taking away the sins of the world.

Cycle 2: 'The Son of Man is master of the Sabbath.' – In yesterday's gospel, Jesus, as teacher of wisdom, promised that his disciples would find his yoke easy. Today's gospel gives us a glimpse of what the other 'yoke' could be, for the Pharisees spoke of 'the yoke of the law'. Around the single Decalogue precept to keep the Sabbath day holy, their scruples had built a hedge of thirty-nine kinds of work forbidden on the Sabbath. Plucking ears of corn they would regard as the forbidden 'reaping'. Jesus rebuts their scruples by two Old Testament exceptions they would have to respect. David, who did not hesitate to take the Temple bread offering for his followers on the Sabbath. And the Temple holocaust and libation, which was work meant to continue on the Sabbath. How much more, he suggests, should they respect the authority of the Son of Man, present in the person of Jesus.

Prayer-lines: God our Father, we thank you for sending your son Jesus into the world to show us the true way to you at all times.

Week 15: Saturday
Cycle 1: Ex 12:37-42; Cycle 2: Mic 2:1-5; Gospel: Mt 12:14-21
Cycle 1: 'All the array of the Lord left the land of Egypt.' Thus was Yahweh's promise to Abraham in the now distant past fulfilled: 'Your descendants will be slaves and oppressed for four hundred years … After that they will leave with many possessions.' In the death of the first-born of the Egyptians, Yahweh had indeed passed judgement on the people that oppressed Abraham's descendants. He would now lead them out by Moses to the desert where they could worship him, the God of their ancestors, and by solemn covenant become his chosen people. And 'as the Lord kept vigil for them that night to bring them out', this coming out, or exodus, would be commemorated every year by the Hebrews by a solemn vigil. And so Christians keep vigil on Holy Saturday night for God's great deliverance of the baptised by Christ's rising from the dead.

Cycle 2: 'So the Lord says this, "Now it is I who plot".' Micah is the last of the 8th century BC prophets who would witness the downfall of the kingdom of Israel, and the deportation of the ten northern tribes by Assyria. He is a contemporary of Isaiah, but from a small town in the lowlands of Judah, not a city man like Isaiah. He is, therefore, all the more competent to plead the cause of the small people, the socially oppressed. With the inauguration of kingship the original sense of equality in Israel has suffered, and class distinction became the rule. Micah denounces the greed with which those in power took over the lands of the poor. We think, for example, of the rape of Naboth's vineyard under Ahab. Now it will be God's turn to plot against the rich, and to despoil them by an alien invader. And then the unjust will lose even their share 'in the community of the lord'. – Can we claim that prophetic warning against social injustice is irrelevant in our generation?

Gospel: 'Here is my servant, the favourite of my soul.' The hostility of the Pharisees towards Jesus with which our gospel today opens is contrasted by Matthew with the Father's attitude to the Suffering Servant, Isaiah's prophetic portrayal which Jesus has fulfilled by his healing, his teaching and in his person. We are familiar with Jesus leading us to his knowledge of the Father. 'No one knows the Father except the Son, his Image. We should learn to see Jesus more through the Father's eyes: his beloved messenger who 'does always the things that please him'.

Prayer-lines: God, our Father, may our daily discovery in your Scriptures of your loving plans for our salvation lead us to the knowledge and love of Jesus Christ in whom they are fulfilled.

Week 16: Monday
Cycle 1: Exod 14:5-18; Cycle 2: Mic 6:1-8; Gospel: Mt 12:38-42
Cycle 1: 'The Lord will do the fighting for you'. But the high drama of Israel's Exodus is not yet completed. The full revelation of Yahweh's supremacy has still to be revealed. Our passage captures all the conflicting emotions of the dramatis personae. The exultation of the Pharaoh and the Egyptians as they vengefully pursue such an easy prey. The panic of the sons – and even more, no doubt, of the daughters of Israel at the sight of the Egyptian army in rapid pursuit of them. Finally, the prophetic calm and courage of Moses, who has total confidence in God. The story is a model to inspire every generation with hope in God's saving power in the face of overwhelming odds.

Cycle 2: 'This is what the Lord asks of you'. Yahweh is here pleading a lawsuit against Israel, as he has already done through Amos, Hosea and Isaiah. The whole cosmos is the lawcourt: mountains, hills and foundations of the earth. In the context of our Good Friday liturgy, at the adoration of the Cross, the reproaches are unbearably poignant. 'My people, what have I done to you?' The people's confession of guilt, then, is understood before the triple query of, what is the right way to serve God. The answer is 'No' to all three suggestions. What Yahweh wants is an internal conversion, issuing in just dealing, fidelity and goodness, and a sincere love in return for God's.

Gospel: 'The only sign it will be given is the sign of the prophet Jonah'. Jesus referred, of course, to the sign of his death and burial. For the unbelieving, a sign of total failure. In reality it meant for him life with God, the only triumph that matters. The scribes and Pharisees were asking for a flamboyant exhibition of Jesus' power: a sign of victory. It is not to be Jesus' way: the way of the Suffering Servant: God's way. And God's way demands the leap of faith. And it seems that it is the most unlikely people that God makes capable of this leap of faith. Jesus refers to the Gentiles. Nineveh of the dreaded Assyrians: the Queen of Sheba. And these too as impelled only by an obscure Judaean prophet and a distant Judaean king. Are we too in danger of being one day condemned at not making better use of the means of faith so lavished on us since our childhood?

Prayer-lines: Lord Jesus, make us daily more receptive to the guidance of your Spirit, that we may trust you at all times, especially when difficulties arise.

Week 16: Tuesday
Cycle 1: Exod 14:21 - 15:1; Cycle 2: Mic 7:14-20; Gospel: Mt 12:46-50
Cycle 1: 'Israel witnessed the great act the Lord had performed'. The whole event of Israel's rescue and Pharaoh's defeat has been ritualised for observance in later generations. Two different prose traditions are combined. In one Moses extends his rod; the waters part and the people walk across the piled-up waves to the far side. In the second account Yahweh, the storm-God leads his people in a holy war against Pharaoh and his host. By a strong wind he drives back the sea, thus provoking the Egyptians to pursuit. At dawn he blows again and the waters re-

turn to their bed and the Egyptians are drowned. ('Red Sea' we may note is a traditional mistranslation of 'Reed Sea', indicating a swampy area). At all events the narrative remains for us a parable of what God has done for us in Baptism, and continues to do in every Mass.

Cycle 2: 'As you swore to our fathers long ago'. In the chapter before our first Reading today Micah has given us one of the gloomiest of prophetic oracles about Jerusalem's guilt. But our passage would seem to have been added after the return from exile, and sounds a contrasting note of hope. It follows a liturgy of repentance, in which Zion admits her former sin. Then comes Yahweh's assurance of forgiveness and restoration. He will remember his promise to the patriarchs, wipe out Zion's sin and show his mercy, his 'loving-kindness'. It is a message of hope for every Christian generation too. The opening image of Yahweh's 'shepherd's crook' reminds us that our Good Shepherd is always ready to go in search of his lost sheep.

Gospel: 'Who is my mother? Who are my brothers?' The fact that it was not easy to get close to Jesus when he was teaching indoors is clear from all the synoptic Gospels. Mark, who is often Matthew's source, also relates this episode. But a few lines earlier, he tells us that on a similar occasion in Nazareth his relatives set out to take charge of him, saying, 'He is out of his mind'. Matthew, like Luke, omits this Nazareth reference. He simply makes Jesus avail of this opportunity of designating his disciples as being his true family. He is not denying his natural ties, but emphasizing the priority of the bond of common discipleship in the new family he was forming. When we exchange the sign of peace at Mass we should renew in our will the primacy of Christian family-hood given us in baptism.

Prayer-lines: Lord Jesus, may our scripture reading at Mass renew our joy and gratitude at the union with you and one another given us through baptism.

Week 16: Wednesday

Cycle 1: Exod 16:1-15 Cycle 2: Jer 1:1-10 Gospel: Mt 13:1-9

Cycle 1: 'Then you will know that I am your God.' The escape of Israel and the rout of the Egyptians was indeed a memorable victory. But many more trials still awaited the people to test and strengthen their faith in Yahweh. Food, of course, is the first concern of a people in the desert. 'An army marches on its stomach'. Manna was God's first answer to this problem, that light glucose secretion on desert bushes, which Arabs still call 'mann'. And, as for meat, a sudden change in the wind carrying migratory quails causes them to collapse from fatigue and be easily caught. No reproach is made so far against the people for their murmuring. They have not yet reached Sinai, and made their covenant with Yahweh. They are only 'novices' in desert life. But we have been 'professed' by our baptism – to trust God as our Father for our 'daily bread', and all our other needs.

Cycle 2: 'I consecrated you as a prophet to the nations'. For the next two weeks we shall be following the fortunes of Jeremiah, the prophet whom Jesus, for many of his contemporaries, resembled most. Like Moses at the burning bush, Jeremiah shrinks in dismay at being called by God for a mission. He is still only a young man. God brushes aside this excuse. Nor may fear have any place in him now, for 'I am with you to protect you'. And, with a single gesture, God places his message in Jeremiah's mouth. It is a two-fold message: to uproot what is evil, but also to build up what is good. To some extent it is indeed a forecast of Jesus' Good News of the kingdom. And in fact every Christian has the same guarantee of God's protective presence.

Gospel: 'Other seeds fell on rich soil'. Jesus certainly preferred an outdoor audience, and a boat on the lakeside provided a useful pulpit. And the mainly rural audience in such a rural setting would suggest an appropriate image for his message: 'a sower going out to sow'. Although the seed sown would meet many difficulties in bearing fruit, some of it was destined to be fruitful, though in varying degrees, 'some a hundred fold, some sixty, some thirty'. We are asked to listen and reflect, and no doubt, try to identify ourselves among these varied seeds.

Prayer-lines: Lord Jesus, may your Holy Spirit give us willing ears to hear what God is telling us through these messages in Scripture.

Week 16: Thursday
Cycle 1: Exod 19:1-20; Cycle 2: Jer 2:1-13; Gospel: Mt 13:10-17
Cycle 1: 'The Lord came down on the mountain top'. Three months after Israel's victorious escape from Egypt the people arrive at Sinai, the central stage of their historic exodus from slavery to the Promised Land. God descends upon the mountain in a dense cloud, traditional symbol of divinity. Moses' credibility, always somewhat in jeopardy with a volatile people, will be upheld as they hear God speak to him from the cloud. But the people must purify themselves from the profane world before God comes down upon them. The entire mountain becomes sacred by God's descent on it. Our description shows signs of the later liturgical celebration of this momentous religious occasion by trumpets and incense. The letter to the Hebrews reminds us of our Christian privilege of being spared such a terrifying introduction to God by being brought instead to Jesus, the mediator of a new covenant.

Cycle 2: 'I remember the affliction of your youth'. Two, generations have passed since Isaiah and Micah have prophesied, but the reign of good king Hezekiah in Jerusalem has been followed by the long and religiously deplorable rule of Manasseh. Now under Assyrian sway, Jerusalem and Judah have relapsed into idolatry. Once again, therefore, through Jeremiah, Yahweh is pleading a law-suit of marital infidelity against Jerusalem. Israel's desert period is idealised as a honeymoon with Yahweh, fresh from their marriage covenant at Sinai. The bridal imagery of Hosea is renewed. But priests, political leaders and court prophets have all proved false. The whole cosmos is invoked to deplore such unimaginable infidelity and folly on Jerusalem's part. 'I remember the love of your bridal days'. Penitent review of one's relations with God are never irrelevant to Christians either, collectively as in Lent, or individually.

Gospel: 'I tell you solemnly, many longed to see what you see, and never saw it'. Scholars have remarked on the uniqueness of Jesus using. 'I tell you solemnly' before a statement. Are we listening here to his own very words, and not just the evangelist's? At all events, it is a summons to pay special attention. And the theme is our special privilege as Christians. We are not even a very large fraction of the world's population. If we find it hard to bring home to ourselves that blessedness, let us at least follow St Paul's example of ceaselessly thanking God, in faith, for our faith, however lightly it may seem to sit upon us. And in counterpoint to this motive for gratitude is the motive for unease at the prophecy of Isaiah: 'They listen without hearing'. Far better off then those who haven't heard of Christ than, say, countries of the west who have heard and still hear, but fail to accept. Again too an object of prayer. As Paul prayed for the conversion of his people, so must we that the once-Christian lands of Europe return to Christ.

Prayer-lines: Lord Jesus, help us increasingly to value our faith and do all we can to share it with others.

Week 16: Friday

Cycle 1: Exod 20:1–17; Cycle 2: Jer 3:14-17; Gospel: Mt 13:18-23

Cycle 1: 'I am your God who brought you out of the house of slavery'. Yahweh has indeed shown himself to be the true master of Israel by rescuing then from Pharaoh. Will his people now accept him as such and agree to do his will? The framing of the Ten Commandments in the second person singular suggests an intimacy grounded upon a personal relationship with God rather than on an impersonal legislative system. They are indeed a summary of man's duties in life to God and his fellow creatures. But even from the beginning they were not looked on by Israel as restrictions on its freedom. In Hebrew they are called simply the ten words. And in the words of the Psalmist they were looked on as ten lamps for man's steps. The negative form indicated the wide sweep of freedom of conduct which God allowed his people. Christ would fulfil this teaching by showing that all God's requirements were fulfilled by love – 'the fulness of the Law'.

Cycle 2: 'Come back, disloyal children, for I alone am your Master'. Jeremiah has reproached Jerusalem with not learning from the fate of Israel, the Northern Kingdom, deported by Assyria one hundred years earlier for her infidelity to Yahweh. Instead, Jerusalem has continued her cult of false gods. Yahweh himself, therefore, will take the initiative and give her worthy shepherds, that is rulers, to lead her wisely. The Ark of the Covenant in the Holy of the Holies on which he had formerly been enthroned will no longer be the seat of his presence. The whole city of Jerusalem will be his throne instead. And to this presence the other nations will come flocking, disowning their own gods. As Christians we may still pray for these promises of Jeremiah to be fulfilled. There will always be need for wise rulers in Church and state, and the acceptance in all lands of Christian values.

Gospel: 'And so he produces nothing'. We have already heard the parable of the sower a few days ago. Or perhaps better the parable of the seeds, who are the centre of attention. We have already seen the main point of the parable. The ultimate good harvest from the sowing. But today Matthew treats the parable as an allegory, with each item having its particular meaning. He is writing in the light of early church experience, some fifty years after Jesus. And it makes clear that there is no easy harvest in store for the seeds: trials and traps lie in wait for its growth. The key to growth for Matthew is 'understanding'. That is, the seed is not merely an abstract message. It is a deep invitation by God to the hearer to love him with all our heart and all our soul and all our strength. That understanding is the gift we must pray for as we listen to God's word.

Prayer-lines: Lord Jesus, word of God and sower of the seed, open our hearts and minds to the riches of eternal life which your sowing holds out to us.

Week 16: Saturday

Cycle 1: Exod 24:3-8; Cycle 2: Jer 7:1-11; Gospel: Mt 13:24-30

Cycle 1: 'This is the blood of the Covenant the Lord has made with you'. We are now at the heart of Israel's religion. The people 'with one voice' have agreed to all the commandments and ordinances laid down for them by Yahweh. This agreement is now enshrined in solemn ritual. The altar symbolises Yahweh. The blood sprinkled on it and on the people unites them in what the prophets see as a marriage bond: of protection on Yahweh's part, obedience on Israel's. For Israel blood is the symbol of life. This Covenant was the pivotal event of Israel's history and remains I suppose the paradigm of all religious commitment. Psychologists of religious development would call it the 'central stage', after the preparatory stage of childhood. But it is the subsequent stage of 'actualisation' that matters most: when the conscious commitment has to be lived out and integrated into the whole of life. – The rest of Israel's history will show how irregularly and fitfully this 'actualisation' followed.

Cycle 2: 'Do you take this Temple for a robber's den?' Jeremiah had been called by God in his youth to begin by 'tearing up and knocking down' – all that was opposed in Israel to the Covenant at Sinai. Here we see him at the heart of his prophetic task. King Josiah had indeed brought off a sweeping reformation of idolatry in Judah, emphasising that the only authentic worship was to be that of Yahweh in the temple of Jerusalem. But the people had understood that in a one-sided way. If Yahweh was indeed enthroned in the Temple, in the Holy of Holies, that made Jerusalem safe from any hostile power. But Josiah had recently been slain in battle, and the people had relapsed into their idolatry, oblivious of their commitment to the Covenant. 'Steal, would you, murder, commit adultery? and then come in this Temple?' Yahweh answers his own rhetorical question. 'I, at any rate, am not blind. It is Yahweh who speaks.'.

Gospel: 'Let them both grow till the harvest'. Perhaps every generation is impatient to see Christ's victory 'sealed and signed', with evil overthrown. After the resurrection the disciples ask

Jesus, 'Lord, has the time come. And you going to restore the kingdom to Israel? 'Even in the second century, 'Second Perer' records sceptics asking, 'well, where is this coming?'. And he replies, "The Lord is being patient with you all, wanting nobody to be lost, and everybody to change his ways'? God's plan, in other words is that the good be not separated from the evil before the end. And the separation be not by human assessment, but by God's. It is for us then not to judge people or movements prematurely. And to have patience and trust in God even in face of the apparent triumph of evil.

Prayer-lines: Lord Jesus, thank you for making the new and eternal Covenant with us in your blood. By our daily celebration of that covenant help us to be as faithful as you to the work of our salvation.

Week 17: Monday

Cycle 1: Exod 32:15-34; Cycle 2: Jer 13:1-11; Gospel: Mt 13:31-35

Cycle 1: 'If it pleased you to forgive this sin of theirs'. After the solemn sealing of Yahweh's covenant with Israel, Moses goes up the mountain for instructions about the dwelling in which Yahweh will live among his people. But the people get tired of waiting for his return, and persuade Aaron to make them a golden calf as an effigy of their God. On the mountain Yahweh informs Moses of this apostasy. He threatens to destroy the people for such infidelity, and make a new people for Moses to lead. Moses nobly pleads for them and Yahweh relents. But when Moses comes down on the plain again he vents his wrath on Aaron and the people. He returns to Yahweh on the mountain to beg forgiveness for them. He himself is prepared to share their punishment if that forgiveness is not given. But Yahweh does forgive the people and promises to go with them to the Promised Land. In the whole episode Moses' nobility stands out in stark contrast to Aaron's weakness and the undeserving people.

Cycle 2: 'I had intended Judah to cling to me, to be my boast'. We may treat the text as a parable. A parable of what God thinks of the people of Judah and Jerusalem. He had intended them to be his glory by their fidelity to him and his Covenant at Sinai. Instead they have ignored the commandments and followed false gods. They have, therefore, become for him like a 'spoiled loin-cloth, good for nothing'. – We recall that as Christians we too have been chosen to cling to God and be his people, his honour, his glory.

Gospel: 'I will speak to you in parables and expound things hidden'. Chapter 13 of Matthew is a discourse consisting entirely of parables about the kingdom, the climax we may say, of Jesus' teaching. Today the first message is the mysterious growth of the invisible seed into its full impressiveness. If the seed is the word of God, 'and the Word was made flesh', then the kingdom is a Person who grows in us to his full stature. The leaven teaches us the surprising effect a small group can have in society. These are the mysteries we must watch, cherish and cultivate:

the growth of Jesus' mind, manner and Spirit in others and ourselves.

Prayer-lines: God our Father, open our eyes to the presence of
your kingdom in Christ, in our own lives, and the lives of others.
May we foster the growth of Christ in our thoughts, words and
deeds at all times.

Week 17: Tuesday
*Cycle 1: Exod 33:7-11, 34:5-9, 28; Cycle 2: Jer 14:17-22; Gospel: Mt
13:36-43*
Cycle 1: 'The Lord would speak with Moses face to face, as a man
speaks with his friend'. A high-water mark, indeed, in Old
Testament revelation, a high point in the mystery of God's presence with humankind. For in a sense the whole Bible can be
summed up as the mystery of the presence of God. A friendly
presence from the beginning, with Adam and Eve. But a presence
rejected by them, and lost for their children. The rest of the Bible,
we may say, is the restoration of that presence with the 'children
of men'. Fugitive apparitions to individuals at first, in different
places and under symbols. It is for each of us to ponder these
and see how they are repeated for us. Today it is the symbol of
the Tent, God dwelling in our midst, in his mysterious way. A
presence fulfilled in the Incarnation. Jesus is God's perfect Tent.
In order to speak to us as to Moses, as friend. A God of tenderness.

Cycle 2: 'Have you rejected Judah forever?' If the Old Testament
can have its high points of joy, it has also its moments of deep
depression, almost despair. Our first Reading today expresses
one such dismal situation. War and famine have smitten Judah,
and Jeremiah gives voice to the misery of all. 'Lord, we do confess our wickedness'. He knows so well that the disasters are fitting punishment for the people's infidelity. Yet his faith in God's
fidelity to the Covenant of Sinai does not waver. He, at least,
does not trust in any other god to send the needed rain. Yahweh
is in fact responsible for the drought. ('It is you who do all this').
Yet Yahweh remains Jeremiah's hope because of the compas-

sionate God he is. – And we too, whenever we feel that our trials are due to our failing God, we must not forget St John's assurance. 'God is greater than our conscience'.

Gospel: 'The harvest is the end of the world'. Today's gospel explains the parable of the darnel sown among good grain as an allegory, giving a specific meaning to its seven elements. 'The world' here means humanity, with its evil elements as well as the good. The owner of the harvest has already explained that to root out the weeds before the harvest might damage the good grain. That does not mean that evil will go unrequited at the end of time. Nor indeed does it mean that evil in the world should go unchecked until then. No one parable can carry the full truth. Vatican II was not afraid to declare that the church is in constant need of reformation. Not indeed in order to make of its members a purist elite, but to aim at that difficult balance between patient tolerance and indifferentism.

Prayer-lines: God our Father, Lord of the harvest, increase our faith in your presence in us and in the world, and in your wise guidance of humanity towards salvation.

Week 17: Wednesday
Cycle 1: Exod 24:29-35; Cycle 2: Jer 15:10, 16-21; Gospel: Mt 13:44-46
Cycle 1: 'They would see the face of Moses radiant'. The Old Testament believed that no one could see God and live, Moses was the great exception who could talk to God face to face as a friend. It was natural, therefore, to believe that he would carry afterwards on his face something of divine splendour. St Paul later would ask if the giving of the (now superseded) Law could have such an effect, what must be the effect on Christians who bear the likeness of Christ? But what is at issue here is not one's facial appearance: it is a Christian's inward conformity to Christ. It is only the Father, 'who sees in secret': that can detect the glory of such an inward reflection of his beloved Son in us.

Cycle 2: 'I am with you, to save you and deliver you'. Jeremiah is unique among the prophets in revealing what we might call his 'spiritual life', his intimate relations with God. These intimate glimpses of his dialogues with God have been styled his 'Confessions', and can indeed serve as a model for our own prayer in time of distress. For, in today's passage, Jeremiah is on the point of despair. 'Why is my wound incurable?', he groans. He even accuses God of being a 'deceptive stream' for him, 'letting him down', as we say, to be a target for people's curses and insults. – But God's reply is quite firm. From the start he warned Jeremiah of the trials that lay ahead in his mission, but also of his protective presence with him. If Jeremiah will drop his complaining and 'utter noble, not despicable thoughts', then God will renew his prophetic commission, and will 'redeem you from the clutches of the violent'.

Gospel: 'He sells everything he owns and buys it'. Only Matthew has these twin brief parables, but they are striking ones. For all their brevity they have the power of an Impressionist's sketch. There are two major points being made. First the 'super-value' of the treasure and the pearl. Then the surrender of all one has for this once-in-a-lifetime bargain. But in common with these two messages is the rapidity and joy of the decision made to buy. Every aspect of the parables deserves pondering. They are both condensations of heavenly wisdom. Nothing can be compared with the treasure or pearl of the kingdom. And no half-measures are enough to win it. 'I count everything else as loss', St Paul will write. And this message of 'do it now and with joy', is counsel for us not only in major decisions, but for daily action in little things.

Prayer-lines: God our Father, open us up daily to the action of your Holy Spirit, that he may repeat in us the eagerness of Christ always to do the things that please you.

Week 17: Thursday
Cycle 1: Exod 40:16-21, 34-38; Cycle 2: Jer 18:1-6; Gospel: Mt 13:47-53
Cycle 1: 'The glory of the Lord fills the tabernacle'. Catholics are at a disadvantage with this translation: from infancy we have as-

sociated 'tabernacle' with the box containing the Blessed Sacrament outside Mass. The Hebrew word means 'dwelling'. And the dwelling of God with his people is the central feature of our first Reading today. We can see the intense importance this account had for Jerusalem priests, who edited it for a people in exile in Babylon, who longed to see their Temple restored. God's presence with his people is the heart of their faith, and Moses the Lawgiver their unique mediator with God. It is he, in today's account, who puts all the final touches on God's dwelling place. And the cloud, the only sign of God's presence that was allowed, was now to be their fellow-traveller, dictating every stage of their journey, to the Promised Land. –It is a symbol for us to remember in times when God's 'absence' may seem more real to us that his presence.

Cycle 2: 'As clay in the potter's hand, so are you in mine.' Perhaps this is the most typical example of a prophetic symbol of God's relationship with his people. Very simple, but very evocative. The origins of humanity in clay is a very common idea in the ancient neat East, and we met it already in the story of Adam's creation in Genesis. Here, however, it is a question of God's designs in history, not in creation. If the damp clay is not turning into the exact shape the potter wants, a flick of his fingers can remodel it. Here God is the potter. He can alter his decree of punishment for his people if they repent. And the converse is true. A prospective blessing on God's part can be changed by a people's perversity. Surely this is a vivid model to be kept in mind as we pray for ourselves and society. Our free will and our prayer have an important part to play in life and in world affairs.

Gospel: 'Brings out things both new and old'. The parable today of the dragnet is also proper to Matthew's Gospel. It has the same message as that of the darnel sown among the wheat. The world, and therefore also the church, is not an Èlite of perfect souls, but a mixed bag. We must be patient and tolerant within reason with evil elements in society, and trust that final judgement will be made by God. – But what of 'the scribe who became a disciple of the kingdom' and brings forth new things and old?

Matthew is not urging innovation in the moral law of the Bible, but fresh ways (like new parables) in presenting Christian teaching. It is an invitation to all who are responsible for passing on Christian truth. Clearly there were such Christian scribes in Matthew's own community. And Matthew has always been regarded as the prince of them. These words, therefore, about the Christian scribe are as it were his signature to his gospel.

Prayer-lines: Lord Jesus, increase our faith in your constant presence in our midst, and mould us in your image day by day.

Week 17: Friday
Cycle 1: Lev 23:1-37; Cycle 2: Jer 26:1-9; Gospel: Mt 13:54-58
Cycle 1: 'These are the solemn festivals of the Lord'. If God, as we saw, was to dwell in the midst of his people and be a fellow-traveller with them, this awe-inspiring presence had to be acknowledged regularly by solemn and festive ritual. Israel in fact borrowed much of its worship from older peoples, but she distinctively stamped it by linking their feasts with the saving events in her own history. These annual feasts were the normal and commonest ways in which people encountered the presence of their God. It was not only a matter of offering sacrifices. Prayer and song (in psalms, etc.) allowed people to share their personal lives, their joys and sorrows, with God in his presence. And this presence, though invisible was felt to be a powerful and dynamic force. Ritual indeed could lapse into formalism, as the prophets would point out. But that too could be offset by the strong communitarian sense in which Israel prayed. If we have inherited a number of Israel's feasts let us also borrow something of its joyful and social ethos as we come into the real Presence of God.

Cycle 2: 'The prophets whom I send so persistently to you without your ever listening to them'. We last saw Jeremiah learning the lesson of God's control of Israel's destiny as the potter has of his clay. Today we catch a glimpse of how unyielding to God's hands that clay can be. 'Perhaps they will listen ... Then I will relent'. Jeremiah, on Yahweh's behalf has already exposed the hypocrisy of the Temple worship of his day: grave social injustice as well as recourse to false gods. What should have been a house of prayer they have turned 'into a den of thieves'. But today he speaks God's ultimate sentence. Unless they repent he will destroy the Temple, as he had already let the Philistines destroy the sanctuary at Shiloh. This, of course, on Jeremiah's part was rank blasphemy, and 'you shall die' the inevitable reply of the religious leaders. We can see how this episode rang an ominous bell for the evangelists in their account of Jesus' trial.

Gospel: 'Where did this man get it all?' There is food for disquiet in today's Gospel. As we know, we listen to the gospel not just as history, as the record of what happened in the past, but primarily for its meaning to us in the present – Such as the accounts of Jesus' eagerness to heal the sick; his power to heal those with faith, etc. All three synoptic gospels testify that Jesus' powers, so dramatically shown after his baptism by John at the Jordan, astonished his townsmen. 'And they would not accept him'. How often may our own familiarity with good people not conceal from us the answer that evaded the Nazarenes: 'They got all this from God', and thereby glorify God for his gifts.

Prayer-lines: God our Father, increase our faith in your presence and power in your midst, and may your Spirit of love and justice inspire all that we do or say in our daily lives. Amen.

Week 17: Saturday

Cycle 1: Levi 25:1, 8-17; Cycle 2: Jer 26:11-16, 24; Gospel: Mt 14:1-12
Cycle 1: 'This is to be a jubilee for you'. The word 'jubilee' is defined from the Hebrew word for a ram's horn (*Yobel*) which was blown at the beginning of this 'year of liberation'. First to be 'liberated' was the land. Every 50 years it would remain unplanted, unpruned and unharvested. 'You will eat what comes from the fields'. Like the annual feasts, this was to be a deeply religious symbol. A symbol that land, with its homes and harvests belonged to no one but God. The Israelites wee in fact only his tenants. 'The jubilee is to be a holy thing to you'. The consciousness

that even the land belonged to Yahweh was intended to sanitise and hallow all social relations too, buying and selling especially. Even if the growing complexity of civil and urban life would mean in practice that this legislation remained largely an ideal, a blueprint, it was – and should be still for us – a salutary reminder of the basic principles of social justice.

Cycle 2: 'The Lord has truly sent me'. This indeed was the sign of a true prophet. And we recall how frequently in the gospel of John Jesus speaks of himself as 'the one whom the Father has sent'. The civic authorities are therefore emboldened to challenge the death penalty for Jeremiah pronounced by the priests and the court prophets. For one hundred years earlier the prophet Micah had also threatened the fate of Shiloh for the Temple. Then the king, Hezekiah, had heeded the warning and instituted a religious reform, which in fact had saved the besieged city. For the moment, then, Jeremiah is saved by a family that had supported the recent reform under King Josiah. Yahweh has kept his word to stand by his faithful prophet.

Gospel: 'John's disciples took the body and buried it; then they went off to tell Jesus'. There is something particularly poignant about the death of John the Baptist. The last time we met him in this Gospel he had sent two disciples to ask Jesus. 'Are you the one who is to come, or have we got to wait for someone else?' He had indeed baptised Jesus at the Jordan. To the crowds he had promised, 'The one who follows me will baptise you with the Holy Spirit and fire'. But the reports he had of Jesus were not of one who had come for condemnation and judgement. Jesus sent John back another prophetic description of the Messiah. 'The blind see again and the lame walk, lepers are cleansed and the deaf hear … And the Good News is proclaimed to the poor'. In other words a Messiah who was a blessing for the needy. – He went on then to praise John as 'the greatest', though the least in the Kingdom was greater than him, for John belonged to the Old Dispensation. He would not live to see the Spirit descend at Pentecost. And yet he would not be denied a share in Christ's glory. For, as we read today, he would precede him into death, so as to follow him into life after the Resurrection.

Prayer-lines: God our Father, fill us with the Spirit of your Son that we may bear worthy witness to you by our lives.

Week 18: Monday
Cycle 1: Num 11:4-15; Cycle 2: Jer 28:1-17; Gospel: Mt 14:13-21
Cycle 1: 'Who will give us meat to eat?' It is easy to see why the desert was so often looked on in the Bible as a place of trial, of testing and temptation. It was normal enough when the Israelites were newly come from Egypt. But now they had been over a year at Sinai. And they had become a covenanted people, with God dwelling in their midst, and committed to be their protector. It is their faith in Yahweh that is being tested. And Paul will warn the Corinthians that 'these things all happened as warnings to us. You can trust God not to let you be tried beyond your strength. And with any trial he will give you a way out of it and the strength to bear it'. He was certainly speaking from his own harsh experience. If our faith and our prayer lead us to look to God in our trials we will often find them the source of unexpected blessings in the rest of our life.

Cycle 1: 'Hananiah, the Lord has not sent you'. It is a crucial time for Jerusalem. A few years before, the king and many of the nobles had been carried off to captivity in distant Babylon, the remnant remaining vainly clung to a hope of a speedy return, and things as before. These were not God's plans, nor his message. He tells Jeremiah to appear before the people with a wooden yoke across his shoulders.

A symbol that God's design was that for the moment Babylon's power would prevail. Hananiah, a court prophet, confident that he spoke for popular hopes, challenges this message. He takes the yoke from Jeremiah and smashes it, as a sign of restoration for Jerusalem. But as God has not sent Hananiah, he is giving a false message. For this he will die. God will use Babylon's power as an instrument to purify his people. – Perhaps this is a lesson for us today in this century of unprecedented wars: may they purify humanity for an era of justice and peace.

Gospel: 'They ate as much as they wanted'. The gospels constantly set Jesus and his deeds in contrast to Moses in the Old Testament. In today's episode again, 'one greater than Moses' is shown. As Moses led Israel through the desert he frequently met the problem of a hungry and rebellious people. At one stage Moses seemed to have lost all hope and complained to God of his unendurable burden. Here Jesus meets a parallel situation with compassion and power. Having first healed their sick he now turns to the question of a meal for them. All of 5,000 men, mind you, not to speak of women and children. Perhaps then up to 30,000 or more. For Matthew, however, the whole account looks not so much back to Moses in the desert. 'He took the loaves, raised his eyes to heaven, said the blessing, broke the loaves'. All this solemn detail of the ritual looks forward to the institution of the Eucharist. So should it too for us – God's gift of himself for the salvation of the world.

Prayer-lines: Lord Jesus, nourish us daily with the wisdom of your word and the sacrament of your Body and Blood.

Week 18: Tuesday
Cycle 1: Num 12:1-13; Cycle 2: Jer 30:1-22; Gospel: Mt 14:22-36
Cycle 1: 'O God, please help her, I beg you'. While the Bible's value is primarily its revelation of God, and the kind of person he is, it is also prepared to show us human nature, even in its weakness. This is perhaps particularly true of the narrative of Israel's days in the desert. It was all very well for the people to know that God had made a covenant with them. That he had de-signed a tent-dwelling in which he would live among them and journey with them; that he would even communicate with them through Moses. But human egoism and pride would have its say too. And so today we hear Aaron and Miriam (for she too had shown herself a prophetess at the crossing of the Reed Sea'): 'Has God not spoken through us too? 'It is the primordial sin of trying to 'play at God', and is rightly punished. But the whole

incident serves to enhance Moses' magnanimity – in praying for the rebellious Miriam – as well as God's own witness to his unique intimacy with God.

Cycle 2: 'Now I will restore the tents of Jacob'. There is so much bad news for Jerusalem in the oracles of Jeremiah that he has entered the English vocabulary in the word 'Jeremiad' for a doleful complaint. But he is also the bearer too of great good news. And for the next three days we shall be hearing from what is called his 'Book of Consolation': certainly a high-water mark in all Old Testament prophecy. Today he does not gloss over Israel's desperate plight, her moribund condition, because she is already gone into exile: 'no medicine will make you well again, so great is your guilt, so many your sins'. And Yahweh admits, 'I have done all this to you'. But at once he adds a promise of restoration. 'The city shall be re-built on its ruins, the citadel restored on its site'. It is a prophecy that individuals as well as communities can read with consolation at times when all may seem lost.

Gospel: 'Man of little faith, why did you doubt?' We can take Jesus' prayer by himself at night as an historical model, and so it was imitated by the early Christian centuries. But the narrative as a whole would have been read or heard by Matthew's generation as a parable relevant to every Christian generation. There have always been times in the church's or some church's history when Jesus seemed if not asleep in the boat with them, at best remote, on the shore in a safety which his church lacked. And even when they rallied their wavering faith, he may have seemed 'a ghost', someone of the past and unable to help. In such times Jesus' message of comfort comes across the waves: 'Courage, it is I. Do not be afraid'. There have been perils for the church in every age, but Christ is always there, and 'the gates of hell shall nor prevail'.

Prayer-lines: Lord Jesus, may our daily Mass strengthen our faith in your presence with us and you power to save us.

Week 18: Wednesday
Cycle 1: Num 13:14; Cycle 2: Jer 31:1-7; Gospel: Mt 15:21-28

Cycle 1: 'This perverse community that has rebelled against me'. This would indeed seem the climax of Israel's failure to trust God. They are now within striking distance of the Promised Land. The scouts have brought back encouraging reports of its attractions, 'flowing with milk and honey'. And Caleb urges the people to go in boldly and take it over. But others make much of the size of the inhabitants, and the people's courage evaporates. They even vote to go back to Egypt, to undo, as it were, the Exodus, God's saving plan for them. Their lack of trust in Yahweh, despite all he has hitherto done for them, brings condign punishment. They shall die in the desert they refuse to exchange for the Promised Land. In moments of decision we too must often put trust in God before excessive caution.

Cycle 2: 'The Lord has saved his people, the remnant of Israel'. In our first Reading today we continue Jeremiah's 'Book of Consolation'. Its basic principle lies in God's, 'I have loved you with an everlasting love'. We might say that this sounds like the unconditional love of a mother for a defiant child, even if the child must first be punished, as Israel was by exile. – But now all that is over. Thee will be a new deliverance, a new Exodus. God will rebuild her ruins, and she can renew her feasts. For vine-yards will again produce on the sunny slopes of Samaria. And the northern tribes will be re-united with Judah, flocking down to worship at Zion. It is all a joyful rehearsal of the final happi-ness, when Christ will come in glory.

Gospel: 'Woman, you have great faith. Let your wish be granted'. Jesus' remarkable three-fold refusal is overcome by a mother's persistence. Obviously a model of persistent prayer in face of God's apparent deafness. But Matthew also sees another lesson here. Jesus has already worked a miracle for a pagan centurion, congratulated him on his faith, and prophesied a Gentile entry instead of Jews into the legacy of the patriarchs. For Matthew this is a parallel case. Jesus goes out of his way, twice, to state that the first offer of salvation is to Jews. But, though a Gentile, she has hailed him as 'Son of David', namely, 'Messiah'. So her faith is in him as Messiah, Master of the messianic table, where he dispenses the messianic bread of the kingdom to the church.

Prayer-lines: God our Father, we thank you for admitting us to the table of your children in the Promised Land. Grant that our lack of faith may never deprive us of our favours from you.

Week 18: Thursday
Cycle 1: Num 20:1-13; Cycle 2: Jer 31:31-34; Gospel: Mt 16:13-23
Cycle 1: 'Order this rock to give water'. After many years in the desert, which Israel is now preparing to leave, we are not surprised in today's first Reading at yet another round of Israel's complaints about the lack of water. This time, however, it would seem that even the leaders were weakening in their faith in God. Even though they did produce water from the rock, it was not simply by an oral command, a way in which God's mercy and 'holiness' would be revealed. As a result of this failure neither Moses nor Aaron would be allowed to enter the Promised Land. Perhaps St Paul is our best guide in considering this puzzling episode. Writing to the Corinthians he makes a parallel between the rock which could supply the needs of the Israelites and Christ who is all-sufficient for us as Christians. Certainly that was Paul's own key to life. 'All I want is to know Christ and the power of his resurrection' – in me. (Phil 3:10).

Cycle 2: 'I will plant my law, writing it in their hearts'. This is indeed a summit of Jeremiah's 'Consolation', for all of us as for Israel. Nowhere else does the Old Testament speak of 'a new covenant'. It is as if Yahweh, through Jeremiah, had plumbed the depths of Israel's' age-long infidelity, and resolved that it is flawed beyond repair, Certainly reading the narrative of the desert journey from Egypt alone would tend to that impression. And all its later history would show how fugitive the occasional national 'conversions' had proved. Yahweh will therefore recreate a new heart in them, which would give the people the power to observe his laws faithfully. Later prophets will speak of this as a new spirit, and of an 'eternal covenant'. At all events the

New Testament will see this promise fulfilled in Christ's paschal mystery and its memorial in the Eucharist. Let us brood with faith and gratitude on the gift of the new covenant in Christ.

Gospel: 'Simon, you are a happy man ... Get behind me, Satan'. What is striking in today's passage is the sudden juxtaposition of Jesus' congratulation of Peter, and his stinging rebuke. He is blessed by God's special revelation; he is decried, 'because the way you think is not God's way but man's'. It is a reminder of the mixture that is found in all of us: the alliance, in Pauline terms, of 'flesh' and grace. 'Flesh' in the sense of our flawed human nature. And grace as God's gift, supremely of his Spirit. As Paul will say, 'we carry this treasure in earthenware vessels'. A thought perhaps, to make us tremble, for ourselves. But also to prevent our sitting in judgement on others, who embody the same mystery. But a thought, finally, to comfort us when we reflect that God did not revoke his gift to Peter even after his denial of Christ.

Prayer-lines: God our Father, make us always gratefully conscious of your gift to us in Christ. Implant in us the law of your Spirit that we may walk always in Christ's footsteps.

Week 18: Friday

Cycle 1: Deut 4:32-40; Cycle 2: Nah 2:1, 3:1-7; Gospel: Mt 16:24-28
Cycle 1: 'Keep his laws and live long in the land'. Moses is giving the last counsel to his people as they prepare to enter the Promised Land. He is looking back over their eventful history together since he led them out of slavery in Egypt. He recalls the great marvel of their first encounter with Yahweh at Mount Sinai, and the revelation there of God's plans for them. And even before Sinai, the wonders he had wrought for them in Egypt. By these signs and wonders he had wanted to teach them that he was the unique and incomparable God. And all these great favours were due to his preferential love for them above all peoples. His final benefit to them will be his dispossessing more powerful peoples, and giving their lands to Israel. But on its part Israel must be faithful to God's laws.

Cycle 2: 'Nineveh is a ruin. Could anyone pity her?'. Nineveh, as capital of Assyria on the Tigris River, had indeed straddled the Near-Eastern world like a colossus for nearly 400 years. We have caught glimpses of the great shadows it threw over the kingdoms of Israel in the north and Judah in the south. Alliance of such minor powers with Egypt on the Nile had proved futile. But now Assyria's day was coming to an end, and Nineveh its proud capital would be humbled in the dust. The petty powers, Nahum tells us, may now rejoice in a newfound peace, but Nineveh would have to face the pillage and destruction it had so often wreaked on others. 'The rumble of wheels, jolting chariots, hosts of dead, countless corpses'. It is a perpetual warning for all earthly so-called Super Powers. Ruin is their destiny.

Gospel: 'Who loses his life for my sake will find it'. Jesus has just sharply rebuked Peter for trying to dissuade him from the destiny of suffering and death that is the Father's plan for him. He now develops this correction of Peter's human recoiling from suffering by insisting that it is the unavoidable cost of discipleship for his followers. And yet it is really an updating of the Old Testament first Commandment. 'Thou shalt love the Lord thy God with thy whole heart (that is, effectively); with all thy soul (thy life by martyrdom if called for): and all thy strength (thy possessions). Jesus updates this commandment from Deuteronomy by making himself, rather than 'the Lord thy God', the object of this total love. And the promise to some of his listeners to see 'the Son of man coming with his kingdom' would be fulfilled on the day of his resurrection.

Prayer-lines: Lord Jesus, fill us with your Holy Spirit that we may gladly face the cost of being your disciples, conscious always of your risen presence with us in your kingdom.

Week 18: Saturday
Cycle 1: Deut 6:4-13; Cycle 2: Hab: 1:12–2:4; Gospel: Mt 17:14-20
Cycle 1: 'You shall love the Lord your God'. The name 'Deuteronomy', fifth book of the Bible, is from the ancient Greek translation of the Old Testament, and means literally 'the Second

Law', or 'final edition' of the Covenant law of Sinai. Written long after Sinai and the desert days, it reflects the long history of Israel in the Promised Land, with a guilty consciousness of an often violated covenant, and an awareness of God's anger with his people and the punishment foretold by the prophets. Inspired especially by the prophets Hosea and Jeremiah ('prophets of the heart') it seeks to reduce the multiplicity of the laws to one: and to root that one in people's hearts. In other words, to sum up man's relationship to God as the duty to love. For St Paul, it is the law of freedom in the Spirit. St. Augustine will put it another way for the Christian era: Love God – and do as you will.

Cycle 2: 'Lord, why do you look on while men are treacherous?'. If Habakkuk has told us nothing more about himself than his name, we must still be grateful to him for leaving us an important prophecy for every era when war and violence seems to hold sway. A prophet for today then? At all events he has no qualms about challenging God who is, he believes, in supreme control of nations, for his seeming indifference, even apparent assent to the oppression that goes on. 'Why do you look on?' he asks. Yet he is prepared to listen for God's reply. God has a vision. His own vision. 'If it comes slowly', he says, 'wait'. The upright man will live by his faithfulness, and his trust in God. An Old Testament version perhaps of Jesus' 'why are you so frightened?' to his disciples in the boat.

Gospel: 'Because you have little faith'. Where Mark in his gospel has no inhibitions about revealing the shortcomings of Jesus' apostles, Matthew is noted for his more reverential treatment of these twelve pillars of the new Israel. Jesus will address the crowd as a 'faithless generation', but to the disciples his reproach is softened to 'you have little faith'. For Matthew's succinct six verses Mark's probably more familiar narrative will take sixteen, and give us the ideal riposte of the sick boy's father: 'I do have faith. Help the little faith I have'. It is a model prayer for the occasions, which few of us escape, of being forced by life to move what seem like 'mountains'. We can always remind

Jesus of what he has said of the power of even a mustard-seed of faith.

Prayer-lines: Lord Jesus, teach us always to pray with the faith proper to those whom you have adopted as your brothers and sisters.

Week 19: Monday
Cycle 1: Deut 10:12-22; Cycle 2: Ezek 1:2-28; Gospel: Mt 17:22-27
Cycle 1: 'What does the Lord your God ask of you?'. Moses has rehearsed the narrative of Israel's past forty years: the ordeals in the desert: the covenant with Yahweh at Sinai; the repeated backslidings, and finally the hazardous journey to where they are now on the east bank of the Jordan. He concludes with an impassioned summary of Israel's God-centred faith. The essential elements are reverential love of God, and fidelity to the laws of the Covenant. 'Circumcise your heart' is a metaphor for inward 'conversion'. Echoes of the grave sins of social injustice that the prophets had denounced in Israel and Judah come across in Moses' special concern for the widow, the orphan and the stranger. His 'love the stranger' foreshadows Jesus' injunction in the Sermon on the Mount to 'love your enemy'.

Cycle 2: 'Something that looked like the glory of the Lord'. For the next two weeks out first Reading will be from the prophet Ezechiel. He has been called 'one of the greatest spiritual figures of all time'. He will echo Jeremiah, his contemporary's, denunciations of Israel's faithlessness and his doom – prophecies. Like Isaiah he will stress Yahweh's 'Holiness' in its sense of total transcendence of all created things. But he sharpens their message by drawing on the imagery of the pre-classical prophecy of Elijah and Elisha, and of Babylonian art-forms. Yahweh appears to him not in a burning bush (as he did to Moses), but as a storm-god. He is enthroned on a fantastic chariot drawn by redoubtable celestial beings. We do well to imitate in spirit Ezechiel as he prostrated himself before God's unutterable majesty.

Gospel: 'And a great sadness came over them'. Despite the appearance of the obliging fish who provides the shekel to pay, the tax for Jesus and Peter, Matthew does not intend this as a miracle story, for he doesn't describe the catch. What matter's most for Matthew is the practical principle of not giving scandal, 'so as not to offend these people'. But we might more profitably ponder the first part of our passage. Where Matthew speaks of the sadness of the disciples at Jesus' second prediction of his passion. The details of the passion given in the other two predictions were no doubt added by hindsight, after the event had happened. But the cloud of hostility and menace gathering round Jesus as they make for Jerusalem must have weighed frequently at least on Jesus' spirit. We should share with Jesus our own times of depression when they come.

Prayer-lines: Lord Jesus, help us by your Holy Spirit, enter into your reverence for your Father, and your redemptive love for all humanity.

Week 19: Tuesday
Cycle 1: Deut 31:1-8; Cycle 2: Ezek 2:8-3:4; Gospel: Mt 18

Cycle 1: 'The Lord himself will lead you. Have no fear'. Keywords indeed, 'The Lord will lead you', as Moses comes to the end of his review of what it means to be God's covenanted people. He is also about to surrender his unique authority over them to Joshua, his lieutenant. It is a major transition in Israel's history as it leaves the desert and enters the Promised Land west of the river Jordan. It will certainly not be the same without Moses to instruct them, rebuke them, plead to God for them. Joshua and subsequent guides of Israel will never reach Moses' stature. But, amid all the changes and challenges that are bound to follow, the one unchangeable reality is God. It is a lesson for all generations and for all leaders in social, political and religious life. 'Have no fear. God will not fail you or desert you'.

Cycle 2: 'Son of man, tell them what I have said'. Ezechiel has been told, like Jeremiah in different terms, that his mission is to a

rebellious audience. But he is warned not to be contaminated by
their rebelliousness. Rather he is to digest fully his God given
message and make it as it were his own. This will be made clear
for him by the symbolic action of eating a papyrus scroll. 'It tasted',
Ezechiel says, 'sweet as honey', even though 'its message was
lamenting, wailing and moanings'. The sweetness came from
Ezechiel's faith in the saving purpose of God's punishments. In
our turn we must learn to trust a loving God even when the
news we receive is not at first to our liking. 'God will not fail us
or desert us'.

Gospel: 'Unless you change and become like little children'. Our
gospel today is from the fourth of Matthew's five great discourses on which his Good News rests. It stresses the contrast between the leaders and the led, 'the little ones', in the Christian
community. We are not to take 'become like little children' literally. Elsewhere Jesus urges his disciples to be adult, in not fearing death, for instance. The children are a symbol of an attitude
of spirit lacking in the apostles as they debate 'greatness' in the
kingdom of heaven. James and John were ambitiously planning
ahead. Children are predominately carefree beyond their daily
work and food and games. They know they are dependent. It is
the spirit of the 'Our Father': dependence on God as a child on
its father. Jesus himself is the best role-model of this 'childlike-
ness'. 'I do always the things that please him'.

Prayer-lines: Lord Jesus, send into our hearts the Spirit of adoption that will free us from all anxiety, and keep us ready at all
times to do and accept the Father's will. Amen.

Week 19: Wednesday

Cycle 1: Deut 34:1-12; Cycle 2: Ezek 9, 10; Gospel: Mt 18:15-20
Cycle 1: 'There has never been such a prophet in Israel as Moses'.
Today's first reading brings the book of Deuteronomy to an end,
and with it the Pentateuch, the first five books of the Bible, the
Torah or Teaching of Moses. It is fitting that it should end with a
eulogy of Moses, who was the embodiment of that teaching.
There are other 'greats' in the Old Testament. King David (The

Anointed one); Solomon (the Wise): Elijah (the Prophet), but, unlike Moses, none of them met God face to face. It is not surprising that the first Christians, being Jews, would compare Jesus to Moses. St Matthew's five great discourses from Jesus' lips are a parallel to Moses' Pentateuch. Jesus himself will refer the Jews to Moses' teaching, but is not afraid to cap it at times. For Moses was only a servant in the house of God: Jesus the Son. The Law was given through Moses: grace and truth by Jesus.

Cycle 2: 'Defile the Temple; fill the courts with corpses'. In the midst of the exiles in Babylon Ezechiel has a vision of the idolatrous abominations going on in Jerusalem, even in the Temple itself. It is a fearful vision, especially for a priest like Ezechiel. Idols and unclean animals are being worshipped by priests and layfolk alike. There will be only a few who merit to have the cross marked on their foreheads. King Josiah's abortive religious reform has been indeed shortlived. The corpses will of themselves, of course, defile the sanctuary. But greatest disaster of all is the sight of the numinous cloud,' the glory of the Lord', symbol of the Lord's invisible presence over the Ark leaving its throne between the cherubim, and coming out of the Temple. With this sight all hope for Jerusalem is fled. – The hope, however, is not dead. For 'the glory of the Lord', and with it the hope of Israel will now be transferred to the colony of Jews in Babylon. And with it will come their hope of resurrection.

Gospel: 'Where two or three meet in my name, I shall be there with them'. We sometimes meet a phrase that sums up the meaning not only of a whole passage, but even of the whole Gospel. – We should be on the look out for them. 'I shall be there with them', is one such phrase. Jesus is teaching about the period after he has 'gone to the Father', and the ensuing relationships between the disciples. Sin will not have ended with his resurrection. Even within the church. But all must share Jesus' desire to save, to win back those who stray, to be other 'redeemers'. But with the gentleness of Christ himself, as for example with the woman taken in adultery. The church is the Body and the Temple of Christ. And thereby, if the common prayer of

Christians is efficacious with the Father, it is because of his, 'I will be there'. May our Eucharist always deepen our sense of Jesus' saving presence with us; and our share in his mission to serve and save.

Prayer-lines: Lord Jesus, increase our faith in your presence with us, and our willingness to serve you in others.

Week 19: Thursday
Cycle 1: Josh 3:7-17; Cycle 2: Ezek 12:1-12; Gospel: Mt 18:21-19:1
Cycle 1:'I am going to be with you even as I was with Moses'. Moses has bequeathed to Joshua his wisdom by laying his hands on him. But it is above all Yahweh, 'the Lord', who is going to continue the protective work he has up to now done through Moses. The continuing presence of Yahweh, visibly symbolised in the Ark of the Covenant, is celebrated as a liturgical event in which priests play a central role. For us too the protective presence of God's power with us always remains the bedrock of our faith and hope in life.

Cycle 2: 'Perhaps they will admit then that that they are a set of rebels'. Ezechiel is commissioned to disabuse the deportees at Babylon of their vain hopes of a return to Jerusalem. He has to mime in front of them what way things really are. Jerusalem is still under siege. The regent and some of the nobles try to escape by breaking through the city wall. But they are captured, the regent blinded and deported to Babylon. Grim news indeed for the deportees. Many disbelieve till later news is brought that Jerusalem has in fact been destroyed. Are we also unreceptive of our prophets of doom today? Are we unmoved at their protests to world leaders against the debts of countries economically crippled, or the destruction of the earth's resources through economic greed? Are we too living in a world of rebels against God's saving plans?

Gospel: Peter: 'As, often as seven times?'. Jesus: 'No. Seventy-seven times'. A pity there wasn't a camera there to capture Peter's face at this reply of Jesus. Matthew is still treating of relationships in the Christian community. 'How good and how sweet it is', the psalmist sings 'when brothers live in unity'. But in practice it may not always be so. For St Augustine we are earthenware jars knocking against each other, wittingly or not. Forgiveness does not come easy to human nature. 'An eye for an eye' (instead of two eyes for an eye) represented a real step forward in restraint for Old Testament morality. This lesson in Christian ethics is as relevant today as ever in cases of grave injustice and violence. It is part of the daily news on the media. It is true we are an 'Easter People'. But to be that in practice we need to believe first that we are a forgiven people. St Paul reminds us: Christ died for us while we were still sinners.

Prayer-lines: Lord Jesus, fill us with your Spirit that we may know you and your Father as a God of forgiveness, and live up to our adoption as God's children.

Week 19: Friday

Cycle 1: Josh 24:1-13; Cycle 2: Ezek 16:1-15, 60, 63; Gospel: Mt 19:3-12
Cycle 1: 'I gave you a land where you never toiled'. The conquest of the Promised Land under Moses' lieutenant is now at least nominally over. Joshua gathers the twelve tribes of the Chosen People together at their central shrine of Shechem where even Abraham had worshipped Yahweh. (Jerusalem had not yet been captured). It is now Joshua's turn, as it had been that of Moses before him, to remember God's many favours to his people. First he recounts the events described in Genesis, Exodus and Numbers. He then recalls the victorious overrunning of the country since they had crossed the Jordan. – So much on God's part. What will be Israel's response? We too should regularly revisit the various stages of our life to detect in them God's interventions on our behalf, and ask ourselves how we have responded.

Cycle 2: 'I had clothed you with my own splendour'. One of the most astonishing passages in the Old Testament for the freedom of its imagery. Long before Ezechiel, Hosea had used the imagery of marriage to convey the depth of Yahweh's relationship by covenant with Israel. Today Ezechiel traces that fantastic love-affair back to its roots. Yahweh had adopted Israel for his love from her beginnings, 'exposed in the open fields as you were born'. At every stage of her growth to womanhood he had heaped his favours upon her, till finally he made her his queen. Unbelievably, she had from earliest times prostituted herself to idols. 'Remember', he says, 'and be covered with shame'. For the last word is not Israel's shame, but God's faithful resolve to pardon her for all she has done wrong. How far can each of us apply this dramatic parable to ourselves?

Gospel: 'What God has united man must not divide'. We have always something to learn from Jesus' way of treating moral problems. 'Is it against the law?', the Pharisees ask. And that is sometimes the way people approach problems of sexuality: 'is it against the law?'. Jesus bids the Pharisees, and us too, to look behind and above the legal problems of human relationships to the basic personal relationship of all humanity: the relationship with God. What does God want of us? This is the question we too must ask ourselves in regard to our daily conduct. But even the Jewish law, in its account of creation, records that God meant man and woman to be united in marriage for life. For human nature that can sometimes be quite difficult. But for the sake of the Kingdom, for a total love of God, it is possible, as is also voluntary celibacy. Of this latter Jesus himself is the supreme model.

Prayer-lines: Lord Jesus, we ask you to make us grateful for all your gifts to us, and may both married and celibate Christians strengthen their fidelity to their respective vocation by mutual example.

Week 19: Saturday
Cycle 1: Josh 24:14-29; Cycle 2: Ezek 18:1-32; Gospel: Mt 19:13-15
Cycle 1: 'It is the Lord our God we wish to serve. Then, cast away the alien gods among you, and give your hearts to the Lord'. Here at Shechem, in the heart of the Promised Land Joshua is now appealing to all the tribes of Israel, even those that had not

been in Egypt and shared the instructive experiences of the
Exodus. And even those who had come out of Egypt had, we
know, been deprived entry to the Promised Land by their lack of
faith in God. So we are not really surprised that the explicit
promises of obedience to the true God and his Covenant in
today's Reading is soon followed by a series of relapses into the
idolatry which still pervades Canaan. This will be the theme of
the Book of Judges, which follows. – Has this history of these
promises of fidelity to God no lesson for us in the light of our
Baptismal promises? How far have we put away 'the alien gods'
among us – of consumerism, human respect, laziness or whatever?

Cycle 2: 'Make yourselves a new heart'. Ezechiel is still among
the exiles in Babylon. He is still trying to wean them from their
vain hopes of a return home to 'the good old days' before
Jerusalem's destruction. Now that they know Jerusalem has perished, it is a question of encouraging them in a proper relationship with God. Up to now the common belief had been that the
guilt of one's ancestors lingered over their descendants. Not so,
Ezechiel insists. God takes pleasure in no one's death. The unjust will indeed be punished as is fitting, but the individual who
keeps the ritual and moral laws will surely be rewarded.
Elsewhere the prophet makes clear that it is God himself who
will grant them the new heart to achieve such fidelity. – We too
must remind ourselves that God's power is always at hand for
the asking, no matter what moral background we may come
from.

Gospel: 'To such as these the kingdom of heaven belongs'. It is
not at first clear what Jesus meant by teaching that 'of such is the
kingdom'. It is certainly not the expression of a sentimental attachment to children, or even a reference to the moral innocence
of children, for elsewhere he speaks of adult sinners entering the
kingdom. We must first remember that the kingdom of God
means allowing God to rule in each of us as king. That, for example, was St. Therese's way! She really treated Jesus as her king.
We also remember Jesus' words to Nicodemus! Unless we are
born anew, we cannot enter the kingdom. A Christian is reborn

not merely in baptism. He/she must be ready to re-learn how to love, as led not by self or the world, but by the Spirit of Christ. As our Lord puts it elsewhere: by hearing the word of God and keeping it. And that, he tells us means not only being a child, but his 'mother, brother and sister'. Of such, need I say, our Lady is the supreme model: his mother, while remaining to the end, led like a child by his Spirit.

Prayer-lines: God our Father, create in us a new heart, that we may serve you always with docility after the examples of your Son Jesus and his Mother.

Week 20: Monday

Cycle 1: Judg 2:11-19; Cycle 2: Ezek 24:15-24; Gospel: Mt19: 16-22

Cycle 1: 'The Lord was with the judge and rescued them.' For the next few days our first reading will be taken from the Book of Judges, seventh book of the Old Testament. The title is misleading. 'Judges' in the Hebrew means military leaders, sent by God, and filled with his power to rescue Israel from the enemies that surrounded them in the Promised Land. And, like other parts of the Bible, this seventh book sets out to teach theology rather than history. The theological message is that of the prophets. If Israel does not remain faithful to the Covenant of Sinai, then the God of the Covenant would, as he had warned them from the start, punish them through other peoples. But he would not abandon them. 'He appointed judges for them and rescued them.' It was a relevant message for Israel later on in the age of the prophets. No doubt it has its relevance for us Christians too in every age.

Cycle 2: 'Ezechiel is to be a sign for you.' Ezechiel's bizarre visions, which he recounted to the exiles in Babylon, had been startling enough: the dazzling glory of God enthroned on the cherubim as on a chariot, leaving the Temple of Jerusalem which idolatrous worship was desecrating. But now God's message was to come to them in the flesh and blood of the prophet's life rather than in his words, however startling. What could be more

moving for a people where family ties were so closely knit than
the sudden death of a man's wife. 'I told this to the people in the
morning. My wife died in the evening.' But the message is not
yet complete. 'You are not to lament, not to weep.' When the
news of Jerusalem's fall would reach them, the people must not
mourn for her, 'delight of their eyes though she was'. For she
had deserved this ultimate fate by her own guilt. And thus will
be made clear to them the reality of God's justice. 'Then you will
learn that I am the Lord.'

Gospel: 'If you wish to be perfect ... then come, follow me.' We
may take the story of the rich young man as a parable: a symbol
of his people. The commandments he had kept summed up for
the Jews the fullness of the good life. And surely it was a good
one. And it still is for the Jews whose fidelity to them can shame
us Christians who claim to follow a higher ideal. For that is what
Jesus is inviting us to in this story. Not to a special category of
virtue, but to be a Christian disciple and follower of Christ. The
Ten Commandments mapped out the good life on earth. But,
with Jesus that life had entered its last days. And with his death
and resurrection a new life began for humankind. He did not
abolish the commandments; he perfected them. He made us able
to observe them with a new vision, heart and joy. The commandments had regulated our conduct with God and neighbour. But now God was visible as our neighbour, in everyone.
Henceforth all goodness would consist in following him 'with
all one's heart and soul, and mind and strength'.

Prayer-lines: God our Father, fill us with the Spirit of your Son
that we may want only to know him and the power of his resurrection in walking joyfully in the way of your commandments.

Week 20: Tuesday
Cycle 1: Judg 6:11-24; Cycle 2: Ezek 28:1-10;Gospel: Mt 19:23-30
Cycle 1: 'Gideon built an altar there to the Lord, and called it
The-Lord-is-Peace!' Gideon, I presume, has been chosen by the
Lectionary as the first sample of the Judges because he is better

known than the others. But in the Bible he is preceded by the more noteworthy Deborah, a prophetess, who wins an outstanding victory over the Canaanites. It is certainly a story worth reading on your own. But Gideon's story also emphasises that the chief agent in Israel's deliverance is, as always, Yahweh. 'Do I not send you myself' is the angel's assurance to the diffident young warrior. Gideon is, however, 'variant warrior' enough to complain to the Angel of Yahweh of Yahweh's apparent abandonment of his people. 'He has abandoned us to Midian'. And, afterwards even when it has been clearly, and frighteningly shown that he is really dealing with the divinity, he is not afraid to ask for his famous sign of the fleece. Perhaps a model for our free speech in prayer at times.

Cycle 2: 'You are a man, not a god'. If Ezechiel could be unsparing in revealing Yahweh as a God of judgement for Israel, he would also, like other prophets, foretell God's judgements on the other nations around. But a saving God too for them. We read in Isaiah, 'Blessed be my people Egypt, Assyria my creation, and Israel my heritage'. Tyre (here personified in its ruler) was a very wealthy city on an island off the coast of modern Lebanon, then Phoenicia. Its economic success was proverbial in the Near East. This was its 'wisdom'. But such financial 'wisdom' led to the folly of pride: 'your heart has grown arrogant'. For the prophets this fall from wisdom recalls the primordial myths of human beings arrogating for themselves divine stature. Reminiscent of the picture of Adam and Eve in Paradise. Is it too far-fetched to be relevant to our modern myths of Asian and Celtic Tigers?

Gospel: 'Who can be saved, then? For God everything is possible'. For the twelve Jesus' strictures on riches seemed to challenge the whole Jewish concept of the temporal reward of goodness. And indeed it is not wrong for man to own things: nor even to become rich. It is natural for man to want to own many things. So when we see people freely giving up not merely possessions, but all the other things that Jesus mentions and that nature desires, brothers, sisters, etc., then the power of God is freely at work. The same is true when we see virtue in any form: patient acceptance of suffering, even of injustice: strict honesty in trade: perfect fidelity in marriage: forgiveness of injuries. All these are palpable signs of God's active presence and power in our midst. We should thank God constantly for making humans capable of this God-like conduct. And we should ask him to show his power in the same way in our lives.

Prayer-lines: Lord Jesus, enable us to recognise your presence in human goodness, as well as in human want.

Week 20: Wednesday
Cycle 1: Judg 9:6-15; Cycle 2: Ezek 34:1-11; Gospel: Mt 20:1-16
Cycle 1: 'They proclaimed Abimelech king of Shechem'. The success in battle of a 'judge' in Israel would naturally suggest the value of making him king, and his family a dynasty. But Gideon, after his success over the Midianites, refused the kingship. 'Yahweh will be your Lord', he loyally insisted. One of his sons by a polygamous marriage however, Abimelech, ruthlessly seized power by butchering all his siblings at Shechem, Of these only Jothan escapes. In our passage today he harangues Abimelech's followers at Shechem by an allegory portraying the folly of a kingship not willed by God. The sequel, which is not given in our reading, will bear this out. Abimelech is ignominiously killed by a woman, and his followers dispersed. The unity which Joshua had established at Shechem is undermined. The ambiguity of the kingship option in Israel will again be debated in the Books of Samuel.

Cycle 2: 'I am going to look after my flock myself'. The gospel overtones of this line alone are enough to alert us to the importance of this prophecy of Ezechiel not only in the Old Testament but also in the New. Designating gods and rulers as shepherds was common imagery in the ancient Near East, where flocks of sheep and goats are a normal part of the landscape even today. God himself is addressed as shepherd in the psalms and David is treated as the shepherd – king. Here Yahweh indicts the leaders of Israel for neglecting their duty. They seek their own profit rather than preserving their flocks from injury. They, therefore, are the ones chiefly responsible for the exile to Babylon. As the good shepherd of his people, God will reverse the people's misfortunes and look after his own flock.

Gospel: 'Why be envious because I am generous?'. When Jesus told this parable he was rebuking the Jews for their attitude to the Gentiles. The Jews felt that because God had made them his Chosen People ('Israel my heritage'), all other peoples were second-rate in his eyes. Even after Jesus' Death and Resurrection, where many of the Jews, even of priests and Pharisees, had become Christians, they still tended to look on pagan converts as second-class Christians, wanting them to follow the Law of Moses in order to be 'proper' Christians. All that controversy is now past history. What remains of permanent truth for us is that we must not look down on others. We are all objects of God's mercy. Above all, we must not try to anticipate God's verdict on anyone. We cannot read God's mind. But we do know that 'he wants all to be saved', and that he is a God of infinite mercy. Let us show ourselves true sons and daughters of his by always being merciful in our judgements.

Prayer-lines: Lord Jesus, freely we have received your mercy and your blessings; fill us with your Spirit to enable us to mirror your generosity to all those we meet.

Week 20: Thursday
Cycle 1: Judg 11:29-39; Cycle 2: Ezek 36:23-28; Gospel: Mt 22:1-14
Cycle 1: 'And he treated her as the vow he had made bound him'. The story of Jephthah as 'judge' in Israel illustrates the rough times of this period, and the ethically deficient character of these 'judges'. We are now east of the Jordan in Gilead, and the Ammonites are the enemy. (Amman is today the capital of the kingdom of Jordan). But the religious condition of the people has again lapsed since the last Judge-leader. Jephthah is a swashbuckling guerilla leader, but he is successful against the

Ammonites. However, he rashly and unjustifiably vows to sacrifice the first thing he meets on his triumphal way home. His horror is genuine when this proves to be his only daughter. However, the rough religious code of the day – as she herself admits – demands her death. Is it any wonder that in the Sermon on the Mount Jesus condemns unnecessary oaths?

Cycle 2: 'I shall give you a new heart and a new spirit'. Yahweh is indeed going to show himself the good shepherd of his people as he has promised in yesterday's passage. Not merely will he defend them from their enemies. He will give them a share in his divine holiness. 'A new heart' means a new way of thinking and loving: a new way of considering people and things. The 'new spirit' will be God's Spirit in them, enabling them to live up to God's covenant. This really sums up Ezechiel's theology. Israel will then display Yahweh's holiness before the nations, not merely through individuals, but as Yahweh's own holy people.

Gospel: 'Many are called, but few are chosen'. God's call, his invitation to the messianic banquet of his kingdom, is free and generous. But acceptance of the invitation and perseverance are not automatic. There is no room for complacency. Jesus is talking to the religious leaders of his time. His Father's invitation to the kingdom has long since gone out to his people through his servants, the prophets. They have ignored the urgency of the invitation: 'Everything is ready. Come to the wedding'. They have even maltreated the prophets (here Matthew has slipped in a historical reference to the destruction of Jerusalem by the Romans in 70 AD as evidence of God's anger). So the banquet is now thrown open to the marginalised: 'bad and good alike'. It is a church of saints and sinners, wheat and darnel, till the final judgement. All will then be required to be wearing a wedding garment: a converted life expressed by good living. – It is a parable for all seasons.

Prayer-lines: God our Father, grant us all a new heart and new spirit that we may live according to your will and be welcomed into your kingdom.

Week 20: Friday

Cycle 1: Ruth 1:1-22; Cycle 2: Ezek 37:1-14; Gospel: Mt 22:34-40

Cycle 1: 'Your people shall be my people, and your God my God'. The idyllic charm of Ruth's story apart (and no one should omit to read all of its four short chapters), the book is a welcome relief from the grimness of so much in the Book of Judges. Like the book of Tobit, it is a story of transition from grief and bereavement to joy and fulfillment. It gives a vivid picture of the hardships of life for the 'little folk' (of all times): famine and exile; death and widowhood; poverty and separation. These natural calamities are softened by the charm of this rare love between daughter and mother – in law. The real happy ending is not merely the marriage of Ruth and her motherhood. It is that she would be thereby the great-grandmother of King David, she a Moabitess. Like the Book of Jonah, that of Ruth is a prophetic plea for the equality of all peoples in God's sight and saving plan.

Cycle 2: 'I shall put my Spirit in you, and you will live'. Our first reading today shows Ezechiel at his most typical as the prophet of Israel's re-creation by Yahweh. He has already damped, even swamped their hopes of Jerusalem's survival by his mute acceptance of his wife's sudden death. But now he gives a surrealistic vision of Israel's revival from dry bones into 'a great, an immense army'. Ezechiel's laconic reply, 'You know, Lord' to Yahweh's query about the possibility of Israel's revival is not just evasion of a difficult question. It is a statement of his belief in the mystery of the resurrection: by God's 'knowing', and power and initiative. It is, of course, a message for all time. When so many are asking what future the new millenium holds for us, the Christian answer must be one of confidence in God. He is a God of resurrection, of new life.

Gospel: 'A question to disconcert him: which is the greatest commandment?' The answer was not far for the Pharisees (or Jesus) to seek: in their daily Morning Prayer from Deuteronomy. And Jesus had already used the same passage to repel the devil's temptation in the desert after his baptism in the Jordan. For the great temptation is not to love God so totally: 'with all one's heart and soul and mind'. A love, indeed, not of feeling but fidelity; of willing and doing God's will according to his covenant. A love in fact, which includes God's other children: 'our neighbour as ourselves'. This additional clause from Leviticus was certainly a bonus for the Pharisees' question. They were showing no neighbourly love of Jesus in their question. As St John would put it later. 'Whoever does not love the brother whom he can see, cannot love the God whom he has not seen'. Is it the Pharisees, and ourselves, who are disconcerted by Jesus' reply?

Prayer-lines: God our Father, send forth your Spirit to enkindle in us the fire of your love and our love for one another.

Week 20: Saturday

Cycle 1: Ruth 2:1-11, 4:13-17; Cycle 2: Ezek 43:1-7; Gospel: Mt 23:1-12

Cycle 1: 'Your daughter-in-law is more to you than seven sons.' The four chapters of the Book of Ruth have been telescoped into our two short Mass readings. This obscures the brilliant play-writing ability of ancient Israel. It is a drama, we may say, in four acts. Naomi has known the extremes of suffering, by the famine, which makes her an exile across the Jordan in Moab; then by the deaths of her husband and two sons. Thus totally-widowed, she returns in Act II to Bethlehem. God now sends in a potential benefactor, Naomi's elderly blood-relative Boaz, a well-to-do bachelor farmer. In Act III Boaz meets Ruth, who has loyally left her own people of Moab to assist Naomi. Boaz befriends Ruth because of her generosity. Today's account of Ruth 'gleaning among the alien corn' is from Act III. As Naomi's kinsman Boaz is entitled to buy back the land of Naomi's dead husband, and also marry his daughter-in-law, Ruth. It is a story of encouragement for us all in showing us God's power to reap a harvest of success from apparent disaster.

Cycle 2: 'I shall live here among my people forever'. The last chapters of the Book of Ezechiel are a blueprint of Israel's restoration. The guilt which had been the reason for their punishment by exile had been described mainly as the pollution of Yahweh's worship by the practice of idolatry, even in the temple itself. Ezechiel, therefore, describes the erection of a new temple where Yahweh will be worthily worshipped. In earlier chapters he had described Yahweh's mysterious presence between the cherubim leaving the temple to move eastwards to join the exiles in Babylon. In today's reading his prophetic camera shows us 'the glory of the Lord' in the same form returning to 'fill the Temple' with its numinous cloud, as it had done at its dedication by Solomon. Ezechiel's careful design was never in fact followed but his prophecy would be fulfilled surpassingly by the coming of the Word of God in flesh, and dwelling among us.

Gospel: 'The greatest among you must be your servant'. Mark's Gospel can show us Jesus praising a Pharisee; and there were good men among them. Matthew's account today reflects Christian controversy with Pharisees at the time (some fifty years after Jesus) when his gospel was written. But Jesus certainly did condemn trenchantly the vainglorious spirit with which they are here identified. Too often we find it among the apostles; according to St Luke, even at the Last Supper. That spirit can be alive in the world and the church in every age. At the United Nations in the 1970's Pope Paul VI claimed that pride was the real obstacle to justice and peace. If that spirit is, therefore, so pervasive we are all called to be on our guard against it. And here certainly, 'we have only one Teacher, the Christ', who showed himself so dramatically among his disciples at the Last Supper 'as one who serves'.

Prayer-lines: Lord Jesus, fill us with your Spirit that he may make us ever more humble and obedient to your will.

Week 21: Monday

Cycle 1: 1 Thess 1:1-10; Cycle 2: 2 Thess 1:1-12; Gospel: Mt 23:13-22

Cycle 1: 'You are now waiting for Jesus, his son'. The particular interest of this first letter of Paul to the Thessalonians is that it is the oldest extant Christian document, written about 50 AD. That is only twenty years after Jesus' death and resurrection. We are, therefore, here at the first flowering of Christian faith as preached to Gentiles. It reminds us thus of the kernel of our own faith. We believe in the first place in God's love for us. His special choice of us. But, of course, faith came more dramatically to these former pagans in this part of northeastern Greece. It meant for them 'breaking with idolatry' – to become instead 'servants of the only true God'. The fact that they could take this great leap is for Paul a sign of God's power namely the Holy Spirit, at work. And this Spirit has continued this work in them. 'You have shown your faith in action, worked for love (of God, of course) and persevered' under the trials their new faith exposed them too. A blue-print for every Christian generation.

Cycle 2: 'We are continually thanking God for you'. Paul is well aware of what the Thessalonian converts have to suffer. The Jews there had tried to kill him, so that he had to escape down south to Athens. But he wastes no time, as we might, in his second letter to the Thessalonians expressing mere human sympathy. He goes straight to the Christian point – the positive character of the sufferings of these Christians. They are strengthening them in faith, mutual love, and patience. And then it is 'for God's kingdom' they are suffering. The noblest work we can do in the world is to extend God's rule over it. That is the grace Paul asks for his converts. It is the grace we ask for daily at Mass. 'Thy kingdom come'. May that be our goal in all we do.

Gospel: 'You shut up the kingdom of heaven in men's faces'. One cannot help asking why Jesus is so harsh, as in today's gospel, against the Pharisees; he who was reproached as being the friend of sinners. The answer is in the word, 'hypocrites'. By outward observance they pretended to be religious, but they omitted all religion's true demands: humility before God, mercy towards men. By refusing to accept Jesus they ended up, as Gamaliel would put it in regard to the apostles, 'fighting against God' – But the many religious wars that have occurred since then have shown how the spirit of Pharisaeism can always be a danger for religious people – to the great dishonour of God and religion. Our constant goal and principle in life must be, as Vatican II puts it, 'that the Church be a sign and instrument of communion with God, and unity among all people'.

Prayer-lines: Lord Jesus, grant us always 'to act justly, to love tenderly, and to walk humbly with our God'. Amen.

Week 21: Tuesday

Cycle 1: 1 Thess 2:1-8; Cycle 2: 2 Thess 2:1-17; Gospel: Mt 23:23-26
Cycle 1: 'Eager to hand over to you our whole lives as well'. If Paul can claim that he has taught his converts by the example of his life, our first reading today justifies his claim. In various ways we can hear Christ's words in the gospel echoing for us. The Beatitude, for example, of suffering 'in the cause of right' in the tradition of the prophets. Again his claim that he is trying 'to please not men but God' – the reverse of so much hypocritical religious observance that Jesus condemned. And finally we might say perhaps that he surpasses Jesus' imagery of the Good Shepherd laying down his life for his sheep by the comparison with 'A mother feeding and looking after her own children'.

Cycle 2: 'To turn to the coming of Our Lord Jesus Christ'. In one sense this is to turn to perhaps the most debated point in biblical theology today. A number of sects who believe in a literal interpretation of the New Testament will seek the answer in the figures and symbols of the Book of Revelation. Our first reading today is a warning against this sort of interpretation. Most scholars today agree that the overall New Testament message clearest in Acts and the letters of St Paul, is that the kingdom of God and Christ's coming in power is already realised in the church. The all-important saving event of Christ's coming has already happened. 'We are the people' as Paul writes to the Corinthians, 'on whom the end of the ages has come'. It is for us to pray and work earnestly for the 'how we shall all be gathered round him' in the unity of the Spirit.

Gospel: 'These you should have practised without rejecting the others'. Our gospel readings this week continue to hold up mercilessly before us the dangers that lie in wait, not for the wilfully sinful, but for the crypto-sinners that complacently pious people can be. And our honest experience can tell us how we can 'feel good', as the saying goes, because we have attended to small matters dutifully, and are then aggrieved if someone, perhaps of our family or our friends reveal to us that we have failed in a more serious domain. Prudence indeed, the mother of all virtues demands that we keep a proper balance in our good deeds. And 'the weightier matters of the Law' are indeed 'justice, mercy and good faith'.

Prayer-lines: God, our Father, help us to make Jesus the centre of our lives that the coming of your kingdom may be realised in us even now.

Week 21: Wednesday
Cycle 1: 1 Thess 2:9-13; Cycle 2: 2 Thess 3:6-18; Gospel: Mt 23:27-32
Cycle 1: 'God's message is still a living power among you'. God's message, or his Good News as St Paul calls it earlier in our first reading, is not for Paul something abstract. It is not a definition in the Greek manner of God's nature, his essence. It is a dynamic power, like the whole Bible. An account of what God has done in creation and in history. But 'among you who believe it'. Faith unlocks the door to the action of that power. We recall Jesus' insistence on faith for exercising his healing power over the sick. That, for St Paul, is the difference between 'God's message and some human thinking'. We should thank God that he gave so many of those who broke away from the church of Rome in the 16th Century a strong and effective faith in the innate power of the Bible.

Cycle 2: 'Peace all the time and in every way'. However deep the theological teaching that Paul will give in the first part of his letters, he does not end them without attention to Christian practice. 'Brothers who refuse to work' would be better translated as 'disorderly'. No doubt the man who is inattentive to his work will often misuse his time by making mischief. And Paul has himself given the example of how serious application to work has not hindered his full attention to his mission as apostle. At all events idleness is no mark of the Christian. And it is certainly no way to earn the peace, which Paul wishes to be the hallmark of his disciples.

Gospel: 'We would never have joined in shedding the blood of the prophets'. We shall not be sorry, after today's gospel passage to say goodbye to this scathing objurgation of the Pharisees in Chapter 23 of Matthew. Yet we must, as best we can, keep in mind the times in which Matthew's Gospel was written. Jerusalem had been taken and destroyed by the Romans some ten years earlier. The Pharisees were now the religious leaders in Israel, since the priests were no longer required for sacrifice in the Temple. The Nazarenes, as Christians would still be called in Jerusalem, were seen by Pharisees as outrageous dissidents. So these violent words we read today with such astonishment simply reflect the high tensions which ran between the Judeo-Christians and the Pharisees as Jewish authorities.

Prayer-lines: Lord Jesus, grant us an increase of faith in the power of your word that we may be always committed to living a life worthy of God. Amen.

Week 21: Thursday
Cycle 1: 1 Thess 3:7-13; Cycle 2: 1 Cor 1: 1-9; Gospel: Mt 24:42-51
Cycle 1: 'When our Lord Jesus Christ comes with all his saints'. A central idea for St Paul's teaching was that Jesus' death and resurrection had brought about the ultimate stage in humanity's history of salvation. It is especially in writing to the Thessalonians that he refers to this dramatic coming of Jesus at the end of time. His Greek word for it, *Parousia*, meant the solemn arrival at a place of a king or the emperor. In this belief, as we see from today's Gospel, he is echoing Jesus' own teach-

ing. While Jesus speaks of it as a warning against complacency in the faith, the vision of Jesus' saving return, was also for the Thessalonians, a stimulus to constancy under the strains imposed by living in a hostile Jewish or pagan society. It is indeed a vision for every Christian generation to cultivate, especially in times of natural disasters.

Cycle 2: 'God will keep you without blame until the day of our Lord Jesus Christ.' Our first reading is an echo of St Paul's prayer to the Thessalonians that they will be ready for Jesus' Second Coming. And it will be the theme of the second last chapter of First Corinthians. We shall be reading this long letter for the next few weeks. In the variety of the topics that it treats ,it is perhaps the most relevant for the many-faceted society we are living in. For the moment we may notice the repetition of 'Our Lord Jesus Christ' nine times in our short passage today. It foretells the emphasis, which Paul will later place on the pre-eminence of Jesus over any of those who have preached him at Corinth. It is, perhaps a reminder also to us that our devotion to Jesus, in his Person, word and sacrament, must always take precedence over our particular devotions to this or that popular saint.

Gospel: 'Stand ready for the Son of Man is coming'. The theme of vigilance (literally, 'keeping awake') covers more than one idea in the Bible. In the Old Testament it refers mostly to faithful and diligent observance of God's will, as expressed in the law. This concept also obtains in the gospel. The faithful servant must provide for the household at the proper time. But in the New Testament the predominant idea is that of constant watchfulness for the coming of Jesus. We have met it frequently in St. Paul's letters in the context of his wishful belief in an early return to save the elect. This need of watchfulness in the gospels is all the more understandable in relation to Christ's Passion. There was no ambiguity in Gethsemani in Jesus' asking the disciples to stay awake with him. Their subsequent shame at having failed him in that fateful hour would henceforth mark their whole lives.

Prayer-lines: God our Father, may your Spirit fill us with a constant desire for the coming of your Son Jesus Christ, and prompt us to be ready to receive him faithfully. Amen.

Week 21: Friday

Cycle 1: 1 Thess 4:1-8; Cycle 2: 1 Cor 1:17-25; Gospel: Mt 25:1-13

Cycle 1: 'God wants you all to be holy.' In today's reading Paul passes from his general commendation of the Thessalonians' faith to practical spiritual counselling. For their faith must be dynamic, and issue in goodness of life. 'Make more and more progress in the life that God wants'. The goal, therefore, of the Christian is growth in Christ. And, writing as he is in the context of a Greek pagan society, he was to pinpoint the question of sexual morality. The first chapter of the letter to the Romans gives us an idea of the prevalence of sexual immorality in the first century. Can we claim that our own century is very different? At all events, for the first Christians, 'God gives the holy Spirit' to enable us, whatever society we live in, to grow in holiness according to God's plan.

Cycle 2: Our first reading today omits Paul's urgent appeal to the Corinthians to maintain unity, instead of party spirit, in their Christian faith. He proceeds then to outline the faith he had preached to them. It is not based on human wisdom, which was the tradition of Greek philosophy. Still less did it satisfy the messianic expectations of the Jews. It was a message about 'God's way to save. And, against all human reasoning, to save by a crucified Messiah. Yes, by human standards, that is sheer folly. But God's foolishness is wiser than human wisdom'. It is a maxim for every Christian generation to hold on to; for each one of us too. With Paul we should be ready to acknowledge God's saving power at all times, and thank him for it.

Gospel: 'You do not know the day nor the hour'. Our gospel today continues with the teaching of the need for Christian vigilance. Some of the details of the story may be puzzling (where is the bride, for instance?) but the over-all message is clear. A wedding-feast was a commonplace rabbinical image for the relationship between God and his people. Here it is the individual Christian that is in question. The oil is an allegory for the good works that can be shown on the day of 'judgement'. The midnight cry, 'the Bridegroom is here' reflects the early Christian longing for the return of Christ. The wise virgins are not being selfish in not sharing their oil with others. Good works cannot easily be transferred to another.

Prayer-lines: Lord Jesus, teach us by your holy Spirit to live our lives by the wisdom of your saving cross, and to grow in holiness according to your Father's plan.

Week 21: Saturday

Cycle 1: 1 Thess 4:9-11; Cycle 2: 1 Cor 1:26-31; Gospel: Mt 25:14-30

Cycle 1: 'You have yourselves learnt from God to love one another'. In his letter to the Romans Paul will give the principle: 'Do not be mastered by evil, but master evil by good'. This fraternal love ('philadelphia' in Paul's Greek) is, therefore, the Christians' surest armour against the pagan way of life, which surrounds the Thessalonians. Not that it is a cliquish, exclusive love. He has already told them it will extend, like God's love, 'to the whole human race'. And, to be a practical love, it will mean living economically self-sufficient, 'earning your own living'. Paul was the first to give them an example of this, even though his commission to preach the Good News could exempt him from other work. 'The labourer', Jesus said, 'is worthy of his hire'.

Cycle 2: 'To shame the wise God chose what is foolish'. Paul today continues to elaborate the mighty paradox of Christianity by applying it to the Corinthians themselves. Could they honestly claim that they had deserved the gift of their faith by reason of any human dignity or excellence? (It would seem, in fact, that while none of them were from the very bottom of the human scale, neither were any of them from the upper layer). In themselves, therefore, God had repeated the paradox of the crucifixion, the saving power of Christ's abasement. An end therefore, at once to their partisan divisions, pitting one evangelist against another, Peter against Paul and Apollos. The only one to boast about is the all-wise God. – Would that all the Christian churches today find unity in their contemplation of Christ crucified, and in surrender to his will: 'That they may all be one'.

Gospel: 'Everyone who has will be given more'. We can read this well-known parable in several ways. In Matthew it is practically the end of Jesus' great teaching discourses before he enters on his climactic Passion narrative. Psychologically Jesus is already beginning to 'take off' from this life, and he is leaving his disciples a general programme of life for their guidance till he returns in judgement. He has by now given many 'talents' to his disciples. Blessed are their eyes for what they have seen, their ears for what he has told them. They must now turn these gifts to good use, both for themselves and for others. What he condemns in the buried talent is a reception of God's gifts, his light, in a static way, unwilling to face up to change and development. Over-conservatism can always be a danger in religion.

Prayer-lines: Lord Jesus, teach us to appreciate all the gifts you have given us, and bestir us to bear fruit in ourselves and in others for your glory. Amen.

Week 22: Monday
Cycle 1: 1 Thess 4:13-18; Cycle 2: 1 Cor 2:1-5; Gospel: Lk 4:16-30
Cycle 1: 'So we shall stay with the Lord forever'. It would seem that some of the Thessalonica community had died since Paul had left them, and that this unduly disturbed the living. Paul does not forbid their natural grief over their loss. But it must not be the grief of pagans – 'who have no hope'. He repeats briefly for them the core of their Christian creed: 'Jesus died and rose again'. But that is also the pattern of the Christian's death: it will be followed by a sharing in Jesus' resurrection. The vital good news, for us as for the Thessalonians, is the continuity in union with Christ both in our death and our resurrection to eternal life.

Cycle 2: 'Your faith should depend on the power of God'. Paul continues to deflect his converts from their excessive concern with human gifts or abilities. He had made no attempt to convert them to the faith by a display of oratory or human intelligence. His message was the unvarnished truth of a saviour, a Messiah, who had saved by being crucified! The fact that this paradox had led to their belief, therefore, must be due purely to the power of God's Spirit. We may well learn from Paul's reasoning here to look around us, and indeed in our own lives, for evidence of the same power at work: in parents, for example, courageously bringing up their children in a family-unfriendly age; in sick people cheerfully bearing their illness; in the devoted care and patience the sick and elderly receive from their carers.

Gospel: 'Everyone in the synagogue was enraged.' Luke starts his account of Jesus' public life with an episode that gives the pattern of his whole career: initial success; admiration of the crowds, later turning into scepticism. Finally the attempt to do away with him. On a different plane the episode illustrates a theme of St Paul's: the war of the flesh against the Spirit. In his letter to the Galatians Paul lists the fruits of the flesh, and they are well illustrated here. Jealousy! The jealousy of the Nazarenes that a mere carpenter's son should be so gifted. Jealous of the miracles Jesus had worked elsewhere. Above all jealousy of the non-Jews healed and helped by the prophets. – But the Spirit is a spirit of freedom. Freedom from poverty, captivity, blindness and oppression. And not only in their physical senses, but above all captivity to man's inward slavery and darkness. This is what the Nazarenes, like the Pharisees, rejected. And with it their own salvation. God grant that we may be more open to God's greatest gift.

Prayer-lines: Lord Jesus, teach us to rejoice with you in seeing your Spirit at work in the lives of others, as well as in our own.

Week 22: Tuesday
Cycle 1: 1 Thess 5:1-6, 9-11; Cycle 2: 1 Cor 2:10-16; Gospel: Lk 4:31-37
Cycle 1: 'Alive or dead, we should still live united to him'. St Paul has reassured the Thessalonians about the fate of their dead members: they will return with Jesus. But he now deals with the

significance of that expected return of Jesus for us who are living. First of all, it will be a sudden one, and catch the unwary by surprise while they say complacently, 'How quiet and peaceful it is'. Christians, however, must 'stay wide awake and sober' to be ready for it. We are reminded of Jesus' parable of the foolish bridesmaids whose oil-lamps had gone out when the Bridegroom arrived. Those who are unready for Christ's return can expect only 'the Retribution', the Judgement. But for Christians it is meant to be their salvation. A vital motive for us, then, to encourage one another in living in such a way as to meet Christ without fear.

Cycle 2: 'We have received the Spirit that comes from God'. Paul is quite familiar with the impressive pretensions of Greek philosophical ideas which were current in the world of his time. Apollos, who had come from Alexandria to Corinth, was no doubt an able exponent of them. But, in what concerns God, and 'the gifts he has given us', especially through Christ, only God's own Spirit is a reliable guide. We think of the amazement of the teachers in the Temple at the wisdom of Jesus at twelve years old. We too may marvel at the spiritual depth and insight of many souls who have not been given the opportunity of a proper education. It is to the wisdom of the same Spirit we too must look for guidance amid the enigmas and problems of life. 'Veni, Sancte Spiritus …'.

Gospel: 'I know who you are, the Holy One of God'. Let us learn from that devil today – as so many of Jesus' compatriots failed to learn. 'The Holy One' means the anointed one, alias the Messiah. – How anointed? Filled with the Holy Spirit, as were the Old Testament prophets. But if John the Baptist was, in Jesus' words 'more than a prophet', how much more was Jesus himself! The Jews were expecting one final prophet. He would not only, like the others, speak on God's behalf. He would also launch 'the kingdom of God'. It would be the final showing of God as king over the forces of evil, both outside and within the Chosen People. We have clearer views now on that programme of God's. At times it may seem to be failing in the face of all the in-

justice, violence and hatred in the world. But this is only a continuation of the triumphant 'failure' of Christ on the cross. It is
for us to believe that even on the cross Jesus is 'the Holy One of
God' – even in the apparent failure at times of Christianity to
proclaim the Good News. 'Have faith in me', Jesus assures us, 'I
have overcome the world'.

Prayer-lines: Lord Jesus, strengthen in us the faith we have been
given in Baptism, and make us instruments of your Spirit's holiness and power.

Week 22: Wednesday
Cycle 1: 1 Col 1:1-8; Cycle 2: 1 Cor 3:1-9; Gospel: Lk 4:38-44
Cycle 1: The letter to the Colossians will lead us into deeper
waters than that of the Thessalonians. The return of Christ is, indeed, still prominent in the Christian perspective. But not so
much as an event ahead, as an experience already realised. For
Christians must be aware of their relationship with Christ as
members of his Body, 'in Christ', and sharing therefore not only
in his death and resurrection, but in his ascension to heaven too.
That is why he can address the Colossians as 'saints', for they already share in God's holiness. And Christ is visualised not
merely in his individual person, but in his cosmic reality, as centre of creation. The churches too are not just communities of individual believers. They are united in Christ's Body as fellow-
members.

Cycle 2: 'Only God matters, who makes things grow'. In our first
reading Paul continues his criticism of the Corinthians. By failing
to see that by their partisanship for this leader or that, they have
shown they are still 'infants in Christ', in their faith. They lack
the enlightenment of the Spirit which would teach them what
was happening in their midst. Paul indeed had evangelised
them. Apollos came along later as a catechist, clarifying their
ideas. But all the time it was the one God who was at work
though his human instruments. 'You are God's farm, God's
building'. We must regularly reflect on how God is at work in

our communities in various ways, as parents, teachers, priests, whatever. But always by the power of his Spirit, building up the Body of Christ.

Gospel: 'They wanted to prevent him leaving them'..., but 'I must proclaim the Good News of the Kingdom of God. That is what I was sent to do'. Mark's Gospel highlights this summary of the gospel manifesto by dramatising the search for Jesus after the spectacular healings. The disciples were clearly disappointed that this success story was not to continue. But it would have been to betray his mission: 'what I was sent to do'. The Good News he was given to proclaim was not healing for men. The Good News is: God is king, and God is near, is here: in Jesus' word, deeds and person. 'King' is an empty title today. On Jesus' lips it means what the Old Testament had promised, and Jesus confirmed in his own way. 'Blessed are you, the poor. Yours is the kingdom. God is here as judge of mankind: of nations and individuals. But not by human criteria – as the Jewish leaders judged. No. As He who sees the heart. Who pities the poor, the weak, the despised, the repentant: 'This day thou shalt be with me in Paradise.'

Prayer-lines: Lord Jesus, increase our faith in your presence within us, and in the power of your Spirit to grow in your likeness, committed to your mission in the world.

Week 22: Thursday
Cycle 1: Col 1:9-14; Cycle 2: 1 Cor 3:18-23; Gospel: Lk 5:1-11
Cycle 1: 'He has taken us out of the power of darkness'. From thanking God for what Epaphras has told him of the ready reception of the good news by the Colossians, Paul proceeds to a prayer of petition for them. For the seed that is sown must grow and bear fruit. For Paul the essential fruit of the Christian faith is the wisdom and spiritual insight into what God wants of us. It is not an intellectual or abstract knowledge this, but a matter of practice, of conduct appropriate for those who have been adopted by God. We think of Jesus' assention in the Fourth Gospel: I do

always the things that please him. This is not a facile fruit to bear
in life. It calls for strength and constancy. But these are supplied
by God himself. If our native condition before grace is one of
stumbling in darkness, God has lifted us out of it, and let us
walk in the light shining from the life and death and resurrection of Christ.

Cycle 2: 'You belong to Christ, and Christ belongs to God'. Paul
wishes to conclude his dismissal of the foolish partisanship of
the Corinthians. In the Old Testament God said, 'My thoughts
are not your thoughts'. And only in God's thoughts can there be
wisdom. The Corinthians must learn to accept the folly of the
Cross if they want to be truly wise. It is sheer folly to cry, 'I belong to Paul, Apollos or Cephas'. All such teachers of the Good
News are merely the Corinthians' servants in handing them on
the faith. So too are the world, life and death, present and future
their servants. How? In Christ, to whom they belong. For he is
Lord of all. Yet he too is subordinate to his Father – by his loving
obedience to the infinitely loving will of the Father.

Gospel: 'From now on it is men you will catch'. We read the
gospels at several levels: as a record of an event in Jesus' life; as
recorded later by an evangelist for the needs of his own generation; and, of course, also for ourselves. The second level of our
gospel's relevance is strongly suggested by the very similar miracle given in the last chapter of John's gospel: and in that gospel
all Jesus' works are 'signs', that is, symbols of a deeper reality.
Here, of course, it is a miracle at the start of Jesus' public life, but,
like the post-resurrection account in John, it too is an 'epiphany'
(appearance) of Jesus' person and his power. And Jesus himself
points out its symbolic sense by his reference to 'fishers of men'.
Peter is promised a rich harvest of believers for the good news.
As regards ourselves, we may note what a great act of faith it was
for Peter to 'put out into deep water' for a catch in broad day-
light. Galilean fishermen do their fishing by night, preferably a
moonless one. – We too must at certain times be prepared to fly
in the face of reason if that seems to be God's will for us. If we feel
our faith is inadequate we can pray to God, 'help my unbelief'.

Prayer-lines: Lord Jesus, Grant us the wisdom to trust your saving love and power in doing what we know is your will.

Week 22: Friday
Cycle 1: Col 1:15-20; Cycle 2: 1 Cor 4:1-5; Gospel: Lk 5:33-39
Cycle 1: 'He should be the first in every way'. If our last passage
from Colossians reminded us that in Christ we have been lifted
out of our native darkness, in today's reading we are fully exposed to the radiance in which we are now meant to live.
Scholars agree that we have in this remarkable passage an early
Christian hymn which lends itself to the over-all message of
Colossians. It stands as a mighty rock of Truth against the tides
of false ideas about the supernatural powers, which were rife at
the time in Asia Minor. The inspiration for presenting Christ as
the image of God and 'the first-born of all creation' is the Old
Testament description of personified female wisdom working
with God in creation. Christ is, therefore, superior to all angelic
powers. And while, as head of the church he is the source of its
unity, he is also the reconciling bond of the whole multifarious
cosmos. What food here for our adoration!

Cycle 2: 'There must be no passing of premature judgement'. In
our first reading Paul returns once more, to the topic that had revealed to him the immaturity as Christians of the Corinthians.
None of the various religious mentors they were comparing, he
insists, have any proprietary rights over the faith they preach or
teach. They are only mediators of God's mysteries. It is not for
any of them to win adherents to himself. They have only to be
faithful to their commission as stewards of the Good News. And
for others to compare their relative merits is pointless; in fact it is
premature before the only verdict that matters is given: that of
Jesus on his return. A timely censure this for all of us, on judge-
mentalism in our daily lives.

Gospel: 'While the Bridegroom is still with them'. St Paul records
that Jesus said somewhere, 'it is more blessed to give than to receive'. And certainly his answers to his opponents give them

more than they deserve. He never just snubs them. He tries to lead them onto the truth. For he came to call the Pharisees too, as well as the sinners. He always remains the Saviour. And, in today's passage he reveals the profound mystery lying behind the cheerful 'eating and drinking' of his disciples while John's disciples fast. 'The Bridegroom is still with them'. The term 'Bridegroom' is not referred to himself. It is the symbol of the messianic times that have arrived with him. God was at last come in him, Jesus, to save all who believe. This is a time of joy – but, a time for tears will come too, when the bridegroom is taken away. Yet it will not be the tears or fasting of the Pharisees. For Jesus always remains as Bridegroom. And the spirit of Christian Lent is joy of the Holy Spirit, who has raised Jesus from the dead.

Prayer-lines: Lord, help us always to live in the radiance of your Son's presence, and in the joy of his Spirit.

Week 22: Saturday
Cycle 1: Col 1:21-23; Cycle 2: 1 Cor 4:6-15; Gospel: Lk 6:1-5
Cycle 1: 'Now God has reconciled you'. After yesterday's blinding vision of the splendour of Christ in God's cosmic plan, our first reading returns to the contrast of this with the darkness of the Colossians' former condition. How have they been rescued from that state of 'foreigners and enemies' of God? Purely by the free gift of God. ('God' in St Paul's letters refers to God the Father). But the means of this great space-lift from darkness into light has been the 'body', the physical humanity of Christ. This humanity of Christ needed to be thus emphasised in an area with so much speculation about angelic intermediaries. Paul's own role as servant of the Good News will be developed in a subsequent passage.

Cycle 2: 'To bring you as my dearest children, to your senses.' Paul has patiently explained to the Corinthians that their setting up of Apollos and himself on rival pedastels is all-wrong. For they are only servants of the Good News. To be done with this sorry affair of partisanship in Corinth Paul now pulls out all the literary stops he knows. Sarcasm first. What right has any of you to pass judgement on Apollos or Paul? All you possess of Christian knowledge comes to you from and through them. – Then irony. You're carrying on as if you were already in full possession of the promised kingdom. Would that your were! And that we could share it with you. Instead, spare a thought for the tough life we have to put up with, 'without food and drink and clothes' – social outcasts. Still, if you blush to hear me say all this I'm not trying to wound you. For you are as dear to me as his children are to a fond father.

Gospel: 'Why are you doing something that is forbidden on the Sabbath day?' The conflict stories of Jesus clashing with the Pharisees might seem the least relevant parts of the gospel today. It is true, of course, that orthodox Jews today can still be as scrupulous as the Pharisees in not breaking the Sabbath rest. And from the rest of their conduct, it is clear that this attitude is compatible with real piety and love of God. Abbot Marmion wrote, 'Fidelity is the fairest flower of a love for which nothing is unimportant'. But Jesus is not reproaching the Pharisees on these occasions for their fidelity. He is reproaching them for putting slavery to a system of their own devising before God's stated plan and will. 'The Sabbath', Jesus said 'was made for man', that is, made by God for man's benefit. But the Pharisees' fidelity to their own Sabbath regulations had disfigured the image of God. From the true image of a loving Father to that of more or less a policeman or a kill-joy. God preserve us all from such an invidious spirit of legalism.

Prayer-lines: God our Father, grant us your Spirit in abundance that we may share your only Son's love and freedom in our relations with you.

Week 23: Monday
Cycle 1: Col 1, 24-2:3; Cycle 2: 1 Cor 5:1-8; Gospel: Lk 6:6-11
Cycle 1: 'The mystery is Christ among you, your hope of glory.'

Paul will now develop the theme of his pastoral role as servant of the Good News. At Damascus years before when Ananias expressed his misgivings at Jesus sending him to baptise Saul, the notorious persecutor, Jesus had foretold the sufferings that Saul was destined to endure for Jesus' sake. Here Paul refers to them as part of his service of Christ. For his task is to make clear to everyone the truth that all God's plans of salvation are fulfilled only in Christ.

Paul's programme is to instil in his converts the love of one another which discloses to them God's secret wisdom and designs. May we all today strive to share that secret by our mutual love.

Cycle 2: 'That his Spirit may be saved on the day of the Lord'. Paul now turns to deal with questions of moral behaviour among the Christians of Corinth. Presumably one of them wished to marry his widowed step-mother, perhaps of his own age. But Paul takes literally the Old Testament condemnation of marrying one's stepmother. Paul insists that the man be excommunicated by the community's decision, not by Paul's. The ultimate goal of this severe penalty is the man's being forgiven on the day of judgement. As the Jews scrupulously cleaned their houses from all trace of leaven in order to celebrate their annual Passover festival, so should Christians avoid all taint of sin in reverence for Christ's paschal mystery.

Gospel: 'Is it against the law to do good?' No reply would come from the scribes and Pharisees, for they were hoping to find something in Jesus' conduct to use against him. Their hatred of Jesus had blinded them to 'the weightier things of the law: mercy and not sacrifice'. Jesus would gladly have healed their withered minds as well as the man's withered hand. We too must watch Jesus in every gospel passage and take in all his teaching. For he practised what he preached: 'do good to those who hate you', in his Sermon on the Mount. He comes before us in the gospel to lead us into a share in his own attitudes to our life situations. In today's passage his message is quite clear: it cannot be against God's law to do good, to save. That was the mainspring of his own life. Indeed also of his death. The key to

Jesus as our model is his name. It means 'saviour'. It is the programme for all his followers.

Prayer-lines: 'Your word is a lamp for our steps'. May we always walk in the light of Jesus' example to do good at all times to others.

Week 23: Tuesday

Cycle 1: Col 2:6-15; Cycle 2: 1 Cor 6:1-11; Gospel: Lk 6:12-19

Cycle 1: 'In Christ you find your own fulfilment'. Our first reading today makes reference to religious errors into which Colossians may be led by false teachers. We are not given a clear picture of what these errors were beyond belief in supernatural powers outside Christ: 'sovereignties and powers'. It is, however, enough for us to grasp the positive doctrine that Paul teaches. By his cross and paschal mystery Christ has cancelled any moral debt due to our sins. Paul dismisses any other views as worthless, and based on 'the principles of this world'. In our own age, which is not yet free from such empty speculations, we may well heed Paul's advice to put all our hope in what Christ has achieved for us, once for all.

Cycle 2: 'You are doing the wronging, and to your own brother'. Sexual misconduct is not the only matter Paul has to reproach the complacent Corinthians about. They are going to law in civil courts against their fellow-Christians. 'What kind of Christian witness is this to be giving to the pagans? Surely the Christians should be able to judge their own disputes. Better still, they should live up to the Sermon on the Mount, and 'let the man have your coat as well'. Paul then reminds them of the various swamps of immoral living they have been rescued from by their faith and baptism. They must be then more conscious of the cleanness of life that has thereby been grafted on to them. Can we claim that Christians of our own age are sufficiently conscious in their social lives of the moral requirements of their baptism?

Gospel: 'He spent the whole night in prayer to God'. Our gospel today gives us a very basic example of how we can make our oneness with Christ a reality in our lives. 'Jesus went out into the hills to pray'. Prayer (as also praise and joy) is a key concept in St Luke's Gospel (and Acts of the Apostles). But Luke, more than the other evangelists makes Jesus the subject of this praying: e.g. at his Baptism, etc. This is not a contemplative form of prayer, but a practical one: seeking his Father's guidance in his life and mission: today, before calling the Twelve; again before he asks them the key-question. 'Who do you say I am?'; and before teaching them the 'Our Father'. This is one of the many interesting links between Luke and John. For John Jesus is primarily 'the one sent by the Father'. And his prayer would be one of asking the Father, ' what do I do next? Where, do I go from here'. It recalls Ignatius of Antioch's profound reflection on Jesus as the Word! 'Word of his own, from silence proceeding, in all that he was and did, he gladdened the heart of Him who sent him'.

Prayer-lines: God our Father, fill us with the Spirit of Christ that we may seek to gladden your heart in all we say or do today.

Week 23: Wednesday
Cycle 1: Col 3:1-11; Cycle 2: 1 Cor 7:25-31; Gospel: Lk 6:20-26
Cycle 1: 'There is only Christ. He is everything and he is in everything. 'We read part of today's first reading on Easter Sunday. It is particularly convincing in that baptismal context. No doubt the Colossians had been given the same vision of the Christian life at their (obviously recent) baptism. But their transformation in Christ's paschal mystery was not meant to be a magical one. It would be an ongoing process: 'putting off (a technical baptismal expression) their old way of living'. Not merely flagrant sensuality, but human selfishness in all its ugly reactions of passion and speech. The source of such a profound transformation could only be a concentration of one's whole life on uniting with Christ and imitating him. It is a permanently relevant programme for us all.

Cycle 2: 'The world as we know it is passing away'. Already, in writing to the Thessalonian community, Paul has shown that he expects an early return (parousia) of Christ in glory. This will in-evitably form the background of his answers to the Corinthians' questions about marriage. Apparently, for some of them the idea of an early end to the world as they knew it would do away with marriage altogether. Paul's answer is carefully balanced. Those already married should continue as they are. The unmar-ried are also free to marry. But in Paul's opinion, the unsettled times predicted in the gospel before the world ends will bring hardships for them. For everyone, however, detachment from the world is wise.

Gospel: 'Fixing his eyes on his disciples.' We recall that the gospels reflect the interests and needs of an evangelist's commu-nity, as well as recording Jesus' words while on earth. Inevitably we contrast the Beatitudes of Luke with Matthew's: 'Blessed are the poor in spirit'. Luke here is not lauding one social class and censuring the other. The poverty that Jesus proclaims blessed belongs to those that accept the kingdom in his person and teaching. For to become his follower will be to share his hard-ships. The rich who are destined for woe are those who refuse to accept the Christian way. We can catch here an echo of the con-trast in the Magnificat, and a glimpse of Luke's ideal of the poor but unselfish fraternal community of the Acts of the Apostles.

Prayer-lines: God our Father grant us abundantly your holy Spirit that we may be one with Christ in all our dealings with others.

Week 23: Thursday

Cycle 1: Col 3:12-17; Cycle 2: 1 Cor 8:1-7, 11-13; Gospel: Lk 6:27-38

Cycle 1: 'Let the message of Christ in all its richness find a home within you'. In our first reading today Paul continues to unwrap the riches which Christ's teaching holds for the Colossians. The love of God for them he pictures as a garment, muticoloured in the virtues which the Christian behaviour exhibits: compassion, humility and patience. Its clearest expression will be the ready forgiveness which social living constantly demands. This will ensure the peace, which is the sign of Christian unity. 'Always be thankful'. Are we as sharp as Paul was to find motives for thanking God in the goodness we see in the lives of others?

Cycle 2: 'A brother for whom Christ died'. St Paul turns today to another question raised by the Corinthians: may Christians eat food that has been sacrificed to idols. In pagan towns in those days food in the market-place would be advertised as having been offered to this or that deity. Such food was prohibited for Jews, and Judaeo– Christians may have said they should also be taboo for Christians. But some Corinthians, claiming to know their theology better than others (a common trait, apparently, for Corinthians!) felt that as there is only one God, and one Lord, Jesus Christ, the alleged link between market food and idols was meaningless. Paul would indeed agree on the theological principle, but argues that such 'knowledgeable' Christians respect the weaker conscience of others. In other words, one may have to sacrifice one's Christian liberty for fear of scandalising 'a brother (or sister) for whom Christ died'.

Gospel: 'You will be sons of the Most High'. However lofty St Paul's programme of Christian behaviour may seem, it seems tame beside the demands of Jesus' teaching in today's gospel. There would seem to have been no previous parallel in the Jewish world for Jesus' command. 'Love your enemies'. And he leaves no room for ambiguity in practising this love. Our enemies are those who really hate us, who curse us, slap us in the face, rob us. And failure to obey this rock-face moral climb means we are no better than sinners. Worse still, we shall fail in our family likeness as sons and daughters to the Father. How far in practice are we really concerned with developing that family likeness in our daily life?

Prayer-lines: God our Father, may our desire to live in the likeness of Christ show itself in our readiness to love and forgive one another.

Week 23: Friday
Cycle 1: 1 Tim 1:1-14; Cycle 2: 1 Cor 9:16-27; Gospel: Lk 6:39-42
Cycle 1: 'To Timothy, true child of mine in the faith'. Timothy was from Lystra, where Paul had preached on his 'first missionary journey' with Barnabas (Acts 14). His father was a Gentile, his mother a Jewish Christian. On his 'second missionary journey' as he passed through Lystra Paul took him with him as a reliable helper even into Greece. He helped Paul in evangelising Thessalonica and Corinth, and from then on was Paul's trusted lieutenant. The two letters to Timothy and that to Titus are called Pastoral letters because they are concerned with the 'pastoral' care of the churches after the period of expansion. Nearly all critical scholars would regard them as written some decades after Paul's death in the 60s. They are, however, in the Pauline tradition, and of course are inspired.

Cycle 2: 'The slave of everyone to win as many as I could'. In today's first reading we hear St Paul at his best, defending his rights as an apostle against those who would impugn them. Yes, unlike other preachers, he has not asked to be supported for his work of preaching. His whole aim has been to pass on *gratis* the Good News of Christ. He has made every effort to win over every human category, looking for recompense, only the gospel rewards. They, as Corinthians, were all familiar with the rigorous way Greek athletes trained to win a prize at the national games. He has done the same for the higher crown of Christ's rewards.– Does it not greatly simplify our programme too as Christians once we set out, like Paul, to be 'saviours' in some sense of all those we meet?

Gospel: 'Take the plank out of your own eye first'. Jesus is not above using humour when teaching morality. One can sometimes hear the guffaws from the crowd at his more outrageous hyperboles like the above. The obvious model of hypocrisy in the gospels is the Pharisees ('blind guides' he calls them elsewhere). The 'plank' in their eye he has identified as omitting the 'weightier things of the law, justice, mercy and good faith', while cavilling at details. But Luke addresses his words today to 'his disciples'. And St Jerome bewails the fact that we so often show ourselves heirs of the Pharisees' vices: criticising others' faults, and treating ourselves as faultless. Is any remedy available for such a common infection? Perhaps we might find one in St Paul's listing of the signs of the Spirit (the 'fruits') at work in people. Perhaps if we set out to cultivate the habit of looking regularly for the sparkle of the Spirit at work in others, often the unlikely ones too, instead of the facile 'speck-spotting' that can come so instinctively to us.

Prayer-lines: God our Father, make us sincere imitators of your Son Jesus, that we may share his work of saving the world.

Week 23: Saturday
Cycle 1: l Tim 1:15-17; Cycle 2: 1 Cor 10:14-22; Gospel: Lk 6:43-49
Cycle 1: 'Christ came into the world to save sinners'. Paul has left Timothy at Ephesus both to counter false versions of the faith that were circulating there, and to reinforce the truth of the Good News. The plan of God is one of salvation through Jesus Christ. Paul is speaking from his own experience. From being a persecutor of the church, Christ has rescued him to be an apostle. As an outstanding example of God's saving patience with him, he can assure others that they can amend their ways. A spontaneous prayer of praise and gratitude to the transcendent God must follow, in which we too can join.

Cycle 2: 'The bread we break is a communion with the body of Christ'. In today's first reading Paul returns to the dangerous practice of believers who think themselves 'strong' enough to share in temple banquets without damage to their faith. Now they admit that their sharing in the Eucharist established them in a real communion with the risen Christ and other believers. They should realise therefore, that by sharing in Temple banquets they enter into a union with pagans. And these pagans, by their belief in idols, give them a subjective existence, which bolsters the activity of anti-God forces ('the demons'), at work in the world. Are we Christians today sensitive enough to the support we may be giving to anti-God forces in the world?

Gospel: 'Everyone who listens to my words and acts on them, what is he like?'. At times the gospel might seem mainly, if not exclusively, a moral teaching. And surely it is that: a new way of life. But in it's entirety the gospel shows that this way of living is only the expression of a new way of being. Perhaps the text of our Alleluia acclamation is not a bad summary of it: 'I am the Way and the Truth and the Life'. The Truth which Jesus brings is a Way, but only because it is a life– in Him.– It is useful to see our Christian lives as a house we've got to build (St Paul would say, 'a temple for the Holy Spirit'). The vital rock on which we have to build is none other than Christ, the cornerstone of the building. Only by union with him, clinging to him especially when the river bears down upon our house, will it stand firm for us.

Prayer-lines: God our Father, strengthen us in our faith that by baptism we are one with Christ and sharers in his saving mission in the world.

Week 24: Monday
Cycle 1: l Tim 2:1-8; Cycle 2: 1 Cor 11:17-26, 33; Gospel: Lk 7:1-10
Cycle 1: 'First of all, there should be prayers offered for every one'. The Pastoral letters to Timothy and Titus are distinctively concerned with the organisation of Christian life in the churches, which Paul has founded. The first thing to be regulated in the corporate life of Christians is public worship. Even in his first Letter to the Corinthians Paul refers to the misunderstandings and disorders caused by lack of supervision in the common prayer. And this prayer should be for all, not exclusive of any group. Prayer for civil authorities will allow for peaceful practice of the faith. But in any case, salvation, by God's will, is intended for all mankind. The brief statement of belief in the one God, and of Jesus as mediator, would seem to be a familiar catechetical formula. The passage is a fleeting glimpse of the early Christians at prayer.

Cycle 2: 'You are proclaiming his death until the Lord comes.' Another source of division in Corinth, we see in this first reading, was class distinction. Possibly the fact that the assembly for the Eucharist took place in a private house of a wealthy member meant that the better off came early and had a good meal, while the poor arrived later and perhaps still hungry. At all events Paul is highly indignant at this flagrant lack of unity on an occasion which called for the fullest expression of unity between Christians. It is the earliest account we have of the institution of the Eucharist, and like St Luke's differs somewhat from Mark's and Matthew's. It is a timely reminder for us too of our Christian unity above all at our Mass – 'that the world may believe'.

Gospel: 'I am under authority myself'. One of the key themes of St Luke's Gospel – as of his 'Acts of the Apostles' – is the universality of the Good News. So we are not surprised at his complimentary presentation of the centurion of Capernaum. He will have a counterpart in Cornelius, the centurion of Caesarea later on. But it is not often that Jesus is recorded as being astonished. Faith, of course, is what Jesus required of anyone who came to him for healing. But the centurion's faith had a plus-value that Jesus had looked for in vain from the Jewish religious leaders. Unlike them, the centurion believed that Jesus' power came from a higher source. In Jesus he sensed that the kingdom of God had come. May we too be alert for signs of that kingdom come in our midst today.

Prayer-lines: God our Father, increase our faith in the presence of your Spirit in our midst, a Spirit of unity where so much division exists today.

Week 24: Tuesday
Cycle 1: l Tim 3:1-13; Cycle 2: 1 Cor 12-31; Gospel: Lk 7:11-17
Cycle 1: 'They will be rewarded with great assurance for their work for the faith'. The Pastoral letters outline how the early Christian churches were organised. The terminology of the various ministries involved is not, however, very clear. And we must be careful not to project back to such early times the terms and structures of our own. 'Presbyter' in Greek may be literally translated as 'elder', being the comparative of the adjective for

'old'. But the wisdom of a younger person would be recognised too. The whole group of elders in a church would guide the policy of a community. But they were also responsible for the pastoral care of individual Christians in belief and moral behaviour. Our first reading makes clear the integrity required of an elder. Of deacons too and deaconesses (the Greek word is common gender). They may have rendered more menial services than did the elders. But they would find a real reward in their Spiritual growth as committed Christians.

Cycle 2: 'You together are Christ's body, but each of you is a different part of it'. The primary lesson the Corinthians needed to learn was their oneness in Christ. The church was an organic whole, a body, with Christ as its head. No one member could fulfil all its functions. Each one depended on the others. And this was not a matter for ill feeling, for discontent or feeling superior to others. 'In the one Spirit we were all baptised'. But as a body we must respect our diversity.

Gospel: 'God has visited his people'. One of the essential ways of listening with profit to a gospel is to note which evangelist has written it. To know what particular angle he views the Good News of Jesus from, his special interest in Jesus. Luke is the only evangelist who has given us this story. He portrays Jesus especially as a man of compassion for the marginalised. Here its object is a widow, a classic biblical personification of the afflicted. She is mentioned four times in this short passage. For her sake Jesus has no hesitation in incurring the ritual uncleanness of touching a dead body. Even more important is to see Jesus with faith in his presence here and now. The gospels were written to make their mystery and power present for every generation.

Prayer-lines: Lord Jesus strengthen our faith in your presence and power to help us here and now, and to recognise you in others as fellow-members of your Body.

Week 24: Wednesday

Cycle 1: l Tim 3:14-16; Cycle 2: 1 Cor 12:31-13:13; Gospel: Lk 7:31-35

Cycle 1: 'The mystery of our religion is very deep indeed'. Our passage in the first reading is a bridge between the first part of the letter to Timothy (about prayer and the ministry) and the practical directions on 'how people ought to behave in God's family'. But it also gives the theological foundations for the rules and regulations, and a corrective for false teachings that are abroad. Christ is indeed the heart of 'the very deep mystery of the Church'. An excerpt from an early Christian hymn sums it up. Christ, though fully man, 'visible in the flesh', was shown (by his resurrection) to be righteous and Son of God. The angels looked on in admiration as he ascended. This faith was preached everywhere while Christ sits in his divine glory beside the Father. Much food here indeed for adoration and thanksgiving.

Cycle 2: 'The greatest of these is love'. This perhaps most famous passage of St Paul's writings might seem to demand no commentary on it. It has been called 'a hymn to love'. But it is important also to see it as an integral part of Paul's message to the actual community at Corinth that we know so well from other parts of I and II Corinthians. Paul clearly, and admirably, personifies love instead of defining it. The aspects that he emphasises are attitudes that the different groups were failing to cultivate. The so-called 'strong' in faith were not patient and kind enough. The rigorously ascetic were not ready to excuse others. The community in general seemed to take pleasure in others' sins. All this 'childishness' will have no place at the 'face to face' stage. – A charter indeed for us Christians to live by.

Gospel: 'Wisdom has been proved right by all her children'. Our Gospel passage is a sequel to a scene where John (from prison) sent a deputation to ask Jesus, 'Are you the One who is to come?' – Jesus answered by sending back some references in Isaiah to the Messianic times which showed that Jesus' activity was indeed a sign those times had come. He then went on to eulogise the Baptist to the crowds. But now he turns on the religious leaders to rebuke them for paying heed neither to himself nor the

Baptist. They had recognised the latter's asceticism, but refused his baptism of repentance. Jesus they dismissed as being too careless about their laws of food and drink and acceptable company. Yet God, in his wisdom, Jesus asserts, can be served in both life-styles. Have we any lesson of Christian tolerance to learn from this?

Prayer-lines: God our Father thank you for the inestimable gift of your revelation in Christ. May he be our model in everything, especially in the practice of tolerance and love.

Week 24: Thursday
Cycle 1: l Tim 4:12-16; Cycle 2: 1 Cor 15:1-11; Gospel: Lk 7:36-50
Cycle 1: 'Be an example to all the believers'. Paul here exhorts Timothy to be a model leader for all the believers. Five aspects of his conduct are detailed for his being an example to others. In the next chapter Paul specifies kindly treatment of the elderly, and appropriate reserve with simplicity in regard to younger men, and women of different ages. As in the synagogue, the 'reading' will be of the Old Testament; 'preaching' means the homily, and 'teaching' catechetical instruction. He should rely on the powers given him at ordination, when the elders pressed their hands on his head.

Cycle 2: 'The gospel I preached to you ... believing anything else will not lead to anything'. We cannot help feeling grateful to the group in Corinth that disbelieved the resurrection, seeing that it provoked for us the most vital passage in first Corinthians. Paul makes it crystal clear that the resurrection of Jesus is an essential part of the Christian tradition, and of any kind of Christian preaching. Note, for example, the clause, 'that he was buried', which confirms the reality of Christ's death, and also of his later appearances. His appearance to Paul himself is very important. He is the only New Testament writer who claims personally to have seen the risen Jesus. The emphasis on the appearances is that the initiative is taken by Jesus, not the subjective experience of those who saw him. Yet the last word for us will remain Jesus' statement to Thomas: 'Blessed are those who have not seen and yet believed'.

Gospel: 'He who is forgiven little shows little love'. With the people at table we too can ask, 'who is this man that he even forgives sins?' The answer is implicit: he can only be God. In the parable of the Pharisee and the tax-collector at prayer, it is the latter's, 'God be merciful to me a sinner' that alone pleases God. Here again it is the sinner who has repented who is superior to the Pharisee who sins less. Is this a travesty of justice? No. It is an insistence on the primacy with God of our love. Simon had indeed hosted Jesus at a meal, but given no sign of love to him beyond this. This woman, conscious beforehand that she had won Jesus' forgiveness is now able literally to fulfil the first commandment of loving God 'with all your heart and soul and strength'. For the Pharisee these words had been only a routine formula in his Morning Prayer, the Shema.

Prayer-lines: God our Father, help us to feel the power of your Son's resurrection in our lives, especially by loving you with all our hearts.

Week 24: Friday
Cycle 1: l Tim. 6:2-12; Cycle 2: 1 Cor 15:12:20; Gospel: Lk 8:1-3
Cycle 1: 'As a man dedicated to God, avoid all that'. Paul draws his advice to Timothy to a close by portraying the contrast between the true and the false teacher. The latter is clearly conceited, and arguesome in defending his views. However, in the tradition of Greek Sophists peddling their wisdom, such sectaries seek to make money out of their teaching. And we all know the evils that the pursuit of money leads to. The man, however, who is dedicated to spreading 'the sound teaching of Our Lord Jesus Christ' presents a very different picture: one of faith and love, of patience and gentleness. This is what Timothy pledged himself to at his public baptism. – How often, outside the Easter vigil, do we recall our baptismal commitments?

Cycle 2: 'Christ has in fact been raised, the first-fruits of all'.

What folly then, Paul goes on, to claim there is no resurrection after death! It would be paramount to challenging the basic truth of Christ's resurrection. If that were possible, Paul's preaching would have been useless. And their faith, of which the Corinthians had been so complacent, would be meaningless. They are still unredeemed, and their members who have died are lost. If Christianity means simply living for Christ in this life only, living merely for a dead man, then it is sheerest misery. – But all this is idle speculation. For Christ is risen, and we will follow him in our resurrection.

Gospel: 'The Twelve, as well as certain women who had been cured'. Yesterday's gospel account of the woman who had lavished such gratitude on Jesus at Simon's table should have prepared us for today's remarkable disclosure that Jesus' travelling companions included women as well as the Twelve. The fact of being cured by Jesus would easily explain their devotion to him. But from this chapter 8 on to the end of Luke's gospel, and into the first chapter of Acts, we must also keep in mind that the word 'disciples' covers women as well as men. Only Luke, of the evangelists, has given us this precious insight. For his Greco-Roman as well as his Jewish readers, the idea of women, respectable or not, being among Jesus' travelling companions would have been scandalous. Do we think Jesus worried?

Prayer-lines: God our Father, grant that by the power of your Spirit our lives and attitudes may be modelled on those of your Son Jesus, our Lord.

Week 24: Saturday

Cycle 1: l Tim 6:13-16; Cycle 2: 1 Cor 15:35-49; Gospel: Lk 8:4-15

Cycle 1: 'God the source of all life, and Jesus Christ before Pontius Pilate'. Scholars tell us that we have here the core of an early baptismal formula, the seed of our Apostles Creed. This would explain the mention of Pontius Pilate, to show that our faith is rooted in history. The Apostles Creed does not speak of Jesus as 'who spoke up as a witness' (*martyresantos* in the Greek). But it is important for us to remember that Jesus was the first martyr, the first 'witness' to the Christian truth whom we are pledged to imitate. The final doxology to God as 'King of kings and Lord of lords' (familiar to us from Handel's 'Messiah') is a reminder to the first century Christians that no human rulers, not even the emperor can compare with the transcendent God.

Cycle 2: 'We will be modelled on the heavenly man'. Was Paul not a bit severe on the (imaginary?) Corinthian who would ask 'what sort of body do the risen have?'. For resurrection does imply rising with a body. Paul is right, of course, to answer the question by reference to the mystery of the seed that is sown and grows into something better, higher; that great sacrament of nature that is all around us. He will then clinch his argument by referring to the then current belief in apocryphal writing about the existence of a heavenly Man. For the Christian, of course, he is Christ, who will share his risen life with us as 'a life-giving Spirit'. How far is the Christ we listen to and receive at Mass that risen Christ? Or must the angels at the tomb challenge us too with their, 'why are you looking for the Living One among the dead'?

Gospel: 'Some seed produced a hundred fold'. Growth and fruit-bearing are two of the basic phenomena of life, its basic mysteries. No wonder they are referred to so often in the Bible. From the first account of creation in the Book of Genesis to Jesus' words at the Last Supper: 'it is to my Father's glory that you bear much fruit'. And finally to the last chapter in the Book of Revelation, with the tree of life in Paradise which yields twelve crops of fruit, one for each month of the year. – The last is really the development of Luke's parable. So what? It means that the 'last word' of the Word of God is not man's sin and infidelity, proclaimed down the pages of the Bible, but the victory of God's mercy, the Good News indeed. However, the early church which also treated the parable as an allegory is realistic. God's victory is certain, no matter what the frustrations from the powers of evil. But it is up to each one of us to make that victory her/his own – or else lose the one thing that matters.

Prayer-lines: God our Father, we thank you for these incessant reminders to hope in you, and yet tremble at our own frailty. Help us always to maintain a proper balance between fear and love. Amen.

Week 25: Monday
Cycle 1: Ezra 1:1-6; Cycle 2: Prov 3:27-34; Gospel: Lk 8:16-18
Cycle 1: 'All whose spirit had been roused by God prepared to go and rebuild the Temple'. When we last read from the prophet Ezechiel we had left the Judaean exiles in Babylon. All their hopes had been shattered by the destruction of Jerusalem and the Temple. Yet not quite all. For Jeremiah had prophesied that some of them would one day return. That distant hope was realised when tolerant Persian king Cyrus took over Babylon. As we see from our first reading, he gave the Jews permission to return to Jerusalem and rebuild the Temple. He would see to the necessary funding. To the Jews who did return, as the Responsorial Psalm puts it, 'it seemed like a dream, on our lips there were songs'.

Cycle 2: 'The Lord confides only in honest men'. With our first reading for the next few days we enter a new source of biblical enlightenment, the wisdom books. They do not refer to Israel's sacred history or traditions. Instead they clearly show the influence of the wisdom of other traditions, notably of Egypt. Their theme is the proper conduct of life: how to cope with its different situations. But an essential ingredient of this successful living is a proper relationship with God. 'He blesses the home of the virtuous; he accords favour to the humble'. The pithy two-lined structure of each proverb helps to drive its message home. 'Do not say to your neighbour, I will give it to you tomorrow; if you can, do it now'. A timely reminder to us of our act of contrition for 'what we have failed to do'.

Gospel: 'So that people may see the light'. Luke places the parable of the lamp after that of the sower and the seed. We can take it that it is giving the same message. Jesus is not only the Sower, but the Light of the world, showing us by word and example the way to the kingdom of light. But as seed can be stifled or stolen or have its growth arrested, so the light given us by Christ can also fail in us, instead of growing and being shared by others. Israel too, we remember, had been chosen by God to be a light to the nations. The gospels often see her as a people who has failed in that mission. When Jesus, the true light came into the world his own received him not. We too can be faithful to our mission to the Good News of Christ only if we make him, his message and his conduct a light 'for our own steps' in how to live.

Prayer-lines: Lord, grant us by the inspiration of your holy Spirit to shed the light of the Good News of Christ wherever we go.

Week 25: Tuesday
Cycle 1: Ezra 6:7-20; Cycle 2: Prov 21:1-6, 10-13; Gospel: Lk 8:19-21
Cycle 1: 'I rejoiced when I heard them say, let us go to God's house'. The rebuilding of the Temple of Jerusalem began seriously only twenty years after Cyrus's edict of repatriation of the Jews, and today's dedication ceremony was only five years later, 515 BC. Those twenty-five years had seen serious setbacks for the Jews who had returned. The neighbouring Samaritans to the north, in occupation already for 200 years were suspicious of them. And when the Jews refused their help in the rebuilding work, the seeds of mutual enmity were sown which the gospels refer to. Darius, however, Cyrus's successor, had confirmed the rights of the Jews and the prophets and Zechariah spurred them on to work. It was, not, when finished, a patch on Solomon's edifice, but even as it was, it could now be, till Jesus' time, the centre of Jewish worship and piety.

Cycle 2: 'To act with justice is more pleasing to the Lord than sacrifice'. In proverbs like this we can often catch echoes of the prophets' teachings, and even of Our Lord's, 'what I want is mercy, not sacrifice'. References to a king, frequent enough in handbooks for those preparing for court life in Egypt, may seem indeed an anachronism for our times. But most of the proverbs are of perennial value, 'A man's conduct may strike him as upright', might seem irrefutable. But conduct is put in its proper place as secondary to motivation: 'The Lord, however, weighs the heart'. The supreme arbiter of a life's value is God: 'The Just One watches the house of the wicked'. He who neglects the poor 'shall himself plead – and not be heard'.

Gospel: 'My mother and my brothers are those who hear the word of God, and put it into practice'. This is a short passage, but full of meaning, Mark sees the episode in another way. He has Jesus asking, 'who is my mother and who are my brothers?'. As if he was denying his family for his disciples. But Luke never identifies Jesus' family with the general unbelief of the Nazarenes. In chapter 1 of Acts he has them, especially Mary, with the 12, awaiting the coming of the Spirit together. And several times already in the gospel he has portrayed Mary as hearing God's word and acting on it. 'Behold the handmaid of the Lord. Be it done to me according to thy Word'. Again, when a woman in the crowd lauds the privilege of Mary's physical maternity, Jesus corrects the emphasis to, 'Nay, rather is she blessed because she heard God's word and kept it'. In that respect Mary will always be the model of our discipleship. Listening attentively to God's word for its light, and then walking towards Him in that light.

Prayer-lines: In every Mass may we look for Jesus not only in the sacrament of his Body and Blood, but first in his word – that it may be 'a lamp for our steps'. Amen.

Week 25: Wednesday

Cycle 1: Ezra 9:5-9; Cycle 2: Prov 30:5-9; Gospel: Lk 9:1-6

Cycle 1: 'God has not forgotten us in our slavery?' Ezra was a scribe, an expert on the law of Moses, who came back to Jerusalem from Babylon empowered to teach and enforce that law as the law of the land. He found that since the first return of the exiles several generations earlier the law had been seriously infringed, especially by intermarriage with alien peoples. He holds a public penitential service. While he embodies the rigid attitude of Judaism to the law, which we find in New Testament times, we have no reason to doubt the sincerity of his compunction, and his gratitude for God's abiding mercy towards his Chosen People. We may read such a prayer as our own personal history writ large, for we need to grow in awareness of 'what we have done and what we have failed to do'. Our prayer will always be that of the tax-collector in the Temple: 'God, be merciful to me a sinner'. It is the prayer, Jesus assures us, which justifies us.

Cycle 2: 'Every word of God is unalloyed'. Or, as the second letter to Timothy puts it, 'is inspired, and useful for making us holy'. So the wisdom of the Old Testament in the Book of Proverbs is not dated. 'Give me neither poverty nor riches, only my bread to eat'. 'Our daily bread' we ask for in the Our Father. The reason given by the sage for wanting neither poverty nor riches is a fair description of today's world. The rich (even on a collective level, including the rich countries) seem to have forgotten God. The poor are often driven to flout the moral law. Even modern ecologists are urging the need for more frugal living in the developed countries. As Christians, however, we have deeper motives than ecology to inspire us. We share in varying degrees the mission of the Twelve in the gospel to proclaim the Good News of Christ, the blessedness of the poor in spirit.

Gospel: 'He gave them power and authority to proclaim the kingdom of God'. By now Jesus had initiated the Twelve into his mission, his message, and his power – over sickness and even nature. But people were now coming to him in ever-greater numbers. John the Baptist's death in Herod's prison, and the growing hostility of religious authorities made it clear to him that his time was limited. If the seed had to be sown everywhere in Palestine he would have to share the sowing with others. The scantiness of the equipment he allowed them showed that success would depend not on themselves but on the power that he had given them. It is a lesson that many a needy foundress/founder would learn in the centuries ahead.

Prayer-lines: Lord Jesus, sower of the Good News of the kingdom, deepen our sense of responsibility for passing on that Good News to others.

Week 25: Thursday
Cycle 1: Haggai 1:1-8; Cycle 2: Eccles 1:2-11; Gospel: Lk 9:7-9

Cycle 1: 'Rebuild the house. I shall be glorified there'. Our first reading is from Haggai, one of the 12 'minor prophets'. But his message was an important one. Some twenty years after King Cyrus's edict allowing the Jews to return to Jerusalem and rebuild the Temple, it would seem that not many had taken advantage of it. Life in Judaea had not been easy for them. Those who had the money built houses for themselves. But crops were bad and they excused themselves from doing anything about the Temple. Haggai, however, would point out that God's dwelling place, and his worship must come first. The poor crops were due to their religious apathy. With support from the civil and religious leaders he succeeded in spurring them into action.

Cycle 2: 'For all his toil, what does man gain by it?' A bleak vision indeed, and one not calculated to make Ecclesiastes popular reading. Nor is its pendant today in the Responsorial Psalm much better. The wisdom books in general are marked by a lack of interest in 'the marvels that God worked' in Israel's history. They would look instead for his presence in creation. But Ecclesiastes doesn't seem to find him even in creation. 'There is nothing new under the sun'. He seems to fall back on the non-Hebrew Near Eastern view of reality: a never-ending cycle of phenomena leading nowhere. It is fitting that the Bible should find a place for this sort of existential despair. It can be a prelude to the Good News of Christ, which gives life its true meaning.

Gospel: 'And Herod was anxious the see Jesus'. Luke likes to give us beforehand a clue to events that lie ahead. In his Passion narrative he alone of the evangelists will tell us of Herod's actually 'seeing Jesus' during his trial in Jerusalem, and venting his anger on him for not answering his questions. What is significant for us, however, is that Jesus could have been identified by people with such very different characters to Jesus: the fiery prophet Eijah, and the sternly ascetic Baptist. Luke will shortly have Jesus asking his disciples who they think he is. It is the vital question for each of us to answer in assessing our 'spiritual life'.

Prayer-lines: Lord, in times of discouragement, may we be given the grace to ask ourselves are we giving your rights over us the priority they deserve.

Week 25: Friday
Cycle 1: Haggai 1:15-2:9; Cycle 2: Eccles 3:1-11; Gospel: Lk 9:18-22
Cycle 1: 'The new glory of this Temple is going to surpass the old'. What a daring prophecy this must have seemed to Haggai's hearers of 500 BC. The returned exiles from Babylon were poor and dispirited. They lacked unity. They had reason to fear their neighbours, the Samaritans. So, not surprisingly, Haggai, speaking as God's prophet, calls incessantly on the leaders, Zerubbabel and Joshua to 'have courage' and rebuild the Temple. 'To work. I am with you'. Was Haggai's prophecy of a greater glory for this second Temple ever fulfilled? St Luke, for one, would see it as fulfilled when Mary brought her 40-day old baby there to be presented to the Lord. Simeon and Anna personified those who had the courage to wait 500 years for it. And hope in God's promises will always be a major virtue for Christians too.

Cycle 2: 'A time for giving birth; a time for dying'. Yesterday's reading from Ecclesiastes might portray Ecclesiastes as purely pessimistic; pagan even. But the hymn on the futility of human toil is simply a poetic description of the aimlessness of a purely worldly outlook on life: the life of man without God. Today he presents the span of human life as a seesaw of opposites: 'a time for every occupation under heaven'. But now, while admitting the mystery of life, he also accepts that this pattern is of God's making, and therefore must be good. – Only in the gospel is the last word said about the mystery of life and its paradoxes. The time that fulfils all others is Christ's time , his 'hour'. For dying and living again. It is the time we celebrate at every Mass.

Gospel: 'Who do you say I am?' The vital question for us all. Peter is given the honour of answering the question for all. His primacy has already been emphasised in the miraculous catch of fish. 'The Christ of God' for Peter means the 'anointed' wonderworker he has seen at work so often since he was called. The Saviour, in other words. Luke will significantly omit Peter's remonstrance at Jesus' forecast of his sufferings. Omit, therefore, Jesus' stinging reprimand – Jesus will just insist on the Twelve not talking about his Messiaship. For his Messiaship is going to be totally at variance with popular messianic expectation. He will indeed be the Saviour-Messiah. But only by his willing death. A programme he wants us to share with him. Do we really believe that?

Prayer-lines: God, our Father, help us to trust your love and wisdom in all the vicissitudes of life, and see in your Son Jesus the one you sent to save us.

Week 25: Saturday
Cycle 1: Zech 2: 5-15; Cycle 2: Eccles 11:9-12:8; Gospel: Lk 9:43-45
Cycle 1: 'I will be her glory to the midst of her'. Zechariah, like Haggai, is one of the minor prophets, and belongs to the last part of the Old Testament. The exile in Babylon is over. A remnant of them has returned to Jerusalem. But the great prophets are figures of the past. Those of the present will only echo them, especially Ezechiel, who foretold the construction of a new Jerusalem. But this quiet period is a distant preparation for the

New Testament, for the religious culture in which Mary and
Joseph, Elisabeth and Zechariah, Simeon and Anna lived. It is
centred on Jerusalem and the worship in the temple. The annunciation to Mary will confirm the fulfillment of God's promise to
dwell in the midst (The Hebrew word can also mean 'womb'!) of
'the daughter of Zion'.

Cycle 2: 'The breath returns to God who gave it'. Ecclesiastes will
end his sceptical teaching with predictable sobriety. He has no
hint of an after-life to look forward to. That would hardly come
to the Hebrews before the second century, BC. He is not, indeed,
a kill-joy. We should enjoy the normal pleasures of youth and
health. But nor to forget the judgement that is to come. He ends
with an impressionist portrait of the failing of one's powers in
old age. Walking is an effort. One by one our senses fail us. – It is
the darkest hour before the Good News of Christ and his resurrection. 'O death, where is thy sting?'

Gospel: 'They were afraid to ask him about what he had just
said'. Jesus had been transfigured on the mountain before Peter,
James and John. He came down and heals an epileptic boy
whom his disciples were unable to cure. As usual, his miraculous
healing power caused astonishment. But it was vital, particularly
for his disciples, to realise that Jesus' saving mission was not to
be realised in that facile way. His power would be fully shown
only by his willing surrender to death.

But for the moment it was totally beyond their comprehension. – And so, we too must not be surprised when we find it difficult to accept the saving mystery of the cross in our lives.

Prayer-lines: God our Father, increase our faith in your presence
with us at every stage of our life, and our readiness to share in
your Sons's paschal mystery.

Week 26: Monday
Cycle 1: Zech 8:1-8; Cycle 2: Job 1:6-22; Gospel: Lk 9:46-50
Cycle 1: 'Boys and girls playing in the squares.' This attractive vi-
gnette of a restored Jerusalem is a pleasant surprise in our first

reading. It is one of the very rare references to the joys of children being an element of messianic happiness. When Zechariah
talks of Yahweh's anger at Zion's sufferings at the hands of
Gentile powers he is simply echoing the pre-exilic prophets.
Jerusalem's restoration is, of course, always in view of a restored
covenant: 'They shall be my people and I will be their God'. But
the blessings to come were not merely spiritual ones. After all, it
was only very late in Israel's history that the concept of an after-
life emerged. Meanwhile God's blessing were also to come in
the form of 'the good life' as envisaged by a simple pastoral and
agricultural people. We too are entitled to pray for temporal
blessings for ourselves and others.

Cycle 2: 'In all this misfortune Job committed no sin.' A mistranslation in the Letter of James has given us the misleading phrase,
'the patience of Job'. The word should be 'endurance'. The book
of Job has been described as 'the supreme effort of the Hebrew
literary genius'. – In the form of a poetic dialogue the author has
faced up to a profound theological problem, that of the just man
suffering. This masterly dialogue has been inserted into the
framework of an ancient near-eastern story: Job's sudden descent from high prosperity into utter misery; and his restoration
in reward for his steadfastness under suffering. In the heavenly
court, conceived in mythological terms. 'Satan' is simply an official whose function was to report to God the misdemeanors of
men. He cynically challenges the possibility of a disinterested
service of God: 'Not God-fearing for nothing is he?' But God has
faith in Job.

Gospel: 'The least among you all is the one who is great.' So we
are back to the perennial lesson, problem, challenge, of Christian
humility. The gospel can also be Good News in letting the apostles portray their weaknesses. For rivalry is universal in human
nature. 'If my self-esteem dies five minutes before my self', St
Francis de Sales used to say, 'I'll be quite content.' At the United
Nations in the 1970s Pope Paul spoke of pride as the root cause
of wars. But it is more important to look for the cure. St Paul is
clearly suggesting that 'pride is the sin of the world' when he de-

clared that our salvation comes through the humility of Christ. 'Divine in nature, he emptied himself to assume the condition of a slave.' For each of us the way to salvation must be the daily echoing of Christ's words in Gethsemani, 'Not my will, but yours be done.'

Prayer-lines: Lord Jesus, may your word and example teach us the lesson of humility, especially when we meet suffering.

Week 26: Tuesday
Cycle 1: Zech 8:20-23; Cycle 3:1-3, 11-17, 20-23; Gospel: Lk 9:51-56
Cycle 1: 'Seek the Lord of hosts in Jerusalem.' This is the last prediction of the prophet who wrote the first eight chapters of 'Zechariah'. A contemporary of Haggai, that is, about 520 BC. But his gaze goes further than Haggai's unique concern with rebuilding the Temple. For both of them the rebuilding of the Temple meant above all the return of Yahweh's presence to his people. But Zechariah would see a Jerusalem unwalled for the reception of a greater population than ever before. In today's reading he will see Jerusalem as the centre of a great pilgrimage of other peoples to the presence of Israel's God. Can we see here the influence of the 'Second Isaiah', where Israel is addressed as 'a light to the nations'?

At all events, let *us* join Jesus in the gospel as *he* takes the road to Jerusalem – and 'to pass from this world to the Father'.

Cycle 2: In the end Job cursed the day of his birth.' – So far, so good. We saw yesterday, Job had justified God's trust in him. But Satan still had a card to play. 'You've still left him his health,' he objects to God. With new permission to afflict Job in his body ('but spare his life'), Satan now reduces Job to total misery by a revolting illness that drives him to sit on a refuse heap outside the town. His three friends, who hear of his plight, come from afar to console him. Aghast at his frightful condition, they observe the ritual of sitting beside him in silence for a week. When Job finally breaks the silence, it is to curse the day of his birth. He turns his gaze from God to himself. But then he asks the inevitable question: Why? 'Why give light to a man whom God baulks on every side?' This unlocks the great debate which follows. For his friends are only too happy to give him the answer of traditional wisdom. Job must have sinned. Let him repent, therefore, and regain God's favour.

Gospel: 'Jesus resolutely took the road to Jerusalem.' St Luke's Greek says literally 'Jesus stiffened his face to go.' Why? 'The bell was tolling' – for 'his being taken up'. Jesus had discussed with Moses and Elijah at the transfiguration, his death and burial, his assumption to heaven and sending of the Spirit. This is therefore a turning point for Jesus in Luke's gospel. For the next ten chapters, replete with Jesus' teaching and example, Luke will remind us regularly that he is on the way to Jerusalem. – It is, of course, a parable of our life as Christians on our pilgrimage to share Jesus' 'passing from the world to the Father'.

Prayer-lines: God, our Father, fill us with the Spirit of your Son, Jesus, that we may always seek to do your will in our lives.

Week 26: Wednesday

Cycle 1: Neh 2:1-8; Cycle 2: Job 9:1-13, 14-16; Gospel Lk 9:57-62
Cycle 1: 'The kindly favour of my God was with me.' Nehemiah is one of the most attractive characters in the Old Testament, if not the whole Bible. We are not told in this, his memoir, how he had risen to a position of such trust and distinction in the royal household of Persia. In chapter 1 he has told us of his grief at hearing of the dilapidated state of the walls of Jerusalem. He prays to God that he may succeed in his daring request to the king to travel the long distance from Persia to rebuild these walls. The ease with which this request is granted bears witness to how high he was in the king's favour. But the success of his project is also foreshadowed by his practical foresight in planning the necessary permission and materials. Should he be made a patron for Christian men and women?

Cycle 2: 'He whom I must sue is judge as well.' Yes, Job's friends can wax eloquent about the cause of his misfortunes. Job in reply surprised them by taxing them as false friends for not consoling him. But the only consolation they can offer him is to bring him to see things as they do. 'Does the Lord pervert justice? If you are innocent and upright, then indeed he will watch over you … Can a creature be purer than the Creator?' Job replies once more in today's passage. He does not claim that God will pervert justice. But his justice is his power, with which no one can contend. As God's works in nature are a mystery, so are his dealings with humans. I can't bring him to court, because he would be my judge as well as my defendant. Could I rely on his even hearing my case?

Gospel: 'No one who looks back is fit for the kingdom of God.' Our gospel today is relevant for us all. It tells us the cost of discipleship. There is a certain crescendo in this cost. No resting place: No home on earth: No funeral celebrations, even for a dead father. Not even bidding farewell to a living family. No need to apply each single saying to ourselves. But there is a common message of renunciation for us all. God himself will decide the application for each of us, be it possessions, ambitions, family ties, or whatever. And whatever the renunciation costs it is only half the story. The important part is what we buy with it: the kingdom of God, shared with the Son of Man. Jesus' disciples were surely baffled by his words here, above all by the fulfilment of them in his death. But they followed him somehow, and received the kingdom.

Prayer-lines: Grant us your holy Spirit, Lord, to enable us to follow you wherever you lead us.

Week 26: Thursday
Cycle 1:Neh 8:1-12; Cycle 2: Job 19:21-27; Gospel: Lk 10:1-12
Cycle 1: 'The people listened attentively to the Books of the Law.' Scholars debate how much of the five books of Moses were read by Ezra to the people on his return from Babylon. Was it the whole five books, or just Leviticus and Deuteronomy, the legal ones? At all events we know that the priests of Jerusalem exiled

in Babylon did intensive study of the law codes while there. The need to codify and edit these laws could explain the delay – nearly one hundred years after Cyrus's edict of restoration – before Ezra was able to return and impart the details to the people at large: 'the people of the land'. In our reading Nehemiah is now pictured as being civil governor in Jerusalem at this period.

Cycle 2: 'He whom I shall see will take my part.' Much attention has been given by scholars from patristic times to this passage. But the text is not clear, and its meaning therefore greatly debated. Job, however, in preceding passages has revealed his sense of being totally abandoned by his family, by his friends, by men, and it would seem, by God. Yet, by his conviction of his own innocence, he makes a leap of faith. Even after his death, God, the just God, will vindicate him, and he, Job, will somehow be allowed to witness that vindication. We cannot, however, read into this leap of faith a belief in the resurrection of the body. – How much, therefore, do we as Christians owe to God's mercy for his revelation of our resurrection in Christ'!

Gospel: 'I am sending you out like lambs among wolves.' Our gospel today gives us St Luke's view on the nature and problems of mission. The seventy-two would seems a reference to the nations of the world mentioned in Genesis. – At all events it is meant to be a world-wide mission. Why 'In pairs'? No doubt for mutual support, but also as an embodiment of the message of peace. Saul and Barnabas were a classic example of it. 'Lambs among wolves' could mean not only defenceless among savage enemies. It could also refer to the messianic peace promised by Isaiah, of the lamb lying down with the wolf. On the negative side, of course, the mission may sometimes meet with failure. But the ultimate triumph of God's work is assured.

Prayer-lines: God our Father, make of us 'children of the resurrection', in bringing the Good News of hope and peace to the world we live in.

Week 26: Friday

Cycle 1: Bar 1:15-22; Cycle 2: Job 38:1-21; 40:3-5; Gospel: Lk 10:13-16

Cycle 1: 'We have taken to serving alien gods.' Baruch is first introduced to us in the Book of Jeremiah as the latter's secretary. The book which goes under Baruch's name is a collection of short pieces set against the background of the fall of Jerusalem and exile to Babylon. Certainly the confession of guilt in today's first reading graphically reflects the despondent guilt-feeling of the exiled people of Jerusalem. It harmonises with the theology of Deuteronomy. Israel's history has been a sorry succession of disloyalties to its covenant with Yahweh through its idolatry. Their present disaster had been (vainly) foretold by the prophets. Nor is the doleful picture without instruction for Christians. The 'alien gods' may have changed their names, but the possibility of being unfaithful to our baptismal commitments is always there.

Cycle 2: 'Which is the way to the home of the light?' With our first reading today we come to the climax of the book of Job. Now God himself will join in this long and tangled debate. It is no anti-climax even after the poetic eloquence of Job's speeches. But God opens up vast visions which make the problems of the preceding debate seem irrelevant. Yahweh makes no statement to Job; no reference to whether he is innocent or guilty. As all-wise creator of all he puts a series of ironical questions to Job, which neither he nor any creature can answer. The implicit conclusion is that if such be the case in the material universe, the same must be true in the moral order. As the prophet Isaiah would put it: 'As the heavens are above the earth, my ways are above your ways.'

Gospel: 'Who rejects me rejects the one who sent me.' Jesus has warned the disciples that they must expect to find disbelief and opposition in their mission. Here Jesus is addressing not merely individuals but whole towns which will be held responsible for their refusal to accept his teaching. We must also recall that, writing his gospel some fifty years after the Ascension, Luke is also warning the churches of his own time to give sincere welcome to Christian teaching. For it is not merely human preachers that are being rejected. It is God himself who is offering us the Good News of salvation.

Prayer-lines: Lord, help us to pay heed to your word as it is read to us in the Scriptures, and live according to its light.

Week 26: Saturday

Cycle 1: Bar 4:5-29; Cycle 2: Job 42:1-17; Gospel: Lk 10:17-24

Cycle 1: 'He will rescue you and give you eternal joy.' The confession and prayer of Baruch which precede our first reading show that Israel's conversion has in fact taken place. The writer, as prophet, assures her that God recognises this, and will pardon her. He had sold her 'to the nations', because they were his property as slaves when he had bought them from Egypt. And this 'sale' plunged their mother, Jerusalem, into deep sorrow. Jerusalem now speaks, personified as a widow, bereft not merely of husband but of children too; with no one to support her. A reminder for us as Christians that our sins do damage to the church, as well as offending God.

Cycle 2: 'I obscured your designs with my empty-headed words.' The Book of Job, in today's first reading ends with his vindication by God. He is now content, for Yahweh has let himself be found in his unfathomable mystery. (The three friends, however, who have caused Job such anguish, are severely rebuked by God for misrepresenting *Him* in their speeches.) It is Job who has spoken the truth. The three are ordered to offer holocaust in expiation. Job forgives them and intercedes for them. God then restores Job's fortunes on the double. The author here rejoins the original ancient tale of the just man rewarded for his patience under suffering. Is he here foreshadowing the vicarious suffering of the 'Suffering Servant' of Isaiah?

Gospel: 'Revealing them to mere children, Father, is what it pleased you to do.' The incredulous joy of the disciples at their power to expel demons occasions Jesus' prophetic vision of the total defeat of Satan and the power of evil. Characteristically then he turns to thank the Father for according such revelation to the unlearned disciples, and not to those who feel no need of God. It has been entrusted to Jesus to share with his disciples knowledge of the mutual relationship between the Father and himself. This is the great privilege that the religious leaders and political rulers of the past had never been granted. Do we thank God enough, as did the early Christians at their Eucharist (see the *Didache*), 'for the knowledge and faith and immortality' he has revealed to us in Jesus?

Prayer-lines: God our Father, fill us with your holy Spirit to be more grateful for all you have done and are constantly doing for us in your church.

Week 27: Monday

Cycle 1: Jon 1:1-2:1, 11; Cycle 2: Gal 1:6-12; Gospel: Lk 10:25-37

Cycle 1: The little book of Jonah, like the Bible in general, seeks to tell us about God, and man, and the difference between them. It opens with the familiar God of justice sending his prophet to de-clare to a sinful people its sins . But Jonah is not a typical prophet, his story is not an historical one. It is a parable. Like other prophets Jonah dreads his task. Nineveh is a sinister city, of very ill-repute. But he thinks he can escape his commission by flight – to Tarshish in Spain, in the far west, instead of east to Nineveh. He reckons, however, without God's power – to raise a storm at will. And the unsolicited conversion to Yahweh of the Gentile sailors underlines his guilt.

Cycle 2: 'The Good News I learnt through the revelation of Jesus Christ.' What is the background of this 'most Pauline of Paul's epistles'? It was Luther's 'pet epistle'. The Galatians were former converts of Paul a few years earlier. He is now writing from Ephesus in the west of Asia Minor. After Paul had left them, Jewish Christians, (possibly former Pharisees), who had already opposed Paul and Barnabas at Antioch and at the 'Council of Jerusalem' (Acts 15), came to Galatia with a different version of the gospel. We know this version only through Paul's attack on it. Briefly it was that justification for the Gentiles was not really complete without also obeying the Law, especially the law of circumcision, given, after all, to Abraham by God. (Gen 17).

Gospel: 'Which of the three proved himself a neighbour?' Jesus is always a model in his conduct. He not merely avoids the traps his opponents set for him, he leads them also into greater truth. The lawyer today would seek to involve Jesus in the current casuistry about whom exactly a Jew could consider as neighbour – to be loved, according to the Law – as oneself. Jesus tells a simple story which shows that the lawyer is asking the wrong question. The point of the command is not about identifying one's neighbour. The point is: what is neighbourliness? To whom can I show the love which God's law enjoins? The priest and the Levite wanted to make sure they were not touching what might be a dead man, and thereby defiling themselves. The Samaritan – whom the lawyer would certainly not consider a neighbour, has a truer sense of what the love of God and neighbour meant.

Prayer-lines: Thank you, Lord, for coming to us daily in Word and sacrament to strengthen us in holiness. May we always be doers of the Word, not hearers only.

Week 27: Tuesday

Cycle 1: Jon 3:1-10; Cycle 2: Gal 1:13-24; Gospel: Lk 10:38-42
Cycle 1: 'And God did not inflict on them the disaster he had threatened.' So Jonah gets a second chance to play the prophet. The cheerful use of exaggeration (vastness of Nineveh, etc.) continues to emphasise the irony of the story. But Jonah's taking a day's journey in the city before delivering his prophetic message bears out his reluctance in the whole affair. What a contrast is the total contrition of the Ninevites! They take the timid little prophet from Israel seriously. All must fast and wear sackcloth, from the king to the cattle! And they credit God with the freedom of his boundless compassion to change his decree of destruction. 'And God relented.' Only Jonah remained to be converted. Tomorrow we'll see how God does it.

Cycle 2: 'They gave glory to God for me.' As with Paul's opponents at Corinth we can be grateful for those in Galatia occasion-
ing this firsthand account of Paul's 'faith journey'. His history as
a persecutor of Christians is a guarantee that it was by God's intervention he has been converted. Christ was revealed to him as
'the Good News to the pagans'. It was only after his stay in
Arabia, (i.e. the desert east and south of Damascus), and a subsequent three years spent in Damascus that Paul made contact
with the Jerusalem church, notably with Peter, for information
about Jesus' ministry. And after only a two-week stay there Paul
has returned to his homeland in Cilicia. Hence he was personally
unknown to the Christians in Judaea.

Gospel: 'Mary has chosen the better part.' Luke's is the only
gospel that has this little story. The popular medieval use of it to
exalt the contemplative over the active life misses the point.
Elsewhere Jesus has pronounced the blessedness of those who
hear the word of God and keep it. Mary here seems to be the personification of that beatitude. But Jesus is not belittling the
virtue of Martha's warm-hearted welcome of him. He does correct her concern with the elaborate arrangements of hospitality.
(For Luke, Jesus is the real host of the occasion, feeding the sisters both by his presence and his word). And, above all, in defending Mary's total attention to him, Jesus is giving us an important reminder. There are more ways than one of welcoming
Christ, of serving him, of pleasing God.

Prayer-lines: Lord Jesus, help us to remain detached in *our* work
and free from tendencies to judge others in theirs.

Week 27: Wednesday
Cycle 1: Jon 4:1-11; Cycle 2: Gal 2:1-4, 7-14; Gospel: Lk 11:1-4
Cycle 1: 'Am I not to feel sorry for Nineveh?' Jonah, we are told,
fell into a rage at seeing Nineveh repent and therefore being forgiven by God. Now we know what his problem has been all
along. Hate! He hated this city of notorious ill-repute, and with
all his being wanted to see it punished. He goes outside the city

to sit down and sulk. He has therefore to be taught a lesson. Nineveh was near modern Baghdad, where the heat can be unbearable. God provides a castor-oil plant which gives Jonah a very welcome shelter. When it dies at dawn Jonah begs for death. But at least he has learnt to be sorry for the loss of something treasured. Perhaps even to glimpse God's right to be sorry to lose even sinners. A lesson for us all in our angers and frustrations. Above all the unfathomable mystery of a God so merciful to the undeserving.

Cycle 2: Paul's second visit to Jerusalem in our first reading would seem to be the same as Luke narrates in Acts 15 in connection with the debate in Antioch over the necessity of circumcision for salvation. Acts tells of the public discussion; the impact of Peter's intervention; and the final decision to ask of the Gentiles only conformity to some dietary laws. In Galatians Paul talks of a private meeting with the leaders of the Jerusalem Christian community, James, Peter and John. It was agreed that Paul's mission was chiefly to the Gentiles. But he should remember to help the poor Christians in Jerusalem. At a later meeting with Peter in Antioch Paul publicly rebukes him for dropping his practice of taking meals with the Gentiles for fear of losing face with the Judaeo-Christians.

Gospel: St Luke's 'Our Father' is shorter than that in Matthew. In that respect, scholars say, it is probably closer to Jesus' formula. For the first Christians it was a revelation of how Jesus prayed himself. And so we find its phrases recurring on his lips in the gospels, especially in his Passion. 'Father, glorify thy name …' 'Thy will, not mine be done' at Gethsemani. 'Father, forgive them', on Calvary. Above all, the secret of all Jesus' prayer – given to us as the secret of ours: the address, *Abba.* Too familiar for God for any Jew but Jesus, and 'those he is not ashamed to call his sisters and brothers'.

Prayer-lines: God, our Father, grant us your holy Spirit in abundance, that he may lead us into the full truth of your love for sinners.

Week 27: Thursday

Cycle 1: Mal 3:13-20; Cycle 2: Gal 3:1-5; Gospel: Lk 11:5-13

Cycle 1: 'For you who fear my name the sun of righteousness will blaze out.' 'Malachi' in Hebrew means 'my messenger'; but it may also be the prophet's name. He is the last of the minor prophets. Later than Haggai and Zechariah, for the Temple has been rebuilt, and regular worship is going on there. However, the priests are not giving proper instruction or example. Even divorcing their wives, which Malachi deplores. The general morale is low. Those who flout the law seem to prosper. Malachi warns, however, that God's judgement is coming – with punishment for the evil, and comfort for the faithful ones.

Cycle 2: 'Are you people in Galatia mad?' Strong words, indeed, for Paul is really angry with these converts of his. He – and they – have seen miracles, especially of conversion, among them without any practice of the (Mosaic) Law. Can they not, therefore, see that these wonders are the work of the Spirit among them? And they have been brought about by Paul's preaching to them the saving power of Christ's crucifixion. Their own experience therefore, should convince them of the truth of what he taught. As he has already said, 'I live by faith in the Son of God, who loved me and gave himself up for me. I will not nullify the grace of God.'

Gospel: 'How much more will the heavenly Father give the Holy Spirit.' This parable is a sequel to Jesus' teaching his disciples the 'Our Father'. It is one of his 'how-much-more' parables. In these he contrasts the certainty of God's power and generosity to the doubtful guarantee of human sources of help. Another is the parable of the importunate widow forcing a ruthless judge to grant her request by sheer dint of her incessant pleading. – And remember, Jesus adds, that what God gives is infinitely more precious than anything humans can give, namely his Holy Spirit. This he gives not merely for our personal sanctification, but, in Luke's context, also to meet the intentions of the 'Our Father': hallowing of God's name; coming of the kingdom, etc.

Prayer-lines: God, our Father, fill us with you Holy Spirit that we may realise the wonders you have done for us through your Son, Jesus, and your readiness to continue your benefits endlessly as we pray.

Week 27: Friday *c. 400 B.C.*

Cycle 1: Joel 1:13-15, 2:1-2; Cycle 2: Gal 3:7-14; Gospel: Lk 11:15-26

Cycle 1: Joel is one of the minor prophets. He is dated in the era after the return of the exiles to Jerusalem. Liturgy in the Temple is taken for granted. For once, abuses in cult or social justice do not appear in these prophetic oracles. Instead, the topic a disastrous plague of locusts (not unknown even in the 20th century). They are omnivorous. All the crops have perished. And this has had a serious effect on the Temple offerings. The cereal offering has had to be stopped, and the libation of wine. All the grapes too have been devoured. It would seem that the oft-predicted Day of the Lord has come – the day of judgement not merely for Jerusalem, but for the whole world. Worthy occasion, indeed, for priests and people to pray fervently to God in his Temple.

Cycle 2: 'It is those who rely on faith who are the sons of Abraham'. Paul's opponents had argued that as part of the covenant God had made with Abraham he had given the command of circumcision. Paul rebuts this argument by the fact that God had first given a promise to Abraham independent of circumcision, that in him all the nations would be blessed. And, by relying on faith – not on the Law – the Gentiles had shared in Abraham's meritorious faith. People of the Law, however, are subject to the curse laid on those who do not observe every item of the law. Christ saved us from this curse of the law (which falls on a corpse hanging on a tree) so that we might inherit the blessing promised to Abraham.

Gospel: 'If Satan is divided against himself, how can his kingdom stand? Note that Jesus does not deny the existence of Beelzebub, or Satan'. Nor his power. He is 'a strong man, fully armed, guarding his own palace, his goods undisturbed'. The violence

that has been going on for so long in history is only the shadow
of the great conflict between God and demonic evil. But Jesus asserts that he has broken into that palace of Beelzebub – by healing disease, curing mental illnesses, preaching forgiveness and
unity instead of vengeance and division. For Jesus himself is 'the
stronger one' in the parable. It is worth pondering on that aspect
of our faith. It is a religion of God's supreme power. And power
should be a dominant aspect of Christ for us – as it was for St
Paul. The paradoxical power of his crucifixion. It is renewed for
us in the sacraments. But also in our own 'crucifixions', big or
small if we unite them with his. He is always 'the stronger one',
on whom our weakness can rely.

Prayer-lines: Lord Jesus, teach us by your Spirit always to 'gather
with you', so that no 'unclean spirit' may find entry to the house
of our hearts.

Week 27: Saturday

Cycle 1: Joel 4:12-21; Cycle 2: Gal 3:22-29; Gospel: Lk 11:27-28

Cycle 1: 'The Lord shall make his home in Zion'. In yesterday's
first reading we saw the whole people at prayer in the Temple in
view of the great disaster which afflicted them. Now God has
answered that confident prayer. The plague of locusts and the
drought are over. Yahweh will restore again the grain, the new
wine and the oil. For the Day of the Lord has really come. For the
nations it is a day of judgement, and punishment for their cruel
treatment of Israel. The traditional cosmic phenomena in sun
and moon and stars will bear witness at this great judgement
scene. Egypt, Israel's primal enemy will see the Nile dried up,
and the land therefore barren. Edom, home of Jacob's treacherous brother, will become a wasteland. But Jerusalem, with
Yahweh once again residing there 'will be a holy place'.

Cycle 2: 'You are all one in Christ Jesus'. The Old Testament
shows that all humanity, Jew and Gentile, and even all creation
is a prisoner to sin. (The Letter to the Romans will spell this out
more clearly). So the Law was introduced for a time to prepare

for the coming of Christ, as a kind of guardian. Freedom from this discipline came with the advent of Christ and our justification by believing in him. We are incorporated in Christ by faith, and by its sacramental complement, Baptism. We have put on Christ like a garment by adopting his moral dispositions and his outlook. Secondary differences like race, social conditions and gender disappear through our becoming, in the same Spirit, members of Christ's body. – How rich, indeed, is our Christian faith!

Gospel: 'A woman in the crowd raised her voice'. Luke, who alone has this episode, places it effectively as a contrast to the preceding scene where some of the crowd muttered that Jesus was casting out devils by the prince of devils. But this simple woman is full of admiration for this wonderful man, and expresses it in a typical maternal way. What a lucky woman his mother is, to have such a wonderful son. And she gets her reward from Jesus. As he had taught the Samaritan woman to long for the 'living water' of the Spirit. As he invited the crowds he had fed with bread and fish the day before to accept him now as the 'Bread of Life'. So now he invites this simple woman in the crowd to transfer her admiration of an earthly relationship to eternal ones. To rise from earthly family images to the heavenly family where 'whoever does the will of my Father is my brother and sister and mother'.

Prayer-lines: Lord Jesus, increase our faith to accept more fully our unity with one another by our union with you in baptism.

Week 28: Monday

Cycle 1: Rom 1:1-7; Cycle 2: Gal 4:22-5:1; Gospel: Lk 11:29-32

Cycle 1: 'The Good News that God promised long ago'. For the next four weeks we shall be reading from this most important of all Paul's letters. It could be dated with all probability to 57 or 58 AD. Now Paul has not played any part in evangelising the Christians in Rome, but he is planning to visit it, and perhaps make it his base on his way to Spain. Christianity would seem to have arrived there by the early 40s AD, only a few years after the resurrection. And, it would seem, directly through Christian Jews from Jerusalem. In his earlier letter to Galatians Paul has trenchantly rebutted his Jewish – Christian opponents who advocated circumcision for Gentile Christians. In Romans, however, Paul will deal with the problem of faith and good works more serenely. The contribution that this letter has made to subsequent Christian thought is enormous.

Cycle 2: 'When Christ freed us, he meant us to remain free'. In the first reading today Paul shows that his opponents draw the wrong conclusions from the story of Abraham. Hagar does not represent the Gentiles, as they claimed. She represents those who commit themselves to their slavery under the Law. Sarah, Abraham's free-born wife, represents the freedom which has been won for us by Christ. Gentiles are, therefore, descendants of the promise God made to Abraham, independently of the covenant at Sinai. – As Christians, however, we must be careful not to interpret this as an indictment of Judaism. It is an attack specifically on those who would impose the Law on Gentile Christians.

Gospel: 'A greater than Jonah is here'. Matthew's gospel reads 'the sign of Jonah' as his spending three days inside the 'great fish': a foreshadowing, therefore, of Jesus' burial and resurrection after it. But Luke's interpretation is the more likely one. Jesus is reproaching his own generation for not 'repenting', as the Ninevites had done. – And we have seen how minimal Jonah's preaching had been. The other Old Testament example that Jesus invokes as witness against his own generation is the long journey of the queen of Sheba to hear Solomon's famous 'wisdom'. – But there was no comparison between Solomon's proverbs and the wisdom that Jesus, the light of the world, had brought. – We may well, perhaps, place ourselves in the dock with the generation Jesus has reproached. Will anyone rise up on Judgement day to condemn us for not making better use of all our privileges as Christians? Our sacramental life from infancy, and our easy access to Jesus' wisdom in the gospels.

Prayer-lines: Lord Jesus, make us ever more conscious of and grateful for all you have given us.

Week 28: Tuesday

Cycle 1: Rom 1:16-25; Cycle 2: Gal 5:1-6; Gospel: Lk 11: 37-41

Cycle 1: 'The power of God saving all … Jews first, but also Greeks'. Paul is going to explain that the Good News of Christ is the only way of salvation for mankind. The great division of humanity for the Bible is between Jew and Gentile. The picture he paints of the Gentile world is black indeed: 'The anger of God is being revealed against its wickedness… Such people are without excuse'. They have exchanged the truth about God, discernible in nature, for idolatry. The result has been a general lapse into sexual perversion. Such would be the current Jewish view of pagan immorality in Paul's time. But can we say that our present post-Christian western world is any better? Happily the Good News of Paul is still valid for us: the power of God saving all who have faith in Christ.

Cycle 2: 'What matters is faith that makes its power felt through love'. Having dealt with the doctrinal side of the question, Paul now makes a passionate appeal for its proper practice. Hold on to the freedom, which Christ gave you from slavery to the law. To accept circumcision is to reject the freedom given by faith in Christ. However, Paul's remark that 'whether you are circumcised or not makes no difference', shows that he does not think that circumcision is wrong in itself. But the freedom given by faith in Christ is not moral licence. It is the grace to live by love.

Gospel: 'Give alms and everything will be clean for you'. Certainly for St Luke the Jewish tradition of alms-giving was a vital component of Christian morality. But we are taken aback at the violence of Jesus' rebuke of the Pharisees, speaking as a Pharisee's guest. However, we need not take this strong criticism of religious hypocrisy, which will continue in the next two days, as given on that particular occasion alone. It is a parallel to the long denunciation given in chapter 23 of Matthew's gospel.

Luke has simply inserted it into his own narrative sequence. Elsewhere, in his Acts of Apostles, for example, Luke has spoken in more favourable terms of the Pharisees: unlike the Sadduces they believed in the resurrection, and therefore take Paul's part in his trial before the Jewish council. But the lesson of this critique is always valid. Sincerity of heart in religion will ensure that our conduct will be also correct.

Prayer-lines: God our Father, grant us your holy Spirit in abundance that our conduct be always inspired by our desire to please you.

Week 28: Wednesday

Cycle 2: Rom 2:1-11; Cycle 2: Gal 5:18-25; Gospel: Lk 11: 42-46
Cycle 1: 'God has no favourites'. Paul now addresses an imaginary Jewish listener who has been applauding Paul's lurid description of Gentile immorality in the Roman world. But Paul at once challenges the right of such a Jew to condemn the Gentiles. The Jews too are guilty, and in need of repentance. After all the Jew has the Law to guide his conduct. He will be judged according to his fidelity to that law. If he has failed to obey it, he too will have to face punishment. This is a lesson for every Christian generation too. Jesus in his teaching has warned us of the danger of spotting offences in our neighbour's conduct when our own faults are more grievous.

Cycle 2: 'If you are led by the Spirit, no law can touch you'. We get into difficulties in translating the Bible's psychological terms. What is here termed 'self-indulgence' is literally 'flesh' in the Greek. But 'flesh' in the Old Testament is not always pejorative. It simply refers to our unstable, perishable nature, made as we are from clay. Paul's list clearly covers more than physical sins. Anyhow, it portrays pretty adequately the weakness of human nature unaided by grace, 'not led by the Spirit'. In practice, the important task for the Christian is twofold (a) To cultivate the 'fruits' of the Spirit. (b) To practise identifying these fruits in others' behaviour. Becoming alert to seeing the Spirit at work in this way leaves us too more open to his influence.

Gospel: 'These you should have practised without leaving the others undone'. What is Jesus faulting (us?) Pharisees with today? The law did indeed prescribe offering a tenth of their produce to the Temple. Their scruples forced them to extend this normal requirement to even the tiniest plants. At the same time they were not practising the two basic commandments: the love of God and love, in the form of justice, towards their neighbour. Their conduct in public showed that it was human esteem and not God's favour they were seeking. The lawyer, on the other hand, while he was in a position to fulfil the laws himself, made no allowance for those who were not so privileged. Concern for the major virtues would have bred humility, and precluded negative judgement on the conduct of others.

Prayer-lines: Teach us Lord to be aware of your Spirit at work in all of us, and save us from passing negative judgement on others.

Week 28: Thursday
Cycle 1: Rom 3:21-30; Cycle 2: Eph 1: -10; Gospel: Lk 11:47-54
Cycle 1: 'It is the same justice of God that comes through faith'. Paul has already shown that, despite possessing the Law, the Jews were lacking in righteousness'. But that righteousness is now available to them too, as for the Greeks, by faith. Faith in what? Faith in the reconciliation with God won for us by Jesus Christ. This is a further display of God's righteousness. In the past he manifested it by not punishing sins. Now he shows it by sharing his righteousness with all who believe in Christ. Paul's vocabulary here is not always clear to the modern mind. He means that God has acquitted humanity of sin, and thereby made men innocent. But the human contribution is faith; not in doing what a law commands.

Cycle 2: For the next ten days or so our first reading will be from the Letter to the Ephesians. It is a considerable contrast, in thought and vocabulary to Galatians (and Romans), and has been of enormous influence on theology and spirituality. It has been called a summit of Pauline doctrine. However, the large majority of scholars agree that it was written not by Paul himself, but by 'his best disciple'. It opens in the style of a hymn of thanksgiving (in the Jewish liturgical tradition), thanking God for his great plan of salvation. The author details our adoption by him in Christ into his family, freeing us from our sins, and uniting everyone and all creation too in Christ, It is a passage calling more for reflection and prayer than verbal commentary.

Gospel: 'They did the killing, you the building'. In yesterday's gospel Jesus rebuked the experts in the Law for not making allowance in their teaching for those who were unable to fulfil the Law in every detail – as they could do themselves. Today he identifies their guilt with the 'establishment' of Old Testament times who paid no heed to the warnings of the prophets about Israel's guilt and the punishment it merited. We think, for example, of the treatment of Jeremiah by his contemporaries. Now that the prophets are dead (and silent) the lawyers are prepared to honour them by erecting memorial tombs for them. – Yes, they have indeed in their expert knowledge of the Law the key to God's designs. But they don't use it to bring others to God. – In our own allergy to being criticised by others we can readily understand the wrath of these men, which will in fact make them guilty of Jesus' blood too. Have we a lesson here to learn about accepting criticism with a view to our self-knowledge? 'May I know you, may I know myself' was St Augustine's prayer.

Prayer-lines: God our Father increase our knowledge of your saving plans, and our desire to fulfil them.

Week 28: Friday
Cycle 1: Rom 4:1-8; Cycle 2: Eph 1:11-14; Gospel: Lk 12:1-7
Cycle 1: 'Abraham's faith was considered as justifying him'. Paul has already invoked Abraham as the source of blessings for all peoples by reason of God's promise given long before the Law of Sinai. He now proposes him as a model of those who are saved by faith, not by good works. The Jews of Paul's time had regarded Abraham as an observer of the Law before its time: by

his victory over the four great kings who invaded Canaan (Gen 14), and his surrender of Isaac (Gen 22). But Paul points out that these 'works' had in no way put God in his debt. He was declared just by God independently of them. And David too (the putative author of all the Psalms) teaches the same thing. It is the sinner whom God, by forgiving him, can declare sinless.

Cycle 2: 'The Spirit of the Promise, the pledge of our inheritance'. When Paul says that 'we were claimed, as God's own chosen from the beginning', he is not necessarily referring only to the Jews as the Chosen People. From the beginning he has included everyone, Gentile as well as Jew, in God's plan of salvation. The 'you too' refers to the Ephesians the letter is addressed to. 'Stamped with the seal of the holy Spirit' refers to our Baptism – pledge of our adoption as God's children. Pledge too of our inheritance of the kingdom. A kingdom which is one of praise of God for his boundless condescension. 'Stamped with the seal of the holy Spirit' as God's sons and daughters we must try to show our family likeness to Christ our Brother. But we have also the right to depend on his Spirit to guide us in all we do.

Gospel: 'You are worth more than hundreds of sparrows'. And 'not one of them is forgotten in God's sight'. Chesterton used to say that Jesus said this with a twinkle in his eye as he looked at Peter, the Big Fisherman's bulk. At all events, the conviction that we count a lot in God's sight is the clue to our proper conduct in many ways. It will save us from 'the leaven of the Pharisees': that pernicious frame of mind that makes us unduly self-conscious of what others will say of us. (As long-distance taxis in Africa will cheerfully proclaim on their slogans: 'Let them say'). More. It will give us the courage to stand up to opposition. Even to violence, if doing what God wants is at stake.

Prayer-lines: Lord Jesus, fill us with your Spirit that we may imitate you as sons and daughters of your Father and our Father in heaven.

Week 28: Saturday
Cycle 1: Rom 4:13, 16-18; Cycle 2: Eph 1:15-23; Gospel: Lk 12: 8-12
Cycle 1: 'The faith of Abraham, who is father of us all'. Yes, the
Jews believed, God had promised he would be, through 'the
child of promise' the father of 'all the families of the earth'. Paul
has already insisted that the promise was anterior to the command of circumcision, and therefore had priority over it. Now
he claims the same priority for the promise over the Mosaic law
itself. Therefore all depends on faith (through Abraham's faith
in the promise). The Law therefore must yield to the promise.
And this holds true for the Gentile as for the Jew. Abram's first
name ('great is your father') is now charged to 'Abraham' ('father of a throng of nations'). The first of these would be
Ishmael's descendants, but Paul extends it to the Gentiles. 'For
God calls into being what does not exist' refers first to Isaac in
Sarah's barren womb; now to all the Gentiles.

Cycle 2: In today's first reading Paul's 'best disciple' continues
the hymn of thanksgiving to God for his plan of salvation. While
borrowing some ideas and vocabulary from Colossians, it also
draws on Ps 110 and Ps 8 with reference to the exaltation of
Christ and the church. 'The Saints', to whom the Ephesians have
shown love, here means the angels, with whom, in Christ, they
have been joined. Christ's exaltation is above all a manifestation
of God's power. A new statement about Christ is that he is head
of the church, whose members form his Body. And the church
too shares in his exaltation, as 'in the fulness of him who fills all
creation'. A breath-taking comment indeed on Ps 8's, 'what is
man that you should care for him, made him little less than a god.'

Gospel: 'When the time comes the holy Spirit will teach you what
you must say'. To understand the enigmatic phrase, 'blasphemy
against the holy Spirit', we must have some idea of how Luke
presents the holy Spirit in Jesus' life. The immediate context of
the phrase is the refusal of some of Jesus' opponents to see 'the
finger of God', i.e. the holy Spirit as the power behind Jesus'
casting out devils. But for Luke the holy Spirit is pervasive in
Jesus' life. He comes down on Jesus at his conception, presides

over his 'growth in wisdom and age and grace' as a child. And then in his fulness at his baptism. 'Full of the holy Spirit' he goes out into the desert and is 'tempted by the devil'. Returned, he heads again 'full of the holy Spirit' to Galilee. The role of the Spirit is clearly to penetrate Jesus' being as man, to enable him to fulfil his mission as saviour. After our Baptism he continues that work in us.

Prayer-lines: God our Father, increase our faith to realise the wonders you have wrought in us through Christ and his holy Spirit.

Week 29: Monday

Cycle 1: Rom 4: 20-25; Cycle 2: Eph 2:1-10; Gospel: Lk 12:13-21

Cycle 1: 'The faith that was considered as justifying him'. Abraham's faith consisted in believing that God has power to do as he had promised. By this believing, Abraham was held justified. And that remains the model for our faith too. Only that we now have the guarantee of God's power in raising Jesus from the dead. – We are indeed 'an Easter people', we live always in the light of Jesus' resurrection. It is the faith on which our lives in Christ are built. As Paul has said already in his first letter to the Corinthians: 'If Christ is not raised, then our preaching is useless, and your believing is useless. If our hope in Christ is for this life only, we are the most unfortunate of all people'.

Cycle 2: 'You have been saved by a gift from God'. Paul outlines God's great plan of salvation as it concerns humankind. It brings all of us, Jew and Gentile alike, from death to life. Even to share Christ's ascension to heaven. This is the victory over 'the ruler who governs the air'. What is said already of Christ is now said of all Christians. And there is a shift from Paul's stress on faith as opposed to works of the law. Salvation is God's gift and work alone: God's grace rather than our good deeds. What a vision of hope this can be for us: that in Christ we are created, re-created as it were, 'to live the good life as from the beginning God meant us to live it'.

Gospel: 'A man's life is not made secure by what he owns'. This is a recurring theme in Jesus' teaching, highlighted especially by Luke. 'Blessed are you poor' is the first of his Beatitudes. It was a particularly hard lesson for the Jewish tradition – wealth was looked on as a sign of God's blessing. But Paul put his finger on the seriousness of this instinct to hoard, 'avarice', by identifying it with idolatry. Possessions can really become a false god. In the Old Testament the people could not resist the promise of false gods. In the New Testament the Pharisees relied on money. Today the pressure comes from advertisement. Jesus' warning is as necessary as ever. No possessions can protect us from the one thing worth fearing, God's judgement. It is not what we have that counts before God. It is what we are.

Prayer-lines: God our Father, fill us with your holy Spirit to live in Christ the good life you want us to live.

Week 29: Tuesday
Cycle 1: Rom 5:12, 15, 17-21; Cycle 2: Eph 2:12-22; Gospel: Lk 12:35-38
Cycle 1: 'The righteousness that comes through Jesus Christ, our Lord'. From Abraham and his justification by faith Paul now turns to Christ. Christ's death for us as sinners had brought us grace and life instead of our sin and death. He has, therefore, reversed the sin of Adam and its sequel. 'However great the number of sins committed', – and Paul has already sketched a panorama of the sinful world of his time – 'grace was even greater'. And this is due to God's love for us, and the righteousness that comes through Jesus Christ our Lord.

Cycle 2: 'You are being built into a house where God lives'. The Gentiles of Ephesus are now reminded how their lot has been totally changed by their faith and incorporation in Christ. They have been lifted out of their exclusion from God's covenant relationship with Israel, and made fuller partners in it. Jew and Gentile, through the death of Christ, have become a new humanity, reconciled to God. They share, as members of one city, one household, the one Spirit that brings them to the Father.

They form part with the apostles and prophets of a new Temple for God to live in. – We have much food here to meditate on, our Christian riches.

Gospel: 'Happy those servants if he finds them ready'. Yesterday Jesus reminded us that possessions are no security against the day of judgement. Another constant in his teaching is the need for Christian vigilance. 'Happy the one whom Jesus finds ready when he comes'. Jesus was giving his disciples practical and urgent advice in view of the definite crisis he saw coming; his arrest and death. We know that in fact he didn't find them ready in Gethsemani. Coming for what, was it , on that occasion? To ask them, you remember to share in his great struggle (the meaning of Luke's word 'agonia') against the powers of evil. – Our share in that struggle is not denied to us either. In big things or small: death, failure, disappointments of every kind. We will be unable to take our share, unless we are 'watching' for Jesus' coming in them. How do we watch? Above all by daily prayer, that we may remain awake to the presence and demands of Christ in our daily life.

Prayer-lines: Lord Jesus, grant us your Spirit in abundance to be conscious of the riches of our Baptism, and our calling to share in your struggle against the forces of evil.

Week 29: Wednesday
Cycle 1: Rom 6:12-18; Cycle 2: Eph 3:2-12; Gospel: Lk 12:39-48
Cycle 1: 'You are living by grace and not by law'. In baptism, Paul has told us, we died with Christ; died to sin. And we also rose with him; rose as freed from sin. We must live accordingly, letting no sin enter our lives. Instead of that we should dedicate our whole being for God: 'a weapon fighting on the side of God'. So, in other words, we have changed our masters. From being 'owned' by sin, we have been set free to be owned by God, owned by the 'righteousness' God has given us.

Cycle 2: 'The depths that I see in the mystery of Christ'. Paul, though unworthy, has been entrusted with proclaiming this mystery. A manifold mystery; a secret known at creation by only God the creator. It means the full and equal participation of the Gentiles in the mystery of the Church. Only now has that mystery been revealed to the Sovereignties and Powers, those malevolent forces that until the death of Christ held sway over humanity. Later on in his letter Paul will remind the Ephesians (and us) that we must still give battle with them. But now we are able to approach God with confidence through our faith in him.

Gospel: 'When a man has a great deal given him on trust, even more will be expected of him'. Jesus has already proclaimed the need for Christians to be consciously vigilant for his, unpredictable, coming – as slaves wait up for their master at any hour. 'The Son of man is coming at an hour you do not expect'. Luke, mindful of the needs of his own generation, as he is writing some fifty years after the Resurrection, uses Peter's question to focus the teaching of vigilance in a special way on those in authority: Luke's is the only gospel to use the word 'steward'. The key-principle involved is the idea of Christian service in the church. Does the 'allowance of food', therefore, mean more than material food? Does the description of a loose-living servant show that such officials did exist in Luke's time? At all events, failures in the Christian service, that authority in the church requires, will not go unpunished. Authority and privilege also demand responsibility.

Prayer-lines: While we meditate, Lord, with wonder and gratitude on 'the marvels you worked for us', let us never forget the obligations of our Christian service.

Week 29: Thursday
Cycle 1: Rom 6:19-23; Cycle 2: Eph 3:14-21; Gospel: Lk 12:49-53
Cycle 1: 'The present given by God is eternal life'. Paul contrasts the former life of the Gentiles with their new life in Christ. It is important for them to realise that Christian freedom does not mean licence to continue sinning. That was a form of slavery from which they are now ransomed. That means they have been freed to enter a new service: that of the good life of righteous-

ness. They should realise how worthless that former life of sin was. It has left them only with a sense of shame. Their new campaign is that of righteousness. Their new master is God. Death was the miserable return for their former immorality. But now God repays them beyond all their deserts by the gift of eternal life.

Cycle 2: 'Glory to Him in the Church and in Christ Jesus'. Before he concludes the doctrinal part of the Letter to the Ephesians the author continues the prayer he began last Saturday. It is a prayer of thanksgiving to God for the wonders he has wrought for these Gentiles in making them members of the Church. He prays that 'they may be filled with the Spirit', which is the power of God. Through that Spirit may the life of Christ grow ever stronger in their faith and love. In this growth into their understanding of the mystery of Christ they will be 'filled with the utter fulness of God'. And God will thus be glorified in the Church as he already is in Christ.

Gospel: 'I have come to bring not peace but division.' Our gospel today is about the great mystery of the rejection by men of God's offer of salvation in Christ. In the gospel Jesus' teaching is usually about others : his disciples, his opponents. Today he speaks of himself. 'A baptism (of fire) I must still receive, and how great is my distress till it is over'. We are still, according to Luke, on the road to Jerusalem. And these words give us a rare insight into Jesus' thoughts on the way. A perceptive and harrowing foreboding of the Passion that lies ahead – an agony he will have to face alone while his disciples sleep.

Prayer-lines: Lord Jesus, give us by your holy Spirit, a sincere desire to share gladly in your baptism of fire as you know best for each of us.

Week 29: Friday
Cycle 1: Rom 7:18-25; Cycle 2: Eph 4:1-6; Gospel: Lk 12:54-59
Cycle 1: 'Who will rescue me from this body doomed to death?' The exclamatory, 'Thanks be to God' which follows this ques-

tion is not the Letter's answer to it. That will come in chapter 8. Meanwhile Paul wrestles with the confrontation of the self ('Ego' in Paul's Greek) with sin and the law. Paul is not speaking autobiographically of his personal problem. He is looking at the problem of corporate human history, both of Jew and Gentile, before the coming of Christ. Doubtless in practice many today will see his words realised too in their own lives, Both Augustine and Luther thought it expressed Paul's own experience as a Christian. But it is the Pauline perspective that matters first. Only with Christ's coming is the dilemma resolved.

Cycle 2: In Pauline letters the doctrinal section is usually followed by exhortations to behave according to the truths of faith. So it is here. The outline of God's great plan has been given. All things are to be united in Christ and subjected to him. Through his death a new humanity has been created. Jews and Gentiles are made one in the church. All this unity is a dynamic reality, to come about by the behaviour of Christians, inspired by the Spirit. So the virtues of community living are listed: charity, humility, gentleness, patience. 'One Lord' is a vital statement for a Gentile-Christian church in a polytheistic society. 'One faith' will depend on the Church's foundation of authoritative apostolic teaching. The ultimate unity is summarised in the fourfold 'all' of God's supremacy.

Gospel: 'You do not know how to interpret these times'. Jesus is still referring to the mystery of his generation's rejection of the kingdom which he represents, in his teaching and his deeds. He is indeed, as Simeon predicted, set for the fall and rising of many in Israel. 'Blind leaders' he will later call the Pharisees. They have indeed the wit to recognise things like change in the weather! The collapse of their world a few decades later they fail to detect. Even the crowd, 'led by the blind', fail to see how urgent it is to believe in him. Yet, to save money in an expensive lawsuit they are canny enough to make a settlement out of court. – Should we ask ourselves what priority we give in our lives to Christian principles?

Prayer-lines: God our Father, help us to make our own the wisdom which our daily scripture readings make available to us.

Week 29: Saturday

Cycle 1: Rom 8:1-11; Cycle 2: Eph 4:7-16; Gospel: Lk 13:1-9

Cycle 1: 'The Spirit of life in Christ has set you free'. Here at last is the answer to Paul's agonised cry as he personified helpless humanity before Christ's coming, 'who will rescue me from this body doomed to death?'. The answer is, 'the Spirit of Christ'. As he raised Jesus' body from death, so the Spirit will raise ours. As he was the vital principle in Christ's earthly life, so will he be in ours. Where mere nature ('flesh' is Paul's term) was unable to keep the law of God's will, the Spirit will enable us to keep it. For he has made his home in us, as well as our dwelling in him, by our baptism. So the imitation of Christ in our lives is now possible. Not by any effort of our flawed nature, but by yielding to the vitalising power of the Spirit.

Cycle 2: 'So the body grows, until it has built itself up, in love'. Ephesians, in our first reading, has stressed the unity of humanity in Christ and in the church. It now describes the diversity of Christ's gifts within that unity. In the letter to the Corinthians these gifts could be divisive: the contrary here. They foster the growth of the church. 'In this way we are all to come to unity in the faith'. The goal and fruit of that growth of the church is the perfect humanity, 'fully mature with the fulness of Christ himself'. With each part of his Body the church playing its proper role: the authority of the Apostles, the evangelising work of the teachers, and so on, the church shall be preserved from 'every wind of doctrine'. It is the vision of ecumenical unity for which we all pray today.

Gospel: 'Unless you repent you will all perish'. Jesus today continues the warnings to his contemporaries that 'conversion' (the basic meaning of 'repentance') to him is a matter of life or death. He gives examples of recent violent deaths that are not recorded elsewhere, but bring home to the emotions the finality of death.

His parable of the gardener obtaining a remission of life for the fig-tree shows that there is still time for conversion and meeting God's forgiveness. But it is not an endless remission. If the tree bears no fruit next year, the gardener may cut it down.

Prayer-lines: Lord Jesus, help us to seek the guidance of the Spirit in all we do, that we may play our part in building up your church.

Week 30: Monday
Cycle 1: Rom 8:12-17; Cycle 2: Eph 4:32-5:8; Gospel: Lk 13:10-17
Gospel: 'Was it not right to untie her bonds on the Sabbath day?' We'd all agree that it was. And we'd share in the joy of the people who were present, especially at seeing the discomfiture of the synagogue official and, no doubt of other pharisees who were present. We feel it's only what human nature demands in the situation.

But our English translations of the gospel often conceal from us its deeper meaning. Elsewhere in St Luke Jesus also says, 'Was it not right?': about the Passion he had to undergo. In explaining the scandal of his death to the two disciples on the road to Emmaus, the words 'Was it not right?' clearly mean: 'Was it not ORDAINED?' – By whom? By his Father. By God. And here today in the synagogue, as always, Jesus sees his activity as doing the will of his Father. He is, in fact, a revelation of his Father at work. That's the sort of religion God wants of us: not petty laws of what we can do only on weekdays.

Cycle 1: Our first reading from Romans brings the gospel message even further. If, in the gospel stories, God shows himself at work in Jesus' deeds, so he plans to be active in *our* lives too. He does this through the power and activity in our lives of his own Spirit which he has given us. 'The Spirit himself and our spirit bear united witness that we are children of God'. In other ways, we are 'other Christs', revealing God's nature by our deeds.

Cycle 2: And our first reading marvellously echoes that teaching, so dramatically visualised for us by Jesus. 'Be kind, forgiving each other as readily *as God forgave you* in Christ. Try, them, to imitate God ... and follow Christ by loving as he loved you.'

Prayer-lines: God, our Father, fill us with your Holy Spirit, that our lives, like that of Jesus, may reveal your goodness to others.

Week 30: Tuesday

Cycle 1: Rom 8:18-25; Cycle 2: Eph 5:21-33; Gospel: Lk 13:18-21

Gospel: 'The kingdom of God is like a mustard seed ... like yeast in the flour.' One is tempted to say, these tiny parables are themselves a mustard seed, a leaven. For in a sense they contain the whole gospel, the Good News: the presence of God with us, and his power. They are spoken by Jesus to the Twelve to encourage them. All very well for him to promise they would sit on twelve thrones, but at times this seemed to them only a dream. They had few illusions about themselves, a handful of nobodies in the eyes of the people and the Jewish leaders – not to speak of the mighty world of Rome. –So, no wonder that at Jesus' death their faith collapsed like a house of cards.

Yet the truth is here in these little parables. If a seed could become a tree; if a little yeast could make a loaf of a little flour, the same miracle could take place in the world of men's hearts. Why? Because the same power is at work: 'with God all things are possible'. – A lesson for us all to ponder – in the face of our own weakness, our community's powerlessness.

Cycle 1: 'The glory as yet unrevealed which is waiting for us.' St Paul makes no apology when, without warning, he leads us into the deeper waters of Christian thought. – And yet he is not really deserting the basic message of today's gospel: God's hidden power in our midst. Only here, Paul widens our horizons to the cosmic limits of creation. And this sits well enough with our present day ecology consciousness. With our personal redemption in Christ, Paul assures us, will come the harmony of the whole created order which, as Scripture tells us, has been defaced by sin.

Cycle 2: 'This mystery has many implications.' Yes, the mystery of marriage is too vast for a short treatment. But even here the mystery of the hidden power in the mustard seed is not irrelevant. Paul is taking the current code of Jewish, Greek and Roman behaviour and, so to speak baptising it in Christian faith. 'This mystery applies to Christ and the church.' He is indeed the third person in every marriage. It is not too much to say that successful Christian marriage can only take place by bride and bridegroom learning to ponder and accept their entry into that awesome mystery of Christ's loving his church – unto death, and into life.

Prayer-lines: Lord Jesus increase our faith in the words of scripture, that we may grow more aware of the mystery of your divine life in every aspect of our lives.

Week 30: Wednesday
Cycle 1: Rom 8:26-30; Cycle 2: Eph 6:1-9; Gospel: Lk 13:22-30
Gospel: '"Will there be only a few saved?"' Rightly Jesus dismisses this speculative curiosity by a practical injunction: 'Try your best to enter by the narrow door.' For the questioning Jew the door to salvation was not a narrow door for *him*, as a member of the Chosen People. Jesus would shock him by the vision of outsiders 'from east and west, from north and south 'being admitted to the banquet of salvation, and yourselves turned outside'. It is intended as a shock for us too, as Christians, also a chosen people. We cannot take our salvation for granted.

Cycle 1: 'And yet, as our first reading reminds us, our faith is one of joyful confidence, not of fear. For 'the Spirit comes to help us in our weakness'. The Spirit of adoption given us in baptism 'turns everything to our good, co-operating with all those who love him'. As we grow in our knowledge of Christ by sacrament, prayer and fidelity, the door to salvation opens *wide* to admit us.

Cycle 2: Paul talks of relationships today. Here is not the proper place to discuss such a vast and complex subject. Merely to remind ourselves that the key to peace and justice in all our relationships is our common relationship to Christ: as Paul puts it: 'in the Lord … as the Lord does … obedient to Christ'. That is indeed the 'narrow gate' of the gospel through which we must all try to enter. That celtic vision of Christ 'in mouth of friend or stranger'; in wife or husband; in employer or fellow-worker. 'Of all the names in the world given to men, the only one by which we can be saved'.

Prayer-lines: Lord, make us ever more docile to the work of your spirits within us that we may become true images of your Son, Jesus.

Week 30: Thursday

Cycle 1: Rom 8:31-39; Cycle 2: Eph 6:10-20; Gospel: Lk 13:31-35
Gospel: 'It would not be right for a prophet to die outside Jerusalem.' St Luke keeps reminding us in these chapters 9 to 19 that Jesus is on his way to Jerusalem. It is a symbolic as well as an historic journey. Jesus is going as the prophet he is called to be: to lay down his prophetic challenge at the heart of Judaism, and face the consequences. And it is for us a prophetic journey to make with him as Christians. To challenge by our lives a world that is indifferent or hostile to Christian values.

Cycle 1: Christianity is indeed no insurance policy against struggle and suffering, and even death. But Paul's exultant war-cry in the first reading assures us that all the odds in that battle are in fact on our side. 'With God on our side, who can be against us?' And he will go into detail to indicate the variety of harassment that Christian living may cost us. 'If we are troubled or worried,' 'or lacking food and clothes,' 'or being threatened or even attacked.' For Paul, as for us as Christians, 'these are the trials through which we triumph by the power of him who loved us'.

Cycle 2: The Christian's journey is no easy task. But in our first reading St Paul points out how well-armed we can be by the Spirit of our baptism to triumph in that lifelong campaign. We are 'strong in the Lord, with the strength of his power'. And we have only to 'pray in the Spirit on every possible occasion' to receive and experience that almighty power which is God's Spirit in us.

Prayer-lines: Teach us, Lord, to see in our lives, a sharing in Christ's journey to Jerusalem. Make us strong by your love to bear witness before the world to your saving will.

Week 30: Friday

Cycle 1: Rom 9:1-5; Cycle 2: Phil 1:1-11; Gospel: Lk 14:1-6

Gospel: The gospel is one of four occasions where St Luke pictures Jesus at variance with the Pharisees over the question of Sabbath observance. Again it is a question of moral priorities. If the law of mercy holds good for an animal, an ox or an ass fallen into a well, surely it must hold even more for human beings. – But at least in two ways we might learn from the Pharisees in this story: To watch Jesus closely as he moves through the gospel; and to receive his words of wisdom in (willing) silence.

Cycle 1: In the first reading today St Paul's willingness 'to be cut off from Christ if I could help my brothers of Israel, my own flesh and blood', brings home to us what an intolerable shock it was for him that Israel had rejected Jesus as her Messiah. Yet, while Paul is in no way anti-semitic as a result of this, he does not abandon hope for her conversion. As Vatican II declares, following the Letter to the Ephesians, 'Christ, who is our peace, has through his Cross reconciled Jews and Gentiles'. May this be our earnest prayer at every Mass.

Cycle 2: Up to now our first reading has been from Ephesians. It is full of riches, but it is more of a sermon than a real letter to particular people. But today, in Philippians, we have a genuine letter of Paul's which is just as full of Christian teaching. Every line of Philippians would bear comment, but we can single out its central theme: Paul's love for the Philippians. This love is no mere sentiment, though it is that too. But Paul describes it accurately as being identical with Jesus' love for them. Not surprisingly he is echoing Jesus' words to the Twelve at the start of the Last Supper. Paul's longing for the Philippians echoes Christ's longing 'to eat this Passover with them before he suffered'. He prays for the Philippians' growth in love, as Jesus did for the unity of his followers: his 'new commandment'. In a word, we can see how true it is for Paul to claim, 'for me, to live is Christ'.

Prayer-lines: Lord Jesus, fill us with your Spirit, that we may share your joy at recognising his work in others.

Week 30: Saturday

Cycle 1: Rom 11:1-29; Cycle 2: Phil 1:18-26; Gospel: Lk 14:1, 7-11

Gospel: This lesson on how to avoid embarrassment in public is only a piece of worldly wisdom, and Jesus was not the first one to give it. But a parable usually has a meaning below its surface message. And for his hearers, steeped in Old Testament imagery, the wedding feast was always potentially a figure of the Kingdom of God. So Jesus is here really hinting to the Pharisees not to be so proud as a class apart, deeming others inferior in God's eyes. The humbling and exalting can be done only by God ('the person who invited you'). And that will be on the Day of Judgement.

It is also a message for the undying Pharisee in us all. Agreed. But what is our conduct to be when confronted by sin, injustice, cruelty and so on? Again the Pharisees of today's gospel give us a clue: watch Jesus closely. At the Last Supper he knelt to wash the feet of those who would betray or deny him. On the cross he prayed for those responsible for his death.

Cycle 1: Our first reading reminds us of the close bonds Christians will always have with Jews. 'As the Chosen People', as St Paul puts it, 'they are still loved by God, loved for the sake of their ancestors'. Whatever about St Paul's natural optimism about the ultimate conversion of Jews to Christ, we must seek to share God's love for them. As Vatican II instructs us, we 'must try to understand the difficulties for the Jewish soul (with its lofty sense of God's transcendence) when faced with the mystery of God becoming man'. This awareness can only deepen our own reverence for the Incarnation.

Cycle 2: This strategy of 'watching Jesus closely', to imitate him, is also the message of our first reading. Paul is writing to his beloved converts in Philippi from prison, and possibly facing death. For one like Paul, to whom 'life is Christ', death would mean only deeper union with Christ. And yet he can also see Christ personified in the Philippians. So, in fact, he expects that Christ will ask him to live on, to work for him among his converts. Elsewhere Paul will say that we should live no longer for ourselves, but for Christ, who died and rose for us. A memorable statement of our Christian programme.

Prayer-lines: Lord, may Christians everywhere avoid the sin of pride, and imitate their master, who humbled himself even to death on the cross.

Week 31: Monday

Cycle 1: Rom 11:29-36; Cycle 2: Phil 2:1-4; Gospel: Lk 14:12-14
Gospel: 'When you have a party, invite the poor, the crippled, the lame, the blind.' It would seem a forlorn hope to offer such advise to 'leading Pharisees'. But we can't be too sure that none of Jesus' listeners follow his advice. It is on the record that some Pharisees of Jesus' time and earlier, had in fact taught a doctrine as noble as this. And the New Testament elsewhere makes clear that some Pharisees did become Christians after the Resurrection. But if they did practice such high virtue, as indeed Christian movements like l'Arche and the Cheshire Homes in our day, the secret of such virtue is to be found in what St Paul tells us of the power of Christ's Spirit in us.

Cycle 1: 'God never takes back his gifts or revokes his choice.' Our first reading concludes St Paul's reflections on the mystery of God's salvation to the Jews. He had thought that they would switch from their initial rejection of Jesus as Messiah to an acceptance of him when they perceived the rapid conversion of the Gentiles. But then Paul envisaged an early end to salvation history: a return of Christ even in St Paul's own lifetime. It was not to be so, as we can see some 2000 years later. But even St Matthew's gospel, written some twenty years after Romans, had to adapt to a longer perspective than Paul's. God's plans are always mysterious, and inscrutable to us. But we can share in Paul's hymn of abasement before God's unfathomable wisdom, and be at peace in Paul's assurance that God never revokes his choice.

Cycle 2: 'Our life in Christ, the persuasion of his love, the Spirit we have in common, and the sympathy and compassion that Spirit begets in us.' St Paul is writing to his favourite converts, who have welcomed him so warmly on his first arrival in Greece. He is not afraid to expose them (and thereby us) to both the fullness of their wealth in the faith he has shared with them, and its lofty obligations in Christian living. In tomorrow's passage from the same letter Paul will show us what a shining example of the power of the Spirit we have in the humility of Christ. May the church always be a church 'of the poor' to manifest Christ's presence on earth.

Prayer-lines: May Christians everywhere always imitate Christ's option for the poor and the oppressed.

Week 31: Tuesday
Cycle 1: Rom 12:5-16; Cycle 2: Phil 2:5-11; Gospel: Lk 14:15-24
Gospel: 'Happy the man who will be at the feast in the kingdom of God.' We are still in the house of a leading Pharisee, and it is clear that this smug statement of conventional piety comes from one of the Pharisees present. It implies that he, as a pious Israelite, would certainly be at that feast. Our familiarity with the parable that follows may have blunted us to the sternness of Jesus' correction of the man's presumption. 'Sorry', the parable is saying. 'The feast in the kingdom of God has already begun. God has already said, "Come along. Everything is ready." But you, Pharisees, have refused the invitation. It has been given, therefore, to the poor, the crippled, the blind and the lame: the outcasts whom you despise. Christ in his teaching is both the servant and the invitation, the Way, the Truth and the Life. How far have we accepted him into our lives?

Cycle 1: 'In union with Christ we belong to each other.' In the second part of his theological letters St Paul likes to draw out for everyday life the moral consequences of what God has done – and is still doing for us through Christ and the Spirit. Made one in Christ we are parts of a single body: each part needing the other, yet eager to do its special task for the whole. The spirit of love who makes us one will give us patience under trial, and a share of God's friendship for the poor.

Cycle 2: 'He emptied himself even to accepting death on a cross.' Whether this famous passage was composed by Paul himself, or is an earlier Christian hymn, it is, like the hymn to charity in First Corinthians, a high – water mark in all the Pauline writings. It situates the human life of Christ in God's over-all plan to reclaim all things to himself. This plan was achieved by Jesus' selfless obedience in taking on the 'slavery' of a human existence, destined by its alienation from God to death. Paul has already assured the Philippians of their very existence in Christ by sharing his Spirit. – He is now calling on them to share in this selfless attitude of Christ in order to share in the same divine plan.

Prayer-lines: Help us, Lord, by the working of your Spirit in our lives, to bring about by humility and love that unity of Christians for which Christ died.

Week 31: Wednesday
Cycle 1: Rom 13:8-10; Cycle 2: Phil 2:12-18; Gospel: Lk 14:25-33
Gospel: 'First sit down and work out the cost.' We have left the banquet scene, where Pharisees were warned that their places in the kingdom were not guaranteed for them simply as members of the Chosen People. Today we are back on the road – the road, as we've been told by Luke, that leads to Jerusalem. And Jesus is followed by 'Great crowds'. We know how easily a crowd can grow on a road, following a commanding figure. – So here Jesus' message is that one does not become a disciple simply by following him physically. One must clearly know and accept what this following entails.

The first question for the 'would-be' Christian to answer is:

can I take on the commitment – which may demand my giving up all I hold dearest? The second question is equally daunting: can I afford *not* to take up this challenge – to become Christ's disciple? – Disturbing words.

Cycle 1: St Paul will continue today spelling out the moral consequences of our union with Christ. No need to enumerate the different commandments which concern our relations with our neighbour. If we love our neighbour no less than we love ourselves, we are in no danger of neglecting our obligations to him.

Cycle 2: 'It is God who puts both the will and the action into you.' In view of the challenge of today's gospel we are glad of the reassurance that our first reading gives us. 'For his own loving purpose' we are meant to shine in the world (as disciples of Christ)' like bright stars'. And, finally, we have the example of St Paul (and so many others) who 'has not run in the race and exhausted himself for nothing'.

Prayer-lines: That as Christians we may all gladly pay the cost of discipleship in our active concern to combat poverty and injustice in the world.

Week 31: Thursday

Cycle 1: Rom 14:7-12; Cycle 2: Phil 3:3-8; Gospel: Lk 15:1-10
Gospel: 'Rejoice with me. I have found what I lost.' Perhaps we are all familiar with that strange phenomenon, that strange relief we feel at finding something we have lost. But in this parable Jesus is not just reminding us of a fellow-feeling we have with him. Nor is he just defending himself against the complaint of the Scribes and Pharisees at his hobnobbing with disreputable characters. – He is revealing the mind of his father in heaven. Because that is his mission in life. – More than the angels, it is the father who is rejoicing in heaven. – At what? Over whom? Over *us*: the tax collectors and sinners that Jesus this morning has welcomed to eat with him.

Cycle 1: 'We shall have to stand before the judgement seat of God.' Our first reading too will challenge the Pharisee-and-

Scribe tendency in us to pass judgement on others. God alone is the judge of us all. Our only desire should be that through his mercy we may all one day give him cause for rejoicing at our being 'found' by him.

Cycle 2: 'We have our own glory from Christ Jesus.' How can we respond to this prodigal God of ours, this Good Shepherd that rejoices in finding us when we have strayed from him? St Paul has spoken for us in the first reading today. 'Because of Christ' (this recklessly welcoming Christ) 'I believe that nothing can happen that will outweigh the supreme advantage of knowing Christ Jesus my Lord'. May we come today, willingly, to meet him in his search for us. Amen.

Prayer-lines: That our daily nourishment through your word of truth in the Bible show itself in our daily imitation of the life of Christ.

Week 31: Friday

Cycle 1: Rom 15:14-21; Cycle 2: Phil 3:17–4:1; Gospel: Lk 16:1-8

Gospel: 'The children of this world are more astute.' Perhaps the best way to understand this tricky parable is to take Jesus as the speaker. (St Luke often uses the word for 'master', *Kyrios*, to refer to Jesus.) In that case Jesus is holding up the 'astuteness' of men of the world in pursuing material gain as an example to us, his followers, to be equally wise and practical in pursuing Christian goals. For one day we too will be called on by our Master to give an account of our stewardship: how we use our money. But we have also been made stewards of much else. God has given us the greatest possession of all, our Christian faith. But also our human talents. One day he will ask us how much we have done to deepen the knowledge of our faith. Happily many layfolk are attending courses in adult religious education and theology. How far, we may be asked, have we used our natural talents, say, in writing on social activity, to make our world a more Christian world? There can be much food for honest self-questioning here.

Cycle 1: 'What I have said and done by the power of the Holy

Spirit.' Life, for Paul, he says, means Christ: that is, letting Christ take over all his activity. And he does this through his Spirit, who had directed all his own activity on earth, from his conception to his resurrection. The Spirit is God's power in action, and given to us in Baptism. He is meant to be that in our lives too. With God (and his power that is the Spirit) all things are possible. Here Paul marvels in all that he has been able to do in preaching the gospel from Jerusalem right around to modern Yugoslavia. We too must reverence this revelation of the Spirit's power at work in Paul.

Cycle 2: 'Be united', St Paul says to us through the Philippians, 'in following my rule of life'. What kind of talk is this, Paul? Surely you're not boasting of being perfect? Far from it. Paul does not spare words when writing. But they were sometimes inadequate to convey all he thought and felt. (The Second Letter of Peter says: 'There are some things in Paul's letters that are hard to understand.'!) But then there is no mistaking *his* life. He constantly urges his converts to take that life as a model. He can point to his total dedication in spreading the Good News; he works at night (as tent-maker) as well as by day, in order to support himself; he makes himself 'all things to all people' – to gain everybody for Christ. Not at all that he thinks himself a saint. His principle is simple, and absolutely sincere. As he puts it to the *Corinthians,* 'Take me for your model as I take Christ'.

Week 31: Saturday
Cycle 1: Rom 16:3-27; Cycle 2: Phil 4:10-19; Gospel: Lk 16:9-15
Gospel: 'You cannot be slave both of God and of money.' Jesus' warning today about the use and abuse of money is a sequel and a pendant to the parable of the unjust steward which we heard yesterday. There is no great mystery for us in the 'uprighteousness' of money in our lives. We have not far to look to see how it competes with God (and his righteousness) for men's hearts and lives. Nor does it affect only those committed to worldly affairs. The church, the People of God, is not immune to its baneful influence either, whether individually or collectively. How slowly

the principle of being 'a Church of the Poor', proclaimed at Vatican II, is winning its way in developed countries!

Cycle 1: '… the way the eternal God wants things to be.' There is no doubt that Paul has many old friends waiting for him in Rome, even though he has not been able to visit there. They have been his fellow-workers in his missionary journeys; even risked their lives for him. (A number of the names are common names for Roman slaves). But over-arching all these affective bonds rises God's eternal plan that is being realised through the life and death of Jesus, and the spreading of his Good News through his disciples: the secret that must be broadcast to pagans everywhere to bring them to the obedience of faith. – This weightiest of Paul's epistles must have done much to fortify its Christian readers and listeners in the savage persecution which Nero was soon to unleash on them in Rome.

Cycle 2: 'I have learnt to manage on whatever I have.' Our first reading shows us a brighter side of things than the warning of the gospel. Even 'money, that tainted thing' can be used for eternal gain. The whole passage proclaims St Paul's total freedom from all possessions – in his certainty of having God. 'I know how to be poor and to be rich too'. Hence his freedom to be concerned for others. In return for the help sent to him by the Philippians he assures them, 'my God will fulfil all your needs, as only God can'.

Prayer-lines: May we grow daily in our conviction that our lives as Christians are bringing about God's great plan of salvation for the world.

Week 32: Monday
Cycle 1: Wis 1:1-7; Cycle 2: Titus 1:1-9; Gospel: Lk 17:1-6
Gospel: 'Were your faith the size of a mustard seed …' In today's gospel Luke gives us three loosely connected teachings of Jesus. What matters for us though is not their logical connection, but their relevance for our life. The first two are obviously relevant to community living, be it in parish or otherwise. 'Better be

thrown into the sea than lead astray one of these little ones.' The 'little-ones' are not children but fellow-Christians. We must never forget our responsibility to make virtue easier for others; not harder by our bad example. And secondly, our need to cultivate a spirit of endless forgiveness with those who tread on our toes. The cure St Luke gives us for these perennial problems in social life is faith: to pray constantly that the mulberry trees of our moral weakness with their deep strong roots may by God's grace and power 'be uprooted and planted in the sea'.

Cycle 1: The Book of Wisdom may be regarded as the last book of the Old Testament. It was written in Greek in Egypt, where Greek culture flourished and would be a threat to the faith of the many Jews living there. The author draws on the faith of Israel already committed to writing, to reinforce Jewish belief in God's beneficent activity in their midst. 'The Spirit of the Lord indeed fills the whole world'. As with Spirit, and Word, the literary personification of God's Wisdom active in the world was a fertile preparation for the New Testament writers in proclaiming the Incarnation.

Cycle 2: Our first reading, from one of Paul's pastoral epistles, is concerned with church structures. Titus, Paul's convert and companion in his missionary work, is to set up elders in the church of Crete, especially to ensure sound teaching of the faith there. The question of giving good example to the faithful is especially important for those who are God's representatives. In their turn the faithful must not neglect to pray for the spiritual well-being of their pastors.

Prayer-lines: Lord, increase our faith in the power of the Spirit within us to strengthen us in holiness. May he ever guide our conduct by his Wisdom.

Week 32: Tuesday

Cycle 1: Wis 2:23-3:9; Cycle 2: Titus 2:1-8, 11-14; Gospel: Lk 17:7-10
Gospel: 'We are merely servants.' Yesterday our prayer to Our Lord was 'Increase our faith'. Today, however, he warns us

against a danger that can lie in wait even for faith. The pagans in Old Testament times thought they could control their gods by prayer, harness the power for their own ends. The Pharisees were indeed in no danger of this misrepresentation of religion. But, on the other hand, as we can see in the prayer of the Pharisee in the Temple, they thought they could put God in their debt by their scrupulous observance. And observance, not only of the Law, but of their own additions to it. Jesus, elsewhere in the gospels, does in fact assure us of reward for our fidelity to his commandments. But in their parable he cuts the ground from under 'the leaven of the Pharisees': a religion of merit alone: of earning our heaven. God will indeed, we hope, grant us heaven, but thanks to his mercy, not to our merit. If we are faithful, it is not merely that it is our due, it is also by his gift. 'All is grace.' All is God's gift.

Cycle 1: The first reading today continues to probe the mystery of God's presence in the world through his benevolent Wisdom. If there is evil in the world, death especially, it is due to the devil, not God. The death of good people is not a tragedy. 'They are in peace' because they are 'in the hand of God'. And they will share God's ultimate triumph over evil.

Cycle 2: In our first reading Paul continues his portrait of the edifying behaviour that should flow from sound Christian teaching. This good example should not merely be a help to other Christians, but also disarm criticism of Christianity on the part of pagans. In all this our common example is Christ, 'who sacrificed himself for us, to purify a people to be his very own'.

Prayer-lines: Lord, may we thank you daily for any good you have enabled us to do: any evil you have helped us to avoid.

Week 32: Wednesday
Cycle 1: Wis 6:1-11; Cycle 2: Titus 3:1-7; Gospel: Lk 17:11-19
Gospel: 'No one has come back to give praise to God.' Are we surprised at Jesus' disappointment at the nine lepers' apparent ingratitude? The primary form of prayer is, indeed, petition … See the Our Father, Jesus' own prayer at the end of the Last

Supper, and in the Agony. But thanksgiving is a higher form of prayer. The Book of Revelation shows the blessed in heaven thanking God for all he did for them. But we must not wait till heaven to do this. God, it is true, loses nothing by our omitting to thank him. But we lose a great deal by not thanking him: a deeper faith in his active presence among us; a deeper love of him as a person. And we can never be at a loss for motives for thanking him: obvious things like our faith and the life of grace; our natural blessings too. Also the hidden dangers from which he protects us. Above all the hidden glory prepared for us in heaven.

Cycle 1: 'Listen, kings, and understand.' If Solomon here is addressing his fellow-rulers, nowadays men of wisdom are increasingly aware that we are indeed given dominion over the earth and its resources. But with an awesome responsibility before God for the way we use, or abuse, that dominion. 'He himself will probe your acts and scrutinise your intentions.' 'Strict scrutiny awaits those in power.'

Cycle 2: Our first reading takes us further into the theme of edifying Christian behaviour. We must counter the instinct to judge others by remembering the 'plank' in our own eyes. Above all we must be overwhelmed by God's generosity to us in Jesus Christ.

Prayer-lines: Lord, may we learn not only to thank you for the gifts of nature, but also to use them humbly and generously for your glory.

Week 32: Thursday

Cycle 1: Wis 7:22-8:1; Cycle 2: Philem 7-20; Gospel: Lk 17:20-25
Gospel: 'The kingdom of God is among you.' The Pharisees had looked forward, as the fulfilment of God's promises, to a sudden apparition of God in majesty, to make Israel free and glorious; to humble her enemies; and to reward the virtuous. Jesus tells them that the coming of God's kingdom is something far more mysterious. God and his kingdom had already come among

them – but so differently from their expectations. He had come as a carpenter's son in Galilee – to end his life on a cross as a criminal. Only the poor in spirit, the meek and humble would be able to recognise the coming of God, 'with salvation in his wings', in the life, death and resurrection of Jesus. – But there would also be a Second Coming, sudden and unpredictable, of the Son of Man in glory (as Daniel had foretold). But God's judgement would then fall on the Israel that had rejected him in his earthly coming.

Cycle 1: 'In each generation she passes into holy souls.' Here again we have an example of the presence of God among people – by his dwelling among good people. Or, if you prefer, by her dwelling among them. In Greek, the original language of this book, Wisdom (*Sophia*) is a feminine noun. Much of what the New Testament will say about Jesus in relation to the Father, the Holy Spirit and Creation, is being cogently prepared by this description of Wisdom before Jesus was born.

Cycle 2: We can see something of the presence of God's kingdom in the first reading, the shortest of all Paul's letters. He is writing to Philemon from whom Onesimus, a slave, has run away. Both men owe their Christian faith to Paul. So Paul 'trades' on the Christian fellowship of all three of them to recommend friendly treatment (perhaps even freedom) for Onesimus when he returns to his master.

Prayer-lines: Lord, help us to see your kingdom among us, not only as we meet you in Mass and in the sacraments, but in the daily round of Christian living, in justice and charity, in joy and in patience in our trials.

Week 32: Friday

Cycle 1: Wis 13:1-9; Cycle 2: 2 Jn 4-9; Gospel: Lk 17:26-37
Gospel: 'When the day comes for the Son of Man to be revealed.' As in yesterday's gospel Jesus is prophesying the suddenness of the end of the world. As in Noah's day, people will be eating and drinking, buying and selling when the climax comes. But

the warning about not waiting to collect one's possessions refers to an earlier climax, the traumatic fall of Jerusalem, forty years after Jesus' death. Writing after the event, Luke combines the two perspectives. There is no reason to suppose that Jesus, like the Old Testament prophets, did not also see things so. It is a lesson for every generation. The future is today, though 'the world' is still eating and drinking, buying and selling. – But the Coming of the Son of Man is also always today.

Cycle 1: 'How have they been so slow to find its Master ... seeing so much beauty' in his creation. A strongly modern note of sympathy, if not quite tolerance, for those who worship God only in nature: certainly a purer form of atheism than crude idolatry. For the Celtic Christian tradition has shown how fertile a soil for the gospel has been a pre-Christian reverence for the beauties of nature.

Cycle 2: St John, in our first reading sees the Coming of the Son of Man in the Christian's faith and love, 'in Jesus come in the flesh', and in the sacraments. So must we. The end will not be sudden for us if we are in constant dialogue with Christ in those three ways.

Prayer-lines: Lord, thank you for your salutary warnings in the gospel. Through the Mass may we pass over daily with you from 'this world to the Father', from the temporal to the eternal.

Week 32: Saturday

Cycle 1: Wis 18:14-16; 19:6-9; Cycle 2: 3 Jn 5-8; Gospel: Lk 18:1-8
Gospel: 'When the Son of Man comes, will he find any faith on the earth?' Prayer has been well described as 'faith breathing', living faith. So, Luke will include Jesus' sayings about the coming of the Son of Man by his teaching on prayer – one of Luke's favourite topics. The aspect of prayer which he here stresses is perseverance – in the face of discouraging delay. The widow in his parable has no money to influence the judge. Perhaps no influential relations to plead her cause. Perseverance is her only weapon. And it works! It works even on this most unlikely of

persons! The argument of the parable shouts out to us. What then may we conclude about persevering prayer to the *most likely* of persons, 'even when he delays to help them'? The God who all through the Bible has been the defender of the oppressed. Yes, our prayers to God must always have the confidence of much loved daughters and sons. This is what our faith means. And it is by persevering prayer that our faith in God 'breathes', lives and grows.

Cycle 1: What a dramatic conclusion to the theme of God's Wisdom personified in the Old Testament. Not just 'a spirit intelligent and holy ... passing into holy souls, making them friends of God'; but now 'a stern warrior leaping down from the heavens to keep God's children, the Israelites, from all harm', before the might of their Egyptian oppressors. That again is a guarantee of God's readiness to help us in time of crisis.

Cycle 2: Our first reading gives us another example of living faith, 'looking after brothers' (and naturally sisters) 'in the faith, even though complete strangers to you'. It is part of the shortest letter in the New Testament, the Third of St John, and with his typical emphasis on love in action, the new commandment of Jesus. What he calls, 'a proof to the whole church of your charity'.

Prayer-lines: Lord, strengthen our faith in your readiness to help us in our direst needs. Teach us to grow in faith by praying to you at all times, in thanks as well as petition.

Week 33: Monday
Cycle 1: 1 Macc 1:10-64; Cycle 2: Apoc 1:1-4; 2:1-5; Gospel: Lk 18:35-43
Gospel: 'Jesus of Nazareth is passing by.' Bartimaeus is far from the only man whose sight Jesus has restored. But he is a special case. In St Luke's gospel we are coming to the end of that trek of nine chapters from Galilee to Jerusalem where Jesus will meet his death. Bartimaeus is the only one in the gospel to hail Jesus as 'Son of David', that is, 'Messiah'. And, his sight once restored, he 'follows Jesus along the road' to Jerusalem, praising God. Coming as we are to the end of our liturgical year, Bartimaeus is

a role model for us: to follow Jesus whatever sharing in his life and sufferings he may have in store for us.

Cycle 1: The two books of Maccabees describe conditions in Palestine in the mid-second century BC. The Syrian occupying power, heir to that part of Alexander the Great's empire, sought to impose Greek religion and culture on the Jews. While many Jews did yield to the pressure, a resolute minority successfully resisted the assault on their faith. In several ways this courageous resistance on behalf of faith values can be relevant to us today. As Jesus says, 'If anyone declares himself for me in the presence of man, I will declare myself for him in the presence of my Father in heaven.'

Cycle 2: 'Grace and peace to you from him who is, who was, and is to come.' It is appropriate towards the end of the liturgical year to read from the last book of the Bible. A mysterious book which down the centuries has lent itself to many and varied interpretations. The name 'Apocalypse' means 'revelation', and like the whole of the Bible is certainly a disclosure of eternal truths about God and humanity. But its primary message is for people of its own time, as the seven letters to the Seven Churches of Asia Minor indicate. Today's message, to the church in Ephesus, is not untypical in its note of encouragement: the church there has been faithful in spite of difficulties. Yet complacency is ruled out by the weakening of its first fervour. A warning which can always be relevant to Christians.

Prayer-lines: Lord, no matter how many voices tell us to 'keep quiet', may we ever, like Bartimaeus, 'shout all the louder, "Jesus, Son of David, have pity on me!"'

Week 33: Tuesday

Cycle 1: 2 Macc 6:18-31; Cycle 2: Apoc 3:1-6, 14-22; Gospel: Lk 19:1-10
Gospel: 'The Son of Man has come to seek out and save what is lost.' That is the punch-line of the Zacchaeus story. Its deepest message is not the vivid 'scenario' of a hated rich official, small and no doubt correspondingly fat, perched up in a tree; nor the

drama of Jesus calling him down – to be his host that day; nor even the scene of Zacchaeus's overflowing conversion with reckless compensation for his victims. The spotlight is on Jesus' self-declaration as Saviour of the lost, the outcast, the marginalised. He has said it again about a physician's care being for the sick; also in his parables: the lost sheep and the lost coin. His words apart, he has shown this character in his unique and consistent ease in his relationships with women, so marginalised in his time. The Pharisees will be scandalised at letting a notorious woman publicly bathe his feet with her tears; but even the Twelve are nonplussed to find him talking to the Samaritan woman at the well. But, after all that was his name: Yeshua: Yahweh Saves. His identity. There is no other name given to us by which we will be saved …

Cycle 1: Eleazar's willing martyrdom at ninety years is rightly proclaimed as a record of virtue for the majority of the nation. Written little more than a hundred years before Our Lord's time, it reflects the teaching of the Pharisees of that time in regard to the dietary laws of Judaism. The nobility of Eleazar's fidelity to God, 'glad to suffer', as he says, 'because of the awe which he inspires in me', brings home to us how much closer we have come in our relationship to God in Christ.

Cycle 2: 'I am standing at the door knocking'. Today we read from two more of John's letters to the Seven Churches. For both of them the tone is one of reproval. To Sardis: 'You are reputed to be alive, and yet are dead.' To Laodicea: 'You are neither cold nor hot. You are pitiably poor, and naked too.' And yet these severe judgements are not final ones. A chance of amendment is still held out. 'Wake up, revive what little you have left.' And even to the still more wretched Laodiceans, Jesus is standing at the door knocking. If welcomed in he will sit beside his hosts and share their meal. Few more touching appeals from God can be found in the Bible.

Prayer-lines: Lord Jesus, our Saviour, let us ponder the meaning of your name, and hurry down from our 'tree' to make you our guest.

Week 33: Wednesday

Cycle 1: 2 Macc 7:1, 20-31; Cycle 2: Apoc 4:1-11; Gospel: Lk 19:11-28
Gospel: 'We do not want this man to be our king.' We are more familiar with the parable of the talents in St Matthew's gospel. But here we are in a different context, a more ominous one, 'near Jerusalem, and, in the expectation of many', the kingdom of God about to show itself. The parable of the talents, like other parables, was aimed at the Pharisees – who had wrapped up their knowledge of God instead of revealing him to other people. But here St Luke has sewn on a second parable: a nobleman going to claim his kingdom in spite of opposition from his enemies. Jesus is himself, of course, the nobleman, on his way to Jerusalem and his passion – to receive the kingdom from his Father. Both parables have this message for us. To use the 'pounds', the talents God has given us, in grace and in nature, to bear fruit for him. To follow Jesus as our king as he goes up to Jerusalem, there to be the pattern of our life, our death and resurrection.

Cycle 1: The gruesome martyrdom of the seven brothers and their mother in the Maccabean revolt is a climax of heroic fidelity to the Jewish faith. But it is also a precious witness to the explicit Jewish belief of the last centuries BC in a life after death, 'When the Creator will give you back both breath and life'; with reunion with those we loved on earth. Full use of this belief is made by the Christian church in the liturgy of the dead.

Cycle 2: Our first reading lifts us from the road to Jerusalem to see the splendour of God's kingdom as revealed in the court of heaven. The full riches of Old Testament imagery and symbolism are brought into play. All creation, in the fullness of its bewildering variety, joins in an overwhelming chorus of grateful praise to God as creator. We are meant to keep this vision before us as the backdrop of the whole of the Bible story, and of our own lives on earth.

Prayer-lines: Lord Jesus, may we manifest God's kingdom in our lives by our living no longer for ourselves but for you, who died for us and rose again.

Week 33: Thursday

Cycle 1: 1 Macc 2:15-29; Cycle 2: Apoc 5:1-10; Gospel: Lk 19:41-44

Gospel: 'You did not recognise your opportunity when God offered it.' Half-way down the western side of the Mount of Olives there stands a little chapel where one can say Mass facing a large window opening on to a vista of the Old City of Jerusalem. The temple area is in the foreground. The chapel is called the 'Dominus Flevit' (The Lord wept). This is indeed an event worthy of a chapel. Jesus' tears are not often recorded in the gospels. They give us a precious glimpse of Jesus' heart, of God's heart. These tears express all the anguish God has been expressing since the time of Hosea, seven hundred years earlier, over his people's failure to respond to his love for them: 'The more I called, the further they went from me.' If 'it is not fitting' for a prophet to die outside Jerusalem, neither is it fitting for a prophet not to weep for Jerusalem.

And that Jerusalem is the symbol of ourselves: equally the object of God's choice and love; God' invitation, visitation, warnings, tears. On today's passage we must 'recognise your opportunity when God offers it.'

Cycle 1: Our first reading brings us back to the start of the revolt of the Maccabees. It is a shining example of how a resolute display by one family of their fidelity to their ancestral faith can enable a host of others to take courage, and eventually win against overwhelming odds.

Cycle 2: 'The Lamb has triumphed and he will open the scroll.' The vision of God as creator in yesterday's Mass, is matched today by that of the Lamb, once sacrificed, now in triumph. On virtually the same plane as God the creator, he is now hailed in the same way by all the living creatures as redeemer. This vision of God as creator and redeemer must also be the context of our celebration of Mass in which we join with the liturgy of heaven.

Prayer-lines: May the leaders of the world read the signs of the times, and save the world from the fate of Jerusalem.

Week 33: Friday

Cycle 1: 1 Macc 4:36-59; Cycle 2: Apoc 10:8-11; Gospel: Lk 19:45-48
Gospel: 'Jesus went into the temple.' One might easily miss the theological drama behind this short phrase. The long trek from Galilee to Jerusalem begun ten chapters ago is now at an end. We might say that the whole purpose of that long journey for Jesus is that he might take possession of the Temple. It is a central landmark all through the gospel: from the annunciation of John the Baptist to Zechariah in the first chapter, to the return of the eleven apostles there in the last chapter after Jesus' ascension. The prophecy of Malachy, last of the 'writing prophets', is now fulfilled: 'Suddenly the Lord whom you seek will come to his temple'. For Israel the Temple represented the climax of the long history of God's presence with humanity. With Jesus in the Temple it is now visibly fulfilled. But Malachy's prophecy continues: 'I am coming to put you on trial'. And in the subsequent days of Jesus' teaching in the Temple courts, Luke will contrast the positive response of the people with the lethal hostility of the religious leaders.

Cycle 1: Interestingly, in our first reading as in today's gospel passage, the focus is on the Temple: not indeed the splendid edifice of Jesus' day, re-built by Herod the Great, but the more modest one built after the return from the exile in Babylon. The Syrians had desecrated it by erecting an altar to Jupiter in it. The Temple had therefore to be cleansed by putting up a new altar, and establishing the new feast of Hannukah. It is still a popular feast with Jews in mid-December.

Cycle 2: In our first reading the revelation to the Seven Churches of Asia Minor continues in the traditional Old Testament form of prophecy, especially as in Ezechiel. The seer, John, is told to eat a small scroll (on papyrus) containing bad news as well as good, sour as well as sweet. As later passages will show, there is persecution in store for God's faithful. But the good news is always God's indisputable control of history.

Prayer-lines: We thank you, Lord, for the fullness of your presence with us, especially in the Eucharist. Teach us to hand on Jesus' words as did his hearers in today's gospel.

Week 33: Saturday

Cycle 1: 1 Macc 6:1-13; Cycle 2: Apoc 11:4-12; Gospel: Lk 20:27-40

Gospel: 'He is god, not of the dead, but of the living.' Jesus is saying, in effect, that all life here and hereafter consists in friendship with God: nothing less is worthy of the name of life. Inanimate things can have a creator, but only the living can have a God. As a famous New Testament scholar has put it: 'Jesus' reply lights up the whole history of religion. The question that rises to our minds is, why did no one think of that before? Though, looking back, we see it penetrates to the heart of the Old Testament.' Abraham was God's friend. Men lose their friends by death, God doesn't. – For us, 'children of the Resurrection', the focus must be on our relationship with Christ, the Living One. We must not, as the angels at the tomb said to the women, 'look for him among the dead'. Jesus is the great friend with us every moment, from rising to bed-time. We should be haunted by Paul's triumphant cry: 'nothing in death or life can come between us and the love of God made visible in Christ Jesus, our Lord.'

Cycle 1: God's honour having been upheld by the cleansing and re-dedication of the Temple in yesterday's reading from 1 Maccabees, it only remains to record the dismal fate of the great persecutor, Antiochus Epiphanes.

Cycle 2: Our first reading echoes yesterday's passage foretelling the persecution that lies ahead for Christ's followers. But it also foretells their subsequent sharing in his resurrection and ascension to heaven. We need not to be distracted by the medley of Old Testament symbols and allusions by which this message is conveyed.

Prayer-lines: Lord, increase our faith in the constant presence of Christ with us as redeemer and friend, that we may face death, for ourselves and those we love, without fear or anxiety.

Week 34: Monday

Cycle 1: Dan 1:1-6, 8-20; Cycle 2: Apoc 14:1-5; Gospel: Lk 21:1-4

Gospel: 'She has put in all she had to live on.' This well-known episode of the 'widow's mite' follows on a passage where Jesus has warned against the hypocrisy of the Pharisees. 'They swallow the property of widows' while putting on a show of piety. May we be inspired by this generous widow to give also and not count the cost.

Cycle 1: 'You come to us in word and sacrament', we say at Mass, 'to strengthen us in holiness'. The Scripture readings as well as the sacrament of the Eucharist are also our 'daily bread'. On some feast days they can clearly be a feast for us. But an historical account of Jewish boys at the Court of Babylon might well seem a mere crust for our piety. Yet this story has a deeper meaning for us than might at first appear. The Book of Daniel was written at a time of very severe crisis of faith for the Jews. This time it was not, as in the past, the challenge from the idolatry of the nature religions around them. It was the more insidious challenge of Greek culture which had come to the near-east with Alexander the Great, with all the prestige of genuine worldly wisdom. It is easy to see how there can be a parallel crisis of faith for many in the global cultures of today. These passages from Daniel show how God can give us strength to be faithful to our Christian values under even greater pressure.

Cycle 2: Yet the widow is not out of place in today's liturgy among the 144,000 standing on Mount Zion with the Lamb in our first reading. That is indeed a vast throng, and yet it is not identical with 'the huge number, impossible to count, of people from every nation, race, tribe and language' of whom we read on All Saints Day. These 144,000, we are told, 'follow the Lamb wherever he goes'. And as the Apocalypse portrays him as 'the Lamb that is slain', it is clear that these 144,000 have followed him to a sacrificial death of martyrdom. And yet one feels that St Luke's phrase about the widow having 'put in all she had to live on', qualifies her to join the company of martyrs. For she has followed Christ who, as St Paul says, 'made himself poor to make us rich out of his poverty'.

Prayer-lines: Lord, we thank you for the nourishment of your Scriptures. Deepen our faith in them to strengthen our resolve to do always, like Christ, the things that please you.

Week 34: Tuesday

Cycle 1: Dan 2:31-45; Cycle 2: Apoc 14:14-19; Gospel: Lk 21:5-11

Gospel and Cycle 2: 'Do not be frightened … the end is not so soon.' We go astray if we read or hear the Apocalypse as an attempt to describe how the world will come to an end. And, down the ages since the Apocalypse was written, many have read the Apocalypse in that way. Jesus in today's gospel passage is prophesying something else: the destruction of the Temple at Jerusalem. It was one of the charges brought against him at his trial. But we must also remember that, in a way, this was for many Jews an end of the world, a terminal catastrophe. That happened in the year 70 AD. But the preceding decades saw so many world-shaking events: the suicide of the emperor Nero; the wars waged by four claimants to the imperial throne; the eruption of Vesuvius and the destruction of Pompeii – all these happenings also gave justification for those who thought the world was coming to an end. For John, the author of the Apocalypse 'the harvest of the earth is ripe' – ripe for the 'wine-press of God's anger'.

All those first century events may seem very remote from us, and yet what other news do the media give us today but 'wars and rumours of wars', great natural disasters 'and plagues and famines here and there'. The answer given in our first reading is that the timing of the world's end is God's mystery. The end is decided in heaven. In heaven, therefore, lies the sure anchor of our hope.

Cycle 1: Our first reading is the climax of the preceding story. The king of Babylon has had a dream, but can't remember its contents. His wise men are all unable to tell them to him. Only Daniel, the exile of Judah, can do so: clear proof that Daniel's

God is 'the God of gods and revealer of mysteries'. He proceeds to describe the dream: the symbolic succession of empires, from Babylon down to the author of the book's time. This fourth kingdom, he now foretells, will be supplanted by the kingdom of God's chosen people. The purpose of the whole episode is to strengthen the faith of the writer's own generation in the ultimate establishment of God's everlasting kingdom. As such it is, of course, relevant to every Christian generation.

Prayer-lines: Lord Jesus, through a world filled with lights contrary to your own, may our gaze be always turned to you, the true Light of the World.

Week 34: Wednesday

Cycle 1: Dan 5:1-28; Cycle 2: Apoc 15:1-4; Gospel: Lk 21:12-19

Gospel: 'Your endurance will win you your lives.' Jesus in preceding passages has foretold the destruction of the splendid Temple of Herod the Great. But that will be only one part of all Jerusalem's fall. He now goes on to describe the lot of his disciples before the final judgement at the end of the world. Persecution by civil and religious authorities. But again Jesus' message is: Do not be frightened. They will be filled with his Spirit and his Wisdom to confound all opposition. – We think, for example, of the eloquence of Stephen and Paul when put on trial. Perhaps more trying for Christians will be the animosity of people in general, especially on the part of relatives and friends. Yet here too their patient endurance will bring them victory.

Cycle 1: 'You have been weighed in the balance and found wanting.' Once more we see the faithful Daniel's power to interpret mysteries beyond the scope of Babylonian sages. Yet there are some significant differences in this story. Belshazzar is a different king. He is an idol-worshipper, and sacrilegiously profanes the sacred vessels of the Jews. As he is unrepentant, his doom is sealed. Though he belongs to an earlier epoch than the Maccabees, his punishment by God is another comfort for Jews of that later period that *their* oppressor, Antiochus Epiphanes would also incur God's punishment for his crimes.

Cycle 2: Our first reading from the Apocalypse confirms the truth of these gospel promises. 'Your endurance will win you your lives.' We now see Christ's disciples in the moment of victory, echoing the triumphant song of Israel after her escape from Egypt.

Prayer-lines: God our Father, in all the trials of this life may we always pray with faith, 'How just and true are all your ways'.

Week 34: Thursday
Cycle 1: Dan 6:12-28; Cycle 2: Apoc 18:1-23; 19:1-9; Gospel: Lk 21:20-28
Gospel: 'Stand erect, your liberation is near at hand.' Despite the reference to Jerusalem surrounded by armies, St Luke is not necessarily describing the actual siege of Jerusalem by Rome in 70 AD. He is using the prophetic language and detail of the ancient prophecies before the fall of Jerusalem to Babylon in the early 6th century BC. God uses a Gentile kingdom to punish his people for their long unpunished infidelity. The signs of the cosmic powers are symbolic. The sea, as in the Apocalypse, is the reservoir of evil; the powers of heaven, sun, moon and stars are identified with the gods of the heathen nations around Israel, and their shaking refers to the overthrow of pagan supremacy rather than the dissolution of the physical universe.

Cycle 1: Yet another example both of Jewish fidelity in exile to their faith, and God's power to protect them from death. The prohibition mentioned here of praying to anyone other than the king is quite at variance with the religious tolerance of Persian rulers, but was quite characteristic of the Hellenistic kings who followed them. This would make Daniel in the present situation an ever clearer role model for the Jews who suffered under Antiochus Epiphanes. No doubt he is equally a model for Christians today who have to face the 'lions' of so many post-Christian cultural and ethical pressures.

Cycle 2: One could be excused for finding these final readings of the liturgical year depressing. But our first reading from the Apocalypse, encourages us to see in the final scenario the triumph of God's justice over the malignant power of sin in the world. Our part is to gaze calmly at that evil being overthrown, and to rejoice at the ultimate victory of God and his goodness over evil; a victory already won in Christ, and shared continually by him in the goodness of many on earth.

Prayer-lines: Lord, thank you for that 'kindly light' which your gospel sheds on us . Give us the faith to live in that light, and radiate it around us.

Week 34: Friday
Cycle 1: Dan 7:2-14; Cycle 2: Apoc 20:1-4, 11-21:2; Gospel: Lk 21:29-33
Gospel: 'Know that the kingdom of God is near.' St Luke has been using Jesus' prediction of the fall of Jerusalem (only forty years after his own death), as a sort of rehearsal for the end of the world. And today's brief gospel passage invites us to dwell on the fuller, apocalyptic, account of that world's ending given to us in our first reading.

Cycle 1: From portraying Jewish fidelity to the faith in a pagan land, the second half of the Book of Daniel now switches to the literary of apocalypse. Written some 160 years before Christ, during the Maccabean persecution, it portrays in the form of symbolic beasts, the successive destruction of the four great empires which had, until then, dominated the Chosen People. The Chosen People is represented in *human* form (superior, therefore, to the four beasts) – 'One like a Son of Man'. On this people 'an eternal sovereignty would be conferred by God, "the one of great age".' By the close association of king and kingship the meaning of 'Son of Man' would later come to be the messianic king himself. This, of course, is its dominant sense in the New Testament. Our passage, then, in its present context, foretells the ultimate triumph of Christ over all human powers seen as hostile to God and his chosen people.

Cycle 2: We may ignore any literal time references in this passage from the Apocalypse. We recall that it was written not to foretell 'times and seasons' in a distant future, but to give its contemporaries, the Seven Churches of Asia Minor, a sense of the theological realities involved, clothing them in the multi-coloured symbols and imagery of the prophets. The final reality given us today may be summed up as the ultimate victory of Christ over all the powers of evil. Judgement will be passed by God on all humankind according to the merit of their lives. The first world is now replaced by a new one where a redeemed and purified humanity can be reunited to God for ever.

Prayer-lines: Lord Jesus, in the apparent triumph of evil in this world around us and at times within us, strengthen our faith in your ultimate victory, and our desire to anticipate it in ourselves and in the world.

Week 34: Saturday

Cycle 1: Dan 7:15-27; Cycle 2: Apoc 22:1-7; Gospel: Lk 21:34-36
Gospel: 'To stand with confidence before the Son of Man.' Jesus is no longer speaking of the coming fall of Jerusalem. His words today ('which shall not pass away') are clearly addressed to every Christian generation. Even were there no 'wars or rumours of war'; no awesome natural catastrophes, it is always timely for the Christian to be ready for the sudden and unforeseen coming of the Son of Man.

Today we are at the end of a liturgical year, on the eve of a new one. The gospel message today is not simply the cosy one of looking back over the year that is past and thanking God for its blessings. That indeed we should surely do. But our gospel passage strikes a sterner note: 'watch and pray for strength to survive'. 'Stay awake ...' sounds a reveille in an army camp where soldiers are asleep. Sleep, moral sleep, can be the normal condition of our unredeemed human nature in which the gospel finds us, if not in 'debauchery', certainly in the 'cares of life'. That is the great trap in which so many have been engulfed down the ages, both individually and collectively.

Cycle 1: Our first reading on this last day of the liturgical year gives us God's last word on 'the cares of this world', its woes and disasters. Written during the last great disaster of Old Testament times, namely the persecution of Israel's faith and culture by the might of Greek domination, 'with iron teeth and bronze claws', it captures something of the apparent hopelessness of Judah's struggle against impossible odds. But at once it passes from the savage reality of human power to the transcendent serenity of God's final word: 'Sovereignty and kingship will be given (instead) to the saints of the Most High ... and people of every nation will serve and obey him'. Amen. Come, Lord Jesus.

Cycle 2: But our first reading gives us a more positive reason for 'praying at all time'. It is John's final vision of our journey's end. The heavenly city with its river of life, the vision of God, and eternal kingship with him. For us who have faith, that reality has already begun. Jesus' promise, 'Very soon I shall be with you again', may be taken literally today in our Eucharist.

Prayer-lines: Lord, may this ending of the liturgical year be a time for us to bid a resolute farewell to the sleep of nature, and an opening of our hearts in faith to the coming and reign of Christ in our lives.